A HISTORY OF THE ATHONITE COMMONWEALTH

D1594456

This book examines the part played by monks of Mount Athos in the diffusion of Orthodox monasticism throughout Eastern Europe and beyond. It focuses on the lives of outstanding holy men in the history of Orthodoxy who have been drawn to the Mountain, have absorbed the spirit of its wisdom and its prayer, and have returned to the outside world, inspired to spread the results of their labours and learning. In a remarkable demonstration of what may be termed 'soft power' in action, these men have carried the image of Athos to all corners of the Balkan peninsula, to Ukraine, to the very far north of Russia, across Siberia and the Bering Strait into North America, and most recently (when traditional routes were closed to them by the curtain of communism) to the West. Their dynamic witness is the greatest gift of Athos to a world thirsting for spiritual guidance.

GRAHAM SPEAKE is founder and Chairman of the Friends of Mount Athos. He is a regular visitor to Mount Athos and was received into the Orthodox Church there in 1999. Trained as a classicist, he holds a doctorate in Greek from the University of Oxford and is a Fellow of the Society of Antiquaries. His first book, *Mount Athos: Renewal in Paradise* (2nd edn, 2014), was awarded the Criticos Prize.

A HISTORY OF THE ATHONITE COMMONWEALTH

The Spiritual and Cultural Diaspora of Mount Athos

GRAHAM SPEAKE

CAMBRIDGE
UNIVERSITY PRESS

University Printing House, Cambridge CB2 8BS, United Kingdom

One Liberty Plaza, 20th Floor, New York, NY 10006, USA

477 Williamstown Road, Port Melbourne, VIC 3207, Australia

314–321, 3rd Floor, Plot 3, Splendor Forum, Jasola District Centre, New Delhi – 110025, India

79 Anson Road, #06–04/06, Singapore 079906

Cambridge University Press is part of the University of Cambridge.

It furthers the University's mission by disseminating knowledge in the pursuit of education, learning, and research at the highest international levels of excellence.

www.cambridge.org
Information on this title: www.cambridge.org/9781108425865
DOI: 10.1017/9781108349222

© Graham Speake 2018

This publication is in copyright. Subject to statutory exception and to the provisions of relevant collective licensing agreements, no reproduction of any part may take place without the written permission of Cambridge University Press.

First published 2018

Printed in the United Kingdom by TJ International Ltd, Padstow, Cornwall

A catalogue record for this publication is available from the British Library.

ISBN 978-1-108-42586-5 Hardback
ISBN 978-1-108-44432-3 Paperback

Cambridge University Press has no responsibility for the persistence or accuracy of URLs for external or third-party internet websites referred to in this publication and does not guarantee that any content on such websites is, or will remain, accurate or appropriate.

For Thomas

Contents

List of Plates		*page* x
List of Maps		xii
Preface		xiii

PART I

1	Introduction	5
	The Byzantine Commonwealth	5
	The Athonite Commonwealth	8

2	The Monastic Life	15
	Desert Monasticism	15
	Urban Monasticism	23
	Monks as Missionaries and Teachers	26
	The Resurgence of Monasticism after Iconoclasm	29
	Monks as Scholars and Copyists	32
	Monks as Landowners and Merchants	34

PART II

3	St Athanasios the Athonite (*c.*925–1000/1): Founder of Cenobitic Monasticism on Athos	39
	The Beginnings of Monasticism on Athos	40
	The Monastic Programme at the Lavra	44
	The Legacy of Athanasios	48
	The Benedictine Monastery of the Amalfitans	51

4	The Enlighteners of Georgia	54
	St John the Iberian (d.1005) and St Euthymios of Athos (*c.*955–1028)	55
	St George the Hagiorite (1009–1065)	59
	Gregory Pakourianos (d.1086)	61

5   St Antony (983–1073) and St Theodosius (1035–1074)
    of Kiev: Fathers of Russian Monasticism   64
    The Foundation of the Monastery of the Caves   65
    Growth and Prosperity of the Monastery of the Caves   69
    Maturity and Influence of the Monastery of the Caves   72

6   St Sava (1175–1236): Illuminator of Serbia   77
    The Foundation of Hilandar Monastery   78
    Sava's Years on Athos   82
    Return to Serbia   84
    Pilgrimages to the Christian East   87

7   St Gregory of Sinai (c.1265–1346): Initiator of the
    'Hesychast International'   93
    A Travelling Man   93
    The Years on Athos   94
    The Move to Paroria   99
    Interaction with the Slavs   102

8   St Gregory Palamas (1296–1359): Champion of Hesychasm
    on Athos   105
    Gregory the Hesychast   106
    The Hesychast Controversy: Part 1   109
    The Hesychast Controversy: Part 2   114
    Archbishop of Thessaloniki   116
    The Legacy of St Gregory Palamas   120

9   St Theodosius of Trnovo (c.1300–1363) and the
    Bulgarian School of Hesychasm   124
    St Theodosius and the Monastery of Kilifarevo   124
    St Euthymius of Trnovo (c.1325–c.1400) and His Literary Reforms 127
    St Cyprian (c.1330–1406), Metropolitan of Kiev and All Russia   132
    Gregory Tsamblak (c.1365–1419), International Hesychast   135
    St Romylos of Vidin (c.1300–c.1381), Link to Serbia   142

10 St Nikodimos of Tismana (1320–1406): Transmitter
    of Hesychasm to Wallachia   145
    The Arrival of Hesychasm in the Romanian Lands   145
    Koutloumousiou, the 'Lavra of Wallachia'   149
    Romanian Participation in the Athonite Commonwealth   154
    The Dedicated Monasteries   158

11 St Sergius of Radonezh (1314–1392) and St Nil Sorsky
    (c.1433–1508): Revivers of Russian Monasticism   161
    The 'Flight into the Desert'   161
    St Sergius and His Trinity Monastery   162

	The Cult of St Sergius	168
	The Successors of St Sergius	172
	St Nil Sorsky	175

12	St Maximos the Greek (*c*.1470–1556): Enlightener of Russia	182
	From Arta to Italy (*c*.1470–*c*.1505)	182
	From Italy to Athos (*c*.1505–1516)	185
	From Athos to Moscow (1516–1525)	188
	Detention in Moscow (1525–1556)	193
	Maxim's Legacy	196

13	St Kosmas the Aetolian (1714–1779): Teacher of the Greek Nation, Apostle to the Albanians	199
	Early Years and Elementary Education	200
	Athos and the Enlightenment	201
	The Mission of Kaisarios Dapontes	203
	Fr Kosmas's Ministry	205
	Martyrdom in Albania	211

14	St Paisy Velichkovsky (1722–1794): Reviver of Hesychasm	213
	Arrival on Mount Athos	214
	An Athonite Brotherhood	216
	Paisy's Legacy to Mount Athos	217
	The Search for Patristic Texts	219
	The Kollyvades and the *Philokalia*	221
	Paisy's Legacy to Russia	224
	Writers as Disciples of the Elders	226

15	St Nikodimos of the Holy Mountain (1749–1809): Editor of the *Philokalia*	234
	Athos, the Kollyvades, and the *Philokalia*	235
	Reception of the *Philokalia*	240
	Nikodimos's Other Writings	242

16	Athos and the West	249
	The Motor-Boat Age	249
	Athos Comes to England	253
	Athos Comes to North America	258
	Athos Comes to France	263

| | Epilogue | 270 |

Glossary		275
Select Bibliography		278
Index		283

List of Plates

Plates occur after the page number indicated in each case. All photographs were taken by the author unless otherwise indicated.

1. Western and Eastern saints inside the chapel of the monastery of Sts Antony and Cuthbert, Shropshire.   48
2. The Coptic monastery of St Antony in the eastern desert of Egypt.   48
3. A modern statue of Sts Cyril and Methodios in the monastery of the Caves, Kiev.   48
4. The katholikon of Rila monastery in Bulgaria.   48
5. Walls and towers of the Great Lavra on Athos.   48
6. The tower of the Amalfitan monastery on Athos.   48
7. Alaverdi cathedral, part of Alaverdi monastery in eastern Georgia.   48
8. The katholikon of Iviron monastery on Athos.   80
9. The skete of Bogoroditsa on Athos, formerly the monastery of Xylourgou. Photo © Aleksandar Golubović.   80
10. The original site of St Panteleimonos monastery (Rossikon) on Athos.   80
11. The main gate to the monastery of the Caves in Kiev.   80
12. The upper lavra of the monastery of the Caves in Kiev.   80
13. St Sava's tower in the monastery of Hilandar on Athos.   80
14. The east window of the main church of Studenica monastery in Serbia.   80
15. The main church of Ljubostinja monastery in Serbia.   112
16. The west front of the main church of Dečani monastery in Kosovo.   112
17. The church of the Forty Martyrs in Trnovo.   112
18. The area of Athos known as Magoula.   112

19. Milutin's tower, near the monastery of Hilandar on Athos.   112
20. The main church of the monastery of Kilifarevo in Bulgaria.   112
21. The monastery of Zographou on Athos.   112
22. The cathedral of St Sophia in Kiev.   144
23. Interior of the main church of Manasija monastery in Serbia.   144
24. A casket containing the relics of Stefan Dečanski in Dečani   144
    monastery, Kosovo.
25. The main church of Ravanica monastery in Serbia.   144
26. The main church of Moldoviţa monastery in Bucovina,   144
    Romania.
27. The main church of Bistriţa monastery in Moldavia,   144
    Romania.
28. The refectory and defence tower of Koutloumousiou   144
    monastery on Athos.
29. The Trinity monastery of St Sergius near Moscow.   144
30. Icon of the Holy Trinity by Andrey Rublev.   176
    Tretyakov Gallery, Moscow.
31. Walls and towers of the Kirillo-Belozersky monastery   176
    in northern Russia.
32. The entrance to the cathedral of the Ferapontov   176
    monastery in northern Russia.
33. Icon of Solovki monastery and its founders, Sts Savvaty   176
    and Zosima. Icon Museum, Vologda.
34. A skete belonging to the monastery of Valaam on an island in   240
    Lake Ladoga.
35. The katholikon of the monastery of Vatopedi on Athos.   240
36. A casket containing the relics of St Maximos the Greek   240
    in the Trinity monastery of St Sergius.
37. The main church of the Prophet Elijah skete on Athos.   240
38. The main church of Neamţ monastery in Moldavia, Romania.   240
39. The Byzantine tower of Prosphori at Ouranoupolis near the   240
    border of Athos.
40. Archimandrite Sophrony in the garden of his Essex monastery.   240
    Photo © Monastery of St John the Baptist, Tolleshunt Knights.
41. The monastery of St Antony the Great at St Laurent-en-Royans   240
    in the Dauphiné.

List of Maps

1. The Byzantine Commonwealth. *page* 4
2. The monasteries and sketes of Mount Athos. 38
3. The travels of St Sava. After Obolensky. 76
4. The travels of St Gregory of Sinai. 92
5. Monastic centres of the Athonite Commonwealth. 122

Preface

This book is a sequel to my earlier book, *Mount Athos: Renewal in Paradise*, which was first published in 2002. That book was primarily concerned with the monastic revival that took place on the Holy Mountain in the second half of the twentieth century as seen in the context of the history of Athos from when monks first arrived on the peninsula in the ninth century down to the present day. In the introduction I identified four areas of concern for which Athos is important – spiritual, historical, cultural, and environmental – and I tried to do justice to all of them in the chapters that followed. But having written that book, I began to realize that there was more to be said about the importance of Athos, especially about the role that it played in the spread of Orthodoxy, and specifically Orthodox monasticism, throughout Eastern Europe and beyond over the past millennium. Dimitri Obolensky had touched on this in his great work *The Byzantine Commonwealth*, but no one seemed to have pursued it. It is essentially a spiritual story, of a monastic diaspora, but with such broad ramifications that it impacted not just on religious life but on politics, society, and the arts. As the story unfolds, the Holy Mountain emerges in a new light as the chief instigator of what must rank as one of the most significant and wide-ranging movements in the history of the Orthodox Church.

In writing this book I have in mind the same reader as I envisaged for my first book, that is someone who is not necessarily a professional academic or a practising Christian, but who has an inquiring mind and a desire to understand the true meaning and importance of Mount Athos as the spiritual heart of Orthodoxy. You do not need to have visited Athos yourself, or indeed any of the parts of the world over which the text ranges (and they are many), but if any of my readers are persuaded by what I write to do so, then the book will have achieved something. My secondary aim, I should confess, is to convince you that monasteries are worth cherishing as centres of excellence – both spiritual and cultural excellence – and this,

I realize, is a conviction that may not come naturally to those of us who are children of Anglo-Saxon Protestant lands. But if the half-millennium of the Reformation merits celebration, how much more deserving is the millennium and more of the Athonite Commonwealth!

Many friends and colleagues have been generous with their time and their advice. In particular, I should like to thank my spiritual father, Metropolitan Kallistos of Diokleia, who encouraged the project from the start and who provided helpful comments on the entire manuscript. I am also grateful to Fr Andrew Louth, Dame Averil Cameron, and the anonymous publisher's reader, who all read the whole book and made numerous suggestions for its improvement. Guidance on points of detail was kindly provided by Bob Allison (Maine), John Burgess (Pittsburgh), Nicholas Fennell (Winchester), Aleksandar Golubović (Belgrade), Vladeta Janković (Belgrade), Dan Ioan Mureşan (Paris), Fr Romilo (Hilandar), the late Sister Sidonia (Kilifarevo), and numerous members of the Friends of Mount Athos whose conferences and pilgrimages are a continuing source of inspiration on all matters Athonite. I am especially grateful to Sergey Shumilo, Director of the International Institute of the Athonite Heritage in Ukraine, for inviting me to address a conference that he organized in the monastery of the Caves in May 2015 on the theme 'Athos and the Slav World'. The opportunity to spend the best part of a week in the glorious surroundings of that ancient monastery with its deep-rooted Athonite traditions was a most timely spur to me to complete the writing of this book.

My godson Thomas Small has often played devil's advocate and coaxed me in the direction of creating a more readable or more convincing text. If I sometimes appeared reluctant to accept his advice, it was entirely due to my own blinkered intransigence. I hope that the dedication of this book is sufficient indication of my repentance and my gratitude.

Transliteration and nomenclature are a nightmare in a work that ranges over so many different languages and alphabets. I am deeply grateful to my friends Nicholas Fennell and Fr Romilo for their kind efforts to put me right on this. I have tried to retain the most familiar forms wherever possible and at the same time to impose some sort of consistency, but for any errors or infelicities that remain I alone am responsible. I am also grateful to the staff of the Slavonic Reading Room and the Theology Faculty Library in Oxford who have dealt patiently and courteously with all my tiresome requests and failures to find things and understand new systems.

As for the illustrations, I am extremely grateful to the Gerald Palmer Eling Trust for covering the cost of reproducing them. Most of the photographs are my own, but I must thank my friend Aleksandar Golubović for the picture of the skete of Bogoroditsa and the monastery of St John the Baptist at Tolleshunt Knights for the photograph of Fr Sophrony.

It remains for me to acknowledge my debt to my publishers. As a former publisher myself, I know how much work is involved in bringing to birth a book such as this. The staff of the Cambridge University Press have been unfailingly helpful and generous with their time throughout the editorial and production process. Many of their names I shall never know, but I must single out for special mention my commissioning editor, Michael Sharp, who has given the project his wholehearted support and full attention from the very start, my assiduous and most obliging content manager, Lisa Sinclair, and my eagle-eyed copy-editor, Lawrence Osborn, who has saved me from all manner of *bêtise*. My sincere thanks to all concerned.

PART I

The road to the monastery was long, steep, and stony. Stones marked the boundaries of the fields in which contented sheep munched and meditated and enjoyed the far-reaching prospect. No dwelling was to be seen except a distant stone byre, nor was there any shelter other than the occasional wind-swept tree, but beyond the crest of a hill there was nothing but mountain succeeding to mountain succeeding to mountain for as far as the eye could see.

Eventually the track came to a fork and the right-hand turning led down to a small hollow in which nestled a stone-built cottage – or was it a pair of cottages? – with some disused sheds and pigsties attached to the back wall. The sight was welcome after the long, hot walk. Even more welcoming and even more unexpected was the sound of the talanto, *the wooden plank that is used by Orthodox monasteries and struck with a mallet to summon the faithful to prayer. Emerging from behind the house was a monk walking purposefully round the small enclosure, beating his* talanto *to an unmistakable haunting rhythm, summoning his community to vespers in the chapel that he had created from a former stable. We followed him inside. The interior was dark, illuminated only by candles and an oil lamp or two. It took a while to adjust to the dim light, but gradually a host of colourful figures came into view: the entire walls were frescoed with scenes from the lives of the saints and with standing figures; a carved wooden iconostasis screened the tiny sanctuary from the rest of the chapel; and on it shining icons of Our Lord, of the Mother of God, and of other saints bade us welcome and prepared us for the chanting that was to follow. The same monk who had been sounding the* talanto *now appeared from behind the screen, censed the holy icons and then the assembled congregation, and began to intone a psalm.*

Apart from the sheep and the architectural style of the buildings, this could easily have been a remote hermitage near the southern point of Mount Athos, the so-called desert of Athos, where hermits scratch a meagre living from the stony soil while devoting their lives to prayer for a fallen world. But in fact we were in Shropshire, the heart of England (though some of the furthest glimpsed mountains may have been over the border into Wales), and the cottage was none other than the monastery of Sts Antony and Cuthbert! The icons, of English saints, confirmed this, though they were mixed in with other saints whom one might have expected to meet on Athos (Plate 1): there beside St Aidan and St Cuthbert were St Isaac the Syrian and St Athanasios the Athonite, with scenes from the life of St Cuthbert above. And on the opposite wall St George stood next to St Antony of Egypt and St Seraphim of Sarov, below scenes from the life of St Antony. After vespers we were taken on a tour of the estate. A pigsty was in process of being converted to provide accommodation for more monks; attractive wooden huts had already been constructed in the woods to house pilgrims at some distance from the monastery; and hundreds of new trees had recently been planted to ensure long-term supplies of timber, not for fuel, but for icons and for woodcarving.

For this monk, so recently returned from Athos, was already known to be a talented iconographer and was destined to make his name as one of the most skilful writers of icons in the Athonite tradition working in the West. Though he has subsequently left the monastery (where his place has been taken by another hermit-monk who continues the same tradition), his monastic career is typical of what this book is concerned with. From his home in New Zealand and following a period of study in London, he was drawn to Athos where he joined the cenobitic monastery of Iviron under the charismatic leadership of Fr Vasileios, one of the principal architects of the twentieth-century revival of Athonite monasticism. During the years he spent on Athos, in obedience to an encouraging spiritual father, he was enabled to embark on the spiritual path of a monk as well as the spiritual path of an iconographer. Having learnt the rudiments of both, he chose to return to the world and to the West, to establish a hermitage in England where he could pray and work, and where he could operate as an ambassador for Orthodoxy and for the sacred traditions of the Holy Mountain.

As we shall see, this is the way that Athos has operated for centuries, since the first monks were attracted to its secluded, harsh, and numinous terrain. Many stay for life, but a significant proportion return to the world, armed with the fruits of the garden of the Mother of God. Their impact on the world, perhaps not widely recognized, has been immense, wide-ranging, and of huge significance. And this is not a phenomenon restricted to a remote Byzantine period or East European context. It is still happening today, even in the West. Theirs is the story that this book sets out to tell.

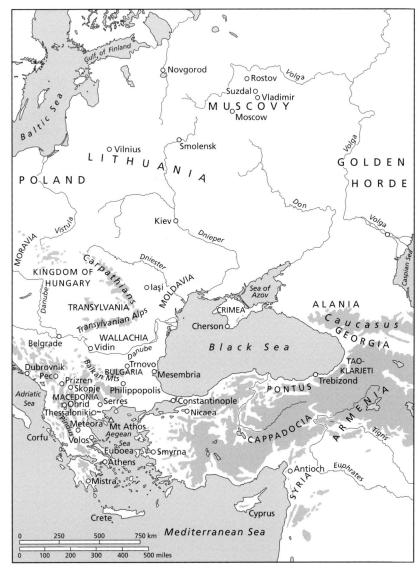

Map 1. The Byzantine Commonwealth.

CHAPTER I

Introduction

The Byzantine Commonwealth

It is no accident that the title of this book is reminiscent of the titles of two other books written by distinguished scholars, to both of which I must acknowledge a debt. The first is the seminal work by the Oxford historian Dimitri Obolensky entitled *The Byzantine Commonwealth*.[1] This book, when it first appeared in 1971, was not without its critics, no doubt because the ideas that it contained were so revolutionary; but perhaps the clearest demonstration of the fact that those ideas have now attained the status of orthodoxy is provided by the historian Jonathan Shepard who entitles his introductory chapter to the recently published volume on Eastern Christianity in the *Cambridge History of Christianity* 'The Byzantine Commonwealth 1000–1550' (and the extension of the closing date from 1453 to 1550 is significant).[2] Rather than paraphrase those ideas here, I prefer to quote Obolensky himself (partly I must confess because he was such a master of English prose) who summarized them quite concisely in the introduction to a subsequent book:

> Some years ago, in a book entitled *The Byzantine Commonwealth*, I ventured the opinion that in the Middle Ages, despite notable differences in social and political life, those East European countries which owed their religion and much of their culture to Byzantium formed a single international community; its nature, I argued, is revealed in a common cultural tradition shared and contributed to by their ruling and educated classes. They were bound by the same profession of Eastern Christianity; they acknowledged the primacy of the Constantinopolitan Church; they recognized that the Byzantine emperor was endowed with a measure of authority over the whole of Orthodox Christendom; they accepted the principles of Romano-

---

[1] D. Obolensky, *The Byzantine Commonwealth: Eastern Europe 500–1453* (London: Weidenfeld and Nicolson, 1971).

[2] J. Shepard, 'The Byzantine Commonwealth 1000–1550', in M. Angold (ed.), *The Cambridge History of Christianity, vol. 5: Eastern Christianity* (Cambridge: Cambridge University Press, 2006), pp. 3–52.

Byzantine law; and they held that the literary standards and artistic techniques of the Empire's schools, monasteries, and scriptoria were universally valid models. This international community I rather intrepidly called the Byzantine Commonwealth.[3]

Some scholars have questioned the validity of the term 'commonwealth' when applied to Byzantium;[4] and it is true, as Obolensky himself admitted in the passage just quoted, that there were often major differences in social and political terms between its members. So there are between members of the British Commonwealth today, but they do not get in the way of it operating very effectively as an economic and cultural umbrella sheltering a motley collection of states that share a common history, culture, and language. But just as with its modern-day British counterpart, membership of the Byzantine Commonwealth was always entirely voluntary; and, as Shepard writes, 'Acceptance of the Constantinopolitan patriarch's profession of faith and the Byzantine-authorised forms of worship – virtually the only stable denominators of adherence to the Byzantine order – did not rule out a variety of other cultural identities or political allegiances.'[5] The Oxford historian Averil Cameron has also pointed to some problems with the 'commonwealth' idea, at least as a general historical model for Byzantium: 'We need now to look less to the religious agendas emphasized in previous scholarship than to "connective history" – networks, connections, and interacting systems, including trade, diplomacy, and indeed these aspects of religion.'[6] Indeed, it is 'connective history' and the networks of Orthodoxy that this book is about and for our purposes the 'commonwealth' idea seems all the more appropriate. 'The term "commonwealth"', Cameron goes on, 'is inherently favorable, bypassing considerations of power and social macrostructures in favor of a kind of generalized cultural beneficence.' She seems willing to accept the term in a less 'top-down' sense, and in a cultural and religious context where a measure of 'generalized beneficence' is surely not out of place; and she writes, 'when applied to the post-Byzantine period the idea is even more closely associated with the influence of Orthodoxy, and especially that of

---

[3] D. Obolensky, *Six Byzantine Portraits* (Oxford: Clarendon Press, 1988), p. 1.

[4] See, for example, the books by the American Byzantinist Anthony Kaldellis: *Hellenism in Byzantium: The Transformations of Greek Identity and the Reception of the Classical Tradition* (Cambridge: Cambridge University Press, 2007), *Ethnography after Antiquity: Foreign Lands and Peoples in Byzantine Literature* (Philadelphia, PA: University of Pennsylvania Press, 2013), and the provocatively titled *The Byzantine Republic: People and Power in New Rome* (Cambridge, MA: Harvard University Press, 2015).

[5] Shepard, 'The Byzantine Commonwealth 1000–1550', p. 45.

[6] Averil Cameron, *Byzantine Matters* (Princeton, NJ: Princeton University Press, 2014), pp. 39–40.

the monastic milieu on Mount Athos during the Ottoman period.' There could scarcely be a more ringing endorsement for the writing of the present book.

The second book to which I am indebted is the collection of studies more recently put together by the Greek scholar Paschalis Kitromilides and entitled *An Orthodox Commonwealth.*[7] While acknowledging his debt to Obolensky's *magnum opus*, Kitromilides narrows the geographical focus from Eastern Europe as a whole to the Ottoman Balkans and the succeeding national states of south-eastern Europe, and he changes the chronological focus from Byzantium to the early modern period. His concern is not to establish the survival of the 'bonds of Commonwealth' in the post-Byzantine era but rather to question whether it really was a 'commonwealth' and, if so, how long it lasted, how it changed over time, and what forms of transition it experienced.

Kitromilides identifies the most significant historical event in the formation of the Orthodox Commonwealth as the baptism of Prince Vladimir of Kiev in 988 and the subsequent adoption of Orthodox Christianity by his subjects. After the symbolic dissolution of the Christian empire on 29 May 1453, the patriarchate of Constantinople assumed a truly ecumenical role and its subsidiary institutions (notably the monasteries) a collective responsibility to provide guidance for the faithful.

> As a historical phenomenon, the 'Orthodox Commonwealth', the cultural creation of Byzantium, remained a hallmark of the post-Byzantine period, and the provision of its spiritual leadership was understood as an essential element in the historical mission of the Church in the years following the Fall of Constantinople. In the post-Byzantine period, Orthodox religious institutions (patriarchates, monastic foundations, places of pilgrimage) in the broad geographical area from the Baltic to the Red Sea functioned as substitutes for the Christian Empire, and became the focal points in the collective life of the Orthodox communities ... In this sense Byzantium survived after 1453 and, as a cultural heritage, retained its organic unity until the nineteenth century.[8]

As to how long this Orthodox Commonwealth lasted, Kitromilides suggests that it died with Joachim III, patriarch of Constantinople, in 1912, the year which saw the outbreak of the Balkan Wars.

[7] P. M. Kitromilides, *An Orthodox Commonwealth: Symbolic Legacies and Cultural Encounters in Southeastern Europe* (Aldershot: Ashgate, 2007).
[8] Ibid., ch. 6, pp. 6–7.

His death had the same symbolic significance as his belief in the Orthodox Commonwealth, which led him to welcome to the Ecumenical Patriarchate, with equal warmth, the Grand Dukes of Russia, the King of Serbia and the princes of Greece. These scions of ancient dynasties and the world they symbolised in the eyes of the Patriarch were, on the threshold of the twentieth century, no more than the last embers of a lost world. The new century was dawning as imperialism was reaching its zenith, bringing the deadly conflicts of rival nationalisms to their climax. The millennium-long shared past of the peoples of East and South-Eastern Europe seemed to have fallen into oblivion.[9]

The Athonite Commonwealth

In writing about what I term the 'Athonite Commonwealth', I am particularly conscious of taking up a statement made by Obolensky which, as far as I am aware, he never attempted to develop but which seems to me to invite amplification and illustration over a dauntingly broad canvas. In the context of the persistent southward migration of the peoples of the Balkans and Central Europe into Byzantine territory he writes:

> These migrations of peoples were, we have seen, followed by a reverse movement from south to north, instigated by the statesmen in Constantinople with the aim of taming and civilizing them. The alternate movements of commodities, men and ideas to and from the Mediterranean world, which have been compared [by Braudel] to the rhythmic pulsations of the living heart, brought the periphery of this world into close contact with its centre on the Bosphorus, and carried the civilization of Byzantium up rivers, across plains and over seas to the farthest borderlands of Eastern Europe.[10]

Later in the same book Obolensky refers specifically to the part played by the Holy Mountain in this two-way process:

> The analogy, suggested earlier, between the alternating current of men and ideas flowing to and from the Mediterranean and the pulsations of a living heart, finds a further illustration in the role of Mount Athos, drawing to itself men from all over Eastern Europe who sought training in the monastic life, and then sending back, through these Slav monasteries founded on its soil, the results of their labours and learning to their native lands.[11]

It is self-evident that Obolensky has here identified a role of immense importance that was played by the Holy Mountain throughout the latter

---

[9] Ibid., p. 18.   [10] Obolensky, *The Byzantine Commonwealth*, p. 360.   [11] Ibid., p. 383.

part of the Byzantine period. It is my contention that it has continued to play this role down to the present day and that, as long as Athos survives as the spiritual heart of the pan-Orthodox world, that will always be a defining part of its identity.

In my earlier book, *Mount Athos: Renewal in Paradise*,[12] I attempted to sketch a history of Mount Athos from its beginnings as a centre of monastic activity in the ninth century, through its many vicissitudes, periods of growth and periods of decline, down to the end of the twentieth century when it was clearly enjoying a strong revival after a long period of uncertainty. This was very much an internal history, focused on the Mountain itself and its indigenous institutions. My purpose in this new book is to attempt an external history of Athos. I shall be examining the relationships that the monasteries developed with the outside world, 'the networks, connections, and interacting systems' as Cameron would define them, the impact that they had on the development of monasticism, the gifts that they showered on a world that was hungry to receive them. As before, I shall aim to avoid the tedium of a chronicle by focusing on the individuals concerned in these spiritual movements, the relationships that they enjoyed with the Holy Mountain, and the ways in which they shared them with the outside world.

Athos has often been described as the spiritual heart of Orthodoxy. It is worth pausing to consider exactly what that phrase means in practice. It means, as Obolensky adumbrated in his classic study, that throughout its history the Holy Mountain has drawn men from far and wide to come and experience for themselves its seclusion, its sanctity, and the teaching of its holy fathers. Some have come to stay, but many have returned to the outside world, charged by the strength of the spiritual gifts that they have received there and inspired to make use of those gifts in whatever way they can. In many instances they have gone on to found (or revive) monasteries in other parts of the world which have in turn become centres of spirituality. Sometimes gradually, sometimes remarkably rapidly, a network of such centres can be seen to have spread all over the heartlands of the Orthodox world and even beyond, as spiritual fathers have attracted and inspired groups of disciples who have in turn become spiritual fathers to new groups of disciples, who have carried the torch of Athonite monasticism to parts of the world which it had never previously illumined. This monastic diaspora is what I have, 'rather intrepidly', chosen to term the Athonite Commonwealth.

---

[12] G. Speake, *Mount Athos: Renewal in Paradise*, 2nd edn (Limni: Denise Harvey, 2014).

The geographical focus of this 'commonwealth' throughout most of its history has been the Orthodox heartlands of the Balkans and Eastern Europe. During the so-called middle Byzantine period, when the empire was at its height and stood in a position of influence over most of its neighbours, the monastic thrust followed the political one into Georgia, Kievan Rus', Serbia, and Bulgaria. After the Mongol invasions and the Latin empire, when there was a realignment of political forces, there sprang up a new spiritual movement known as hesychasm which turned the Holy Mountain into a hotbed, first of controversy, and subsequently of missionary zeal. As a result, Athonite monasticism was championed by a panoply of charismatic elders from all over Eastern Europe who swiftly transmitted it back to their own lands where it spread like wildfire and became the backbone of an entirely new literary as well as spiritual culture. The fire was dampened, but never quite extinguished, by the Ottoman conquest of the greater part of this area, when the focus shifted to those areas that remained free (or less strictly controlled), namely Russia and Romania. In the second half of the eighteenth century, partly in response to the encroachment of secularizing ideas from the West, another creative burst of Athonite spirituality brought about a spectacular renewal of traditional Orthodoxy and a revival of the monastic network, initially in the neighbouring territories of Romania and Ukraine, but spreading swiftly north to Muscovy and then east over the Urals and the wastes of Siberia to the borders with Central Asia and the Far East whence it took ship across the Bering Strait and found new footholds in the Aleutian Islands and Alaska.

By the early decades of the nineteenth century the Athonite Commonwealth seemed to have reached its natural extent and to have covered the entire Orthodox world. Meanwhile, waves of nationalism swept over what under the Ottomans had been a subject territory with no frontiers. Suddenly there were boundaries where none had been before and demands for autocephaly of the various national Churches. At the same time there were moves to restrict the wealth and power of the monasteries: estates were confiscated, monasteries were closed, and many links with Athos were broken. As the Ottoman Empire started to break up, new tensions arose, the countries of the Balkans found themselves at war with one another, and finally 'holy Russia' itself was engulfed by revolution. A pall of communism spread over almost the whole of the Orthodox world and monasticism was forced into a steep downward path.

Meanwhile, Athonite spirituality, though superficially in sympathetic decline, sought new outlets for its unquenchable springs. While traditional routes to the north and east were now blocked, it took a new direction – to the west. New centres sprang up in Western Europe and North America, and suddenly the Mountain's web became a global phenomenon. With the fall of communism and the reopening of borders in Eastern Europe, freedom has returned to the Orthodox heartlands, monasteries have begun once more to flourish and to fill with men and women thirsting for spiritual waters, and Athos has the opportunity to assume a new role for itself as the seminary of a new monastic revival. Whether it will rise to this challenge is beyond the scope of this book to foretell, but the widely publicized mission in 2011 of an Athonite abbot taking one of the Mountain's holiest relics, the Virgin's Girdle, on an extended tour of Russia to be venerated by millions, reciprocated by an equally high-profile pilgrimage to Athos in 2013 by the patriarch of Moscow, and the celebrations held to mark the millennium of the Russian presence on Athos in 2016 suggest that the possibilities are limitless.

It was the third week of May and the streets of Kiev were decked out in countless sprays of pink and white as the celebrated chestnut trees were in full bloom. The sun shone hot from a cloudless sky, and the city went about its business with the usual noise and bustle of trams and taxis and street cries. But Kiev is a city that takes great pride in its monastic tradition and does not allow the visitor to ignore it. Even in the city centre I found oases of calm: the magnificent cathedral of St Sophia (sadly now a museum; Plate 22) with its glorious eleventh-century Byzantine mosaics is set in a walled enclosure amid lawns and trees where anyone can stroll or sit at leisure; and the nearby monastery of St Michael, newly restored, resplendent in blue and gold and housing the holy relics of St Barbara, offers a functioning church where passers-by, hurrying between appointments, may enter just to light a candle and venerate an icon.

Only two or three kilometres south of the centre is the spiritual symbol of the city, the incomparable Pecherskaya Lavra or monastery of the Caves, founded in 1051 on the west bank of the river Dnieper. Inside its gates all was calm and peaceful. The trees were as festive as those in the streets outside and the flowerbeds responded with sheets of white and yellow irises. A paved path leads straight from the main entrance to the great golden-domed cathedral of the Dormition, some 250 metres away, and from various directions the faithful were making their way towards its open north door, outside which a man with no legs begged for alms. As I drew near, the ground began to vibrate under my feet and the massive bells in the nearby tower gradually stirred themselves into seismic action. I entered through a side chapel where six or seven queues of penitents waited patiently for confession. Inside, the lofty nave was already densely packed with pious Kievans, for this is a monastery wholly integrated with the local community; a deacon, colourfully vested, was slowly rotating on his heels and censing the congregation; a male-voice choir was chanting loudly but mellifluously from a hidden gallery; the Divine Liturgy for the feast of the Ascension was about to begin. The royal doors were opened and at last the celebrant appeared, supported by six other priests and numerous acolytes. As he turned to face the congregation, we were able to identify him as none other than Archimandrite Methodios, abbot of the holy monastery of Hilandar on Mount Athos.

What was a Serbian archimandrite doing serving the Liturgy for the Ascension in this great cathedral inside the monastery of the Caves in Kiev, some 1,500 kilometres away from his home on Mount Athos? Why were there several other Athonite clergy (but no bishops) among those conceleb-rating with him? And why did the congregation include so many laymen and women, drawn from all over the Orthodox world and beyond, wearing official badges of identification?

The occasion was an international conference held from 21 to 23 May 2015 and devoted to the theme of 'Athos and the Slav World'. At the end of the service more than a hundred hierarchs, monastics, academics, and other worthies made their way to the nearby monastery refectory where they would spend the next three days listening to learned papers on all manner of topics connected with this all-embracing topic.

After the conference was over, I spent a day exploring the monastery, its buildings, and its grounds which cover an area of more than 20 hectares. Either side of the approach to the main gate the high walls are painted with frescos that date from the early twentieth century and give a foretaste of what is to be found inside: on the left the so-called Synaxis of the Saints of the Near Caves shows St Antony holding an icon of the Dormition among a crowd of saints whose bones are to this day preserved in the Near Caves; and on the right the Synaxis of the Saints of the Far Caves has St Theodosius holding a cross also among a crowd of saints whose relics lie buried in the Far Caves. Above the gate itself is the imposing church of the Holy Trinity which dates from the early twelfth century, though most of what you see dates from an eighteenth-century restoration. Still it is one of the oldest buildings in the monastery and the ensemble makes an awesome aperitif to the spiritual and architectural feast that is within (Plate 11).

The present cathedral of the Dormition, the principal church of the monastery, dates only from the late twentieth century, its predecessor having been blown to smithereens by a bomb in World War II. The first church, said to have been built in 1075–7, was destroyed by the Mongols in 1240 and it was 200 years before it was replaced. That fifteenth-century church was in turn reduced to ashes in 1718 but was soon rebuilt on a much more lavish scale and survived for another two centuries. Thus the history of this church broadly mirrors the history of Russian monasticism: a humble but confident start in the eleventh century; two centuries of decline under the Mongols; renewed growth in the fifteenth century, halted by a sharp temporary setback in the eighteenth; a swift return to renewed splendour, lasting until the twentieth century when suddenly everything was destroyed, only to be brought back to life in the years before the start of the third millennium. Appropriately enough, the present structure was reconsecrated on the feast of the Dormition, 28 August 2000 (Plate 12).

The most 'authentic' part of the monastery is of course the eponymous caves. St Antony had lived in a cave on Mount Athos and when he returned to Kiev in 1051 he naturally looked for a cave. This underground labyrinth in due course became the kernel of the monastery. The subsequent history of the caves is *described on pp. 69–75. They may still be visited, and they give an idea of what monastic life must have been like in those early days when there were no buildings above ground. In fact, there are two sets of caves, the so-called Near Caves, which are nearly 400 metres long, and the Far Caves, which are somewhat shorter, though deeper. Both sets of caves lie some 10 to 15 metres below ground and comprise a system of passages, lined with tombs and occasionally punctuated by chapels. The tombs, mostly set back in niches, are those of former abbots, saints, and monks of the monastery; the chapels, dimly lit by candles and oil lamps, are still used for worship; and the entire complex serves as a major focus of pilgrimage. The passages seem endless and are quite dark in places, so I was glad of the lighted candle that one is encouraged to carry. They are just high enough to enable someone of average height to stand up, but they feel quite claustrophobic all the same, and I was happy when I finally emerged into the sunlight.*

I felt hugely privileged to be able to spend six consecutive nights in this ancient and numinous place. It was the antithesis of the monastery of Sts Antony and Cuthbert on top of the Stiperstone Hills in Shropshire; and yet they were both living reminders of the strength and breadth of the spiritual diaspora of Mount Athos. And why was our conference being held in this most glorious and most hospitable of all possible monastic venues?

In fact, nowhere could be more appropriate to the theme, for Kiev was one of the earliest and one of the most important outposts of the Athonite Commonwealth. For almost a thousand years the monastery of the Caves has flourished as a major representative of Athonite spirituality, disseminating its fruits to all Russia and beyond. Some of the papers delivered at the conference were more apposite to this theme than others, but the fact that the conference was taking place in this auspicious location and evoking so many associations and links with the entire Orthodox world, was a clear indication that both the Holy Mountain of Athos and its far-reaching Commonwealth are alive and well and reaching out to all those who care to listen to their message. In the pages that follow we shall attempt to identify these associations and these links and draw together the diverse strands that combine to create what is surely the most important spiritual and cultural movement that the Orthodox Christian world has ever seen. But first we need to go right back to the beginning . . .

CHAPTER 2

The Monastic Life

According to the fourth-century theologian Evagrios of Pontos, a monk is someone who is separated from all and united with all.[1] This is surely the essence of monasticism for all time: a monk chooses to separate himself from the rest of the world in order to devote himself to a life of prayer, but through that prayer he is united with the whole world – separated from all and at the same time united with all.

Desert Monasticism

Christian monasticism was initially a phenomenon of the desert (Plate 2). Egypt was one of the first centres, and by the year 400 the Egyptian deserts blossomed with monastic establishments of all kinds. Traditionally known as the 'father of monks' and the first hermit, St Antony the Great was born to a prosperous Coptic family at Kome in Upper Egypt around 251. At the age of eighteen Antony withdrew into the desert for a life of solitude which he maintained for nearly forty years. Then he started to receive visitors and a group of disciples gathered around him. His fame as a spiritual guide spread far and wide and many came to seek his advice, so many in fact that he became a 'physician given to Egypt by God', as his biographer St Athanasios (295–373) put it. He persuaded large numbers of them to follow the ascetic life for themselves, 'and so, from then on, there were monasteries in the mountains and the desert was made a city by monks, who left their own people and registered themselves for the citizenship in the heavens'.[2]

Antony was a hermit, and the 'monasteries' that sprang up in his wake were not really monasteries in the sense of organized and structured

[1] See *The Philokalia*, trans. G. E. H. Palmer, Philip Sherrard, and Kallistos Ware, vol. 1 (London: Faber & Faber, 1979), p. 69.
[2] Athanasius, *The Life of Antony and the Letter to Marcellinus*, trans. R. C. Gregg (New York: Paulist Press, 1980), pp. 42–3.

institutions but groups of hermits who chose to live in caves in the vicinity of other hermits. These monks were not bound by any rules and took no vow of obedience, nor did they eat together or worship together, though as each community was formed it would commonly appoint a more experienced monk as 'elder' to be a guide or father to newcomers. In the course of time, these communities became more structured and acquired a few buildings such as a church and a refectory in which the monks would worship and eat a communal meal once a week. More than once Antony found himself the focus of such a community, but each time the pressure of disciples was too burdensome for him and he withdrew again into total solitude. So he remained, separated from all and united with all, for the remainder of his life until he died, apparently at the age of 105, in 356. 'Antony has had many successors,' writes Bishop Kallistos,

> and in most of them the same outward pattern of events is found – *a withdrawal in order to return.* A monk must first withdraw, and in silence must learn the truth about himself and God. Then, after this long and rigorous preparation in solitude, having gained the gifts of discernment which are required of an elder, he can open the door of his cell and admit the world from which formerly he fled.[3]

This notion of 'a withdrawal in order to return' we shall find cropping up time and again in the course of this book. It is fundamental to the story that is to be told.

One of Antony's successors was St Pachomios (286–346) who was born to pagan parents near Esna in Upper Egypt and converted to Christianity while he was serving in the army. On leaving the army, Pachomios received baptism and embarked on the ascetic life in a lavra under the guidance of a hermit.[4] Some years later he had a vision in which he was called to found a community of his own, for which purpose he moved to Tabennisi, about 80 kilometres north of Esna. Here he was joined by a growing number of disciples who formed the nucleus of a community and who agreed on two important principles: that they would live a common (i.e. cenobitic) lifestyle and that they would do so under the guidance of Pachomios. This became the first truly cenobitic monastery, and Pachomios, armed with his military

---

[3] K. Ware, *The Orthodox Church: An Introduction to Eastern Christianity*, 3rd edn (Harmondsworth: Penguin, 2015), p. 38. Emphasis in the original.

[4] A lavra (literally a narrow street or lane in a city) initially meant a group of monastic cells associated with a cluster of common buildings such as a church, refectory, hall, etc. The monks would live as hermits during the week and come together on Saturdays and Sundays in order to attend the services and share meals. From the eighth century the term was applied to much larger cenobitic monasteries such as the Great Lavra on Mount Athos and the Caves monastery in Kiev.

training, set about establishing its buildings and organizing the way that life would be lived there. The buildings consisted of a church and a place of assembly, a refectory with a kitchen, a library, a workshop, a hospital, and cells for the monks, all surrounded by a circuit of walls with a gatehouse at the entrance. As for the way of life, each monk wore a simple monastic habit, joined the other monks for prayer, and ate with the other monks twice a day in the refectory. The monastery aimed to be self-sufficient, and work on the land as well as in the house was shared out among the brethren. The regime was strict and well regulated: there was a rule of silence during working periods, the diet was simple but wholesome (with no meat or wine), and not much time was allocated for sleep. Life in the monastery was governed by a set of written rules which survive (in a Latin translation made by St Jerome) and which, as far as possible, were enforced.

> No one shall enter the cell of his neighbour without first knocking.
>   Nor should one go in to eat at noon before the signal is given. Nor shall they walk around in the village before the signal is given.
>   No one shall walk in the community without his goat skin and his hood, either to the *synaxis* or to the refectory.
>   No one shall go to oil his hands in the evening unless a brother is sent with him; no one shall oil his whole body unless he is sick, or bathe or wash it immodestly contrary to the manner established for them.
>   No one shall oil or bathe a sick man unless ordered.
>   No one may speak to his neighbours in the dark.
>   Nor shall you sit two together on a mat or carpet.
>   No one may clasp the hand or anything else of his companion; but whether you are sitting or standing or walking, you shall leave a forearm's space between you and him.[5]

But Pachomios had a reputation for kindness as well as wisdom, the model proved popular, and by the time of his death in 346 there were already eleven such monasteries in existence in the area, two of them for women. Each house contained several hundred monastics, and by the year 350 Pachomios's second monastery at Pebou had a population of 600.

   In Lower Egypt groups of ascetics first formed at Nitria, about 60 kilometres south of Alexandria, and subsequently in the Wadi Natrun (Shiet in Coptic, Scetis in Greek), an arid valley in the desert some 65 kilometres north-west of Cairo. One day a camel-driver from the Delta known as Makarios (*c.*300–90) visited the valley and decided to take up the ascetic life there at the age of thirty. Soon others joined him and the

[5] A. Veilleux (trans.), *Pachomian Koinonia*, vol. 2 (Kalamazoo, MI: Cistercian Publications, 1981), p. 161.

community in due course formed the nucleus of the monastery of Baramus, which was founded *c*.340. By the end of the fourth century two other monastic communities had been founded in the Wadi Natrun, one named after Fr Makarios and the other after another local ascetic, St Bishoi. And by the sixth century a fourth monastery, first named after the Theotokos, was founded, but early in the eighth century this house was bought by Syrian traders for the use of Syrian monks and since then it has been known as the monastery of the Syrians. All these monasteries were of the semi-eremitic variety and, since they were unprotected, they were subject to frequent attack by Bedouin from the desert and, after the conquest, by Arabs. From the ninth century the monks at Wadi Natrun began to fortify their monasteries, eventually surrounding them with high walls, but the attacks continued and the population fluctuated considerably – from a high of at least 3,500 in the fifth century to a mere 700 in the eleventh. The monks were practically wiped out by the Black Death in the fourteenth century, but all four monasteries are flourishing again today, having enjoyed remarkable renewal in the 1950s.

The fourth-century fathers of the Egyptian desert set standards for the ascetic life that have inspired future generations of monastics and lay people from that day to this. Renowned for their wisdom and their insight as spiritual fathers, they are perhaps best remembered for the deceptively simple words of advice that they dispensed freely to all who sought them out. These *Sayings of the Fathers* (or, more formally, *Apophthegmata Patrum*) constitute a new literary genre, somewhere between parables and folktales, on themes that have a timeless and universal application, and have exercised wide-ranging influence not only on contemporary writers in late antiquity and in the Middle East but on subsequent generations in Byzantium, in nineteenth-century Russia, and throughout the Orthodox diaspora. They are widely read today and often form part of recommended reading as passed on by confessors to penitents and spiritual children. One or two examples must suffice here. First a saying of John Cassian (360–435), whose writings about Egyptian monasticism were recommended by St Benedict as 'tools of virtue for good-living and obedient monks':

> There was a monk living in a cave in the desert. His relations according to the flesh let him know, 'Your father is very ill, at the point of death: come and receive his inheritance.' He replied to them, 'I died to the world before he did and the dead do not inherit from the living.'[6]

---

[6] Benedicta Ward (trans.), *The Sayings of the Desert Fathers: The Alphabetical Collection*, new edn. (Kalamazoo, MI: Cistercian Publications, 1984), pp. 114–15.

Next Arsenios (*c*.360–449), a Roman by birth who became a hermit in Scetis:

> One day Abba Arsenius consulted an old Egyptian monk about his own thoughts. Someone noticed this and said to him, 'Abba Arsenius, how is it that you with such a good Latin and Greek education, ask this peasant about your thoughts?' He replied, 'I have indeed been taught Latin and Greek, but I do not know even the alphabet of this peasant.'[7]

Finally, a saying about St Makarios the Great, founder of the first Scetis monastery:

> When Abba Macarius was returning from the marsh to his cell one day carrying some palm-leaves, he met the devil on the road with a scythe. The latter struck at him as much as he pleased, but in vain, and he said to him, 'What is your power, Macarius, that makes me powerless against you? All that you do, I do, too; you fast, so do I; you keep vigil, and I do not sleep at all; in one thing only do you beat me.' Abba Macarius asked what that was. He said, 'Your humility. Because of that I can do nothing against you.'[8]

Their English translator, Sister Benedicta Ward, sums up the purpose of the *Sayings* as 'radical simplicity and integrity', while the key to the spirituality of the desert is to be found in a saying of St Antony: 'Whatever you find in your heart to do in following God, that do, and remain within yourself in Him.'[9]

One of the most important successors of St Antony as a founder of Christian monasticism was St Basil the Great, bishop of Caesarea in Asia Minor (*c*.330–79). Basil visited the monastic communities in Egypt, as well as those that had sprung up in Syria, and became a convinced supporter of the cenobitic way of life. After living as a hermit for five years in the desert of Pontos he concluded that the communal life was in fact superior to the eremitic and that only by living as a member of a community could one carry out Christ's second commandment: 'Whose feet then wilt thou wash?', he wrote. 'Whom wilt thou care for? In comparison with whom wilt thou be last if thou livest by thyself? How will that good and pleasant thing, the dwelling of brethren together, which the Holy Spirit likens to unguent flowing down from the High Priest's head, be accomplished by dwelling solitary?'[10] He therefore founded a number of coenobia in Cappadocia and made recommendations as to how they should be governed which have remained fundamental to the subsequent development

---

[7] Ibid., p. 10.   [8] Ibid., pp. 129–30.   [9] Ibid., pp. xxvi–xxvii.
[10] Basil, *Regulae Fusius Tractatae*, 7; W. K. Lowther Clarke (trans.), *The Ascetic Works of Saint Basil* (London: SPCK, 1925), p. 166.

of Eastern monasticism, but he also made provision for solitaries to retreat to nearby cells where they could more easily concentrate on the first commandment ('thou shalt love the Lord thy God with all thy heart . . .'). Basil went further than his predecessors in recommending also that monasteries should develop a social dimension to their work, that they should set up hospitals and orphanages that would enable them to care for the sick and the deprived and thus make a direct contribution to the well-being of their neighbours. In this respect he was probably more influenced by the Syrian model than the Egyptian, since Syrian monasticism was not only a desert phenomenon but also had an urban dimension. From as early as the fourth century then, monastics have fulfilled a role in the community not only as physicians of the soul but also of the body, though their primary task has always remained a life of prayer.

In order to devote themselves to this primary task monks have tended to show a preference for lonely places, mountains and deserts and caves, where they can withdraw from the world and be alone with God. The slopes and summits of mountains were especially favoured in the Levant and the Balkans, and indeed the Greek word for 'mountaineer' (*oreivatis*) was sometimes used as a synonym for 'monk'.[11] Such places might first be home to a charismatic hermit or elder, who would then attract a group of disciples to gather around him. Sometimes more than one monastery, or more than one form of monasticism, would emerge and in time the area would become known as a 'holy mountain'. Such mountains were dotted around much of Asia Minor, for example Mount Olympos and Mount Kyminas near Bursa, Mount Latros near Miletus, and Mount Galesion near Ephesus. Elsewhere a few survive to the present day, notably the monastery of St Catherine on Mount Sinai founded by the Emperor Justinian in the sixth century, the rock monasteries of the Meteora, which first came to prominence in the fourteenth century, and most famous of all the holy mountain of Athos.

One of the great figures of desert monasticism associated with St Catherine's monastery was St John Klimakos ('of the Ladder') (*c*.579–*c*.650) who lived as a hermit for forty years before eventually becoming abbot. John's principal work, *The Ladder of Divine Ascent*, aimed primarily at an audience of monks, remains to this day the most widely used handbook of the ascetic life. Each of the ladder's thirty rungs represents either

---

[11] Cf. e.g. Simeon the Mountaineer. The late Archimandrite Ephrem Lash enjoyed referring to his erstwhile fellow Athonites as 'holy mountaineers' (e.g. 'Athos: A Working Community', in A. Bryer and M. Cunningham (eds), *Mount Athos and Byzantine Monasticism* (Aldershot: Variorum, 1996), p. 87).

a virtue to be aspired to or a sin to be jettisoned. Two of its recommendations are of particular interest. The first is the need for a spiritual father.
The ascent of the ladder is not to be attempted alone but under the
direction of a spiritual director. Recalling the wisdom of St Antony, John
writes in step 1 of the monk's need for 'some Moses to be our intermediary
with God, to stand between action and contemplation, and stretch out his
arms to God';[12] and later, in step 26, 'a man, no matter how prudent, may
easily go astray on a road if he has no guide. The man who takes the road of
monastic life under his own direction may easily be lost, even if he has all
the wisdom of the world.'[13] The need for a spiritual guide has always been
and remains one of the fundamental requirements for an aspiring ascetic, as
for example when the young man later known as Elder Joseph the
Hesychast (1898–1959) consulted the discerning Elder Daniel of
Katounakia, he received the following advice:

> Do you have an elder? Without the blessing of your elder, nothing can
> prosper. Without this seal of a paternal blessing, no spiritual work in our
> own monastic life bears fruit. This is why I insist that you pass through this
> requirement, that the grace of God may be with you throughout your lives.
> Go to an old man, however simple he may seem, and submit yourselves in
> obedience to him; and when he dies and you have laid him in his grave, you
> will receive as your inheritance the blessing of God, accompanying you and
> leading you to advancement of every kind.[14]

John's other piece of advice that we should especially note is set out in
step 28, 'On Prayer'. 'Prayer', he writes, 'is by nature a dialogue and a union
of man with God. Its effect is to hold the world together . . . Prayer is future
gladness, action without end, wellspring of virtues, source of grace, hidden
progress, food of the soul, enlightenment of the mind, an axe against
despair, hope demonstrated, sorrow done away with. It is wealth for
monks, treasure of hermits, anger diminished.'[15] And he goes on to lay
particular emphasis on the Jesus Prayer, the invocation of the name of
Jesus, though he does not spell out the prayer in the form that was to
become standard: 'Lord Jesus Christ, Son of God, have mercy on me.'
In step 15 he writes, 'Let the remembrance of death and the concise Jesus
Prayer go to sleep with you and get up with you, for nothing helps you as

---

[12] John Climacus, *The Ladder of Divine Ascent*, trans. C. Luibheid and N. Russell (Mahwah, NJ: Paulist
Press, 1982), step 1 (*Patrologia Graeca* [PG] 88. 636A), p. 75.
[13] Ibid., step 26 (1089B), p. 259.
[14] Elder Joseph, *Elder Joseph the Hesychast: Struggles – Experiences – Teachings*, trans. E. Theokritoff
(Mount Athos: Monastery of Vatopaidi, 1999), p. 47.
[15] John Climacus, *The Ladder of Divine Ascent*, step 28 (1129A), p. 274.

these do when you are asleep.'[16] And later, in step 27, he writes, 'Stillness (*hesychia*) is worshipping God unceasingly and waiting on Him. Let the remembrance of Jesus be present with your every breath. Then indeed you will appreciate the value of stillness.'[17] Here John links the remembrance of Jesus with stillness (*hesychia*), and by 'stillness' he means not only the external way of life of the hermit or solitary but also the internal disposition of continual prayer. As Bishop Kallistos has written when commenting on this passage,

> For the true hesychast, inward prayer is not so much an occasional occupation as a continuous state; it is not merely one activity among others, but *the* activity of his whole life . . . In this way the hesychast is not someone why *says* prayers from time to time, but someone who *is* prayer all the time. His prayer becomes in the true sense *prayer of the heart*.[18]

In the fifth and sixth centuries the focus of monastic activity shifted to Palestine where holy men such as St Euthymios the Great (d.473) and his disciple St Sabas (d.532), both Cappadocians in the tradition of St Basil, took up residence. St Sabas had spent twelve years in a monastery in Judaea before he was instructed by his elder to withdraw to a cave and live the solitary life for five days of the week, returning to his community in order to attend the services on Saturday and Sunday. The monastery founded by him in the valley of the Jordan, initially a community of the semi-eremitic type, survived the Arab conquest and continues to function amid very difficult circumstances to this day.

In the seventh century the Byzantines were taken by surprise by the speed with which Islam spread throughout the Middle East and North Africa. The empire swiftly lost its eastern provinces, the patriarchs of Alexandria, Antioch, and Jerusalem found themselves under infidel rule, and before the end of the century the Arabs were threatening the walls of Constantinople itself. The monasteries, however, though frequently subjected to attack, for the most part survived, largely because most Muslims are serious about their religion and have an innate respect for others who do the same. This respect, which was mutual, was to stand the monks in good stead for much of their history. There has, for example, been a mosque inside the walls of St Catherine's monastery in Sinai since the eleventh century, which symbolizes the symbiosis between the monks and their Muslim neighbours; and in later centuries after the fall of the empire

[16] Ibid., step 15 (889D), p. 178.   [17] Ibid., step 27 (1112C), pp. 269–70.
[18] K. Ware, Introduction to John Climacus, *The Ladder of Divine Ascent*, p. 53. Emphasis in the original.

it may have been their awe for the monks' supernatural powers and the efficacy of their prayers that persuaded the Ottomans to deal lightly with the Athonites.

Urban Monasticism

Certainly, the majority of Byzantines were extremely serious about their religion and for the first three or four centuries of the empire's existence they devoted much of their intellectual energy to establishing a creed that would provide an acceptable basis for their faith. A series of six ecumenical councils were convened to identify what was heresy and what was Orthodoxy. No sooner had these questions concerning the person of Christ been resolved than a new controversy arose in the eighth century over the use of icons and relics in Orthodox worship. Some have argued that the inspiration for iconoclasm, as the movement for the destruction of icons became known, came from Judaism and Islam, but there had always been a 'puritan' element within Christianity that had regarded the use of icons as idolatrous and so, when the Emperor Leo III published his edict attacking their use in 726, he found many inside the Church who were ready to support him. Few of them were monks.

The period of iconoclasm stretched over 120 years but was divided into two phases. In each phase it was monks who were the leading opponents. During the first phase (726–80) persecution of iconophiles, as the champions of icons were known, was concentrated in the capital, was less intensive in the provinces, and lost all its force beyond the boundaries of the empire. Thus St John of Damascus (*c*.675–749), a monk of the lavra of St Sabas in Palestine and a scholar from an influential family, was able to write with impunity numerous polemical works against the iconoclasts. It took the courage of an empress to bring the persecution to an end, and it was during Irene's regency for her son Constantine that a seventh council was convened in 787 that proclaimed the veneration of icons to be Orthodox. The second phase of iconoclasm began in 815, when Emperor Leo V the Armenian repudiated the decrees of Irene, but it lacked the vigour of the first phase. Again, the opposition to it was led by a monk, this time St Theodore the Stoudite (759–826). Theodore refused to take part in the local council of 815 for which he was exiled, first to Bithynia and subsequently to Smyrna. Despite publishing a robust refutation of iconoclasm in which he developed the ideas of St John of Damascus, he was later recalled to the capital. But it took another empress, this time Theodora, to drive the final nail into the iconoclasts' coffin and proclaim the Triumph of

Orthodoxy in 843. By now monasticism was firmly established as an urban phenomenon, and the victory over iconoclasm was celebrated nowhere with greater enthusiasm than in the monasteries. For, as St John of Damascus wrote, 'the image is a triumph and manifestation and inscribed tablet in memory of the victory of the bravest and most eminent and of the shame of those worsted and overthrown.'[19]

Theodore had already made a name for himself by restoring the Stoudios monastery in Constantinople and establishing a strong cenobitic community there. The monastery had been founded by the consul Stoudios in the mid fifth century, but by the time Theodore arrived in 798 it was almost derelict. He immediately set about refurbishing the buildings; he restored the church and added a school, a library, and a scriptorium. He linked Stoudios to a network of monasteries outside the city that acted as a channel for the recruitment of novices and within a decade the community was said to number as many as 1,000 monks, drawn from all walks of life. Building on the tradition received from St Pachomios and St Basil, Theodore devised a cenobitic rule that governed every aspect of monastic life.[20] He created a pyramidal structure for administration of the house with the abbot as head of the entire community and with particular responsibility for spiritual concerns. He retained absolute control over the appointment of subordinates, the drafting of regulations, and the maintenance of discipline. But because the abbot could not be personally responsible for every area of activity, he established a hierarchy of officials, each with his own department but each reporting to the abbot, whose burden was thus lightened. Immediately below the abbot was the deputy abbot (*deutereuon*) who was ready to stand in for his superior should the need arise and who was one of the abbot's chief advisers. Next came the steward (*oikonomos*) who took charge of the monastery's material needs with a staff of his own, which supervised the operation of the kitchen, the refectory, the wine cellar, the bakery, the tailor, and so on. Equal in rank to the steward was the director of discipline (*epistemonarches*) who also had a staff charged with detecting and punishing any infringement of the regulations. Other officers were responsible for tuition in the school, the organization of services in the church, manning

---

[19] St John of Damascus, *Three Treatises on the Divine Images*, trans. A. Louth (Crestwood, NY: St Vladimir's Seminary Press, 2003), p. 68.

[20] The version of the rule that has come down to us was put together by disciples of Theodore after his death in 826 and dates from not before 842. An English translation, by Timothy Miller, is published in J. Thomas and A. Constantinides Hero (eds), *Byzantine Monastic Foundation Documents* (Washington, DC: Dumbarton Oaks, 2001), vol. I, pp. 84–119.

the gate, supervising the library, and caring for the sick. More than forty departments were listed in the administration of the monastery, each with its own dedicated staff, and as a result there was a place in the hierarchy for every single member of the brotherhood. Such a complex structure for a monastery was unprecedented in the capital, but there had never before been a monastery of the size of Stoudios nor an abbot with the administrative skills of Theodore.

Theodore established a similar structure for the spiritual welfare of his monks which was based on discipline. He urged his monks to rejoice in the virtues of obedience, poverty, and self-control, but, disclaiming any originality of his own, he always protested that he was restoring the old monastic ways of the early Fathers. More specifically, he encouraged a return to the old ideals of primitive monasticism, basic necessities, and a restricted diet, and he laid stress on the spiritual benefits of manual labour. 'He who is fervent in bodily tasks', he wrote, 'is also fervent in spiritual ones.'[21] In summer at least eight hours a day were to be devoted to work and in winter at least four or five. But work might include intellectual activity such as the copying of manuscripts, for which Stoudios became renowned, or social activity such as caring for the sick and the poor. Monks were also required to be literate, to devote themselves to reading of Holy Scripture, and to be fervent in prayer and hymnody. Theodore was following the model of the earliest desert monasteries in creating a scriptorium and encouraging his monks to read:

> It should be known that on the days when we rest from our corporal work, the keeper of the books sounds the wooden semantron once, and the brothers assemble at the book station; each one takes a book and reads it until the evening. Before the signal for the office of lamplighting, the man in charge of the books sounds the semantron again, and all the brothers come to return their books in accordance with the register. If anyone is late in returning his book, he should suffer some penalty.[22]

The Stoudite way of life, or 'rule' as it is sometimes called, was soon adopted as the basis for the administration of many monasteries throughout the Orthodox world. By the end of the ninth century it had reached southern Italy where it became the foundation for the charters (*typika*) of the Greek monasteries there; in the tenth century it was introduced at the Great Lavra on Mount Athos; and in the eleventh century it was translated

---

[21] See R. Morris, *Monks and Laymen in Byzantium 843–1118* (Cambridge: Cambridge University Press, 1995), p. 15.

[22] Thomas and Constantinides Hero, *Byzantine Monastic Foundation Documents*, vol. 1, p. 108, §26.

into Slavonic for use in the monastery of the Caves near Kiev by its abbot, St Theodosius (*c*.1062–74). Dimitri Obolensky sums up its influence thus:

> The monastery of Studios . . . played during the early Middle Ages a role in Eastern Europe comparable in some degree to the position occupied in Western Christendom by the abbey of Cluny. The austerity of its rules on corporate worship, manual work and study was tempered by a moderation in the practice of asceticism which on the whole was characteristic of Byzantine cenobitic monasticism . . . In the liturgical field Studios set a pattern for the whole of Eastern Christendom, and many hymns still in current use in the Orthodox Church were composed during the ninth century within its walls. Its constitution claimed to be, in the words of its preamble, 'the best and the most royal rule which indeed avoids both extravagance and inadequacy'.[23]

Monks as Missionaries and Teachers

The defeat of iconoclasm in 843 was followed by a remarkable flowering of the empire's fortunes in political as well as spiritual and artistic terms. Largely free from internal controversy, the Byzantines were now able to turn their attention to external affairs and the developments taking place beyond their own borders. In the Balkans, the Bulgarian empire was expanding and incorporating more and more of the Slavic tribes. Great Moravia had emerged as the first organized Slavic state in central Europe, covering more or less the territory of the present-day Czech Republic and Slovakia, while further east the principalities of Kiev and Novgorod had been established. It was time for Byzantium to reach an accommodation with the Slavs and to bring them within the cultural and spiritual fold of the empire.

In 862 Prince Ratislav of Moravia sent an embassy to Constantinople. It is to be assumed (though it is not stated in any contemporary document) that the two powers sought and concluded a political alliance against their common foe, Bulgaria. What is stated, and what was to have much greater long-term significance, was the request from Ratislav that the Byzantines send a bishop and a teacher to teach the already Christian Moravians in their own language, for the reason that 'good law' came from Byzantium. Ratislav's motives were largely political, as Moravia had been infiltrated by German priests who were agents of Frankish imperialism, and his hope was that the introduction of Slavic-speaking clergy would tip the balance in

---

[23] Obolensky, *The Byzantine Commonwealth*, p. 382.

favour of Constantinople and help Moravia to acquire an independent intellectual culture. In the event, it did far more than that.[24]

The emperor did not select a bishop for this mission, but two brothers from Thessaloniki, the deacon Constantine (826–69) and the monk Methodios (?815–85). Coming from a family with a tradition of public service, both had received a good education and were fluent in Slavonic. They were also experienced missionaries, having been sent two years earlier by Emperor Michael III and Patriarch Photios on an embassy to the Khazars, a Turkic people living to the north of the Caspian Sea. They were therefore well qualified to serve on this new mission, which would require them not only to preach to the Moravians in Slavonic but also to provide them with translations of the Scriptures and of the Orthodox liturgy. They made a start on their translations before they left home, and for this purpose they had to invent a suitable alphabet. The language they used was the local Macedonian dialect of Slavonic with which they had been familiar since childhood in Thessaloniki, but which would be readily intelligible to the people of Moravia. The alphabet, however, later to be known as Glagolitic, was according to their biographers revealed to Constantine by God (Plate 3). Thus Michael was able to write in response to Ratislav's request that God 'has now, in our time, revealed letters in your tongue ... so that you may be included among the great nations which praise God in their own tongue ... Therefore, accept a gift greater and more valuable than gold and silver and precious stones and all transient riches.'[25]

Constantine and Methodios spent about three years in Moravia, during which time they established the basis for Slavonic to be used as a written language both in school and in church. Their mission completed, they departed, no doubt intending to return to Constantinople. On their arrival in Venice, however, they were attacked by Latin bishops, priests, and monks for contravening the doctrine of trilingualism, which insisted that there were only three languages in which it was lawful to praise God, namely Hebrew, Greek, and Latin. Such a doctrine was unheard of in Byzantium, and Constantine replied to their charges with a lengthy, elegant, and confident speech, beginning with these words:

[24] *Vita Constantini-Cyrilli*, ch. 14. See A.-E. N. Tachiaos, *Cyril and Methodios of Thessalonica: The Acculturation of the Slavs* (Crestwood, NY: St Vladimir's Seminary Press, 2001), p. 65. For the Life of Constantine, see also A. Vaillant, *Textes vieux-slaves* (Paris: Institut d'études slaves, 1968), vol. I, pp. 1–40.

[25] *Vita Constantini-Cyrilli*, ch. 14. See Tachiaos, *Cyril and Methodios*, p. 75.

But does the rain not fall equally upon all peoples, does the sun not shine for all, and do we not all breathe the air in equal measure? Wherefore, then, are you not ashamed to recognize but three tongues and command the other nations and races to be blind and deaf? Say, will you have God weak, as though unable to bestow this [script], or jealous, that He does not wish to? For we know many peoples who have a script and give glory to God, each in its own tongue.[26]

There follows a list of peoples who had received their Christianity from Byzantium, designed to demonstrate not only what close relations the empire enjoyed with its neighbours but also how, by respecting their spiritual freedom, it ensured recognition of its own superiority.

News of the debate taking place in Venice soon reached the ears of the Pope, and the two brothers were no doubt gratified to receive an invitation to Rome to defend their position before the supreme authority of the Western Church. They came bearing the relics of St Clement, which they had carried with them from the Crimea, and this guaranteed them a warm welcome, which they duly received. They also brought with them of course books containing the Scriptures and the divine services in Slavonic. The Pope took these, placed them on the altar, and consecrated them, indicating that they were accepted as sacred, and he promptly celebrated a Mass in which the books were used, banishing any suggestion that they were not suitable for liturgical use. He went on to ordain Methodios as a priest and arranged for three of the brothers' Slav disciples to be similarly ordained. The new priests were then invited to concelebrate a Mass in Slavonic in St Peter's basilica.

Exhausted by the rigours of travelling, the intensity of his labours, and the bitterness of the many subsequent disputes, Constantine now collapsed and, anticipating his death, was tonsured as monk Cyril. Only now did he receive the name by which he is more commonly known and the name that is associated with the alphabet subsequently adopted by the entire Slavic world. In fact, the Cyrillic alphabet was not created by Cyril but by Slav disciples of Methodios, who adapted the Greek uncial (capital) script to the phonetic requirements of the Slavonic language.

Meanwhile in Rome, Methodios was consecrated a bishop and installed as archbishop of Pannonia, serving as papal legate to the Slavs. He returned to Moravia where he applied himself to strengthening the Slavonic Church but where he faced growing opposition from a variety of quarters: first the Franks, whose clergy did all they could to undermine his authority; then

---

[26] *Vita Constantini-Cyrilli*, ch. 16. See Tachiaos, *Cyril and Methodios*, p. 83.

the new ruler of Moravia, whose allegiance had switched from Byzantium to central Europe; and finally, the papacy, which withdrew its support for the Slavonic liturgy and eventually banned it. Increasingly isolated, Methodios was invited back to Constantinople where he presented the emperor with two of his disciples and some Slavonic liturgical books, which would no doubt facilitate the acculturation of the Slavs in other areas such as Bulgaria. Returning to Moravia, he devoted his remaining years to his work of translating the Scriptures and other ascetical texts into Slavonic. With the help of two disciples, he completed his task and bequeathed to his followers an entire library in Slavonic that would serve as the basis of their spiritual and political life.

After Methodios's death in 885, however, his followers were expelled from Moravia by the Germans. Over the next two centuries all traces of a Slavonic Church there were eradicated and the country reverted to the Latin rite. But Cyril and Methodios had not laboured in vain, and their disciples, notably Sts Clement and Naum, continued their work of transmitting Eastern Christianity to the Slavs. Bulgaria, whose ruler Boris had accepted baptism from Patriarch Photios in 864/5, was the principal beneficiary of this effort and adopted the principles of the Moravian mission, replacing Greek with Slavonic in church services and receiving and assimilating Byzantine culture in Slavonic dress. The Bulgarians themselves made a major contribution to this legacy when in 893 they convened a council at which it was decided formally to adopt the new 'Cyrillic' script. This had recently been invented by one of Methodios's disciples, was much simpler than its predecessor, the Glagolitic, and was based on the Greek alphabet, which was already familiar to the Bulgarians. Glagolitic remained in use for some centuries alongside Cyrillic, but in due course it was the simpler script that gained universal recognition and was adopted by all the countries of the Slavic world. It is a mark of the deep respect in which St Cyril was held that the new alphabet was named after him twenty-four years after his death. Able now to number Bulgarians, Serbs, and Russians among their 'spiritual children', the two brothers from Thessaloniki had laid the foundations for the creation of what was to become the Byzantine Commonwealth and richly deserved their posthumous title 'Apostles to the Slavs'.

The Resurgence of Monasticism after Iconoclasm

During the period of iconoclasm religious art representing the human form was suppressed, but it did not entirely disappear. Iconophile monks in

remote monasteries, for example in Sinai (which was safely outside the
borders of the empire) and in Cappadocia, continued to paint icons,
though not surprisingly they lacked the sophistication of the earlier art of
the capital and presented a more provincial style. The Triumph of
Orthodoxy in 843 made it possible for artists, many of whom had suffered
persecution and even torture under iconoclast emperors, to come out of
hiding and practise their art openly. Suddenly artists of the calibre of the
monk Lazaros (*c*.810–65), for example, were in great demand not only for
their artistic skills but also as ambassadors and negotiators. Having completed the icon of Christ that was to be displayed prominently on the
Chalke gate near the imperial palace, he was sent on an embassy to Rome,
and in the 860s he was called on to help settle the political wrangling over
control of the patriarchal throne. Lazaros is just one of many painters, but
he typifies the emergence at this time of a large circle of intellectuals and
artists from both inside and outside the Church who had received an
education and who, in the more stable conditions of the day, had the
leisure, the competence, and the enthusiasm to bring about a flowering of
culture that has come to be known in some quarters as the ninth-century
renaissance. As the French cultural historian Paul Lemerle remarked, it
would be a mistake

> to blame the iconoclastic controversy as being destructive or barren when,
> on the contrary, it was a stimulus. . . . The iconoclastic controversy pro-
> voked on both sides a great burst of intellectual activity, and though the
> triumph of monks and the iconodules is not usually taken to be that of
> a broad-minded and innovative spirit, at least it should not prevent us from
> noting a remarkable coincidence: namely that the final re-establishment of
> the images and the first renaissance of Byzantine humanism coincided in
> time.[27]

The triumph of the monks of course also provoked a great burst of
monastic activity as throughout the empire all forms of monasticism
enjoyed revival and resurgence. A number of new foundations sprang up,
notably in the capital, some of them very grand indeed, which would not
have been possible without imperial support. Basil I (867–86) is credited
with having endowed many new religious institutions, and his successors
clearly continued the practice. Indeed, if the twelfth-century historian
Zonaras is to be believed, some of them had been so extravagant in
expenditure on 'their own pleasure and the construction of religious

---

[27] P. Lemerle, *Byzantine Humanism: The First Phase*, trans. H. Lindsay and A. Moffatt (Canberra:
Australian Association for Byzantine Studies, 1986), p. 82.

houses' that by the accession of the Emperor Isaac I Komnenos (1057–9) the imperial treasury was empty.[28] No doubt the latter practice was in part a conscience saver for the former. Basil himself built the Nea Ekklesia inside the imperial palace, though this did not become a monastery before the twelfth century. Early in the tenth century the enormous Lips monastery was founded (or restored) by the city dignitary Constantine Lips, a contemporary of Leo VI (886–912). And around 920 the Myrelaion was built, probably by Emperor Romanos I Lekapenos, initially as a monastery for women, and endowed with estates in Greece and Asia Minor.

In the provinces, new foundations were created in southern Italy, including the cave monasteries of Calabria and Lucania, and in Asia Minor, where many of the rock churches and monasteries of Cappadocia date from this period. We are told that monks from the holy mountains of Ida, Olympos, Athos, and Kyminas took part in the processions at the first Feast of Orthodoxy in 843, and those of Latros, Mykale, and Auxentios also are known to have been active by the start of the tenth century.[29] Some of these foundations may have come about as a result of monks fleeing either from Muslim invasion from the east or from iconoclast persecution from the west, but another factor to be taken into account was the reassertion of Byzantine naval power, which resulted in the reconquest of the islands of Crete (961) and Cyprus (965) where major monasteries were subsequently founded.

There was further monastic activity beyond the borders of the empire. In Bulgaria the Tsar Boris had been baptized in 864 or 865, and a council in Constantinople in 870 placed the Bulgarian Church under the control of the Constantinople patriarchate, so when Sts Clement and Naum, the former disciples of Cyril and Methodios, arrived in 885 they were made welcome. Clement was sent on south to Macedonia where he became a bishop and founded the monastery of St Panteleimon at Ohrid. Naum remained in Bulgaria where he helped Boris lay the foundations of a Slavic Christian culture. But in 889 Boris himself received the tonsure and retired to his own monastic foundation in Preslav, and Naum followed Clement to Ohrid. There he too founded a monastery, known today as Sveti Naum, where he died in 910. By this time all forms of monasticism were well

---

[28] M. Pinder and T. Büttner-Wobst (eds), *Ioannis Zonarae Epitomae Historiarum libri XIII usque ad XVIII*, 3 vols, Corpus Scriptorum Historiae Byzantinae [CSHB] 47–9 (Bonn, 1897), vol. 3, p. 667. See also Morris, *Monks and Laymen in Byzantium*, p. 19.

[29] See A. Lesmüller-Werner and I. Thurn (eds), *Iosephi Genesii Regum libri quattuor*, CFHB 14 (Berlin/New York, 1968), p. 58. See also R. Morris, 'The Origins of Athos', in Bryer and Cunningham, *Mount Athos and Byzantine Monasticism*, p. 38 n. 9.

established in Bulgaria, including the eremitic. Perhaps the best-known hermit was St John of Rila (*c*.876–946) who founded the Rila monastery in about 930, which to this day remains the largest functioning Bulgarian men's monastery outside Athos (Plate 4).[30] All these monastic foundations in Bulgaria were of great importance not only as bases for spreading Orthodoxy in Slavic dress to the Bulgarians at the time but also as spiritual centres from which ecclesiastical activity could begin again when the political balance of power changed.

Political instability in Greece, which included raids by Slavs, Magyars, Muslims, and Bulgars, meant that monastic activity there was inhibited during the tenth century with the one notable exception of Mount Athos. The first church at Hosios Loukas monastery in Phokis was built around 950, but further expansion and decoration of the monastery had to wait until conditions improved in the early eleventh century. Bulgaria was incorporated into the empire in 1018, after which more peaceful times allowed for many new foundations of which the finest surviving exemplars are the churches at Hosios Loukas (1020s), Daphni (before 1048), and the Nea Moni on Chios (1042).

Monks as Scholars and Copyists

The Stoudios monastery was not the first to have a scriptorium attached to it for the copying of manuscripts. Most of the major monasteries of the Middle East, such as St Catherine's, Sinai, and Mar Saba in Palestine, already had such facilities, and a high proportion of manuscripts in Byzantine libraries were copied by monks (though very few by nuns, it seems). But we know more about the Stoudite scriptorium than about any other from the writings of its abbot, St Theodore. He was a prolific calligrapher himself, the library at Stoudios contained a number of manuscripts in his hand, and when he was in exile he often asked to be sent materials for copying. In his rule he stresses the importance of calligraphy and reading, and no fewer than eight articles are concerned with discipline in the scriptorium. Sins included the preparation of too much glue at the risk of its spoiling, careless treatment of the page being written on or of the model, carelessness with paragraphing, accents, and punctuation, relying on memory rather than following the model, breaking a pen in anger, and taking another scribe's pages without his consent; punishments (set out in

---

[30] But this is not saying very much: when I visited Rila in 2013, the brotherhood numbered no more than ten monks.

a separate penitential document known as the *Epitimia*) varied from thirty to a hundred prostrations, having to stand in the refectory, receiving food without seasoning, and excommunication for two or three days. Even if the manuscripts were intended to go no further than the monastery's own library, Theodore's disciplined organization of the scriptorium and his insistence on careful use of materials and total accuracy in copying are commendable and set standards that would be passed on together with the rest of his rule to many other monasteries.[31]

The Stoudios monastery seems to have been responsible for (or at least the focus of) a number of important developments in the composition of Greek manuscripts. Until the eighth century all Greek manuscripts had been written in uncial script (capital letters), which produced an elegant page but was slow to compile as each letter had to be formed independently. The speedy cut and thrust of the debate over iconoclasm may well have created a demand for a cursive script that was easier and faster to write. At the same time, monks who had been exiled from the capital may have sought refuge in the west and seen the beginnings of the new Latin minuscule script there. No doubt its introduction in Byzantium was a gradual process, but the earliest dated example of a Greek text written in minuscule was signed by the Stoudite monk Nikolaos on 7 May 835. This is a text of the Gospels, now in the St Petersburg Public Library.[32]

After iconoclasm the use of illustrations in manuscripts was always carefully considered. Images, such as representations of the evangelists in copies of the Gospels, were always included for a reason, like an icon, affirming the historical reality of the saint. Again, the Stoudios monastery seems to have taken a lead. The Theodore Psalter, for example, now in the British Library, was made there in 1066 by the monastery's proto-presbyter (chief priest), Theodore, for its then abbot, Michael. As many as 435 marginal illustrations accompany the text of the Psalms. The illuminations following the Psalms are sumptuous and depict episodes in the life of David, each with its caption written in gold minuscule, between well-spaced verses in uncial script composed by Abbot Michael about the psalmist, also in gold. Theodore was clearly not just the scribe but the designer and artist of the book. Abbot Michael is being portrayed as a new David who like David must lead his flock and like David has composed these psalm-like verses. Such a luxurious and opulent volume

---

[31] *PG* 99. 1740A–B. See Lemerle, *Byzantine Humanism*, pp. 137–46; Thomas and Constantinides Hero, *Byzantine Monastic Foundation Documents*, vol. 1, p. 85.

[32] MS gr. 219. This manuscript is illustrated in R. Barbour, *Greek Literary Hands AD 400–1600* (Oxford: Clarendon Press, 1981), pls 12–13.

is indicative of the wealth of the monastery and the esteem in which its abbot was held.[33]

Other monasteries in the capital with scriptoria included the Petra monastery, the Evergetis, and the Hodegon. Petra housed a good library whose holdings included the famous sixth-century manuscript of Dioscorides, now in Vienna. Its scriptorium was active from the eleventh century and monks copied manuscripts not only for their own library but also for other patrons. Hodegon's scriptorium seems to have flourished later, during the Palaiologan period, when it specialized in producing de luxe editions of liturgical texts. Outside the capital, the best-known scriptoria were on Athos, notably at the monasteries of Great Lavra, Iviron, and Philotheou, and also the Prodromos monastery on Mount Menoikeion near Serres.

Apart from the calligraphers and illuminators of manuscripts, other monks were trained as readers and chanters, and some, we are told, composed hymns. Monasteries required all monks to be literate and provided them with a basic education, but they were not great centres of learning in the same way that they were in the west. In Byzantium, institutions of higher learning and scholarship existed independently of the monasteries. Scholars would sometimes retire to a monastery, taking their books with them, which would in due course be added to the library's collection. But a monk's primary duty was to pray, for the empire and for the world.

Monks as Landowners and Merchants

Monks take a vow of poverty. Yet monasteries often become wealthy, generally because of their endowments, which are necessary to ensure their survival. This apparent incompatibility has aroused disputes throughout the history of monasticism. The problem was recognized in the tenth century by the Emperor Nikephoros II Phokas (963–9) who took steps to curb the wealth of the monasteries. In a decree of 964, the emperor claims that the situation had got totally out of hand:

---

[33] Additional MS 19352. This manuscript is illustrated in D. Buckton (ed.), *Byzantium: Treasures of Byzantine Art and Culture from British Collections* (London: British Museum Press, 1994), p. 155, in H. C. Evans and W. D. Wixom (eds), *The Glory of Byzantium: Art and Culture of the Middle Byzantine Era AD 843–1261* (New York: Metropolitan Museum of Art, 1997), p. 98, and in R. Cormack and M. Vassilaki (eds), *Byzantium 330–1453* (London: Royal Academy of Arts, 2008), p. 101. There is also an electronic facsimile produced by Charles Barber and published by the University of Illinois Press in 2000.

> They [the monastic authorities] have turned all the attention of their souls to the care of acquiring each day thousands of measures of land, superb buildings, innumerable horses, oxen, camels and other cattle, making the life of the monk no different from that of the layman with all its vain preoccupations.[34]

The emperor contrasts the current state of the monasteries with that of the lavras of the Desert Fathers, which alone represented the true monastic ideal. He goes on to criticize the wealthy donors who, out of a desire to absolve themselves of their sins, neglect Christ's commandment to sell their property and give the proceeds to the poor and instead establish monastic houses for reasons that are far from laudable:

> And moreover, who will not say that piety has become a screen for vanity when those who do good, do so in order that they may be seen by all the others? They are not satisfied that their virtuous deeds be witnessed by their contemporaries alone, but ask that future generations be not ignorant of them.[35]

The emperor forbade donations of land to monasteries unless they could be shown to have lost all their land and, instead of founding yet more monasteries, recommended that donors should give their money to the 'thousands' of monasteries that had fallen on hard times. He also supported the foundation of cells and lavras, so long as they did not aspire to own land beyond their enclosures. He opposed the donation of land on the grounds that large estates were useless without enough people to work them, and the poorer monasteries were regularly short of labour.

Nikephoros meant well with his decree, but he was not successful in his attempt to prevent people from transferring their estates to the monks in order to ensure the salvation of their souls. The practice continued, and emperors were among the worst offenders. On Athos, for example, the monastery of Great Lavra, which Nikephoros had helped to found (and endow), by 964 already owned land as far away as Chrysoupolis at the mouth of the river Strymon. By the end of the eleventh century its land holdings amounted to about 4,700 hectares and stretched as far afield as the outskirts of Thessaloniki. It also possessed as many as seven ships, and when some of them fell into disrepair the Emperor Alexios Komnenos

---

[34] J. and P. Zepos, *Jus Graeco-Romanum*, 8 vols (Athens, 1931–6; reprinted Aalen, 1962), vol. 1, coll. 3, document 19, p. 249, ll. 19–23; trans. P. Charanis, 'The Monastic Properties and the State in the Byzantine Empire', *Dumbarton Oaks Papers*, 4 (1948), 53–118 (56). See also R. Morris, *Monks and Laymen in Byzantium*, p. 167.

[35] Zepos, *Jus Graeco-Romanum*, p. 251, ll. 4–8; trans. Charanis, 'Monastic Properties', p. 57.

allowed the monks to replace them. Monks were officially forbidden from participating in trade and commerce, and St Theodore had ruled that any surplus produce from their estates must not be sold but given away to the poor. But clearly the monks were breaking their own rules, and they traded extensively in wine, as indeed they still do. In the twelfth century the learned scholar and archbishop of Thessaloniki Eustathios (c.1115–95/6) published a pamphlet *On the Reform of the Monastic Life*, in which he was highly critical of the grasping monks and abbots of his day. He deplored the fact that most monks had no interest in books and singled out an abbot who had sold a beautiful manuscript of St Gregory of Nazianzos 'because his monastery had no use for it'.[36] And the fourteenth-century bishop of Philadelphia Theoleptos (c.1250–1322), who was considered by Gregory Palamas to be a forerunner of hesychasm and was one of the foremost spiritual writers of the day, bitterly attacked the capitalist attitude of the monasteries in the late empire.

For Nikephoros the most perfect form of monastic life was that of the ascetic in his lavra or cell (*kellion*): 'The foundation of cells and so-called *lavrai* we do not forbid. Indeed, we find it praiseworthy, providing that these cells and *lavrai* do not strive to obtain fields and estates beyond their enclosures.'[37] Provision for this sort of withdrawal from the monastery was included in St Basil's rule and in the *typikon* for Great Lavra on Athos that was drafted by St Athanasios in about 970, but it was always the exception. Never again would it represent the mainstream of Orthodox monasticism. As Rosemary Morris concludes her study of Byzantine monasticism to 1118, 'In the twelfth century . . . there was a growing and influential view that the best place for monks was in monasteries and that eccentricity and even individuality in the monastic life was doctrinally suspect.'[38]

---

[36] On Eustathios, see L. D. Reynolds and N. G. Wilson, *Scribes and Scholars: A Guide to the Transmission of Greek and Latin Literature*, 2nd edn (Oxford: Clarendon Press, 1974), pp. 61–3, and N. G. Wilson, *Scholars of Byzantium* (London: Duckworth, 1983), pp. 196–204.

[37] Zepos, *Jus Graeco-Romanum*, p. 251, ll. 19–23; trans. Charanis, 'Monastic Properties', p. 57.

[38] Morris, *Monks and Laymen in Byzantium*, pp. 293–4.

PART II

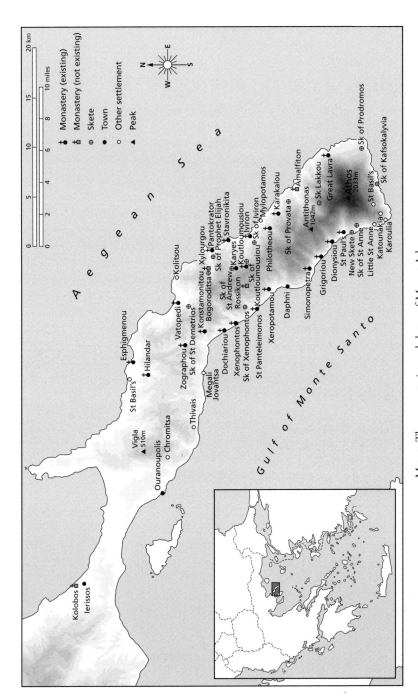

Map 2. The monasteries and sketes of Mount Athos.

CHAPTER 3

St Athanasios the Athonite (c.925–1000/1): Founder of Cenobitic Monasticism on Athos

Some historians have questioned Nikephoros's motives in supporting the foundation of so grand a monastery on Athos and in condoning (contrary to his own decree) the transfer to it of substantial estates not only on the peninsula itself but also elsewhere in Chalkidiki. No doubt, when he became emperor in 963, his priorities changed and he became more concerned to bolster the strength of the empire in what were troubled times. But Athos was too inaccessible and too ascetic to have any serious military potential, as the British surveyor William Martin Leake discovered when he made his exploration of the eastern Mediterranean in 1806, and if it had any geopolitical value at all, it could only be as a contribution to what is nowadays known as 'soft power', at which the Byzantines were past masters.[1] In this respect, however, its potential was of great significance. Rather like the great Gothic cathedrals built by the Lusignans in Cyprus, it was a symbol of Byzantium's intention to establish its presence and display its strength. Over the next two centuries several of the Athonite monasteries were to acquire substantial landholdings in Macedonia and this would be immensely helpful in establishing important cultural links between Athos and what was later to become the kingdom of Serbia. The Athonite Commonwealth was beginning to put down its roots.

Whatever its motives, the foundation of the Great Lavra on Mount Athos in 963 represents a pivotal moment in the history of Orthodox monasticism. For practical purposes it was the first large-scale monastery to be founded in the European provinces of the empire outside the capital. It was also the first outside the Stoudite federation to be established on Stoudite principles, with imperial support, and with an endowment of estates. It was therefore the springboard, either directly or indirectly, for all

---

[1] But Leake did speculate on the potential value of reopening Xerxes' canal to the navigation of the Aegean. See V. della Dora, *Imagining Mount Athos: Visions of a Holy Place from Homer to World War II* (Charlottesville and London: University of Virginia Press, 2011), pp. 130–1.

subsequent monastic foundations in the Athonite Commonwealth. It has always held the first place in the hierarchy of Athonite monasteries and, though it has suffered many ups and downs, it continues to flourish and to hold that primacy to the present day.

Perhaps what is also most singular about the Lavra is that its outward appearance remains more or less unchanged from what it must have been in the time of St Athanasios. Of course, many details will have been changed and many buildings been added over the centuries, but the greater part of the circuit of walls, probably including the defence tower (Plate 5), the central katholikon standing opposite the imposing refectory with its ancient D-shaped marble table-tops, the phiale for the blessing of holy water, even the (somewhat decrepit) cypress trees that overshadow it, all date from the tenth century. Unlike the great majority of Athonite houses, the Lavra has had the good fortune never to have suffered a major fire, which is the main reason for this remarkable continuity. But it must also have benefited from being the most southerly of the monasteries, the nearest to the tip of the peninsula, and the closest to the so-called desert. Beyond it, there are just a few sketes that are its dependencies and then dense forest succeeded by the inhospitable rocky steeps of Mount Athos itself. It is very much the end of the road. The pilgrim who is privileged to enter its awesome portal is immediately struck, more forcibly than when entering any other monastic house, by the sensation that he is travelling backwards a millennium in time and returning to Byzantium.

The Beginnings of Monasticism on Athos

It was as a hermit that Athanasios first came to the Mountain in 958, but he was far from being the first hermit. The resurgence of monasticism in the ninth century was felt in many parts of the empire including the holy mountain of Athos. No doubt hermits had already found their way to its wooded slopes and commodious caves, possibly as refugees from iconoclasm, in the early ninth century. Some of them from later in the century are even known to us by name. St Euthymios the Younger, for example, had moved from another holy mountain, Mount Olympos in Bithynia, to Athos in about 859, because he had heard of its tranquillity, we are told. After three years living alone in a cave, he emerged to find a group of monks had settled around him who wanted him to be their spiritual father. In agreeing to do so, he formed the first lavra, or informal group of hermits, on Athos. Another hermit, John Kolobos by name, a disciple of Euthymios, is said to have founded the first monastery on Athos, somewhere near Ierissos and close to the isthmus in the north of the peninsula, and to have received a chrysobull from Emperor Basil I (before 881) granting his monastery jurisdiction over the Mountain and its hermits. By the end of the century there were several monastic houses on the Mountain, and there had already been a degree of friction between them and the hermits, which the emperor had tried to quell by means of another chrysobull. All the same, the monks decided that there was a need for a central meeting-point or council of elders, and this was duly established at Karyes, where the Holy Community still meets today. This council met three times a year and was made up of representatives of all the monastic communities who now had a forum to discuss matters of common concern. By the start of the tenth century therefore both the eremitical and the lavriot traditions were already well established on Athos.

Athanasios was born in Trebizond on the Black Sea between 925 and 930 and was baptized with the name Avraamios.[2] He received an elementary education in his home town, but to further his studies he had to move to Constantinople. His biographer tells us that he was a brilliant student and in due course became a teacher himself whose courses were very popular. In the capital his circle included Michael Maleinos, abbot of the lavra on Mount Kyminas in Bithynia, and his nephews Leo and Nikephoros Phokas, the future emperor. When Michael returned to his monastery, Avraamios went with him and at Kyminas he was tonsured with the name Athanasios. He worked in the monastery as a scribe for four years, after which he was given permission to become a hermit. But when Michael announced that he would retire as abbot and named Athanasios as his successor, Athanasios took fright at the idea and fled to Athos in search of greater solitude.

At first, he lived peacefully in seclusion at Zygos in the north of the peninsula, but Nikephoros sought him out, and he was advised by his spiritual father to retire to a solitary cell near Karyes. Later he moved down to the southern tip of the peninsula where he lived in a remote cell at Melana, but again Nikephoros pursued him and sent some of his men in a boat to recall him. He was preparing to set sail for Crete in order to free that island from occupation by Arab pirates and he wanted Athanasios to go with him as his spiritual father. Reluctantly Athanasios agreed, and after

---

[2] On Athanasios, see J. Noret (ed.), *Vitae duae antiquae Sancti Athanasii Athonitae* (Turnhout: Brepols, 1982). Also 'Life of Athanasios of Athos, Version B' in R. P. H. Greenfield and A.-M. Talbot (eds, trans.), *Holy Men of Mount Athos* (Cambridge, MA: Harvard University Press, 2016), pp. 127–367; and K. Ware, 'St Athanasios the Athonite: Traditionalist or Innovator?' in Bryer and Cunningham, *Mount Athos and Byzantine Monasticism*, pp. 3–16.

the liberation of Crete in March 961, the two of them laid plans to use the spoils of the Cretan campaign to found a monastery, and Nikephoros promised that he would become a monk.

Returning to Athos, Athanasios started to build. But despite its name, he did not in fact build a lavra like the one he had lived in at Kyminas, but a full-scale cenobitic monastery such as existed at the Stoudios monastery in Constantinople. Nothing on this scale had ever been built on Athos before. The katholikon was completed in 963, and that date has always been understood as marking the foundation of the monastery. In the same year, much to Athanasios's distress, Nikephoros was crowned emperor, thereby reneging on his promise to be tonsured. He begged his spiritual father for forgiveness and assured him that he would abdicate and become a monk as soon as he could. And contrary to his own decree on monastic property (see p. 35), he lavished every gift on the new monastery – great wealth, special privileges, relics and other treasures, a regular income. Nikephoros also appointed Athanasios abbot, gave the monks the right to appoint his successor, and fixed the size of the brotherhood at eighty.

The Lavra still inspires wonder by its very size, but at least there are now nineteen other (if smaller) monasteries in other parts of the Mountain to leaven the visitor's awe. In 963 it was the only one of any size, and the neighbours did not like this new leviathan. The existing population of hermits and lavriot monks found the lavish style of Athanasios's buildings with their conspicuous wealth and imperial connections offensive and out of keeping with their more modest way of life, and they protested that he had introduced 'the world' to the Mountain.[3] In December 969, when Nikephoros was murdered and succeeded by his nephew John Tzimiskes, the monks took their case to the new emperor. But to get a balanced view the emperor also summoned Athanasios who with the assistance of his friend John of Georgia (later to be one of the founders of Iviron) persuaded the emperor to give the monastery even more support: its income was doubled, its brotherhood was increased to 120, and it was given ownership of the monastery of St Andrew of Peristerai in Thessaloniki together with its extensive lands.

The hermits were crushed, and on the Mountain meetings of the whole community were often reduced to bitter disputes. Athanasios realized that something had to be done for them and persuaded the emperor to send Euthymios, a respected elder of the Stoudios monastery in Constantinople, to Athos with a brief to settle the differences between the warring factions. On his arrival in Karyes, Euthymios convened a meeting of the abbots of all

---

[3] See Greenfield and Talbot, *Holy Men of Mount Athos*, p. 241.

the lavras and together they drafted the first *typikon* or charter for the organization of the whole Mountain. This document, known as the *Tragos*, signed by the Emperor John Tzimiskes, by Athanasios, and by all the other forty-six abbots in about 972, is one of the most important to survive on Athos. It is called *Tragos* ('goat') because it is written on goatskin parchment, and it is one of the greatest treasures in the collection of the Protaton in Karyes.[4] Its main provisions are as follows:[5]

> The three customary gatherings of the whole Athonite community, formerly held at Karyes at Christmas, Easter, and the Assumption, are reduced to only one, on the Assumption. In future these gatherings are only to be attended by the Protos, with three followers, by Athanasios, with two, by Paul of Xeropotamou, with one, and by the other hegoumenoi, unaccompanied.[6] This is done to avoid the disorders and disputes which have occurred very frequently at these gatherings.
>
> The Protos cannot legally do anything without the agreement of the assembly of the hegoumenoi, nor can the assembly do anything without his agreement, even if it is a matter for the common good.
>
> A novice must undergo a period of one year's probation before he can take his vows as a monk. All novices must be put in the charge of a spiritual father or the head of their monastery, and must obey him. The novice may not apply to join another monastery without his permission.
>
> Monks who have made their vows in other places and have come to the Mountain are not allowed to buy land or to settle on unoccupied land, unless they get the permission of the Protos and the assembly.
>
> Every hegoumenos may sell, give, or transfer his property, his house, and his cultivated land to his own disciples, or to some other person who has no property, but any gift of a house or land to any monastery is forbidden. Wills relating to such transfers of property are valid, and effect is to be given to them. Any resale for the sake of profit is disgraceful and is forbidden.
>
> Only those monks who have received a training in discipline, under the supervision of a spiritual father, and have proved themselves suitable, may (under supervision) retire to hermitages as solitary ascetics or hesychasts.
>
> A monk may not return to the world after he has taken his vows.
>
> Monks may not go for visits to towns or to country places, act as sponsors, or join in associations with lay persons.

[4] The Protaton was originally a lavra that owned all the buildings in Karyes. It was dissolved in the seventeenth century and all that remains of it is its church, the oldest on Athos, and its treasury and archives.

[5] As summarized by E. Amand de Mendieta, *Mount Athos: The Garden of the Panaghia* (Berlin: Akademie Verlag, 1972), pp. 67–9. The complete text, translated by George Dennis, is published in Thomas and Constantinides Hero, *Byzantine Monastic Foundation Documents*, vol. I, pp. 232–44.

[6] The Protos (formally *protos hesychastes* or 'first hesychast') was the leader of the hermits. Subsequently shortened to Protos, the term is still used for the primate of Athos.

Wine, made in excess of the maker's requirements, and pine-wood may not be sold outside the Mountain. Such goods may be sold to monks who need them. If in need and stricken with poverty, monks may however sell them to laymen living on the Mountain.

During the Great Lent all manual work is forbidden except on Saturdays. All visiting and conversation is forbidden during this season, which must be devoted to prayer and contemplation.

Priests from outside cannot be admitted, unless they bring letters of introduction.

It is forbidden to bring in pack-animals belonging to the monastery of Kolovou, near Ierissos, unless it is threatened with an attack by barbarians. Any question as to the admission of animals which normally enter Athos, is to be decided by the elders.

Eunuchs and beardless youths (even the children of masons and labourers) are forbidden to enter Athos.

The hegoumenoi are forbidden to force kelliots or hermits, living in cells or kellia, to undertake any work.

No pair of oxen may be kept on the Mountain, except for one pair allowed at Lavra. This monastery is very big and clearly needs beasts.

The existing rules regarding the election of the Protos are to be strictly enforced.

The administrator of Mese, the old name for Karyes, must render an account of his receipts and expenditure to the assembly each August. He is eligible for re-election by the Protos and hegoumenoi.

The administrator must prevent all scandalous talk and quarrelling in Mese. If any scandal is reported to him from some other part of the Mountain, he is to go there, accompanied by three or four hegoumenoi living in the district in which the trouble has occurred, and to take such action as is required.

Bearing as it did the emperor's signature as well as those of all the abbots, this document soon acquired the force of law and provided a basis for the resolution of disputes between the various communities and the hermits. It also affirmed the establishment on Athos of the cenobitic system which was already in force at the Stoudios monastery according to the rule of St Basil.

The Monastic Programme at the Lavra

A few years after the ratification of the *Tragos* in about 974 Athanasios drew up a charter or *typikon* for the Lavra itself.[7] This document can be divided

---

[7] The complete text, translated by George Dennis, is published in Thomas and Constantinides Hero, *Byzantine Monastic Foundation Documents*, vol. 1, pp. 245–70. The references in the text are to the paragraphs of that translation.

into four sections. The first section (§ 1–8) is a foundation history, written from the founder's point of view but providing an interesting account of his relationship with his imperial patron Nikephoros. There follows a section (§ 9–29) on constitutional organization and the succession of the abbot. The third section (§ 30–5), the *typikon* proper, consists of numerous unacknowledged quotations from eighteen of the chapters in St Theodore's rule for the Stoudios monastery. This is followed by a section (§ 36–53) of non-Stoudite legislation concerning relations with the monastery's ascetics and with its dependencies elsewhere on the Mountain. The document ends (§ 56) with a final (unacknowledged) quotation from St Theodore urging the brothers to be obedient to the next abbot. This charter shows us the extent to which Athanasios was following the programme established by St Theodore and also the extent to which what he was creating on Athos was new and innovative. It is a matter of some surprise to us, who are trained always to identify the sources of our quotations, that St Theodore is nowhere mentioned by name; but the fact that he is quoted verbatim on so many occasions is evidence of the conscious debt that Athanasios owed to his saintly predecessor and justi-fication of his claim to be following the traditions of the fathers. Let us examine the elements of the programme that Athanasios thought needed to be stressed.

It goes without saying that the monastic life is essentially a life of prayer, so this much is taken for granted in the text, but it underlies everything that is stated. 'Preserve your angelic profession inviolate', is the command, reminding the brothers of their vows. 'Do not depart from your struggle with obedience through negligence and become the sport of demons. ... If you keep these things in mind ... the chorus of martyrs will receive you' (56). Poverty, chastity, and obedience are the essentials of the cenobitic way of life. Quoting directly from the Stoudite rule, Athanasios says,

> You shall always be vigilant that all things in the community be held in common and be indivisible and that nothing be owned on the part of any individual, not even a needle. Your body and your soul, nothing else, should be divided up for all your spiritual children, brothers and fathers. (32)

Quoting St Paul, he describes the virtues of the common life:

> I have found by experience that it is right and beneficial, in fact, it is my judgment, and I declare it best and less fraught with danger for all the brothers to live in common. All together they are to look to the same goal of salvation. Although the entire fullness of the community is joined together

> from diverse links, they form one heart in their common life, one will, one
> desire, and one body, as the apostle prescribes (Rom. 12:4; 1 Cor. 12:12). (38)

And perhaps mindful of the first verse of Psalm 133, he writes: 'if we all
belong to the one Christ, as by his grace we in fact do, and to one mother,
the holy church of God; if we are of the same faith and the one profession,
then let there be no quarrels among you' (28).

Poverty is not just for individuals but also for the community as a whole.
Thus the monastery is forbidden to own slaves: Athanasios, like Theodore,
is a firm believer in the benefits of manual labour for monks. Nor may the
house own female animals, 'since you have completely renounced the
female sex' (31). The main reason for this ban is to ensure that the monks
do not start breeding animals, for that could lead to commercial activity,
and that could lead to immorality. 'I thought it superfluous to make special
mention of sheep and goats, since I believe it is completely out of place for
monks to possess them, especially the monks residing on the mountain'
(53).[8] Vines may be planted to satisfy the needs of the brotherhood and no
more. 'For even if I were to admit that some commercial activity could be
carried on, although it is actually impossible, I do regard it as dishonour-
able and out of place to dispatch monks to sell wine in the villages and
cities, to spend a lot of time visiting with secular persons, to intermingle
with them, to sojourn in their houses, and in this connection to converse
freely with women . . .' (10).

Obedience to the abbot is the principal requirement. Again quoting St
Theodore, Athanasios commands:

> Stick to the race of obedience until the end so that you will obtain the
> 'unfading crown of righteousness' (cf. 1 Peter 5:4 and 2 Tim. 4:8). Led by
> humility, you should always deny your own will and pattern yourselves only
> after the judgment of your superior. If you keep these things in mind and if
> you should guard them to the end, you will be blessed. For the chorus of
> martyrs will receive you. (56).

He devotes a good deal of space to the matter of selecting his successor:
'In my own case, now, I have absolute dominion, so that not even one
person can gainsay my command, and yet I have no intention of leaving
my successor behind without consulting the brothers' (16). He stresses that
the abbot must be selected from among the existing brotherhood and
elected by the 'whole assemblage of the more preeminent brothers':

---

[8] As is clear from other *typika*, there was a real fear of bestiality in monasteries. See the article on
'bestiality' in Alexander Kazhdan (ed.), *Oxford Dictionary of Byzantium*, 3 vols (New York: Oxford
University Press, 1991), vol. 1, p. 286.

> We enjoin and command that the superior must be selected only from this particular community. He should not be a man who has come here from some other monastery, been formed anew in a single day, and right then and there be put in charge. For he brings with him nothing that would aid the brothers in the practice of virtue, except that he wants them to vote for him as their leader, although they know nothing of his manner of life. (17)

Despite the somewhat domineering tone of the *typikon*, we are assured by his biographer that Athanasios was a man of humble character.[9] He proclaimed that the vow of poverty should apply no less to the abbot than to the monks, that the abbot should not set himself apart by wearing fine apparel, and that he should not leave his monastery and neglect his flock; and apparently he practised what he preached. On formal occasions he was dignified and austere, but when alone with his monks he was warm, approachable, and sympathetic. He was said to be a 'most shepherdly' pastor of his flock, a physician and healer rather than a ruler or judge. Many offices within the monastery could be delegated, but the abbot must remain the principal spiritual father of his monks: 'You shall not take charge of the treasury room nor assume the cares of stewardship, but let your key be the greatest care of souls, of loosing and binding according to the Scriptures' (32). Spiritual authority belonged to the abbot alone, and he expected his monks to come to him daily for 'disclosure of thoughts'.

Perhaps with an eye to the future, Athanasios is at pains to insist that his monastery is open to all regardless of their place of origin or 'nationality':

> What we strive for is the eradication of our own will, this is our highest goal, and concentrating on virtue and on comprehending the fact that we have been called to sorrow, not to delights. Each of us must not follow his own desires. Even if some monasteries were established out beyond Cadiz and some monks from those places visited here and then chose to be enlisted among our brothers, we would not call them foreigners. For I am reluctant to designate a monastery as foreign, since that word suggests to me a separation from God. (27)

And in a departure from his Stoudite model, Athanasios concedes that, while the vast majority of the brotherhood should pursue the common life in the monastery, a small number may choose to live apart as solitaries. The circumstances of the Mountain at the time of the foundation of the Lavra required him to consider how the monastery would relate to its existing neighbours, who included hermits and, in particular, the brotherhood gathered around his close friend John the Iberian (47). It may have

---

[9] See Greenfield and Talbot, *Holy Men of Mount Athos*, p. 167.

been partly to assuage their concerns that he made allowances for a few of
the brethren of the Lavra to pursue the eremitic life. They were to number
no more than five, they would be given a small stipend and allowance of
grain, they would remain in obedience to the abbot, and they would each
be allowed just one disciple. These 'hesychasts', as he calls them, though
they are not to be confused with practitioners of the Jesus Prayer, must not
consider themselves in any way superior to the rest of the brotherhood.
Quite the contrary:

> For before God and the angels I bear witness that those who persevere
> in genuine obedience and who remain firm in the love of God and in
> true affection for one another do not take second place to those
> carrying on the struggle special to solitude. But they shall be found
> to be superior and deemed worthy of eternal crowns by the good and
> impartial judge. (46)

The Legacy of Athanasios

Athanasios was abbot of the Lavra for nearly forty years. During his first
fifteen years, the size of the brotherhood increased from 80 to more than
150; and if the servants and the monks living in the dependencies are
included, the figure is said to be 500. But the influx was not restricted to
that monastery, and by the start of the eleventh century there were,
according to his biographer, more than 3,000 monks on the Mountain as
a whole.[10] For comparison, in 1903 there were 7,432 monks; after a low of
1,145 in 1971, there are now about 2,500. The church that Athanasios built
in the centre of the courtyard of the Lavra remains to this day the principal
church of the monastery. When the finishing touches were being put to its
dome, probably in the year 1002, the abbot wished to see for himself how
the work was progressing. As he climbed up the scaffolding on 5 July,
without any warning the dome suddenly collapsed, killing Athanasios and
six others. His tomb lies inside the church, in the chapel of the Forty
Martyrs, and his name is commemorated every year on 5 July in all
Orthodox churches.

Athanasios's legacy is both monumental and enduring. With the emper-
or's help he had founded and built a great monastery, a fully fledged
coenobium modelled on the Stoudios in Constantinople, a completely
independent and self-governing community, that has survived for 1,050
years. At the same time, he had succeeded in reconciling the existing

---

[10] See Noret, *Vitae duae*, Vita A, 238. 5.

Plate 1. Western and Eastern saints stand side by side in the chapel of the monastery of Sts Antony and Cuthbert, Shropshire.

Plate 2. Desert monasticism: the Coptic monastery of St Antony in the eastern desert of Egypt.

Plate 3. Monks as missionaries: a modern statue of Sts Constantine (Cyril) and Methodios in the monastery of the Caves, Kiev. The saints are demonstrating the alphabet that they have devised as a gift to the entire Slav world.

Plate 4. Monastic resurgence after iconoclasm: the katholikon of Rila monastery in Bulgaria, founded *c*.930.

Plate 5. Walls and towers of the Great Lavra on Athos, founded by St Athanasios the Athonite in 963.

Plate 6. A lonely tower rising above the forest: all that survives of the Benedictine monastery of the Amalfitans on Athos.

Plate 7. Alaverdi cathedral, part of Alaverdi monastery in eastern Georgia, founded in the sixth century by Syrian fathers.

population of the Mountain who had objected so violently to this monstrous intrusion into their seclusion. By finding a place for the eremitic life alongside the cenobitic and making the cenobitic houses responsible for the material needs of their eremitic dependants, he had overcome their complaints. His *typikon* has remained the model for Athonite monasteries and their successors from that day to this. No major changes have been made to its rulings (give or take some temporary relaxation of the cenobitic requirements that took place during the period of idiorrhythmic rule) and more than a millennium after they were first drafted they are still in force today.[11]

During the second half of the tenth century, monks flocked to Athos not only from Eastern Europe but from Italy in the west and Armenia and Georgia in the east. Through Athanasios, we are told, 'the whole mountain became a city'.[12] What attracted them to this remote and relatively unknown monastic enclave? Athanasios himself suggests that part of the answer is the very inaccessibility of Athos, which is what drew him there in the first place:

> For lack of distraction means fewer anxieties, and being free of anxiety means fewer disturbances, and the confluence of all this results in a better and more perfect state of being. Many reasons, though, led my lowly self to this decision. The seashore along the mountain was precipitous and without any harbors on both sides, to the north, that is, and to the south, for more than eighty miles. The mountain resembles a peninsula which extends toward the sea in the shape of a cross. The islands in the sea, Lemnos, Imbros, Thasos, and the rest are a great distance away. Because of this, when winter comes, a ship is unable to sail from the mountain to the mainland to procure necessary provisions or to sail back from there to the mountain. It cannot find any sort of anchorage because the seashore on both sides provides no shelter. On the other hand, there is absolutely no way for a person to transport his own provisions by dry land, partly because the road is so long, and partly because the mountain is practically impassable for pack animals.[13]

Such inhospitable conditions are ideal for ascetic endeavour.

---

[11] The idiorrhythmic system, which was introduced to Athos in the late Byzantine period and survived in some monasteries until the second half of the twentieth century, allowed monks to set their own rhythm: they were not bound by the vow of poverty or of obedience to an abbot, and they lived in separate apartments, neither eating together nor contributing to a common purse. See Speake, *Mount Athos: Renewal in Paradise*, pp. 98–100, 107–9, 159–60.

[12] *Vita* A, 164. 37, echoing the Life of St Antony of Egypt, which stated that through him 'the desert was made a city by monks' (Athanasius, *The Life of Antony*, trans. R. C. Gregg, p. 42).

[13] *Typikon*, § 10.

Another factor must have been Athanasios's own personality and background. He was clearly a charismatic figure who made friends easily with everyone he came in contact with, from emperors to hermits. His Pontic origins will have given him an introduction to Georgian society, and he clearly established a name for himself as a brilliant teacher from his time in Constantinople. He made it clear in his *typikon* that his monastery was open to all regardless of their origins, and he seems to have planned it as an international and pan-Orthodox centre from the very start, though the notion of pan-Orthodoxy is somewhat anachronistic at this period. Some monks, himself included, had been tonsured in monasteries elsewhere, but 'such men as these I consider sons and heirs and children of my heart' (21). He was adamant that no one should speak of such immigrants as 'foreign monks', and anyone who did should be excommunicated for three weeks and required to eat alone without wine and oil, and if the insults persisted the culprit should be expelled from the monastery (29).

We have already noted that political instability in the tenth century hindered the development of monasticism in most parts of the empire, but not so on Athos. Despite raids by Muslims, Magyars, Slavs, and Bulgars on Chalkidiki and on Athos itself, recruits were not deterred. Such conditions may even have provided further incentive to those who were happy to sacrifice themselves to attack by the infidel and who were irresistibly attracted both by the charismatic reputations of certain spiritual fathers and by the innate holiness of the peninsula as a whole. Most are likely to have come from neighbouring regions, but others came from a great distance. There were certainly Georgians on the Mountain in the 970s and Amalfitans in the 980s. But as Rosemary Morris has shown, this does not necessarily imply a significant geographical extension of the 'spiritual magnetism' of the Mountain.[14] Georgian monasticism had long been established on Mount Olympos in Bithynia, and several of the first Georgian Athonites had in fact joined monasteries there before continuing their spiritual journeys further west. Similarly, there were close contacts between Athos and several of the monasteries in Constantinople, and many of the new recruits, including perhaps the Amalfitans, may have come via the capital. We shall look more closely at the Georgians in the next chapter, but the arrival of the Amalfitans needs to be noticed here.

---

[14] R. Morris, 'Where did the Early Athonite Monks Come from?', in R. Gothóni and G. Speake (eds), *The Monastic Magnet: Roads to and from Mount Athos* (Oxford: Peter Lang, 2008), pp. 21–40 (33).

The Benedictine Monastery of the Amalfitans

A Benedictine monastery using the Latin rite would be unthinkable on the Holy Mountain today but that is exactly what came into existence some time between 980 and 984, thanks to the atmosphere of inclusive spirituality created by Athanasios. The monastery, dedicated to St Mary of the Latins, was probably founded by Leo of Benevento whose brother was Duke Pandulf II of Benevento. Leo moved to Athos with a group of six disciples from Amalfi around 980, and for a while they were accommodated by the Georgian monks who were already established in some cells of their own near the Lavra and who made them welcome as fellow 'foreigners'. The Georgians, who were themselves already engaged in establishing their own monastery, offered every form of support, both material and spiritual, to the Italians and encouraged them to found a monastery too. The site chosen was a short distance up the east coast from the Lavra on the brow of a hill overlooking a small bay that is still known as Morphonou (which is a corruption of the name 'of the Amalfitans'). In fact, they were not the only Italians to have an establishment on Athos at this time: monasteries both 'of the Sicilians' and 'of the Calabrians' are mentioned in documents, though these were both Greek-speaking and never achieved the same status as the Amalfitan house.

Nothing remains of the monastery today except a tall lonely tower which stands proud of the surrounding forest (Plate 6), but in its day, it was a thriving and substantial house. In the tenth century, the Amalfitans were a wealthy nation who had won for themselves trading privileges with the Byzantines, which included a quarter of their own in Constantinople where they had built both a church and a monastery. The monastery on Athos seems also to have secured special privileges for itself: in the *typikon* of the Emperor Constantine IX Monomachos (1045), which specifically set out to curtail the trading activities of the monasteries and limit the number of ships that they were to keep, an exception is made for the Amalfitans:

> All agreed to another compromise which allowed the monastery of the Amalfitans to own a large boat since they were unable to survive by any other means. They were not to make use of this boat for commercial purposes, but they were to travel with it to the Queen of Cities if they wanted to import anything they needed for their monastery or to be supplied from those who love Christ.[15]

---

[15] Thomas and Constantinides Hero, *Byzantine Monastic Foundation Documents*, vol. 1, pp. 281–93, § 5.

This suggests that the monastery was to some extent dependent on the Amalfitan colony in Constantinople to supply its needs. This was a risky situation, given the volatile nature of relations between Greeks and Latins in the capital and the decline in power and prestige of the Amalfitans in particular. Perhaps for this reason the monastery began to increase its landholdings in Macedonia, of which its possession in perpetuity is confirmed in documents of 1081 addressed to the 'imperial monastery of the Amalfitans'. The designation 'imperial' means that it had achieved equal status with the leading monasteries of Lavra, Iviron, and Vatopedi.

The events of 1054, when anathemas were exchanged symbolizing the break between the Churches of Rome and Constantinople, seem to have had no impact on the fortunes of the Amalfitan monastery, which continued to prosper. Its abbot regularly signs documents near the top of the list, signifying that he represented one of the most senior monasteries. And when in 1198 the monastery of Hilandar was founded as specifically Serbian-speaking, its position is justified by analogy with the other non-Greek-speaking houses of the Georgians and the Amalfitans. After the Fourth Crusade of 1204, there is no further mention of the Amalfitan monastery in documents until 1287, when it is said to be ruinous and deserted, and its property was then transferred to Lavra. Even then there is no suggestion that its position had become untenable on liturgical or theological grounds. The causes of its decline are simply not known but are perhaps most likely a lack of recruits or lack of funds or both. There are a good many reasons why a Latin house might not have flourished on Athos during the thirteenth century. But the fact that it had existed at all, and flourished for as long as it did, is a tribute to the spiritual charisma and monastic vision of Athanasios.

By the turn of the eleventh century, Athos had emerged as the pre-eminent centre of monasticism in the Byzantine world. The empire was prospering and had regained territory and influence in the east, in Greece, and in south Italy. The Holy Mountain benefited from this prosperity, and there was a boom in the foundation of new monastic houses. Many were small and transient; others were more substantial and enduring. Among those that survive to this day we may note, in addition to Lavra, Iviron, Vatopedi, Xeropotamou, Zographou, Xenophontos, Esphigmenou, and the original St Panteleimonos. As Byzantine influence spread across the Balkans and Eastern Europe, the splendour of its ancient and imperial culture made a great impact, and, even if they retained their political independence, the peoples who came in contact with it hastened to become members of this expanding cultural commonwealth. Orthodox

Christianity was the foundation stone of the culture and its most conspicuous element. It was the beauty of the Divine Liturgy in Hagia Sophia that
finally convinced the Russian envoys of Prince Vladimir in 986 that 'only
there God dwells among men'.[16] One by one the rulers of Eastern Europe
accepted Orthodoxy and brought their subjects into the fold of the
ecumenical patriarch. Monasticism spread as rapidly as the faith and it
was natural that each state should wish to have its own representatives
recognized and established on the Holy Mountain. The fact that the
atmosphere of the Mountain was so welcoming was an added attraction
and soon every tongue that was spoken in the commonwealth was to be
heard somewhere on that holy peninsula. Initially the spiritual magnetism
was in one direction only, but the following chapters will show that it did
not take long for it to turn into two-way traffic.

[16] Obolensky, *The Byzantine Commonwealth*, p. 253.

CHAPTER 4

The Enlighteners of Georgia

It is easy to forget that Georgians were among the first non-Byzantines to secure a presence on Athos. In fact, the monastery of Iviron means literally the monastery 'of the Georgians' (i.e. Iberians) and it remained in Georgian hands for almost 400 years. They may therefore claim to be among the very first members of the Athonite Commonwealth.

Unlike the later emerging Slav states of Eastern Europe, the kingdom of Georgia received Christianity as early as the fourth century when St Nino converted King Mirian. In fact, the land now known as Georgia was two separate states until they were united in 978, western Georgia (Egrisi in Georgian, later Abchasia; Colchis in Greek, later Lazika) and eastern Georgia (Kartli in Georgian, Iberia in Greek). Both states spoke languages belonging to the same Georgian family, in which there is a written litera- ture as far back as the fifth century, and the earliest surviving texts are translations of parts of the Bible and the liturgy, but the population as a whole was not fully converted until a delegation of Syrian fathers arrived in the sixth century. Having first bypassed the Council of Chalcedon (451), both Georgia and Armenia in 506 rejected it and became part of the group of churches that distanced themselves from imperial Orthodoxy. But a century later they split, and Georgia chose to return to communion with Constantinople, where it remains. Initially under the patriarchate of Antioch, the Georgian Church gained internal autonomy in the eighth century and complete independence around 1053. Politically, the two Georgias fell under Muslim rule in the seventh century but regained their independence in the ninth, though they were not united until the tenth. They were not incorporated into the empire at any stage, but they were aligned with the Byzantines in their opposition to Islam, their cultural contacts were close, and they enjoyed a relationship with Constantinople that anticipated what was later to become the Byzantine Commonwealth.

Monasticism also came early to Georgia, but perhaps not quite as early as some would have it. According to tradition, the monastery of Bodbe, where the relics of St Nino are preserved, was founded soon after her death in the early fourth century. No doubt there was a shrine, but there is no evidence for a monastery before the ninth century. Certainly a number of monasteries were founded in the sixth century, when the Syrian fathers visited Georgia from Antioch, and several of these are still functioning today, for example at Alaverdi (Plate 7), Nekresi, Jvari, and Davit-Gareja. And an important group of monasteries were founded in the tenth century in the Georgian principality of Tao-Klarjeti (now part of north-eastern Turkey), which was a vassal state of Byzantium.

St John the Iberian (d.1005) and St Euthymios of Athos (c.955–1028)

The two Georgians best known for their presence on Mount Athos are John, known as the Iberian, and his son Euthymios. They came from a rich and noble family in Tao-Klarjeti in southern Georgia, not far from Trebizond, where St Athanasios the Athonite grew up. John and Athanasios seem to have been personal friends, possibly from an early age. Both decided to pursue the monastic life, and John was tonsured in the early 960s at the lavra of the Four Churches in Tao-Klarjeti. He then moved to a Georgian house on Mount Olympos in Bithynia, where he learnt that his son was being held as a hostage in Constantinople. Having rescued him, John moved with Euthymios to Athos some time in the mid 960s where they joined Athanasios at the newly founded Great Lavra. Euthymios was no more than ten or twelve years old and so was below the prescribed age for admittance, but a special case was made for him. The Georgians did not stay long in the monastery, however, and were given some land nearby on which they built their own facilities, as is described rather charmingly in the Life of Fathers John and Euthymios:

> After a certain period of time, their presence on the Holy Mountain became known and the number of Georgians began to increase there, and when this became clear to our fathers, who were filled with all manner of wisdom, they decided: 'It is not fitting for us to stay in the monastery because others come to stay and it is not possible to send them back.' Thus by the decision of Athanasios, at one mile distance from the Lavra, in a beautiful unsettled place the above-mentioned fathers built the Church of St John the Evangelist with a number of cells and stayed there for many years as angels of God.[1]

[1] T. Grdzelidze (trans.), *Georgian Monks on Mount Athos: Two Eleventh-Century Lives of the Hegoumenoi of Iviron* (London: Bennett & Bloom, 2009), p. 57. Life of Frs John and Euthymios, ch. 3. On the Life, see also M. Whittow, *The Making of Orthodox Byzantium, 600–1025* (Basingstoke: Macmillan, 1996), pp. 364–5.

John Tornikios was another member of the same wealthy Chordvaneli family in Tao-Klarjeti. He had had a distinguished military career, serving as a general under David III Kouropalates of Tao, when around 970 he left the army and was tonsured a monk with the name John in the monastery of Oshki. From there he moved first to Mount Olympos in Bithynia and then to Mount Athos, where he joined his relatives, John the Iberian and Euthymios. Monasticism in Georgia was characterized by family relationships and the same trait followed them to Athos. Tornikios had good connections in Constantinople and on at least two occasions petitioned the emperor of the day (John Tzimiskes in 972 and Basil II in 976) for permission to found a monastery for the Georgians on Mount Athos, but each time the request was refused. But later in 976, when the general Bardas Skleros staged a rebellion in the east and marched against Constantinople, the emperor summoned Tornikios to his assistance. At first, he was reluctant to go, but he was persuaded by Athanasios and John the Iberian that it would not be in the best interests of the Athonites for him to refuse. He went therefore, initially as a messenger to the Georgian ruler, requesting military assistance. On his arrival in Georgia, however, David gave him command of the Georgian troops, promising him all the spoils if the campaign was successful. On 24 March 979 Tornikios defeated Bardas and his army in battle, for which he was rewarded with honours by the emperor before returning to Athos.

In gratitude for this victory the emperor granted Tornikios not just honours but also material rewards in the form of great wealth (1,200 pounds of gold), other treasures, and monastic lands both on Athos and elsewhere. The land on the Mountain included the site of the earlier monastery of Clement, some 11 kilometres north of Lavra up the east coast, on which Tornikios personally was now given permission to found the monastery of Iviron ('of the Georgians') (Plate 8). The land off the Mountain included property in Chalkidiki and Thessaloniki which had until 979 belonged to the monastery of Kolobos near Ierissos. Thus Tornikios's military adventure brought the Georgians enormous benefits in kind, which were confirmed by imperial chrysobull, and he was henceforth to be regarded as the principal *ktitor* (founder) of Iviron. These favours, however, also provoked a furious outburst of anti-Georgian xenophobia and jealousy among the Greeks on the Mountain, which was only contained by generous donations to the Protaton. Iviron continued to receive large sums of money from wealthy Georgians and by the end of the century was distributing it to other houses on Athos including the Protaton, the Lavra, and the Amalfitan monastery.

When he returned from his military adventure, we are told that Tornikios was accompanied by many new recruits for the monastery:

> When Tornikios came from the east he brought with him many rasophores and famous monks. His desire was that only Georgians should inhabit the monastery. However, this was an impossible task and it was inevitable that some Greeks were also accepted because we, as you see, have no experience in seafaring and yet all our sustenance arrives by sea. It is difficult to maintain such a large lavra without a blacksmith, carpenters, builders, vineyard workers, sailors and others.[2]

These Greek monks worked as artisans on the construction of the monastery and as servants. They were men of humble origin, chosen deliberately so as not to challenge the social superiority of the Georgian community. John of Iberia's chief concern was to establish a scriptorium where his son Euthymios could work with a team of scribes on his translations of Greek spiritual literature into Georgian. Thus the monastery became an important centre of cultural and intellectual exchange. At this stage, the coexistence of the two linguistic communities did not appear to cause a problem and indeed was even able to further the work of translation since one of the chief scribes at the time was the monk Theophanes, a Greek.

One of Tornikios's decrees stipulated that the abbot should be chosen from the Chordvaneli family, thereby keeping the position in his own family, and this was adhered to at Iviron for at least the first fifty years. John the Iberian was clearly a charismatic figure in the mould of Athanasios, and by the time of his death, around 1005, the monastery is said to have housed 300 monks. As abbot he was succeeded by his son, Euthymios, who was followed in turn by his kinsman George. Athanasios retained his affection and respect for John and Euthymios and named them as the administrators of the Lavra in the event of his own death. It is a mark of the Georgians' good connections with the Byzantine court that John the Iberian named the emperors as administrators of Iviron in the hope that they would not forget the monastery which they had enabled John to build.

Nor did the founders ignore the spiritual development of their monastery. To care for the many novices and junior monks now joining the community, it was necessary also to attract more senior and spiritually

---

[2] Grdzelidze, *Georgian Monks on Mount Athos*, p. 60. Life of Frs John and Euthymios, ch. 7. A rasophore (i.e. wearer of the *rason* or tunic which forms part of the habit) is a tonsured monk of the lowest rank.

advanced monks from Georgia. It was their wish that only native
Georgians should join the brotherhood, and so John the Iberian wrote to
well-known spiritual fathers such as his friends John Grdzelisdze and
Arsenios, the former bishop of Ninotsmida, who had both been monks
at the lavra of Otkhta Eklesia in Tao-Klarjeti but had moved to the desert
of Pontos in search of greater tranquillity. 'Holy fathers,' John wrote to
them,

> your holiness has become known to us and we learned about your life there
> and we regret that you do not wish to come to this holy and eminent
> Mountain so that we also might receive your holy prayer. We entreat your
> holiness to come [here] so that we may reside together because, as you know,
> we too have been in a foreign [land].[3]

Gratified by the invitation, Fathers John and Arsenios came to the Holy
Mountain the next year, much to the delight of the Athonites.

   The newly arrived fathers were put to work in the scriptorium that the
founders had thought to establish for the copying of manuscripts in
Georgian. John the Iberian was conscious of the fact that their homeland
was in great need of books, and he therefore instructed his son Euthymios
to translate as many Greek texts as he could find into Georgian. Many of
the translated texts were sent off to David Kouropalates who responded
joyfully: 'Thanks be to God who in our times has revealed a new
Chrysostomos.' He asked for more books to be sent, and we are told that
Euthymios laboured night and day and that he translated an immense list
beginning with 'Exegesis of the Gospel of John, the teachings of our father
St Basil the Great, also his exegesis on the Book of Psalms, the book of St
John Climacus, the book of St Macarius of Egypt, teachings of St Maximus
the Confessor, the book of St Isaac the Syrian' and at least another fifty
such titles including works by St Gregory of Nyssa, St John of Damascus,
St John Cassian, St Gregory the Theologian, the Book of Revelation, and
numerous hagiographical and liturgical texts.[4] The newly arrived fathers
from Georgia were asked to make copies of these translations, to which
they added colophons of their own in which they express their admiration
for the founders. In one such manuscript, for example, Fathers John and
Arsenios write, 'Christ, bless and give rest to the soul of Fr John and bless
our Fr Euthymios; they faithfully provided spiritual life to the Georgian
people and repay them for their work.' And in another colophon in the
same manuscript,

[3] Ibid., p. 64. Life of Frs John and Euthymios, ch. 11.
[4] Ibid., pp. 67–70. Life of Frs John and Euthymios, ch. 13.

> By the order of our God-bearing Fr Euthymios we, poor sinners, Arsenios of Ninotsmida and John Grdzelisdze and Chrysostom, were deemed worthy to copy by our hands these holy books translated from Greek into Georgian by our holy illuminator Fr Euthymios for the comfort of all the Georgians.[5]

As we have noted, the Georgians already had access to at least some spiritual texts in their own language, but no doubt there were many gaps in the literature and many of the texts they did have were of poor quality. The Athonites had access to the latest Byzantine versions and were therefore well placed to supply their compatriots with books that were based on more authoritative originals and contained superior translations. In this way they made an exceptional contribution to the spiritual, cultural, and liturgical life of Georgia at the time. Euthymios continued the work of translation during his time as abbot (1005–19), and the monastery became the chief entrepôt for the transmission of Greek Christian learning to Georgia.

Euthymios was succeeded as abbot by George I (1019–29), nephew of Tornikios, who unfortunately became involved in an unsuccessful revolt against the Emperor Romanos III Argyros in 1029. Iviron then entered a 'time of troubles', as a result of the growing hostility between its Georgian and Greek monks, and many of the properties it had acquired through the hard work and good connections of the founders were confiscated. Such was the strength of this network of patronage, both Greek and Georgian, that constant appeals to the highest authorities in the empire brought about the restoration of the confiscated estates in 1041; and in 1045 the *typikon* of the Emperor Constantine IX Monomachos listed the abbot of Iviron as back in third place after Lavra and Vatopedi. By the end of the century, the monastery had considerably extended its landholdings and was once again one of the most powerful houses on the Mountain.

St George the Hagiorite (1009–1065)

It was the arrival of George II ('the Hagiorite') in about 1040 that did most to restore the monastery's fortunes. George was born in 1009 to an intellectual Georgian family (two of his uncles were tonsured scribes) and he received a good education in Constantinople. Tonsured at a monastery in Georgia, he made a number of journeys to Antioch and the Holy Land before going at the request of his spiritual father to Athos. His chief purpose was to translate more spiritual texts into Georgian, and for this Iviron was the obvious place to go. He also undertook to write the

---

[5] Iviron MS 13, a translation of theological texts by Euthymios.

Lives of the founders, St John the Iberian and St Euthymios, whose veneration he instituted. But he and his mentors had another aim that was broader and much more challenging: to restore Iviron to at least its former position as the pre-eminent Georgian house and to ensure that it participated fully in the cultural and intellectual developments of the day in what is now known as the Macedonian renaissance.

Elected abbot in about 1045, George continued with the work of translation and revitalized the scriptorium so that multiple copies could be made of the texts. Again the list of texts that he translated is extensive and apparently included the Great Synaxarion, the twelve-volume Menaion, the Acts of the Apostles and the Epistles of Paul, the readings for the year, the Triodion and Pentecostarion, the Catecheses of St Theodore the Stoudite, the book of the Sixth Ecumenical Council, and the Psalter, 'the jewel and crown of all books'.[6] He also obtained recognition of the founders as saints of the Church and with the emperor's support he carried out structural repairs to the katholikon. The magnificent *opus sectile* floor, which still survives, dates from this time, and an inscription around its centrepiece reads in Greek, 'I erected these columns and they shall not be shaken by time. George the Iberian, monk and founder.'[7] But in 1056 George resigned as abbot and left the Mountain, ostensibly so that he could concentrate more wholly on his life's work of translation, but we may wonder if there was not a more fundamental reason for his resignation, possibly connected with the exchange of anathemas which took place between Rome and Constantinople in 1054. There was, after all, a close bond between the Georgians of Iviron and the Latins of the Amalfitan monastery who saw each other as fellow foreigners on the Holy Mountain, and this could have made George's relationship with the patriarch in Constantinople very uncomfortable. George had also been summoned to appear before the patriarch of Antioch in connection with the attempts of the Georgian Church to achieve complete autocephaly, but George was able to persuade the patriarch that this should finally be granted, for which he won great acclaim. George himself had been invited more than once by King Bagrat IV to become primate of the Georgian Church, but he shunned further involvement in the public square.

After a period of seclusion on the Black Mountain near Antioch, where he continued with his translations, George returned to Georgia for about

---

[6] Grdzelidze, *Georgian Monks on Mount Athos*, p. 125. Life of Fr George, ch. 16.

[7] See Dimitrios A. Liakos, 'The Byzantine *Opus Sectile* Floor in the Katholikon of Iveron Monastery on Mount Athos', *Zograf*, 32 (2008), 37–44 (40).

five years from 1060 to 1065. During this time, he helped to establish canon law and initiated a number of reforms to regulate the hierarchy of the Church and its relations with the state. But he never forgot Iviron and in 1065 he gathered together a group of eighty Georgian orphans, rescuing them from starvation, slavery, and other miseries, and took them to Constantinople from where they were shipped to Athos. His purpose in doing this was not purely humanitarian but was also to replenish the complement of Georgians in the monastery:

> Because our country was far away from this land, [only] a few learned men came but even those who came, left again after a while, leaving this splendid church empty. Blessed [Father George] wished to dedicate as an honourable gift to our holy father Euthymios the group of his children, like rational sheep, so that [they might become] singers and priests of this holy church – and thus the commemoration of the God-bearing builders [of the church] would be brilliantly accomplished.[8]

By the middle of the eleventh century the Greek contingent in the brotherhood was so numerous that it was allowed to follow its own *typikon* and attend services in a different church from the Georgians, the latter in the katholikon and the Greeks in the church of St John the Baptist. By the twelfth century the Greeks actually formed a majority, as is confirmed by the distribution of administrative offices, though the abbots continued to be Georgians.

George obtained permission from the emperor for the orphans to be educated at Iviron, but before he could reach the Mountain he died on 29 June 1065. His body was carried to Athos and buried in the monastery, next to that of St Euthymios. He was later canonized by the Georgian Church and his translations were so highly regarded that he was honoured as one of the masters of the Georgian language. His own Life was written shortly after his death by his disciple George the Minor.

Gregory Pakourianos (d.1086)

In the twelfth century there was a decline in the number of works being translated into Georgian paralleled by a decline in the size of the Georgian brotherhood at Iviron, but the monastery continued to prosper, thanks largely to substantial donations of cash and property from wealthy aristo-cratic benefactors. Details of these gifts are provided by the monastery's *Synodikon*, a document in Georgian covering the years from 1074 to the

[8] Grdzelidze, *Georgian Monks on Mount Athos*, p. 141. Life of Fr George, ch. 23.

1180s, that lists the size and source of the benefactions. We may take the case of Gregory Pakourianos as an illustration. Gregory (who is claimed by the Armenians as well as the Georgians) had had an extremely distinguished career as a soldier, serving under several successive emperors in their campaigns on both the eastern and western frontiers of the empire. In return for this service he was rewarded with grand office, impressive titles, and vast estates in the Balkans. In 1074 he and his brother Apasios made a generous donation to Iviron. But in 1083 he decided to found his own monastery at Bachkovo, in the Rhodope Mountains in modern Bulgaria. This remains one of the principal monasteries of Bulgaria with its ossuary surviving from the eleventh century, built as a tomb for Gregory and his brother and including portraits of them dating from the fourteenth century in the narthex. According to the historian Anna Komnena, Gregory was killed in battle against the Pechenegs near Philippoupolis in 1086.[9]

The reason for mentioning Bachkovo here is not that it had significant Athonite connections at the time of its foundation but that it was a Georgian monastery of the eleventh century which functioned as a focus of cultural exchange between Georgia and Byzantium in the same way that Iviron did. In a somewhat surprising display of distrust and indeed dislike for the Byzantines, however, we learn from its foundation document that Gregory intended it to be a house exclusively for Georgians and that no Greek should ever be appointed a priest or monk, except for one secretary responsible for relations with the local authorities.

> I give this instruction and insist upon it for the following reason, lest [the Greeks], being violent, devious, or grasping, should create some deficiency or cause harm to the monastery or lest they appoint someone opposed to the place and eager to gain control over it or gain for himself the office of superior or appropriate the monastery on some other abominable pretext. These sort of things we have often seen happen among our people, caused by simplicity and a gentle disposition. Otherwise we follow these men in the faith as our teachers and we obey their doctrines.[10]

Unlike the founders of Iviron, who went out of their way to keep the abbacy of that monastery within the family, Gregory imposed a ban on the abbot appointing members of his own family to any jobs within his monastery. And he set up a religious school which was attended by

---

[9] Anna Komnena, *Alexiad* 6.14.
[10] Thomas and Constantinides Hero, *Byzantine Monastic Foundation Documents*, vol. 2, p. 547, § 24. It is worth noting that this document was written in Greek, whereas the *typikon* itself was drawn up in three languages: Greek, Georgian, and Armenian. See ibid., p. 510.

a hundred young men whom he imported from Georgia: half of them probably became members of the brotherhood and the other half returned to Georgia as teachers. The monastery retained its Georgian character until the fourteenth century, but in 1344 Bulgarian monks were introduced by Tsar Ivan Alexander (1331–71) who richly endowed it. In the second half of that century the monastery played a major role in the Bulgarian cultural revival, and from 1393 it became the last resting place of the exiled Patriarch Euthymius of Trnovo (*c.*1325–*c.*1400) (see Chapter 9).

The number of Georgian monks at Iviron declined further in the thirteenth century, though they remained formally in charge of the monastery. As at Bachkovo, it was in the mid fourteenth century that their leadership formally came to an end, and in 1355/6 Patriarch Kallistos I decreed that thenceforth the abbot and ecclesiarch must be elected from among the Greek monks. At the same time the Greeks gained the right to conduct services in the katholikon and the Georgians were relegated to a smaller church, probably the chapel of St John the Baptist. Nonetheless a Georgian minority survived at Iviron until the mid twentieth century, and the monastery continued to turn to Georgia for assistance in times of stress.[11] Even today, when there are no Georgian monks there at all, and precious few elsewhere on the Mountain, Iviron remains a powerful symbol in the cultural and spiritual memory of the Georgian people.

---

[11] There was further tension between the Georgians and Iviron in the nineteenth century, for which see N. Fennell, *The Russians on Athos* (Oxford: Peter Lang, 2001), pp. 132–8.

CHAPTER 5

St Antony (983–1073) and St Theodosius (1035–1074) of Kiev: Fathers of Russian Monasticism

In contrast to its southern neighbour Georgia, Russia adopted Christianity rather late. The story is told by the *Russian Primary Chronicle*, which is our principal source for early Russian history. In the year 986, according to the Chronicle, missionaries from foreign parts, presumably at the invitation of Grand Prince Vladimir (reigned 980–1015), visited Kiev. First had come the Bulgars, from the middle Volga, who were Muslims. As soon as Vladimir learnt that Islam forbade the drinking of wine, he exclaimed, 'Drinking is the joy of the Russians; we cannot exist without it.' Next came ambassadors from the Pope, but their doctrines were rejected for reasons that are not made clear. Then came envoys from the Jewish kingdom of the Khazars, but they were forced to admit that the Jews had no country of their own and were scattered among the Gentiles 'because of their sins'. 'Do you want us to share the same fate?', asked Vladimir. Finally came a Greek from Byzantium who spoke at length, confounding the religions of Rome, of Islam, and of Judaism and expounding the beliefs and practices of Byzantine Christianity. Still the prince was unwilling to commit himself and dispatched envoys abroad the following year to obtain more detailed information. They returned with the following report:

> When we journeyed among the Bulgars, we beheld how they worship in their temple, called a mosque, while they stand ungirt. The Bulgar bows, sits down, looks hither and thither like one possessed, and there is no happiness among them, but instead only sorrow and a dreadful stench. Their religion is not good. Then we went among the Germans, and saw them performing many ceremonies in their temples; but we beheld no glory there. Then we went to Greece, and the Greeks led us to the edifices where they worship their God, and we knew not whether we were in heaven or on earth. For on earth there is no such splendor or such beauty, and we are at a loss how to

64

describe it. We only know that God dwells there among men, and their service is fairer than the ceremonies of other nations. For we cannot forget that beauty.[1]

After hearing his envoys' description of their experience of the Divine Liturgy in Hagia Sophia, Vladimir was finally convinced and, in a deal that involved his receiving the Byzantine emperor's sister Anna in marriage, he was baptized by the bishop of Cherson in the Crimea. Just as in the previous decade the Georgian general Tornikios had responded to the Emperor Basil II's request for aid against the rebellion of Bardas Skleros (and had been rewarded with enough land and treasure to enable him to found the monastery of Iviron on Mount Athos), so now Prince Vladimir agreed to assist the same emperor to defeat a rebellion by Bardas Phokas on condition that he be rewarded with an imperial bride; and for the marriage to be valid, the prince had to be a baptized Christian. Returning to Kiev with his bride in 988, he then had the city's population baptized in the river Dnieper, an event that has traditionally symbolized the conversion of Russia to Christianity. The price of military aid had been the award of a bride, but the long-term benefit to Byzantium was beyond price, namely the incorporation of all Russia into the Byzantine Commonwealth.

The Foundation of the Monastery of the Caves

In fact, Vladimir was not the first member of his family to be baptized. His grandmother, Princess Ol'ga, widow of Prince Igor' and now regent, had made a visit to Constantinople and received baptism either there or in Kiev around the year 955, but she had been unable to impose Christianity on her subjects. According to some traditions, her baptism took place at the caves near Kiev, which might suggest the existence of hermits in that area as early as the mid tenth century. But there is no evidence for any monasteries in Russia at this period, and the whole episode is shrouded in mystery. What seems to be clear is that soon after his baptism Vladimir encouraged priests and bishops from Byzantium to visit his realm and assist in the establishment of a Russian Church. Churches were built and decorated in the

---

[1] *The Russian Primary Chronicle*, trans. and ed. S. H. Cross and O. P. Sherbowitz-Wetzor (Cambridge, MA: Mediaeval Academy of America, 1953), p. 111. The Chronicle was most probably compiled early in the twelfth century by a monk of the monastery of the Caves at Kiev.

Byzantine style to replace the old pagan shrines, bishoprics were set up in the main cities, and the consequent development of ecclesiastical organization helped him to impose a unity on the scattered tribes of his territory.

In the wake of the churches there followed monasteries, similarly established on Byzantine principles, and Russia was rapidly incorporated into the Athonite Commonwealth. According to the *Russian Primary Chronicle*, the first mention of a monastery 'tou Rhos' (i.e. of the Rus') on Athos dates from 1016. This was most probably the monastery of Xylourgou, the first cenobitic Russian house, mentioned by name in documents from 1030 on, which stood on the site of the existing skete of Bogoroditsa (Plate 9). The principal church of the skete probably dates from the eleventh century and is dedicated to the Dormition of the Mother of God. This remained the focus of Russian monasticism on the Mountain until 1169, by which time the community had outgrown the buildings and the abbot, Lavrenty, applied to the Protos for a larger monastery. Lavrenty was granted the deserted inland monastery of the Thessalonians (*Thessalonikos*) which was dedicated to St Panteleimon (Plate 10), and this has remained the chief house of the Russians (*Rossikon*) ever since, though in 1765 the decision was taken to move the monastery to its present site on the waterfront. The Russians have retained possession of Xylourgou as a skete.

Meanwhile, sometime in the early eleventh century, the *Primary Chronicle* tells us that a layman from the city of Lyubech in modern-day Ukraine went as a pilgrim to Mount Athos and, having visited the monasteries, was so charmed by what he saw that he decided to enter the monastic life. The abbot of the monastery where he was staying, identified in some traditions as Abbot Theoktistos of Esphigmenou, tonsured him with the name Antony, instructed him in his monastic obligations, and after a few years ordered him to 'return to Rus' accompanied by the blessing of the Holy Mountain, that many other monks might spring from his example'.[2] Antony did as he was instructed and returned to Kiev where, following the example of his Egyptian namesake, he chose to live as a hermit and took up residence in a nearby cave, devoting himself to prayer and fasting.

[2] Ibid., pp. 139–40.

After the death of Prince Vladimir in 1015 the throne passed to his son, Svyatopolk. Svyatopolk did not share his father's piety and instituted a programme of persecution against the Christians. His own brothers, Boris and Gleb, were not exempt from his bloodthirsty campaign and are numbered as Russia's first two Christian Passion-Bearers.[3] To escape this terror, Antony returned to the Holy Mountain where, 'having tasted the honey of *hesychia*', as his entry in the *Synaxarion* puts it, he was given a blessing by Abbot Theoktistos to withdraw to a cave on Mount Samaria, a short distance from the monastery. Here he lived as a hermit, apparently for some decades, though the chronology is somewhat confused between the various traditions.[4]

Meanwhile, in Kiev, Svyatopolk had been defeated by his God-fearing brother Yaroslav (reigned 1019–54), who put a stop to the reign of terror and resumed his father's policy in favour of the Church. 'During his reign', as the Chronicle informs us for the year 1037, 'the Christian faith was fruitful and multiplied, while the number of monks increased, and new monasteries came into being.'[5] Exactly what this means in terms of numbers is hard to say, but the Oxford historian John Fennell quotes the figures estimated by the Russian medievalist B. V. Sapunov. For the 250 years from the baptism of Vladimir to the Mongol invasion Sapunov listed 247 churches to which a construction date could be assigned (25 in the tenth century, 37 in the eleventh, 138 in the twelfth, and 46 in the first forty years of the thirteenth), to which he added a further 76 that could not be dated. But this total of 323 churches he thought was likely to be a small fraction of the probable total, and he concluded that some 2,000 town churches would have been built between 988 and 1240. As for monasteries in the same period, those that can be identified from the sources numbered 7 for the tenth century, 18 for the eleventh, 30 for the twelfth, and 16 for 1200–40, to which he added a further 56 that could not be dated, giving a total of 127. Allowing for unrecorded establishments, he suggested a likely total of about 200, i.e. 10 per cent of the total number of churches. In the absence of firmer data, these figures may be said to constitute a reasonable conjecture.[6]

---

[3] They were not formally classed as martyrs for the faith, but they were canonized as innocent victims in a political dispute.

[4] Hieromonk Makarios of Simonos Petra, *The Synaxarion: The Lives of the Saints of the Orthodox Church*, vol. 6 (Ormylia: Holy Convent of the Annunciation of Our Lady, 2008), p. 97.

[5] *Russian Primary Chronicle*, p. 137.

[6] J. Fennell, *A History of the Russian Church to 1448* (London: Routledge, 1995), p. 63.

According to the entry for Antony in the *Synaxarion*, at about this time a well-known ascetic from Berestovo with the name Ilarion took up residence on the hill above the river Dnieper, where the monastery of the Caves stands today, and dug a cave for himself where he could live as a hermit. In the year 1051 we are told that Ilarion was appointed bishop of Kiev, and at the same time on Athos Abbot Theoktistos received a vision to send Antony back to Russia for a second time. By Sapunov's reckoning there would have been perhaps as many as twenty monasteries already in existence in Russia by this time, and Antony went from one to the next without finding one to his liking for he had already developed a taste for the eremitic life. When God directed his steps to the cave recently vacated by Ilarion, he was happy to settle there. The situation reminded him of his cave on Athos and so he prayed that the blessing of the Holy Mountain should rest there. There he was content to practise the ascetic life and devote himself to unceasing prayer.

Soon, however, as is often the way with charismatic hermits, his renown spread, and after Yaroslav's death in 1054 he was joined by a number of followers, whom he tonsured as monks. Together they dug a whole series of caves to provide a great crypt, a church, and cells, 'which exist to this day in the crypt under the old monastery'.[7] When the number of the brethren reached fifteen, Antony appointed one Barlaam as their first abbot and said to them:

> God has gathered you together, my brethren, and you are under the blessing of the Holy Mountain, through which the prior at the Holy Mountain tonsured me and I have tonsured you also. May there be upon you first the blessing of God and second that of the Holy Mountain.[8]

So saying, he left them and went by himself to resume his eremitical existence in a nearby cave, from where he continued to exercise a fatherly eye over the brotherhood until his death at the age of ninety on 10 July 1073. Meanwhile, the numbers of monks increased, and they came to Antony to ask his permission to found a monastery. Antony turned to Izyaslav, then the ruler of Kiev and the grandson of Prince Vladimir, and the monks were given the land that stood over the cave

---

[7] These are the words of the Chronicle, but in fact the caves do still exist and may be visited to this day. They contain numerous burials but are not otherwise used for monastic purposes, though the Liturgy is still celebrated there.

[8] *Russian Primary Chronicle*, p. 140.

where they laid the foundations of a great church. They also constructed many cells and adorned the church with icons. 'Such was the origin of the monastery of the Caves', the Chronicle concludes. 'This is the monastery of the Caves which issued from the Holy Mountain.' Its principal church, like that of Xylourgou, is dedicated to the Dormition of the Mother of God.

Growth and Prosperity of the Monastery of the Caves

The monastery was blessed to have a series of distinguished, sympathetic, and often saintly abbots under whose direction it flourished for almost two centuries. As the Cambridge historian R. P. Casey has observed, 'Antony was by nature no organizer.'

> The responsibilities of superior were thrust upon him, as upon his prede-cessor in Egypt, and he deputed them as soon as possible to Barlaam. Rigour and regulation was Antony's main concern ... Self-denial, hard manual labour, the cultivation of the interior life, the regular recitation of the Divine Office and ... regular celebration of the Liturgy, constituted life at the Caves before Theodosius's reform.[9]

In 1062 Barlaam was transferred by Izyaslav to the new monastery of St Demetrios, and his place as abbot of the Caves was taken by St Theodosius (1035–74) who had been one of Antony's first disciples.

Our principal source for knowledge of Theodosius is his Life, written soon after his death by Nestor, a fellow monk at the monastery of the Caves.[10] The Life paints a vivid portrait of the saint's upbringing and the battles he fought with his grieving mother who could not bear to be parted from him, a grief that was only finally assuaged by her agreement to take the veil herself in Kiev. The young Theodosius (this was his baptismal name, which he retained throughout his life) identified with the poor from an early age and insisted on dressing in rags to his parents' embarrassment. He went to church every day and, with the assistance of a spiritual director, devoted himself to study of the sacred texts rather than playing with other children. Thus, to the astonishment of those around him, he made rapid strides in wisdom and also in the virtues of

---

[9] R. P. Casey, 'Early Russian Monasticism', *Orientalia Christiana Periodica*, 19 (1953), 408.

[10] An English translation of the Life of St Theodosius appears in G. P. Fedotov (ed.), *A Treasury of Russian Spirituality* (London: Sheed and Ward, 1950), pp. 15–49. There is another, with commen-tary, in M. Heppell (trans.), *The Paterik of the Kievan Caves Monastery* (Cambridge, MA: Ukrainian Research Institute of Harvard University, 1989), pp. 24–88.

obedience and humility (though we may note that he did not always obey his parents' wishes).

Theodosius was thirteen when his father died and after that he applied himself to manual labour in the fields where he took on the humblest work. This offended his mother who wanted him to wear good clothes and mix with boys of his own age, but he refused, and for this the formidable lady beat him often. 'She was robust of body,' writes Nestor, 'and if you could not see her, but could only hear her voice, you might well have mistaken her for a man.'[11] He received another beating when he ran away from home in the company of a group of pilgrims who told him they were heading for the Holy Land. His mother only discovered this after three days and set off in hot pursuit. Eventually she caught up with the pilgrims, whom she rebuked, and administered savage corporal punishment to her son: she flung him to the ground and trampled on him, took him home bound like a criminal, shackled him, and locked him in his room. All this the saintly youth suffered joyfully, we are told, giving thanks to God. Incidents such as this (and there are quite a few more like it) are narrated with such graphic detail in the Life that we can only conclude that Nestor is writing on the basis of fact and not legend.

The final contest with his mother takes place some years later when she is called away from home on a long visit. Theodosius seizes the opportunity of her absence to take himself off to Kiev where he had heard there were many monasteries. He goes from one to another, but none will take him in, dressed as he is in his rags. This is of course God's will who directs his feet to the cave outside the city where St Antony is living as a hermit. When he sees Antony, he goes down on his knees and begs to be allowed to stay. Antony warns him of the hardship he will have to endure if he does so, but he is prophetically aware of what the future holds for Theodosius. When the young man promises obedience in all things to the saint, Antony invites him to remain and asks an elder of the community to tonsure him. From that moment, Theodosius submits himself willingly to God and to Antony, and all the fathers are amazed at the strength of his humility and obedience. Meanwhile, his mother has been searching for him for four years and eventually hears that the boy has been seen in Kiev. Beating a path to the cave, she asks to see

---

[11] Fedotov, *A Treasury of Russian Spirituality*, p. 18.

the abbot. Antony emerges from the cave and listens to her impassioned plea to see her son. Ostensibly unaware of her mischievous intentions, the saint asks her to return the following day, which she does. Theodosius refuses to see her, whereupon she denounces Antony for taking her son away and threatens to commit suicide if she cannot see him. Distressed by her emotional state, Antony begs Theodosius to see her, which out of obedience to his elder he agrees to do. But resisting her entreaties to go back home, Theodosius says that if she wants to see him again she must become a nun herself. After several such meetings she relents and agrees to enter a convent, admitting to him that his teaching has brought her to an understanding of the emptiness of this transient world. All rejoice at this solution to the problem and Antony arranges with the prince's wife for Theodosius's mother to be admitted to the women's monastery of St Nicholas, where she lives happily ever after.

> Such is the life of our blessed father Theodosius from his childhood until the day when he entered the cave [writes Nestor at this point]. His mother related all this to one of the brethren, Theodore by name, who was the cellarer of our father Theodosius. I heard this account from Theodore's own lips, and set it down, in order that all who read may remember his deeds.[12]

If Antony laid the foundations for the monastery of the Caves, inspired by the spiritual and ascetic practices that he had encountered on Athos, it was Theodosius who built on them and set it on the road to fame and prosperity. The regime that he introduced and the style of his rule were to exercise a profound influence over the future direction of Russian monasticism as a whole. Antony and his disciples lived a life of extreme poverty, making ends meet by the work of their own hands, and whatever they earned was contributed to a common purse. But soon they began to attract donations. Some gave them food, others gave them money or treasures such as books and icons, others gave them villages. The monks continued to profess poverty and aspired to be self-sufficient, but the monastery quickly became a significant economic entity, able to borrow money from merchants in Kiev and to spend it on necessities in Constantinople. It was not a princely foundation, but it received regular donations from members of the royal house, wealthy landowners, and senior clergy. These came

---

[12] Ibid., pp. 24–5.

in the form of estates and villages, often including the peasants and therefore the full income deriving from the land, and substantial gifts of gold and silver. Abbots of monasteries moved in high social circles. They often acted as confessors and spiritual fathers to princes and were entertained at grand gatherings. Whenever a list of abbots appears in the records, the abbot of the Caves is always placed first. It was clearly the leading monastery in the whole country.

When Theodosius succeeded Barlaam as abbot in 1062, there were twenty monks at the Caves. By the mid 1060s there were already a hundred. Growth at this rate demands organization, and for this purpose Theodosius sought a monastic rule, though the traditions are divided as to how he actually came by it. According to the Life, he sent one of the monks to Constantinople to obtain a copy of the Stoudite rule that was followed by many of the monasteries there and on Athos. According to the Chronicle, there was at that time in Kiev a monk from the Stoudios monastery from whom Theodosius obtained his copy of the rule. However he came by it, the Chronicle continues,

> he obtained their rule from him, copied it out, and established it in his monastery to govern the singing of monastic hymns, the making of reverences, the reading of the lessons, behaviour in church, the whole ritual, conduct at table, proper food for special days, and to regulate all else according to prescription. After obtaining all this information, Theodosius thus transmitted it to his monastery, and from the latter all others adopted the same institutions. Therefore the Crypt [i.e. Caves] monastery is honoured as the oldest of all.[13]

Maturity and Influence of the Monastery of the Caves

With its adoption of the Stoudite rule the monastery of the Caves was established as a fully fledged coenobium, and Theodosius was thereafter revered as its second founder. As members of a coenobium the monks were expected to attend the services in church, to undertake manual labour, and to practise obedience to the abbot, but the rule was designed to cover every aspect of daily life. There were set stages in the hierarchy through which a monk rose from the novitiate to the highest rank, that of the Great Schema. There was a clearly defined division of labour, and every monk was assigned his own task,

---

[13] *Russian Primary Chronicle*, p. 142.

whether as cook or cellarer, gatekeeper or choirmaster, priest, deacon, or steward. Some specialized in skilled work as icon painters, scribes, or bookbinders. And there was advice for the baker on how to knead the dough and warnings for those reading books not to damage them with candle-wax or saliva.[14]

As an urban institution, the Caves monastery also took on some external philanthropic work for the benefit of the local community. Theodosius established an almshouse for the poor and sick to which he assigned a tithe of the monastery's income, and once a week he sent food parcels to the city's prisons. In the absence of any such service by the state, the monastery adopted the traditional role of charitable welfare provider. With the assistance of the prince he built a magnificent new katholikon dedicated to the Dormition of the Mother of God, the decoration of which he entrusted to artists from Constantinople, and in many ways the Caves was a typical offshoot of contemporary Byzantine monasticism. But in the range of its activities and the breadth of its influence it was far more than that: it was by far the most important monastery of its day and it set the pattern for Russian monasticism for many generations to come.

In the context of this book, its most important contribution is to the spread of monasticism throughout Kievan Rus'. It provided, as we have seen, the first abbot of the monastery of St Demetrios, and Barlaam's successor in that position, Isaia, was also a monk of the Caves. Stefan, who followed Theodosius as abbot of the Caves, founded the monastery of the Mother of God of Blachernae near Kiev in the 1070s, and Nikon, who succeeded Stefan, with two other monks from the Caves founded a monastic community in Tmutarakan on the Taman' peninsula opposite the Crimea. The Caves also acquired a dependency (*metochion*) in Suzdal', and the monastery's rule, introduced by Theodosius, was adopted as the model for all cenobitic houses throughout Russia. The Caves supplied the Russian Church with a large proportion of its senior clergy: writing around 1225, Bishop Simon of Vladimir estimated that some fifty bishops, including himself, had been monks of the Caves; and it may be said that its spiritual network was at least in part responsible for holding together the increasingly divided lands of the Rus' princes. Moreover, the katholikon of the Caves that was built by Theodosius came to be the model for all city cathedrals built throughout Rus' between the 1070s and the 1220s, all of which are dedicated to the Dormition of the Mother of God. It is even said

---

[14] See S. Franklin and J. Shepard, *The Emergence of Rus 750–1200* (London: Longman, 1996), p. 309.

that, when he was making plans for the church in Rostov, Vladimir II Monomakh (reigned in Kiev 1113–25) copied its exact dimensions and its iconographic programme, and that his son Yuri did the same in Suzdal'. And the Caves played the dominant part in creating the sacred literature of the period, both in translations from Greek and in the writing of original works in Church Slavonic, notably Nestor's Life of Theodosius, the *Paterikon* of the monastery preserving details of its greatest alumni, and above all the *Russian Primary Chronicle* itself. It may be said that knowledge of the Kievan period as a whole would be seriously impoverished without the literary output of the Caves monastery.

Dimitri Obolensky concludes his discussion of Russian cenobitic monasticism of this period with a brief sketch of its founder as it emerges from Nestor's Life. 'The impression we gain', he writes, 'is of a man of deep and unassuming humility, balanced moderation in the practice of asceticism, and considerable moral authority. The latter quality was manifest in his relations with the princes and nobles of the land, as well as with his own monks.' But he reserves his warmest tribute for the significance of the monastery itself that Antony and Theodosius co-founded:

> The unrivalled prestige enjoyed by the monastery of the Caves in Kievan Russia, and the personal influence exerted by several of its abbots on the ruling circles of the country, go far to explain the considerable role it played in the early Middle Ages ... The history of this house, at least until the Mongol invasion, shows how rapidly and thoroughly the Byzantine monastic tradition could be assimilated: the three basic elements in this tradition – the writings of the early Egyptian and Palestinian monks, the eremitical practices of Mount Athos, and the Constantinopolitan Studite Rule – combined to shape the life of the leading monastery in early medieval Russia.[15]

Much of the monastery's success, however, must be attributed to the efforts of just one man. At the end of his Life of Theodosius, Nestor writes

> He was respected, not because of fine clothes or rich estates, but for his radiant life and purity of spirit, and for his teachings, fired with the inspiration of the Holy Ghost. To him the goatskin and the hair-shirt were more precious than a king's purple robe, and he was proud to wear them.[16]

---

[15] Obolensky, *The Byzantine Commonwealth*, p. 387.
[16] Fedotov, *A Treasury of Russian Spirituality*, p. 45.

After his death he rapidly came to be held up as the model of spiritual piety, the father of cenobitic monasticism, lauded by some as 'the beacon of all Rus'', by others as 'the archimandrite of all Rus''. In 1108, on the initiative of Abbot Feoktist, Metropolitan Nikifor was ordered by Prince Svyatopolk to write the name of Theodosius in the *Synodikon* as one to be commemorated thereafter in all churches and cathedrals at the Divine Liturgy. As the Chronicle records, all the bishops were instructed to do the same, and they obeyed 'with joy'.[17]

---

[17] Franklin and Shepard, *The Emergence of Rus*, p. 311.

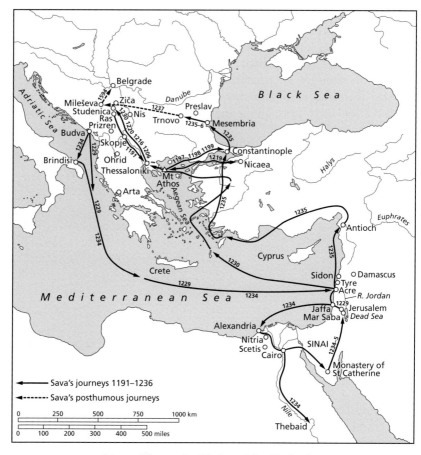

Map 3. The travels of St Sava. After Obolensky.

Places and labels on map:

Belgrade
Danube
Mileševa
Ziča
1594
Studenica
Ras
1230
Nis
1237
Preslav
Prizren
1220
1216
Trnovo
1235–6
Mesembria
Budva
1206
Skopje
1191
1229
1234
Ohrid
1197 1198 1199
1235
Brindisi
Thessaloniki
1219
Constantinople
Arta
Mt Athos
Nicaea
Black Sea
Adriatic Sea
Halys
Aegean Sea
1235
1235
Antioch
Euphrates
Cyprus
1230
Crete
Sidon
Damascus
1229
Tyre
Mediterranean Sea
Acre
R. Jordan
1234
1234
Jaffa
1229
Jerusalem
Mar Saba
Dead Sea
Alexandria
Nitria
SINAI
Scetis
Cairo
1234-5
Monastery of St Catherine
Nile
1234
Thebaid

⟵ Sava's journeys 1191–1236
◀------ Sava's posthumous journeys

0   250   500   750   1000 km
0 100 200 300 400 500 miles

CHAPTER 6

St Sava (1175–1236): Illuminator of Serbia

Serbia seems to have embraced Orthodox Christianity some time during the third quarter of the ninth century, probably between 867 and 874, at the instigation of Emperor Basil I (ruled 867–86). The Serbs had sent ambassadors to Constantinople offering to place themselves under the protection of the Byzantine patriarch. The emperor agreed to their request and sent them priests together with political agents to ensure their incorporation into both the Church and the empire. In the words of Basil's grandson, Constantine VII Porphyrogennetos (945–59), 'When ... they had all partaken of holy baptism and reverted to the submission of the Romans, the emperor's domain again became whole in those parts; and by his benevolent command, all of them accepted chieftains [drawn] from among their kinsmen and people of their own race to rule over them.'[1] The priests were no doubt Greek-speaking and will have had a hard time imposing this foreign religion on the pagan Slavs, but within a couple of decades disciples of St Methodios, who died in 885, arrived bearing Slavonic translations of the liturgy and the sacred texts, which will have greatly assisted the process of evangelization. One or two churches survive from this period, such as the extraordinary little church of St Peter with its circular nave and subterranean font near Novi Pazar. Otherwise we hear nothing of the ecclesiastical history of Serbia until the mid eleventh century.

The two centuries when the country was ruled by the Nemanjid dynasty (c.1167–1371) represent the golden age of medieval Serbia's economic prosperity and cultural flowering. The dynasty was founded by Stefan Nemanja who ruled until 1195. During that period Serbia's boundaries were pushed back to their greatest extent, stretching at one point from the Danube to the Gulf of Corinth and incorporating all of Albania, Epirus,

---

[1] I. Sevcenko (ed.), *Chronographiae quae Theophanis Continuati nomine fertur liber quo Vita Basilii Imperatoris amplectitur* (Berlin: de Gruyter, 2011), p. 197.

Thessaly, and Macedonia. Economic prosperity was assured by the exploitation of rich seams of silver, lead, copper, and iron which were mined by
'Saxon' miners (who probably came from Hungary) notably in Novo Brdo
and Rudnik. Ecclesiastically, Serbia's Church gained independence from
the Byzantine patriarch and established its own autocephalous archbishopric at Žiča (and later Peć). And culturally, Serbia developed its own
schools of architecture, art, and literature, which flourished and produced
monuments to rival those of all its neighbours.

But it is in the visual arts that the ambivalence of Serbia's position,
looking both to the east and to the west, is most apparent. Elements of
Romanesque and Byzantine architecture happily coexist, often in the same
building. The ground-plan of most churches follows the standard
Byzantine type, but details such as intricate tracery around doorways and
windows and sculpted scenes in high relief in the lunettes above provide
clear evidence of Romanesque influence. Similarly, the iconography as
a whole follows the usual Byzantine programme, but occasional elements
in the portrayal of faces are strongly reminiscent of contemporary Italian
schools. Ecclesiastically also Serbia looked in both directions: Byzantine
Christianity was the norm in the hinterland, but the influence of the
Roman Church, spreading inland from the Adriatic, remained strong
until the twelfth century. There is no clearer demonstration of this than
Nemanja's double baptism, first by a Latin priest in his native Zeta and
later by the Orthodox bishop of Ras. And Nemanja's son Stefan (ruled
1195–1227), known as 'the First Crowned', received his crown and the title
of 'king' (in 1217) from none other than Pope Honorius. But he had
married as his first wife Eudokia, daughter of Emperor Alexios III
Angelos, and subsequently received the title of 'sebastokrator', reserved
for members of the imperial family, and the combination of the marriage
alliance and the royal title was enough to symbolize Serbia's incorporation
into the Byzantine Commonwealth at the start of the thirteenth century.

The Foundation of Hilandar Monastery

Nemanja's youngest son, Rastko (later to become Sava), was probably born
in 1175. A passion for monasticism was no doubt in his blood: his father had
already demonstrated his piety by founding several monasteries in Serbia
and would found the greatest of them all, at Studenica, in 1183. But at the
age of fifteen Rastko was appointed a provincial governor by his father,
a position which he held for probably less than two years (1190–1) and then
threw off in favour of the religious life. At the age of sixteen he went in

secret to Mount Athos where he was made welcome by the fathers of the Russian monastery of St Panteleimonos (then recently established on its original site in the hills above the present Rossikon). There is a rather charming story in one of the sources that, when Rastko's father discovered his son's disappearance, he sent an armed guard to bring him back from Athos. The boy played a game of hide and seek with the soldiers, culminating in his appearance at the top of the monastery's tower in full monastic apparel. From there he threw down his shorn locks, his layman's clothes, and a letter addressed to his father, whereupon his pursuers, realizing that he had become a monk and was beyond their reach, returned home empty-handed.[2]

Having eluded his father's attempt to bring him back to Serbia, Sava (who from now on must be known by his monastic name), perhaps wishing to join a larger and longer-established community, made his way to the monastery of Vatopedi where he remained for the next seven years. Athos was by then the leading centre of monasticism in the Orthodox world as well as being an important cultural entrepôt for all members and would-be members of the Byzantine Commonwealth. In addition to the Greeks, who formed the majority, there were already houses for Georgians, Russians, Italians, and probably Bulgarians, so it was natural that Serbs too should aspire to membership of this pan-Orthodox religious society, and this must have been in the forefront of Sava's mind when he left home in 1191. One would like to think that Sava found himself very much at home with the cenobitic regime at Vatopedi and that he communicated this much to his father, for the two must have remained in close touch with each other over the years.

In March 1196, after a turbulent reign of more than thirty years, the already elderly Nemanja abdicated in favour of his second son, Stefan, and entered the monastery of Studenica, his own foundation, as Monk Symeon. After just eighteen months there, he set out to join his son Sava on Mount Athos where, if the sources are to be believed, monks and hermits flocked from all over the Mountain to observe the arrival of this famous former ruler of Serbia as a humble novice at Vatopedi and his emotional reunion with his son.[3] But Sava was a young man in a hurry: he must already have made plans and there was no time to lose if they were to proceed with founding a Serbian monastery on Athos. Funds were

[2] See the Life of Sava by the Athonite monk Domentijan, *Život svetoga Simeuna i svetoga Save*, ed. Dj. Daničić (Belgrade, 1865), pp. 122–7.
[3] Ibid., pp. 154–5.

requested and received from Sava's brother Stefan in Serbia. Meanwhile, Symeon and Sava toured the Mountain and settled on the abandoned monastery of Chelandarion (the Boat), some 12 kilometres north-west of Vatopedi, as ideal for their purposes. To obtain ownership of the monastery, they needed the agreement of the Holy Community of Athos (who currently controlled it), the abbot of Vatopedi (who was Sava's immediate superior), and the Byzantine emperor (who at the time was still the supreme authority on the Holy Mountain). The abbot sent Sava to Constantinople where he was granted an audience with the emperor, Alexios III Angelos (1195–1203), who was his relative by marriage. Sava's request was granted, and early in the year 1198 he returned to Athos with an imperial chrysobull by which title to the monastery of Chelandarion and its environs was transferred from the Protos to the abbot of Vatopedi.[4] Work could now begin on rebuilding the monastery, which from now on would be known to the Serbs as Hilandar, and by July 1198 enough of it was complete for Symeon to be able to move in. Vatopedi will have been sorry to see them go. In the years they spent at Vatopedi, Symeon and Sava had been generous in their efforts to renovate and adorn the monastery. But any disenchantment was soon forgotten and henceforth Vatopedi and Hilandar were to be regarded as one monastery with Sava as father to them both.

Meanwhile, it is to be assumed that Sava and Symeon had done a deal with the Holy Community as to how they should proceed. For when the latter objected to the transfer of the property to Vatopedi, on the thoroughly specious grounds that it was likely to fall into total disrepair if left in the hands of that monastery, the Serbs petitioned the emperor again, this time to grant full ownership to them and permission to found a monastery there. In June 1198 the emperor duly issued a second chrysobull, this one addressed to Symeon and Sava, in which he cancelled the earlier one that had assigned Hilandar and its environs to Vatopedi. His new edict placed the monastery firmly under the authority and management of its founders, Symeon and Sava. From now on, he decreed, the monastery was to be totally autonomous, subject neither to the Protos nor to the abbot of Vatopedi, and to enjoy the same rights and privileges as the other 'foreign' monasteries of the Georgians and the Amalfitans.[5] All three were 'imperial monasteries' and as such came under the ultimate patronage of the

---

[4] Archives de l'Athos, vol. 20: *Actes de Chilandar,* vol. 1: *Des origines à 1319,* ed. M. Živojinović, V. Kravari, C. Giros (Paris, 1998), no. 4, p. 10.

[5] Ibid., no. 4, pp. 8–11.

Plate 8. The katholikon of Iviron monastery on Athos, a reminder of Georgia's early link with Byzantium.

Plate 9. The first Russian house on Athos: the present-day skete of Bogoroditsa probably stands on the site of the eleventh-century monastery of Xylourgou. Photo © Aleksandar Golubović.

Plate 10. The original site of St Panteleimonos monastery (Rossikon) on Athos, known today simply as 'Old Monastery'.

Plate 12. The upper lavra of the monastery of the Caves in Kiev with the bell-tower on the left and the cathedral of the Dormition on the right.

Plate 11. The main gate to the monastery of the Caves in Kiev with the church of the Holy Trinity above it. The monastery was founded by St Antony in the mid-eleventh century after his second visit to Athos.

Plate 13. St Sava's tower at Hilandar dates from the time of the monastery's foundation (1198). It stands as a proud symbol of Serbia's continuing presence on Athos.

Plate 14. The monastery of Studenica in Serbia, founded by Stefan Nemanja in 1183. The east window of the main church is decorated in the Romanesque style with interlaced vines and mythological beasts.

emperor and no one else. Symeon and Sava invited Sava's brother Stefan to be the monastery's principal founder, thereby placing it firmly under the authority of the Serbian ruling family.

Events had moved fast, perhaps too fast for the frail monk Symeon, who at the age of eighty-six died on 13 February 1199. His son Sava remained at his side and has left this vivid description of the scene in his Life of his father, which is contained in the introduction to the *typikon* for the monastery of Studenica:

> He said: 'My child, bring me [the icon of] the most holy Mother of God, for I have made a vow to yield up the ghost [Matt. 27:50] in front of her.' And when his command had been carried out, towards the evening, he said: 'My child, do me a service of love, clothe me in the *rason* [a loose-fitting black overgarment with sleeves] appointed for my funeral and place me in the same sacred position in which I shall lie in my coffin. Spread a matting on the ground and lay me on it and place a stone under my head, that I may lie here until the Lord comes to visit me and take me hence.' And I did all this and carried out his commands. And all of us who looked on wept bitterly ... For in truth, my beloved brothers and fathers, it was a wondrous sight: he whom all men in his country feared, and before whom all trembled, was now seen as a stranger and beggar, clothed in a *rason*, lying on the ground on a mat with a stone under his head, receiving the salutations of all the brethren and asking everyone's forgiveness and blessing with love in his heart. When night had fallen they all took their leave of him, and, after receiving his blessing, returned to their cells to do what they had to do and rest a little. I and a priest whom I had kept with me remained by his side all that night. At midnight the blessed father fell silent and spoke to me no longer. But when morning came and the singing of matins began in the church, the blessed father's face was suddenly illumined, and he looked up to heaven and said: 'Praise God in his sanctuary: praise him in the firmament of his power.' I said to him: 'Father, whom do you see as you speak these words?' He looked at me and said to me: 'Praise him for his mighty acts: praise him according to his excellent greatness.' And when he had said this he straightway yielded up his godly spirit and died in the Lord.[6]

Symeon was buried inside the katholikon of the monastery which had been so recently completed, but he left instructions that in due course his remains should be returned to Serbia. They are now divided between Hilandar and Studenica.

---

[6] For Sava's Life of his father, see V. Ćorović (ed.), *Spisi svetoga Save* (Belgrade-Sremski Karlovci, 1928), pp. 151–75. There is a German translation by S. Hafner in *Serbisches Mittelalter: Altserbische Herrscherbiographien* (Graz: Verlag Styria, 1962), vol. 1, pp. 35–61. Cited in D. Obolensky, 'Sava of Serbia', *Six Byzantine Portraits*, pp. 138–9.

Sava's Years on Athos

Symeon and Sava had achieved much in a remarkably short space of time: it now fell to Sava to consolidate this achievement alone, without his father's assistance. With a view to increasing the monastery's income, Sava made another journey to Constantinople in the spring of 1199. This time the emperor not only issued another chrysobull confirming the monastery's independence and Sava's rights as its founder, but also transferred to it ownership of the abandoned monastery of Zygou on the northwest border of Athos and gave it permission to own a ship. Under its first abbot, Methodios, the monastery flourished and the brotherhood, which had numbered no more than sixteen at the time of Symeon's death, rapidly grew to ninety.

A scriptorium was established at the monastery in which spiritual and ascetic texts were translated from Greek into Slavonic, and its library soon acquired an impressive and wide-ranging collection of manuscripts. Similarly, monks from all over the Slavic world and beyond were soon to be drawn to Hilandar as a place where the theory and practice of 'hesychast' spirituality could be learned from charismatic elders and spiritual guides. And a snapshot of the cosmopolitan character of the Mountain at the time may be gained from Sava's description of his own father's funeral at which Serbian chanters were joined by Greek, Russian, Bulgarian, and Georgian monks.[7] Hilandar was not the only such centre on the Mountain, but for Serbs it rapidly acquired the status of being the principal focus of their religious and cultural life and occupied a unique position in their hearts that it has retained to the present day. As the founders of the monastery Symeon and Sava represent the fountainhead of this cultural stream and as such they are everywhere portrayed and remain deeply revered by all Serbs as the patron saints of their country (Plate 13).

But Sava still had much work to do. He had acquired much of his knowledge of Byzantine monastic life from his frequent stays at the monastery of the Evergetis in Constantinople, and in the summer of 1199 he obtained a copy of that monastery's *typikon* (charter). Having had it translated into Slavonic, he adopted it with some slight modifications as the constitution for Hilandar. With its detailed regulations about behaviour in church and refectory, fasting, monastic dress, confession, liturgy, communion, the appointment of abbots and other officers, and the independence of the monastery, already guaranteed by the chrysobull of 1198, it

---

[7] *Spisi svetoga Save*, p. 171.

stamped Hilandar as a thoroughly cenobitic and imperial foundation. With minor changes Sava introduced the same charter at the monastery of Studenica and from there it was adopted as the model *typikon* for all other monasteries in medieval Serbia, notably Žiča, Sopoćani, Mileševa, Gračanica, and Dečani.

By the turn of the century Sava had become a leading figure on the Mountain, comparable perhaps to St Athanasios two centuries earlier. Not only had he founded a major new house for the Serbs, but also, as a result of his generous benefactions, he was ranked as founder (*ktitor*) of several other Athonite monasteries, including the Great Lavra, Iviron, Karakalou, Xeropotamou, and Philotheou, as well as the main church in Karyes and the dependency of Vatopedi at Prosphori (now Ouranoupolis). He had also provided Hilandar with a dependency at Karyes, close to the Protaton monastery, to facilitate business with the central administration, and a *kellion* which his biographer Domentijan refers to as a *hesychasterion* (or ascetic refuge). This cell, to which he himself would retire for periods of reflection and solitary prayer, was dedicated to St Saba of Palestine. Its *typikon*, also written for it by Sava to ensure its freedom, survives as a marble inscription on the wall of the cell and includes an interesting apologia by its author:

> With this [fear of the Lord] in mind I too, the least of all and a sinner, journeyed to the Holy Mountain. There I saw holy men and spirits who were clothed in the flesh of virtue. I saw angels here on earth and I saw men who belonged in heaven. So, deriving my strength from God, I carried on the struggle to the best of my ability. I established a holy *lavra* and monastery in the name of the most holy Mother of God, and laid solid foundations for a religious community in it. In like manner I managed to acquire a number of cells in Karyes so the monks coming from the monastery on some service would have a place to rest. In addition, there in Karyes I have set up a distinctive form of the solitary life. I constructed a *kellion* and a church in the name of our holy, God-bearing and sanctified father Sabbas, as a dwelling for two or three brothers.[8]

Despite his standing on the Mountain, Sava was still a mere monk, unordained, as most Athonites are. In the year 1200 he was ordained first deacon and then priest by the local bishop of Ierissos, after which he retired to his cell at Karyes. Then, a few years later, perhaps in 1204, he was raised to the rank of archimandrite by three bishops in Thessaloniki. Today all

---

[8] An English translation of the Greek version of the Serbian inscription is printed in Thomas and Constantinides Hero, *Byzantine Monastic Foundation Documents*, vol. 4, pp. 1331–7 (pp. 1333–4). The original Serbian text is found in *Spisi svetoga Save*, pp. 5–13.

abbots on Athos are archimandrites, but then the distinction belonged to
the Protos alone, whose position Sava would now appear to rival. Perhaps
it was for this reason, or perhaps for reasons related to the precarious
situation created by the Fourth Crusade, but most likely in response to
an appeal from his brothers, Stefan and Vukan, that in 1206 he returned to
Serbia. During the years of Sava's absence, his brothers had quarrelled and
invited foreign armies to assist them. Vukan, the elder, asked for aid from
the king of Hungary, who obliged with an invasion that drove out Stefan
and placed Vukan on the throne, whereupon Stefan appealed to the
Bulgarians who restored him to the throne and sent Vukan back to the
Dalmatian provinces that were originally his territory. A fragile peace was
established by 1205, but the country needed the spiritual protection and
national cohesion that could only be provided by Nemanja's posthumous
return. In a sequence of events that is vividly portrayed on the walls of the
katholikon at Studenica monastery, Sava returned to Serbia bearing his
father's relics. The journey was long and arduous, but by early 1207 the
cortege had reached Studenica and the relics were duly interred in the
monastery's church. Shortly after this Symeon, the former Stefan
Nemanja, founder of the Serbian royal dynasty, was proclaimed a saint
and his relics, safely restored to their proper resting place, would from now
on guarantee the safety and prosperity of the kingdom.

Return to Serbia

Now installed as abbot of Studenica, Archimandrite Sava, brother of the
country's ruler, was in a strong position to shape the ecclesiastical future of
the Serbian Church. According to his biographer, Domentijan, Sava
'brought in to his fatherland every model [of monastic life] from the Holy
Mountain'.[9] The first 'model' that he established was the *typikon* for his
own monastery of Studenica for which he used that of the Evergetis
monastery in Constantinople, which he had already adapted for use at
Hilandar. And soon he was putting to good use his experience of founding
monasteries, notably the great monastery of Žiča, which was a joint undertaking with his brother Stefan. For its church of the Ascension, also known
as the Great Church, which took ten years to construct (1209–19), Sava
employed architects, masons, and artists from Byzantium, but like most
medieval Serbian churches its exterior decoration incorporates
Romanesque and proto-Gothic motifs (Plates 14, 15, and 16). In due course,

---

[9] Domentijan, *Život svetoga Simeuna i svetoga Save*, p. 205.

it became the seat of the archbishop of Serbia, the most revered shrine in the land, the place where its rulers were to be crowned, and the model for all the other great churches of the Raska school that were built in the thirteenth century.[10]

During this time Sava also devoted time to the composition of literary works, including most notably the Life of his father.[11] If its first purpose was to glorify the royal house of Nemanja, its second was no less important – to celebrate Serbian monasticism. It was no accident that the founder of the dynasty and his son had become monks, a fact that forged an enduring link between the monasteries of Serbia and the Athonite monastery of Hilandar. As Obolensky aptly put it, 'Athos wove medieval Serbian monasticism into the fabric of Serbian society; it was Sava again who laid the foundations on which his countrymen were to build.' In other words, it was Sava who ensured that Serbia became a full member of the Athonite Commonwealth. Obolensky continues:

> His Life of his father, with its peculiar blend of family chronicle, hagiography, and 'translation' tale, with political concepts derived from monastic foundation-charters, provided the model for future writers who continued, until the fall of the medieval Serbian realm, to record the exploits, secular and religious, of a virtually unbroken line of holy kings. Together with the *Vitae* of the archbishops of Serbia, starting with St Sava, these royal biographies – the best were written in the thirteenth and fourteenth centuries – are the main contribution made by the Serbs to the literature of medieval Europe.[12]

Despite Serbia's strong and enduring Athonite connections, its membership of the Byzantine Commonwealth was put under severe strain in the wake of the Fourth Crusade. As early as 1200 or 1201 Sava's brother Stefan had callously repudiated his first wife Eudokia, daughter of the Byzantine Emperor Alexios III, and married instead Anna, granddaughter of the infamous Venetian Doge Enrico Dandolo, chief instigator of the Fourth Crusade. The balance of power in the eastern Mediterranean changed dramatically with the emergence of a Latin empire based in Constantinople, causing both Bulgaria and Serbia to reassess their foreign policy. In 1204 Tsar Kaloyan of Bulgaria declared his allegiance to the Pope, in return for which he was crowned in his capital, Trnovo, by a Roman cardinal. Stefan of Serbia had to wait a little longer, diverted by

---

[10] See S. Ćurčić, *Architecture in the Balkans: From Diocletian to Süleyman the Magnificent* (New Haven and London: Yale University Press, 2010), pp. 499–505.
[11] See p. 81, n. 6.   [12] Obolensky, 'Sava of Serbia', p. 140.

the machinations of the king of Hungary in support of his brother Vukan, but in 1217 he sent an embassy to Rome asking for a crown. In response, Pope Honorius III sent a legate to Serbia and Stefan became the first ruler of Serbia to receive a crown, and with it his sobriquet 'Stefan the First Crowned'. Our sources are divided over the date of the king's coronation and the person who placed the crown on his head (some insisting that this act was performed by Sava), but it seems most likely that the ceremony took place in Žiča in 1217 or 1218 at a time when Sava was out of the country.

Sava himself seems not to have wavered in his loyalty to the Eastern Church, though there is no reason to believe that he was personally antagonistic to Rome. In 1217 he returned to Athos, having resigned his position as abbot of Studenica; and in 1219 he travelled to Nicaea, which was now the seat of the Byzantine Empire in exile and of its patriarchate. Here he was warmly received by Emperor Theodore I Laskaris, consecrated archbishop by Patriarch Manuel I Sarantenos (1216/17–22), and given permission by the emperor following a decree of the Nicaean synod to set up an autonomous Serbian Church. Both sides had reasons to be gratified by this agreement. Nicaea was anxious to be seen as the legitimate successor of Byzantium and alliances with the Slav nations of Eastern Europe would serve to strengthen that claim. Serbia for its part gained prestige from the award of independence to its Church and its alliance with the empire of Nicaea, widely seen as Byzantium-in-waiting. Nor was this seen to be inconsistent with King Stefan's recognition of the Pope's spiritual authority over Serbia. As Obolensky has written, 'To see in Stephen (as many historians have done) the champion of Latin traditions in Serbia, and in Sava the defender of the Orthodox Church, is to fly in the face of the evidence and to ignore that sense of a united Christendom, which in the first half of the thirteenth century still survived in the Balkans.'[13] It took a long time for the full implications of the Fourth Crusade and the acceptance of the doctrine of papal primacy to sink in.

As its newly appointed archbishop, Sava was faced with the task of organizing the administration of Serbia's independent Church. On his way back to Serbia, he spent the winter of 1219/20 in Thessaloniki where, according to his biographer, he stayed at 'his own' monastery of Philokales and 'copied many books of law, needed by his cathedral church, concerning the emendation of the true faith'.[14] This monastery, to which he had made generous donations in the past, numbered him among its

---

[13] Ibid., p. 153.   [14] Domentijan, *Život svetoga Simeuna i svetoga Save*, p. 227.

ktitores. It had now been taken over by the Knights Templar, though probably Greek monks were still in residence, living under a Latin rule. The 'books of law' that he copied formed the basis of what is known as 'Sava's Nomocanon', a compilation of Byzantine legal texts from various sources that together constituted the principal body of Slavonic canon and secular law. Probably Sava selected the material and supervised the project as a whole, leaving to others the actual copying and translation of the texts themselves. The result, which in the first instance was intended to serve the needs of Sava's new Church, provided the foundation for ecclesiastical and civil legislation not just for Serbia but for the whole of the Slavic world.

Returning to Serbia via Hilandar, Sava set about the organization of his Church, establishing his headquarters at the monastery of Žiča. From Athos he had brought back a number of disciples, some of whom he now appointed to bishoprics in various parts of the country. Of the eleven dioceses that he established, three were in the territory of the archbishop of Ohrid whose Greek incumbents he replaced with Serbian bishops. Others of his disciples he appointed archpriests and sent out to the provinces as his agents to do missionary work and stamp out any remaining traces of paganism or flashpoints of heresy. The Bogomils, a dualist sect whose members rejected nearly everything that the Orthodox Church stood for, had spilled over the border from Bulgaria since the tenth century, and it seems there was a fresh incursion in Stefan's reign which the king had failed to extinguish and Sava was asked to deal with. From his time as abbot of Studenica Sava had acquired a reputation for skilful diplomacy and he had recently been successful in persuading the king of Hungary to cease hostilities against Serbia. Now, by unseating three of his bishops, he had drawn the wrath of the archbishop of Ohrid, Demetrios Chomatianos, who reacted by refusing to recognize the existence of an independent Serbian Church and Sava's episcopacy. The dispute rumbled on for a number of years and no canonical ruling seems to have been given to end it, but within Sava's lifetime the leaders of the other Orthodox Churches agreed to recognize the autocephaly of the Serbian Church and have continued to do so ever since.

Pilgrimages to the Christian East

King Stefan the First Crowned died in 1228 and was succeeded by his eldest son, Radoslav, whom Sava crowned in the monastery of Žiča. Later that year Frederick II, the Holy Roman Emperor, led a crusade to the Holy Land and on 18 February 1229 he received the surrender of Jerusalem from the sultan without a struggle. Perhaps inspired by news of this event, and satisfied that he was leaving Serbia in good hands, Sava set sail in late spring of 1229 on a pilgrimage to Palestine. His biographer Domentijan records his itinerary in some detail. From Jerusalem, where he venerated the holy places, he travelled to Bethlehem, and then to the monastery of Mar Saba (i.e. St Saba) out in the desert towards the Dead Sea. There he was given the pastoral staff of his patron saint, in fulfilment of a prophecy of St Saba the Sanctified that long after his death a man with the same name would come from a distant land who was destined to be the shepherd of his nation and to whom the staff should be given. Until recently the staff was preserved in the *kellion pasteritsa* near Karyes, but it has now been transferred to Hilandar for safekeeping. He was also presented with the miracle-working icon of the Mother of God, supposedly enhanced with a third hand by St John of Damascus, known as the Panagia Tricherousa (Virgin with Three Hands), which he took back to Serbia but which now takes pride of place in the Hilandar katholikon. Both his biographers emphasize the spiritual motive for Sava's journey. He travels as a pilgrim, with money for the journey provided by his nephew King Radoslav. He visits the places associated with Christ's birth, ministry, and passion and venerates the principal shrines. He enters into discussions with Athanasios, the patriarch of Jerusalem, on matters of liturgical concern. And he visits the famous monastery of his patron saint where he connects with its ancient traditions of monasticism, worship, and hymnography and has the opportunity to study its charter, known as the Jerusalem *Typikon*.[15]

On his return journey, Sava stopped off in Nicaea for talks with Emperor John Doukas Vatatzes, in Thessaloniki for a meeting with Emperor Theodore Angelos (the ruler of Epirus), and on Mount Athos for visits to Vatopedi and Hilandar. By spring 1230 he was back in Serbia from what must have been a fairly exhausting tour. As the primate of the Serbian Church, he was in a position to influence its liturgical practices. These were originally based on the liturgical *typikon* of the Evergetis monastery in Constantinople, which reached Serbia via Hilandar and would therefore have been regarded as essentially Athonite. After his visit to the Mar Saba monastery, where he had studied the Jerusalem *Typikon*, Sava decided to combine elements of both traditions to bring about a major revision of the Serbian liturgy. He stayed on as archbishop for another four years, during which time King Radoslav was dethroned by his younger brother Vladislav (1234–43) who had the support of Tsar Ivan

---

[15] Ibid., p. 266.

Asen II of Bulgaria, but Sava remained on good terms with both his nephews. Soon after crowning the new king, Sava announced to a gathering of clergy and laity at Žiča that he would retire from the archbishop's throne, which he had occupied for the past fifteen years, and with the agreement of the assembly he named as his successor his disciple, the monk Arseny.

Sava now embarked on his last great journey, a comprehensive tour taking him back to visit all the principal holy places and ecclesiastical leaders of the Christian East, a journey from which he would not return alive. From the Adriatic port of Budva he set sail in 1234 first for Brindisi and from there, after various adventures with pirates and stormy seas, he continued to Acre. There he lodged at the monastery of St George, which he had purchased from the Latins on his previous visit and given as a dependency to the monastery of Mar Saba. In Jerusalem, Sava was pleased to renew his friendship with Patriarch Athanasios, though in a letter written from there to Abbot Spiridon of Studenica he wrote that he was not feeling well and hinted that his end might not be far off. But he had a long way yet to travel and in Egypt, after a meeting with the patriarch of Alexandria, he made a tour of the major monasteries representative of the earliest monastic traditions – the Coptic monasteries of the Thebaid and Scetis in the western desert and the venerable Greek monastery of St Catherine at the foot of Mount Sinai. From Sinai he began the long return journey via Jerusalem to Antioch and thence by sea to Constantinople where once again he stayed at the Evergetis monastery. Exhausted by the long voyage and weakened by serious bouts of seasickness, Sava was now anxious to return via Athos to Serbia, but he was diverted from this plan by an invitation from Tsar Ivan Asen II of Bulgaria. He then sailed across the Black Sea to Mesembria and continued over land to the Bulgarian capital, Trnovo, where, after a short illness, he died at the age of sixty on 14 January 1236.

Having suffered grievously from the demands made on his health by the responsibilities of office and more recently by the arduous pilgrimages that he chose to make, Sava had yet to endure an even more traumatic post-humous journey. His body was first buried in the church of the Forty Martyrs in Trnovo (Plate 17), but on hearing the news of his uncle's death, King Vladislav travelled to Bulgaria and asked permission to exhume it and take it back to Serbia. The Bulgarians were reluctant to grant his request and the body had to be smuggled out of the city. Once back in Serbia, Sava was first laid to rest in a purpose-built tomb in the monastery of Mileševa in western Serbia. Then the body was transferred to a coffin and placed in the centre of the church where it could be venerated, where it became a focus of pilgrimage, and where it remained for more than 350 years. By 1459 Serbia had become a province of the Ottoman Empire and for another 135 years the cult, in which both the local Muslim and Jewish populations participated, was allowed to continue. Finally in 1594 the grand vizier Sinan Pasha ordered the coffin containing the relics of St Sava to be taken from Mileševa to Belgrade where on 27 April it was consigned to a funeral pyre and burnt.

So ended the terrestrial existence of St Sava and his mortal remains. The burning of his relics was intended by the Ottomans to quell a Serbian rebellion. It had the opposite effect, and the site of the conflagration became yet another centre of pilgrimage. On the same site today stands the massive cathedral of St Sava, one of the largest Orthodox places of worship in the world and a perpetual reminder (if one were needed) of the place occupied by St Sava in the history and culture of Serbia. But Sava is ubiquitous in Serbia. His image appears on the walls of nearly every Serbian church and monastery. In Serbian literature he features in a remarkable number of guises: monk, beggar, boatman, traveller, hunter, shepherd, physician, warrior, to name but a few. He is revered by all Serbs as the greatest of their compatriots and the creator of all that is good in their cultural tradition, a role that sometimes spills over into romantic nationalism. Even Obolensky, master of the measured tone and balanced judgement, comes close to superlatives when concluding his study:

> Yet the historian seeking to encompass the extraordinary variety of his life-work – as prince, monk, bishop, pilgrim, diplomat, administrator, patron of the arts, writer, and teacher of his people – can hardly fail to conclude that in the Greek and Slav world of the East European Middle Ages, it was not given to many, in a life-span of sixty years, to achieve so much.[16]

For our purposes, however, it was the foundation of Hilandar, and the spiritual and cultural links that followed from that foundation, that marked Sava as the father of Serbian monasticism. For over 800 years Hilandar has been the chief symbol of Serbian culture and spirituality. Despite (and perhaps even because of) its remote location on Mount Athos, it has acquired almost legendary status as the guardian *par excellence* of all things Serbian. Hilandar was the principal conduit through which Byzantine Christianity reached Serbia. Its role as such is well summarized by the Serbian scholar Vladeta Janković:

---

[16] Obolensky, 'Sava of Serbia', p. 172.

With the status of an imperial lavra, Hilandar – independent and wealthy – was Serbia's best diplomatic 'envoy' in Byzantium. Moreover, without the mediating agency of Hilandar, medieval Serbia would not have embraced Byzantine culture and civilization and adopted its ancient heritage so comprehensively. Everything that was best in Serbia, its ecclesiastical, political, and cultural elite, all passed through Hilandar, whose radiance cast its light and marked out the country – economically, politically, and culturally – as one of the great powers of medieval Europe.[17]

---

[17] V. Janković, 'The Serbian Tradition on Mount Athos', in G. Speake and K. Ware (eds), *Mount Athos: Microcosm of the Christian East* (Oxford: Peter Lang, 2012), p. 85.

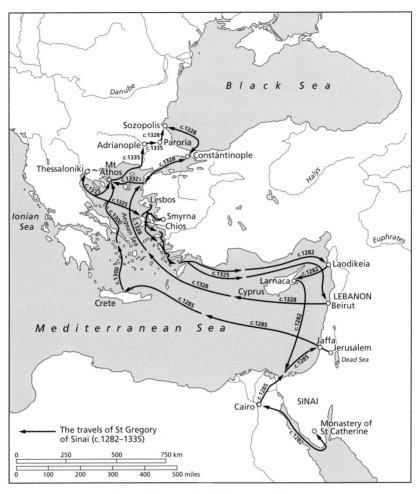

Map 4. The travels of St Gregory of Sinai.

CHAPTER 7

St Gregory of Sinai (c.1265–1346): Initiator of the 'Hesychast International'

In the first half of the fourteenth century Athos was home to two saints, both named Gregory, who were both in their very different ways of pivotal significance in the development and diffusion of hesychasm to the Orthodox world. Gregory of Sinai was the elder by some thirty years, but he was still on Athos when Gregory Palamas arrived in 1316; and although there is no evidence that they ever met, it seems highly likely that they knew each other, as for a number of years they lived as hermits in relatively close proximity.[1] Some scholars have convinced themselves that Palamas was a pupil of the Sinaite, but again there is no mention of this in the sources, and it seems rather odd that the younger man in all his voluminous writings never mentions this if it was the case.[2] Hermits by their nature are not gregarious folk, and it is perhaps wise to conclude that they probably were on nodding terms but otherwise kept themselves to themselves and each got on with his own business.

A Travelling Man

Gregory of Sinai's career is a paradigm of the international nature of late Byzantine monasticism. He was born in Asia Minor, not far from Smyrna, around 1265 to a quite prosperous family. Early in the reign of Emperor Andronikos II (1282–1328) he was taken prisoner by a Turkish raid and sold into slavery at Laodikeia in Syria. Liberated by local Christians, he escaped to Cyprus where he was befriended by a hermit-monk who made him a novice and gave him the *rason* (the habit of the first stage of monasticism). After

---

[1] On St Gregory of Sinai, see Kallistos Ware, 'The Jesus Prayer in St Gregory of Sinai', *Eastern Churches Review*, 4: 1 (1972), 3–22; David Balfour, 'Gregory the Sinaite: Life and Spiritual Profile', *Theologia*, 53: 1 (1982), 30–62; and A.-E. N. Tachiaos, 'Gregory Sinaites' Legacy to the Slavs', *Cyrillomethodianum*, 7 (1983), 113–65. See also *Philokalia*, vol. 4, pp. 207–86.
[2] See, for example, D. Balfour, 'Was St Gregory Palamas St Gregory the Sinaite's Pupil?', *St Vladimir's Theological Quarterly*, 28 (1984), 115–30.

a short time, he left and went, like Moses, to Sinai and was tonsured to the Little Schema (the second stage of the monastic life) at the monastery of St Catherine. Here, according to his disciple and biographer Kallistos (later patriarch of Constantinople, 1350–3 and 1355–63), he led the life of a monkish paragon, the model of obedience and humility, spending all night in prayer, all day in study and reading, eating next to nothing, and climbing every day to the summit of Mount Sinai to demonstrate his devotion to Moses.[3] Allowing for the customary exaggerations of the genre, we may accept that he led a life of exemplary ascetic zeal, which, not surprisingly, soon aroused the envy of his fellow monastics, and after a few years he decided to leave, taking with him Gerasimos, a fellow monk, who became his disciple.

From Sinai they went first to Jerusalem to visit the holy places, and from there they sailed to Crete where they found a remote cave and resumed their austere existence. Already experienced in the practice (*praxis*) of the ascetic life, Gregory was looking for a spiritual guide from whom he could learn contemplation (*theoria*). Here in Crete his prayer was answered by the Holy Spirit who brought to his door a saintly old monk called Arsenios who instructed him in 'guarding of the intellect, true watchfulness, and pure prayer'.[4] The term 'pure prayer' (*kathara prosefchi*) means that here for the first time Gregory was introduced to inner prayer, or prayer of the heart, which will have included the Jesus Prayer. This was a decisive moment in the Sinaite's life which was to have profound implications for the development of hesychasm and its subsequent diffusion throughout the Orthodox world. Gregory was elated and immediately sailed for Athos. We may wonder what he expected to find there.

The Years on Athos

After many years of travelling from place to place Gregory was to remain on Athos for the best part of twenty-five years (roughly 1300–25), though at first his life there was far from settled. Kallistos tells us that he began by scouring the whole Mountain in his search for others familiar with the teaching about contemplation and inner prayer that he had received in Crete from Arsenios but all denied any knowledge of it.[5] His search was apparently focused on the monasteries, which may account for its failure to produce results, since the sort of ascetic practices he was looking for were much more likely to be found among monks following the eremitic

---

[3] Kallistos's *Life of Gregory* has been edited by H.-V. Beyer (Ekaterinburg, 2006).
[4] Kallistos, *Life*, 5.   [5] Ibid., 6.

tradition than the cenobitic. Only when he came to the remote settlement of Magoula (Plate 18), near the monastery of Philotheou, did he eventually find three monks who had some slight experience of it, and here he chose to settle, building some cells for his disciples and for himself a retreat (*hesychasterion*) in which he could devote himself to prayer and the ascetic life.

We may wonder just how thorough a search Gregory had made, since we know from the writings of Gregory Palamas that Nikephoros the Hesychast had been living 'in quietness and stillness' (i.e. as a hermit) on Athos for many years in the second half of the thirteenth century. Not much is known about Nikephoros, except that he was originally from Italy and a convert from Roman Catholicism. But he was well known on the Mountain where he had a considerable following of disciples, and he is the author of a short treatise *On Watchfulness and the Guarding of the Heart*, which is included in the *Philokalia*.[6] From this work it is clear that he was fully conversant with the techniques of hesychasm, including recitation of the Jesus Prayer, descent into the depths of the heart, and guarding over the intellect. He writes of the need for a spiritual guide who will 'unambiguously disclose the spiritual path to us so that we can follow it easily'.

> If you have no such guide you must diligently search for one. If, however, no guide is to be found, you must renounce worldly attachments, call on God with a contrite spirit and with tears, and do what I tell you . . .
>
> Seat yourself, then, concentrate your intellect, and lead it into the respiratory passage through which your breath passes into your heart. Put pressure on your intellect and compel it to descend with your inhaled breath into your heart. Once it has entered there, what follows will be neither dismal nor glum. Just as a man, after being far away from home, on his return is overjoyed at being with his wife and children again, so the intellect, once it is united with the soul, is filled with indescribable delight . . .
>
> Moreover, when your intellect is firmly established in your heart, it must not remain there silent and idle; it should constantly repeat and meditate on the prayer, 'Lord Jesus Christ, Son of God, have mercy on me', and should never stop doing this. For this prayer protects the intellect from distraction, renders it impregnable to diabolic attacks, and every day increases its love and desire for God.
>
> If, however, in spite of all your efforts you are not able to enter the realms of the heart in the way I have enjoined, do what I now tell you and with God's help you will find what you seek. You know that everyone's discursive faculty is centred in his breast; for when our lips are silent we speak and deliberate and formulate prayers, psalms and other things in our breast. Banish, then, all thoughts from this faculty – and you can do this if you want

---

[6] *Philokalia*, vol. 4, pp. 192–206.

to – and in their place put the prayer, 'Lord Jesus Christ, Son of God, have mercy on me', and compel it to repeat this prayer ceaselessly. If you continue to do this for some time, it will assuredly open for you the entrance to your heart in the way we have explained, and as we ourselves know from experience.

Then, along with the attentiveness you have so wished for, the whole choir of the virtues – love, joy, peace and the others – will come to you.[7]

The reason for quoting Nikephoros at such length is to show just how much of the hesychastic tradition was already known, taught, and practised on the Holy Mountain *before* Gregory of Sinai even arrived there. His biographer is strangely silent about this, no doubt because he is anxious to extol as highly as possible the impact made by his subject and the novelty of what he brought with him to Athos. But in fact, it is surely far more likely that Gregory knew perfectly well that the traditions of hesychasm were deeply embedded on the Mountain and that the techniques of 'pure prayer' recommended by the fathers were already being taught and practised by elders such as Nikephoros. This made it a highly suitable place for him to continue his own ascetic regime under the guidance of an experienced spiritual father and this is the reason why he chose to go there.

Based now at the settlement of Magoula, Gregory rapidly acquired a large group of disciples who sat at his feet and learned to practise hesychasm under his direction. His biographer, who was among them and so was writing from personal experience, emphasizes the charismatic qualities that the saint possessed, which brought even experienced monks to seek his instruction:

> Inspired by God with pure wisdom in the Spirit and genuine knowledge, he attracted everyone joyfully with the odour of his virtue, which was more fragrant than precious balm, and with the divine breadth and height of his gift for teaching . . . Like a magnet, he attracted even those who had not seen him and talked to him, for his teaching spread far and wide . . . He urged himself to the extreme limit of both piety and spiritual steadfastness, and by the joy and meekness of his countenance he expressed and revealed the inner illumination of his soul, so that when really eminent men of virtue and doctrine saw him, they abandoned their own preceptors, had recourse to his teaching and company, and submitted to him for the sake of the benefit they aimed to derive therefrom.[8]

This passage encapsulates the two most striking aspects of Gregory's regime, which he imposed both on himself and on his disciples, namely

---

[7] Ibid., pp. 205–6.   [8] Kallistos, *Life*, 13; cited in Balfour, 'Gregory the Sinaite', p. 40.

'the extreme limit of both piety and spiritual steadfastness' and at the same time 'the inner illumination of his soul' as revealed by 'the joy and meekness of his countenance'. The strictness with which he implemented his ascetic programme was tempered by the warmth of his personality and his sense of joy. But the basis of everything is prayer.

And what is prayer? Gregory's answer is: 'Prayer is God, who works all things in all men.' Bishop Kallistos summarizes Gregory's approach to prayer as follows:

> Prayer is God: in the deepest and fullest sense prayer is not our own action but the action of Another in us. It is not we who by our own unaided efforts gather our mind within our heart in prayer, but the indwelling Paraclete; and without him we can achieve nothing. 'No one of himself can control his mind, unless he is controlled by the Spirit.'
>
> True prayer, then, is the prayer offered in us by the Lord Jesus and the Holy Spirit. Gregory develops this point in a specifically sacramental way, observing: 'Prayer is the manifestation of Baptism.' Since prayer is the action of God within us, and since it is through the sacrament of Baptism that God comes to dwell in our hearts, it follows that prayer is essentially the discovery and disclosure of baptismal grace. Our aim in the life of prayer is to bring to light this divine presence within us, to remove the obstacles of sin so that the grace of Baptism may become fully 'active' in our heart. Prayer, then, is to become what we already are, to gain what we already possess, to come face to face with the One who dwells even now within our innermost self. The whole range of the ascetic and mystical life is contained, by anticipation, within the sacrament of Baptism.[9]

In other words, prayer enables us to pass from the stage of baptismal grace, unconsciously present in our hearts, to the stage of conscious awareness of grace, active within us. It is a process of self-discovery, or rather of rediscovery of baptismal grace within us, which can be achieved in one of two ways. Either it can be achieved (very laboriously) through obedience to the commandments and by pursuing the 'active life' such as Gregory did before he met Arsenios in Crete. Or it is revealed to us (more rapidly) through the continuous and methodical invocation of the Lord Jesus and by the 'memory of God'. These are not alternatives, for the second route cannot be pursued without the first as well; and if it is shorter, it is certainly not any easier. This much is clear from the curriculum and daily routine that he prescribes for the would-be hesychast:

[9] Ware, 'The Jesus Prayer in St Gregory of Sinai', p. 7.

He who practises hesychasm must acquire the following five virtues, as a foundation on which to build: silence, self-control, vigilance, humility and patience. Then there are three practices blessed by God: psalmody, prayer and reading – and handiwork for those weak in body. These virtues which we have listed not only embrace all the rest but also consolidate each other. From early morning the hesychast must devote himself to the remembrance of God through prayer and stillness of heart, praying diligently in the first hour, reading in the second, chanting psalms in the third, praying in the fourth, reading in the fifth, chanting psalms in the sixth, praying in the seventh, reading in the eighth, chanting psalms in the ninth, eating in the tenth, sleeping in the eleventh, if need be, and reciting vespers in the twelfth hour. Thus fruitfully spending the course of the day he gains God's blessings . . .

'Like a bee', Gregory says, the hesychast should extract from each of the virtues what is most profitable. Thus, by taking a small quantity from each, he gradually accumulates a great honeycomb overflowing with the honey of wisdom.

Now hear, if you will, how it is best to spend the night. For the night vigil there are three programmes: for beginners, for those midway on the path, and for the perfect. The first programme is as follows: to sleep half the night and to keep vigil for the other half, either from evening till midnight or from midnight till dawn. The second is to keep vigil after nightfall for one or two hours, then to sleep for four hours, then to rise for matins and to chant psalms and pray for six hours until daybreak, then to chant the first hour, and after that to sit down and practise stillness, in the way already described. Then one can either follow the programme of spiritual work given for the daylight hours, or else continue in unbroken prayer, which gives a greater inner stability. The third programme is to stand and keep vigil uninterruptedly throughout the night.[10]

This is a pretty tough regime by any standards. By 'prayer' Gregory means the Jesus Prayer, for which he advocates the form 'Lord Jesus Christ, Son of God, have mercy on me.' And it is clear from the advice he gives about the outward technique and control of the breathing that he is familiar with (and in agreement with) the teaching of Nikephoros the Hesychast (see pp. 95–6). He has two particular concerns: that recitation of the prayer should be continuous and that it should be free from images. Quoting St John Klimakos, he writes 'stillness is the shedding of thoughts.'[11] The prayer is a means of controlling thoughts and concentrating the mind in the heart. Only then can it fulfil its task of discovery.

[10] *Philokalia*, vol. 4, pp. 233–4.   [11] Ibid., p. 278.

But it is not intended to be in any sense a gloomy or depressing regime. The prayer is indeed penitential, a cry for forgiveness, frequently associated with tears; but 'mercy' involves more than sorrow for sin, and tears can be full of joy, so it is intended to arouse a 'joyful grief' (*charmolypi*). Time and again, Gregory's biographer speaks of the warmth of his personality and how the prayer sets his heart on fire, filling him with joy and light. Similarly, in Gregory's own writings there are frequent references to feelings of 'gladness', 'assurance', and a 'leaping up of the spirit' that result from recitation of the prayer. Such words do not imply grief or despondency but rather a joyful trust in God's mercy.

A similar warmth was also apparent in the personality of Gregory's Athonite contemporary, St Maximos of Kafsokalyvia (*c.*1280–*c.*1370). Maximos was a hermit who lived a nomadic existence at the southern tip of the peninsula and was known on the Mountain as both a fool for Christ and a miracle-worker. Hearing of his fame, Gregory expressed a wish to meet him and their conversation is recorded by Maximos's biographer and disciple, Theophanes of Vatopedi. In the course of it, Maximos is asked if he possesses 'prayer of the heart' (*noera prosefchi*). 'Yes,' he replies, 'I have possessed this gift since my youth.' He then describes an occasion before he became a hermit when he was praying to the Mother of God for the grace of prayer:

> And one day, when I was in the church of the all-pure one, as was my custom, I again entreated the Mother of God with tears for this gift; and, immediately after I lovingly kissed her immaculate image, a great warmth arose in my chest and heart, not a burning heat, but refreshing like dew and instilling sweetness and much contrition in me. From that time on, father, my heart began to recite the prayer internally; similarly the rational part of me, together with my mind, remembers Jesus and my Mother of God, and it has never left me.[12]

This linking of the Jesus Prayer with devotion to the Mother of God has no parallel in hesychast literature of the time, but the feeling of warmth that he mentions chimes closely with Gregory's experience.

The Move to Paroria

Gregory seems to have remained aloof from the hesychast controversy that surrounded his namesake Gregory Palamas, though there can be no doubt that he quietly sided with the hesychasts. He himself provoked a certain

---

[12] Theophanes 15, in Greenfield and Talbot, *Holy Men of Mount Athos*, pp. 495–7.

opposition when he took his teaching to the cenobitic monasteries on the Mountain where some of the elders were taken aback by his unfamiliar practices. But the difficulties were smoothed out by the Protos of the time, who was so impressed by the hesychasts that he declared during their conversation, 'Today, I am speaking with the great Apostles Peter and Paul!', and from then on Gregory was made welcome by all the monks as their 'common master'.[13] Like most of the charismatic figures in the history of Athos, sometimes Gregory found the crowds that flocked to his door oppressive and he would take himself off into the desert for a period of quiet. But by around 1325 the danger of attack by Turkish raiders had become so terrifying for those living outside the protecting walls of the ruling monasteries that he and others were forced to leave the Mountain. He went first with a group of disciples (who may have included Gregory Palamas) to Thessaloniki, intending to return to Sinai, and leaving most of his followers in Thessaloniki, he embarked with Kallistos and one other for Chios. They had planned to go on to Jerusalem, but in Chios they were warned against it and instead they went via Lesbos to the Lebanon. Still failing to find anywhere suitable for *hesychia*, they returned to Constantinople where they spent a bitterly cold winter. When their plight came to the ears of the Emperor Andronikos II (1282–1328), he invited Gregory to his palace, promising him 'great things'. But Gregory wanted no such 'great things' and with his disciples sailed across the Black Sea to Sozopolis on the coast of Bulgaria.

Here he met a monk called Amirales who lived in a desert region known as Paroria high in the remote Strandzha Mountains of what is now south-east Bulgaria. Today it is a nature reserve that provides a secure habitat for many endangered species such as wolves and golden eagles. Gregory found the place ideal for his hesychastic purposes and with his disciples built some cells with a view to settling there. After a short time, however, it seems that there was a dispute with Amirales, and after an assault by brigands Gregory and his disciples were forced to leave. They fled first to Constantinople and from there back to Athos where they took up residence for a number of years (perhaps 1332–5) in some cells near the Great Lavra. But once again they were driven out by Turkish raids and, having sailed to Adrianople, returned over land to the seclusion and comparative security of Paroria.

This time Gregory put down firmer roots and established a substantial monastic settlement. For practical purposes we may call it a monastery, and

---

[13] See the entry on Gregory in the *Synaxarion* for 6 April: Hieromonk Makarios, *The Synaxarion*, vol. 4 (2003), p. 353.

certainly it will have been provided with some means of defence against raids, though the regime inside will have been far from cenobitic. In addition, he set up three 'lavras' (monastic settlements, each within a protected enclosure) at various points in the neighbourhood, which were perhaps more like sketes (i.e. monastic villages), to accommodate the influx of monks that began to gather around him, some of whom he trained to live the solitary life as hermits. Still they were not immune from raids, but from now on Gregory stood his ground and fearlessly repelled them, strengthened by a vision from God that this desert was to be populated by monks and become their 'splendid country'. He also appealed to Tsar Ivan Alexander who ruled the second Bulgarian empire from 1331 to 1371 and was known to be an enlightened king, a patron of the arts, and a strong supporter of monasticism. The tsar was pleased to guarantee the safety of the monks, and the support that he provided to Gregory was of mutual benefit. Bulgaria was currently squeezed between the expanding power of Serbia and the relentless advance of the Ottomans. Meanwhile, Byzantium, though disintegrating politically, continued to flourish intellectually, culturally, and spiritually, and Bulgaria was still very much under the influence of both the ecumenical patriarchate and the Athonite Commonwealth. Gregory and his disciples were representatives of that cultural and religious thrust, and with their missionary zeal, unaffected by any ethnic bias, and their enthusiasm for Slavonic liturgy and literature, they may be said to have contributed to it most generously.

Equally generous was the support provided to Gregory and his monks by the tsar. In response to their request for protection he had given them money and nourishment, he had constructed a strong defence tower, he had built them proper cells and a church, and he had given them well-stocked fishponds, sheep and cattle, and stables for their beasts. In return, Kallistos tells us, God enabled the tsar to overcome his enemies. It sounds a far cry from the sort of withdrawn, impoverished, ascetic existence Gregory was demanding for himself and his followers, and indeed Gregory did construct for himself a remote cell not far from the monastery to which he was able to retreat and where he was able to practise hesychasm. But Kallistos emphasizes that Gregory's consuming passion was 'to attract all men to the divine ascent, so that having gone by his side through a course of practical virtue, they might also be raised to the height of contemplation by ceaseless intercession of mental prayer'.[14]

---

[14] Kallistos, *Life*, 18; cited in Balfour, 'Gregory the Sinaite', p. 57.

Kallistos compares Gregory in his missionary activity with three saints: Elijah, Moses, and Antony the Great. He is said to resemble Elijah in the way that he stands up to those who are opposed to the truth. He is like Moses in that he also received God's commands on tablets and dispensed the rules for the ascetic life. And he is like Antony in that he civilized the desert and converted all the monks of Athos to a life of contemplation and endowed them with 'brilliant control of their thoughts'.[15] After a life of travel in which he involved others in his God-pleasing work, he arrived at Paroria where he turned that remote wilderness into a spiritual workshop in which he was able to recast those who came to join him. By the strength of his prayer or the force of his argument or by his sympathy with each person's character, he persuaded most of the notorious brigands of the region to repent and become humble shepherds. He saw it as his duty to bring everyone to a life of virtue, love, and harmony.

Interaction with the Slavs

The first quarter of the fourteenth century, when Gregory was on Athos, had seen the kingdom of Serbia expanding its territory and its influence over large parts of northern Greece under its ambitious and energetic ruler King Stefan Uroš II Milutin (1282–1321). In the first half of his reign he adopted an anti-Byzantine position and captured Skopje, Dyrrachion, and most of Macedonia from the empire. But in 1298 he signed a peace with Byzantium and took the emperor's five-year-old daughter as his fourth wife, and from this point on Byzantine influence in Serbia greatly increased, as did Serbia's influence on Byzantium. Milutin looked not only to the empire for support but also to the Church. He founded many monasteries (Banjska and Gračanica were among his foundations, and at Studenica, where he is regarded as a second *ktitor*, he built the bijou King's Church), endowing them with generous donations, and he was particularly munificent in his support of the monasteries on Athos. At Hilandar, where he was known as a second founder, he rebuilt the katholikon of the monastery on magnificent lines and had it decorated by the best craftsmen and artists of the day. He also responded to the monks' request for protection against raids by pirates and Turks by building a fortress with a tower and a church next to the sea, known as St Basil's, and also restoring an earlier defence tower between the sea and the monastery, known as Milutin's tower (Plate 19). But the influence of the Serbs and other Balkan

---

[15] Ibid., 19.

peoples was beginning to be felt throughout the Mountain and not just in the Slav monasteries. In an important paper on Athonite monastic patronage, Nikolaos Oikonomides identified prestige as the predominant motive of patrons in previous centuries.

> But the fourteenth century added a second motive – competition between nations – which contributed to the cosmopolitan character of Mt Athos. With the threatened collapse of the empire, all neighbours – and even non-neighbours – could force or buy their entrance into the holy community without any hindrance from the haughty Byzantines. And this they did, the Serbs thanks to their military might, others because they were ready to foot a bill. All this took place in a pan-Orthodox atmosphere, where anyone was welcomed by the Athonites themselves.[16]

In this cosmopolitan, pan-Orthodox atmosphere of fourteenth-century Athos it is inevitable that Gregory's fame will have spread not only through all the monasteries on the Mountain itself but also into the neighbouring territories. Thus he will have acquired Slavic-speaking disciples on Athos, his reputation as a teacher will have preceded him when he moved to Bulgaria, and as soon as he settled at Paroria he will have begun to receive a steady stream of serious-minded, high-profile recruits. In fact, Paroria quickly became the principal centre of hesychasm in the Balkans, second only to Mount Athos, and remained so until Gregory's death in 1346.

Their story will be taken up in Chapter 9, but Gregory's disciples, both Greeks and Slavs, included major figures who, having received their monastic training with him, returned to their homelands where they rose to high positions in their respective churches. Dimitri Obolensky describes Gregory's spiritual legacy as diffused by his disciples as follows:

> through them their master's writings and oral teaching spread through the monasteries and royal courts of Eastern Europe. Byzantium, Bulgaria, Serbia, Rumania and Russia were all affected by this new cosmopolitan movement: monks, churchmen, writers and artists, travelling from country to country – 'wandering for the sake of the Lord', as a fourteenth-century writer put it – found themselves in a similar spiritual and cultural environment; and through this 'Hesychast International',[17] whose influence extended far beyond the ecclesiastical sphere, the different parts of the Byzantine Commonwealth were, during the last hundred years of its

---

[16] N. Oikonomides, 'Patronage in Palaiologan Mt Athos', in Bryer and Cunningham, *Mount Athos and Byzantine Monasticism*, pp. 99–111 (102).

[17] The term is first attributed to A. Elian, 'Byzance et les Roumains à la fin du Moyen Age', *Proceedings of the XIIIth International Congress of Byzantine Studies* (London: Oxford University Press, 1967), p. 199.

existence, linked to each other and to its centre perhaps more closely than ever before.[18]

Gregory spent the remaining years of his life at Paroria, humbly and joyfully dispensing spiritual wisdom to all who came to him. But in spite of his work as a teacher he lost none of his desire for solitude and continued to spend time in his hesychastic cell. Forewarned by God that his end was approaching, we are told that he retired to his cell with one disciple and there he fought his final battle with the demons. After three days of tormenting him, they finally gave up the struggle, a divine power put them to flight, and the saint was filled with an unspeakable joy. There, in the company of Kallistos, he died on 27 November 1346.

Gregory lived and died a humble monk who chose to live in some of the most remote parts of the eastern Mediterranean: the Sinai desert, the mountains of Crete, the southern tip of the Athonite peninsula, the uninhabited wilderness of Paroria. He was supported and consulted by kings and emperors; future saints and patriarchs sat at his feet. His regime was strict and made no concessions to rank or riches. He imposed it alike on himself and on all who came to him. His writings were not voluminous, but they are sharply focused, dogmatic, and to the point. According to his biographer, he radiated joy, warmth, and a charismatic personality and this was no doubt the key to his success. He did not invent hesychasm; nor was he the author of the Jesus Prayer, or of the recommended method of praying it. But he inspired a religious and cultural movement that was to have enormous influence over the whole of the Orthodox world and whose ripples are still lapping at all our shores today. Athos had always been and has remained the heart of the movement, attracting to it men such as Gregory and sending them out as missionaries to the wider world. The rest of this book will be devoted to tracing its course, but first we must examine the very different career of the Sinaite's younger contemporary and namesake, Gregory Palamas.

[18] Obolensky, *The Byzantine Commonwealth*, p. 390.

CHAPTER 8

St Gregory Palamas (1296-1359): Champion of Hesychasm on Athos

In the first half of the fourteenth century the Byzantine Empire was in political and economic turmoil. The Emperor Michael VIII Palaiologos, a usurper (r.1259–82), having recovered the empire's sacred capital in 1261, had blinded the legitimate Emperor John IV Laskaris, for which he was excommunicated by Patriarch Arsenios. Michael promptly dethroned Arsenios, which created a schism within the Church. Worse was to follow when Michael forestalled the threat of invasion from the west by agreeing to union with the Church of Rome at the Council of Lyons in 1274. However successful his diplomacy may have been – he kept both the Serbs and the Bulgarians at bay and formed an alliance with the Mongols – he neglected the eastern frontier, divided the empire, and alienated most of his clergy. Michael's successor, his son Andronikos II Palaiologos (r.1282–1328), healed some of the discord by repudiating the union with Rome, but he lacked his father's diplomatic skills and lost favour as a result of his own ineptitude. Despite this, his long reign bore witness to a most remarkable revival in the arts and in culture as a whole. This was the period when Panselinos was at work on the Holy Mountain painting the frescos of the Protaton, when the walls of the katholika at Vatopedi and Hilandar were being painted, and in Constantinople the mosaics and frescos of the Chora were being done. Scholars too were numerous and active at this period, many of them monks, working on a wide range of subjects including philosophy, medicine, astronomy, classical literature, and the so-called queen of the sciences, theology. Nor were they restricted to a single discipline, like today's highly specialized academics, but often wrote on every branch of learning and were highly esteemed for doing so. The liveliest debate of the day was that between sacred and profane learning, between the patristic tradition of the Church and the secular movement of the humanists.

This was the world into which Gregory Palamas was born in 1296 to an aristocratic family originally from Asia Minor which had moved to

Constantinople in the late thirteenth century. His father Constantine was a member of the emperor's court and a senator, a man of piety and learning who was entrusted with the education of the emperor's grandson, the future Andronikos III. But Constantine died when his eldest son was only seven years old and the young Gregory's education then became the emperor's responsibility. Gregory no doubt spent much of his youth in the company of the young Andronikos who was his exact contemporary and who was to be one of his principal supporters in years to come.

We know from Gregory's biographer, the monk and future Patriarch Philotheos Kokkinos (c.1300–77), that he received a good general education and that he particularly excelled in grammar and rhetoric. His chief instructor was none other than the Great Logothete, Theodore Metochites, one of the most erudite humanist scholars of the day as well as being prime minister and a generous patron of the arts. The curriculum Gregory was taught was a secular one and he was no doubt destined for a secular career in the imperial administration. But at the same time he received instruction in spiritual matters from Athonite monks resident in Constantinople and was also much influenced by Theoleptos, the celebrated metropolitan of Philadelphia (c.1250–1322), whose teaching introduced him to 'intellectual prayer'. Inspired by their example, Gregory abandoned his studies in 1316 and at the age of about twenty left the capital together with his two younger brothers to pursue the religious life on Mount Athos, while their mother and sisters entered convents in Constantinople.

Gregory the Hesychast

Gregory's preference, like that of his namesake the Sinaite, was for the eremitical life of the isolated cells rather than the cenobitic system of the ruling monasteries, so to start with, he and his brothers joined the brotherhood of the hesychast Nikodimos, formerly a monk of Mount Auxentios, who lived not far from the monastery of Vatopedi. Here he spent three years as a disciple of Nikodimos, receiving instruction 'in fasting, sleeplessness, spiritual vigilance and uninterrupted prayer',[1] and

---

[1] J. Meyendorff, *A Study of Gregory Palamas* (Crestwood, NY: St Vladimir's Seminary Press, 1998), p. 33. This chapter owes much to Meyendorff's work. See also more recently R. E. Sinkewicz, 'Gregory Palamas', in G. C. and V. Conticello (eds), *La Théologie byzantine et sa tradition*, vol. 2 (Turnhout: Brepols, 2002), pp. 131–82, and A. Louth, 'St Gregory Palamas and the Holy Mountain', in D. Conomos and G. Speake (eds), *Mount Athos the Sacred Bridge: The Spirituality of the Holy Mountain* (Oxford: Peter Lang, 2005), pp. 49–67.

here he was tonsured, which is the root of his connection with Vatopedi. During this time his youngest brother, Theodosios, died. When Nikodimos also died, Gregory and his remaining brother, Makarios, decided to move to the Great Lavra, and for the next three years they remained within the monastery. In search of a more peaceful retreat, Gregory then withdrew to the cell of Glossia, somewhere near the present-day skete of Provata, where he became a disciple of another master of hesychasm with the name Gregory (probably not the Sinaite, though some have tried to connect them).[2] After two years spent at Glossia, Gregory, along with a large group of hesychasts who were living in cells outside the protecting walls of a monastery, was forced by Turkish raids to leave the Mountain in about 1325. This group included Gregory of Sinai and his disciples, who had been living at the nearby skete of Magoula, and together they moved to Thessaloniki, with the intention of continuing their flight to the Holy Land and Sinai. But only the Sinaite and one or two of his disciples went on, while the rest remained in Thessaloniki.

While he was in Thessaloniki, Gregory joined a spiritual circle which had formed around Isidore, a disciple of Gregory of Sinai and future patriarch (1347–50). This group included not just monks but also lay people and even some of the educated ladies of the city, for Isidore subscribed to his master's view that hesychasm was not only meant for monks but for all. Their aim was to extend the practice of the Jesus Prayer beyond the monasteries and so to make the grace of baptism a reality. Thus the intellectual elite of Thessaloniki was brought under the influence of this charismatic hesychast circle.

Gregory did not remain in the city for long but, having been ordained priest in 1326, he retired with a group of ten disciples to a hermitage near Veroia where for five years he lived by a very strict rule of asceticism. His programme was to spend five days of the week in total solitude and on Saturday and Sunday to share in the common life with his brothers and celebrate the Liturgy. This regime, recommended by the hesychast tradition, represented a compromise between the cenobitic life and the complete isolation of the hermit and combined advantages of both. He continued this way of life until 1331, when raids by Serbs made the region unsafe and he decided to return to Athos.

Returning to the more remote southern part of the peninsula, Gregory took up residence in the cell of St Sabas, high on the slopes above the Great Lavra. Here he continued to live with his disciples according to the same

[2] See p. 93.

regime that he had adopted at Veroia, and for major feasts he would descend to the monastery to celebrate the Liturgy with the fathers there. Such visits made him aware of the spiritual decadence that then prevailed in the monasteries: he was, for example, annoyed by monks chattering during the singing of the hymns on Holy Thursday and distanced himself from them by immersing himself in prayer of the heart; but he was later warned in a vision by St Antony not to dissociate himself from cenobitic worship on the grounds that mental prayer was superior. That is why in Thessaloniki Gregory followed the example of his teacher Theoleptos of Philadelphia in preaching a full liturgical renewal at the same time as insisting on loyalty to the cenobitic rule of the monasteries.

While living at St Sabas Gregory began to acquire fame on the Mountain and also began to write. His first work, dating from about 1334, was the Life of St Peter the Athonite. This was followed by the *Treatise on the Presentation of the Virgin in the Temple*, which was a refutation of those who denied the historical truth of that event, possibly aimed at the humanist Nikephoros Gregoras. Other works that he composed at this time included his *Apodictic Treatises* concerning the procession of the Holy Spirit, which were a response to renewed discussions on the union of the Churches initiated by the visit of two papal legates to the court of Andronikos III in 1333–4. These writings indicate that, although Gregory was trying to devote himself to a life of hesychastic prayer in his hermitage, he continued to take an interest in events in the outside world.

Some time in the mid 1330s Gregory was appointed by the Protos and the Holy Community of the Mountain to be the abbot of the monastery of Esphigmenou. Whether he was keen to accept the appointment is not known, but it seems that it was not a great success. Esphigmenou was a cenobitic house with a large brotherhood of some 200 monks. Gregory was still a young man, aged about forty, fired with a reforming zeal, which perhaps did not go down well with the traditionally minded community. For whatever reason, his abbacy did not last more than a year, after which he left the monastery together with a number of disciples and returned to St Sabas. By this time, the area around the Great Lavra must have become renowned as one of the chief centres of hesychasm on the Mountain, for Gregory of Sinai was there at the same time with his disciples, Kallistos and Mark. There is no evidence that they were in contact with each other, and the Sinaite very soon left the Mountain to return to Paroria, but his disciples would later be among Palamas's most ardent supporters in the controversy that was to come. Meanwhile, it was while he was at St Sabas that Gregory began to be made aware of the activities of the monk Barlaam, a Calabrian Greek, in Thessaloniki and Constantinople.

The Hesychast Controversy: Part 1

Barlaam of Calabria (*c*.1290–1348) arrived in Constantinople from Italy in 1330 and quickly established a reputation for himself as a scholar and philosopher through his writings on astronomy and logic. Already a monk, he became abbot of the Akataleptos monastery and was also given a position at the imperial university. In 1333–4, as a protégé of Andronikos III, he represented the Greek Church in dialogue with papal legates on the union of the Churches, and in 1339 he served on an imperial mission to the courts of Naples and Paris, roles which suggest that he had won the trust of the Byzantines and convinced them of his loyalty to Orthodoxy and the empire. Despite the Italian tradition from which he sprang, where the Greeks were formally united with the Church of Rome, Barlaam's Orthodox credentials were considered entirely respectable. It was probably his reading of Dionysios the Areopagite that led him to oppose on existential grounds the Latins' claim to 'know' God and to be able to 'prove' the procession of the Holy Spirit from the Father *and the Son*. His argument was that, since God is unknowable, it is futile to dispute about the procession of the Holy Spirit; and that both the Greeks (who believe that the Spirit proceeds from the Father alone) and especially the Latins (who since the seventh century have inserted the *filioque* clause) are guilty of presumption. This was the basis of Barlaam's opposition to the Latin doctrine, and it drew a swift rebuke from the Athonite.

Gregory wrote at once both to his former disciple and friend Gregory Akindynos and to Barlaam, protesting that the latter's argument was equally damaging to the Greek position and to the Latin. God is indeed unknowable, but was he not revealed? Did he not unite himself with the saints? Does not the incarnation provide man with a supernatural knowledge, to be distinguished from intellectual knowledge, but completely real, and much more real than any philosophical knowledge? In his rejection of the intellectual realism of Western scholasticism, Barlaam had touched a raw nerve in clashing with the mystical realism of the Orthodox monastic tradition. In his *Apodictic Treatises*, Gregory presents his first response to Barlaam's theological agnosticism.

Barlaam decided that he needed to find out more about the way of life of his new opponents and so he spent some time in the company of hesychasts in both Thessaloniki and Constantinople. There he encountered the

psychosomatic method of prayer of the heart in action, whose practitioners
he ridiculed as *omphalopsychoi*, men with their souls in their navel. And
when he was told that the human body could itself participate in prayer
and feel the action of divine grace, it deeply offended his humanistic and
philosophical mentality. He wrote,

> I have been initiated by them in monstrosities and in absurd doctrines that
> a man with any intelligence or even a little sense cannot lower himself to
> describe, products of erroneous belief and rash imagination. They taught me
> almost marvellous separations and reunions of mind and soul, the relations
> of the demon with the latter, the differences between red and white lights,
> the intelligible entrances and exits produced by the nostrils while breathing,
> the shields around the navel and, finally, the vision of Our Lord with the
> soul that is produced within the navel in a perceptible manner with full
> certitude of heart.[3]

Barlaam now launched a series of attacks on the hesychasts, whom he
identified with Messalian or Bogomil heretics, concentrating not on their
spiritual practices but on his doctrine of the knowledge of God and his
concept of prayer and mysticism. He was especially incensed by the monks'
claim to see God himself in the uncreated light of the Transfiguration:

> If they agree to say that the intelligible and immaterial light of which they
> speak is the superessential God himself and if they continue at the same time
> to acknowledge that he is absolutely invisible and inaccessible to the senses,
> they must face a choice: if they claim to see this light, they must consider it
> to be either an angel or the essence of the mind itself, when, purified of
> passion and of ignorance, the spirit sees itself and in itself sees God in his
> own image. If the light of which they speak is identified with one of these
> two realities, then their thought must be held to be perfectly correct and
> conformed to Christian tradition. But if they say that this light is neither the
> superessential essence, nor an angelic essence, nor the mind itself, but that
> the mind contemplates it as another hypostasis, for my part, I do not know
> what that light is, but I do know that it does not exist.[4]

As the controversy became heated, Akindynos tried to moderate
between the protagonists and advised Barlaam to desist from his attacks
on the hesychasts, while assuring Gregory that Barlaam's sole aim was to

[3] G. Schirò (ed.), *Barlaam Calabro, Epistole greche* (Palermo: Istituto Siciliano di Studi Bizantini
e Neogreci, 1954), pp. 323–4, Letter 5 to Ignatius; cited in J. Meyendorff, *St Gregory Palamas and
Orthodox Spirituality* (Crestwood, NY: St Vladimir's Seminary Press, 1998), p. 85.

[4] Quoted by Palamas in his *Triads* 2.3.7, ed. J. Meyendorff in *Grégoire Palamas. Défense des saints
hésychastes. Introduction, texte critique, traduction et notes*, Spicilegium Sacrum Lovaniense 30
(Louvain: Peeters, 1959), pp. 400–2; cited in Meyendorff, *St Gregory Palamas and Orthodox
Spirituality*, p. 86.

confound the Latins. But his advice was ignored and Barlaam declared his intention to humiliate his rival. In 1338 he went to Constantinople and lodged a formal complaint against the hesychasts with the patriarch, John Kalekas (1334–47), which the latter dismissed, urging him to leave the monks alone. Gregory for his part responded by writing his *Triads in Defence of the Holy Hesychasts*, his most important work. He began writing it on Mount Athos, but he felt obliged to leave and settle in Constantinople in order to defend publicly the spiritual traditions of the Mountain and to act as an official spokesman for the monks. These fundamental texts represent a summation of Orthodox monastic spirituality, which identifies the role of hesychasm in relation to its teaching on such basic themes as sin, redemption, the incarnation, and the sacraments. Gregory places himself firmly in the tradition of the Fathers of the Church, citing among others St Makarios the Great, St John Klimakos, and St Dionysios the Areopagite, before listing some of his more immediate predecessors whose example he commends:

> You know the life of Symeon the New Theologian, and how it was all virtually a miracle, glorified by God through supranatural miracles. You know also his writings, which without exaggeration one can call writings of life. In addition, you know of St Nikiphoros [the Hesychast], how he passed many years in quietness and stillness and how he subsequently withdrew into the most isolated parts of the Holy Mountain of Athos and devoted himself to gathering texts of the holy fathers concerned with the practice of watchfulness, thus passing this practice on to us. These two saints clearly teach those who have chosen this way of life the practices which, you report, are now under attack. But why do I refer to saints of past times? For shortly before our own day men of attested sanctity, recognized as endowed with the power of the Holy Spirit, have transmitted these things to us by their own mouths.

He proceeds to list a number of more recent luminaries including his mentor, Metropolitan Theoleptos of Philadelphia, Patriarch Athanasios, who inspired a moral renewal among the Byzantine laity, and some of the leading monks from the monastery of Mount Auxentios, 'who were endowed with the gift of prophecy'.

> You have certainly heard of all these men and of many others who lived before them, with them and after them, all of whom exhort and encourage those wishing to embrace this tradition – this tradition which the new doctors of *hesychia*, who have no idea of the life of stillness and who instruct not from experience but through spurious argument, try to repudiate, deform and disparage, all to no profit for their hearers. We, however, have

spoken in person with some of these saints and they have been our teachers ... Guided by the fathers, take note how they urge us always to bring our intellect back into ourselves.[5]

In order to obtain official and authoritative support for his position, Gregory returned to Mount Athos, the fount of monastic wisdom, whose voice would be heard above the dissonant clamour of the ongoing civil war and political disputes of the empire. He himself drafted in 1340 a document known as the *Declaration of the Holy Mountain in Defence of those who Devoutly Practise a Life of Stillness*, or more simply the *Hagioritic Tome*, but it carries greater weight because it was signed by the leading Athonite abbots and elders of the day, gathered together in the Protaton at Karyes, and also by the bishop of Ierissos. With the publication of the *Tome* the Holy Mountain formally declared its collective opposition to the teaching of Barlaam and acknowledged Gregory as its official spokesman. In the space of just a few pages, it presents a concise response to each objection put forward by the opponents of hesychasm:

> If anyone condemns as Messalians [a heretical sect who claimed that they could perceive God's essence with their senses] those who declare this deifying grace of God to be uncreated, ungenerated and completely real, and calls them ditheists, he must know – if indeed there is such a person – that he is an adversary of the saints of God ...
>
> If anyone declares that perfect union with God is accomplished simply in an imitative and relative fashion, without the deifying grace of the Spirit ... he must know that he has fallen unawares into the delusion of the Messalians ...
>
> If anyone asserts that those who regard the intellect as seated in the heart or in the head are Messalians, let him know that he is misguidedly attacking the saints ...
>
> If anyone maintains that the light which shone about the disciples on Mount Tabor was an apparition and a symbol of the kind that now is and now is not ... he clearly contends against the doctrines of the saints ...
>
> If anyone maintains that only God's essence is uncreated, while His eternal energies are not uncreated, and that as what energizes transcends all it activates, so God transcends all His energies, let him listen to St Maximos ...
>
> If anyone does not acknowledge that spiritual dispositions are stamped upon the body as a consequence of the gifts of the Spirit that exist in the soul of those advancing on the spiritual path ... he inevitably denies that we can enjoy an embodied life in the world of incorruption that is to come ...

---

[5] *Triads* 1.2.12, translated by Palmer et al. in *Philokalia*, vol. 4, pp. 341–2.

Plate 15. The main church of Ljubostinja monastery in Serbia, a fine example of the Morava architectural school with its intricately sculpted windows and blind arches.

Plate 16. The west front of the main church of Dečani monastery in Kosovo combining a remarkable mixture of Byzantine and western motifs.

Plate 17. The church of the Forty Martyrs in the old Bulgarian capital of Trnovo. St Sava was buried inside the church after his death in 1236.

Plate 18. The area of Athos known as Magoula where Gregory of Sinai devoted himself to the ascetic life *c.*1300–25.

Plate 19. Milutin's tower, near the monastery of Hilandar on Athos. As king of Serbia (1282–1321), Milutin incorporated most of Macedonia, including Athos, into his realm.

Plate 20. The main church of the monastery of Kilifarevo in Bulgaria, a major centre of hesychasm in the second half of the fourteenth century.

Plate 21. The monastery of Zographou on Athos, a Bulgarian house since at least 1270.

In conclusion, and for the avoidance of doubt:

> These things we have been taught by the Scriptures and have received from our fathers; and we have come to know them from our own small experience. Having seen them set down in the treatise of our brother, the most reverend Hieromonk Gregory, *In Defence of those who Devoutly Practise a Life of Stillness*, and acknowledging them to be fully consistent with the traditions of the saints, we have adjoined our signature for the assurance of those who read this present document.

There follow the signatures of the Protos and the abbots of the Great Lavra, of Iviron (in Georgian), of Vatopedi, of Hilandar (in Slavonic), and of Koutloumousiou, a number of hieromonks and elders including three from the skete of Magoula, the spiritual father of Esphigmenou, and a (presumably visiting) hesychast from Syria (in Arabic). It is worth stressing that the presence of a Georgian, a Slav, and an Arab among the signatories testifies to the international character of Athos, extending far beyond the boundaries of the empire. Finally, the local hierarch writes:

> I, Iakovos, the humble bishop of Ierissos and the Holy Mountain, who was reared on the traditions of the Holy Mountain and the fathers, testify that by the signatures of these select men the entire Holy Mountain has undersigned with one accord, and I myself, assenting to these things and putting my seal thereto, have undersigned. I add, furthermore, together with all the rest, that we shall have no communion with anyone who is not in agreement with the saints, as we are, and as were the fathers who immediately preceded us.[6]

The Holy Mountain had spoken. This was perhaps its most significant pronouncement to date and demonstrates the self-confidence of the monks and the strength of their influence. Their words were heard in two church councils which were convened successively in June and August of 1341 in the galleries of Hagia Sophia in Constantinople. The first meeting took place on 10 June and was presided over by the Emperor Andronikos III with an entourage of judges, senators, bishops, archimandrites, and abbots. Barlaam was examined on his teaching about the light on Mount Tabor and on his criticisms of the Jesus Prayer. The same procedure was followed in both examinations: extracts from Barlaam's works were read aloud; the monks responded with quotations from the Fathers; and finally, the emperor judged the outcome of the debate. The day did not go well for Barlaam and, on the advice of his defender, John Kantakouzenos, the

---

[6] *Philokalia*, vol. 4, pp. 420–5.

Great Domestic, he admitted his errors and received a free pardon from Gregory. There was general euphoria at this happy outcome, and the emperor made a pretty speech to celebrate the reconciliation. But alas it was not destined to last.

The next day the emperor fell ill and on 15 June he died before he had signed the decrees. Barlaam immediately renewed his attacks on the hesychasts; but seeing that they were not well received, he left the city and returned to the west. There he rejoined the Greek Catholic Church and, as bishop of Gerace, spent his declining years teaching Petrarch Greek.

The Hesychast Controversy: Part 2

After the sudden death of Andronikos, the debate about hesychasm became deeply embroiled in the turbulent political history of the empire. The new emperor, John V (1332–91), was a minor aged only nine, for whom his mother, Anne of Savoy, consequently acted as regent. Despite the support of Patriarch John Kalekas and the Grand Duke Alexis Apokaukos, Anne was not strong enough to quell the influence of John Kantakouzenos, who had been Andronikos's right-hand man and the real power behind the throne. One of the principal sources for this period is Kantakouzenos's own memoirs which he completed in about 1369 when he had retired from politics and become a monk. The third book opens with these words:

> Upon the death of the young Andronikos [III] the worst civil war that the Romans had ever known broke out. It was a war that led to almost total destruction, reducing the great empire of the Romans to a feeble shadow of its former self. For this reason I have deemed it necessary to relate the events of that conflict in detail, so that future generations may learn what evils are generated by jealousy and also so that my contemporaries may have a true account and not have to rely on hearsay.[7]

In August 1341 a second council was called to discuss the issue of hesychasm, over which Kantakouzenos presided in his capacity as Grand Domestic. This time it was not Barlaam who was to be judged but Akindynos, the appeaser and former friend of Gregory Palamas. Akindynos was a traditionalist who found it difficult to accept anything

---

[7] L. Schopen and B. Niebuhr (eds), *Ioannis Cantacuzeni eximperatoris Historiae Libri IV*, 3 vols (Bonn, 1828–32), vol. 2, p. 12; cited in D. M. Nicol, *The Reluctant Emperor: A Biography of John Cantacuzene, Byzantine Emperor and Monk, c.1295–1383* (Cambridge: Cambridge University Press, 1996), p. 45.

new, in particular the new theology of Gregory. As a scholar he was not in the same league as Barlaam, and his writings consist of little more than a regurgitation of his patristic sources. He had problems specifically with Gregory's doctrine of the difference between the divine essence and the divine energies and for this reason found himself thrust into the position of leader of the anti-Palamites.

At the council of August 1341, which was convened because of Gregory's refusal to retract certain statements, Akindynos was condemned, without being named in the decrees. But later that month Kantakouzenos, who had allowed himself to be named co-emperor, was overthrown by his opponents, the patriarch and the grand duke, and for the next five years he waged a bitter civil war against them. Thanks to the support of the landed aristocracy of Thrace and Thessaly and military support provided by both Serbs and Turks, Kantakouzenos eventually prevailed and was crowned emperor at Adrianople in May 1346. Entering Constantinople the following year, he was crowned again and, in an attempt to stabilize his position, married his daughter Helena to the still youthful John V.

Meanwhile, Gregory became a pawn in the hands of those engaged in this political struggle. Deprived of the support of Kantakouzenos, he remained loyal to the Empress Anne but was not willing to accept the politics of the patriarch. Akindynos now launched a vigorous campaign against the 'new theology' of Palamas, as a result of which, for purely political reasons, Gregory was arrested and imprisoned in September 1342. To provide specious justification for the arrest, the patriarch charged him with heresy and ordered Akindynos to publish his *Refutations of the Work of Gregory Palamas Entitled 'A Dialogue between an Orthodox and a Barlaamite'*. In response from his prison cell, Gregory wrote seven treatises *Against Akindynos*. In 1344 the patriarch excommunicated Gregory and his supporters and ordained Akindynos to the priesthood as a first step to higher office. This last move greatly offended the Empress Anne in that it contradicted a decree of the late Emperor Andronikos and ignored the official condemnation of Akindynos. There was even a rumour that she had deposed Kalekas for ordaining a heretic, and from the end of 1344 there was clearly disagreement between her and the patriarch.

In January of 1345 the monks of Athos sent the empress two *Dogmatic Treatises* written by Philotheos Kokkinos in support of Gregory and she began to take an interest in the theology of the debate. She invited Gregory himself to send her his response to the charges brought against him, which he did, recalling the support that he had received from Andronikos in 1341. And she called on a disciple of St Gregory of Sinai, the learned monk David

Dishypatos of Paroria, to provide her with an explanation of the dispute between Barlaam and Palamas and the part that Akindynos had played in it. As the political tide turned in favour of Kantakouzenos, the patriarch started to shift his ground and sought a reconciliation with the Palamites. But it was too late, and Anne had already decided to place her support behind Gregory. Six bishops signed a letter addressed to her in which they encouraged her to bring Kalekas to justice, accusing him of simony, sacrilege, and heresy, and in January 1347 she summoned a council to depose him. She and John V presided over the meeting, which was attended by the Protos of Athos, numerous monks, bishops, and lay officials. Kalekas was condemned, the decrees of the 1341 council were confirmed, and all bishops were required to assent to the condemnation of Barlaam. The next day the Emperor John VI Kantakouzenos entered the city.

Archbishop of Thessaloniki

Kantakouzenos emerged victorious from the civil war, but at enormous cost to the empire, as he was the first to admit. Politically, the state had been greatly weakened by its supplications to the Serbs and the Ottomans; economically, it was on its knees and at the coronation service that took place in May 1347 it was famously recorded that the crown jewels were made of glass because the real ones had been pawned to Venice. To make matters worse, in August the city was stricken by the Black Death, carried on Genoese ships from the Crimea. Countless numbers died – countless because there were no statistics – and the emperor mourned the loss of his youngest son. But there was a new sense of order, a semblance of peace, and a degree of confidence was restored. The real victory went to the Church, which was now the most powerful institution in the state, and the most influential body within the Church were the monks of Athos who were fully supportive of both Kantakouzenos and Palamas.

In February, another council was convened in the palace, which was attended by Anne and Kantakouzenos and a number of monks and senators but not by Kalekas who refused the summons. Once again, the ex-patriarch was condemned and in March, as in 1341, a new decree was issued containing the decisions of two councils, those of January and February, confirming the decrees of 1341, including Kalekas in the condemnation of Barlaam and his associates, and excommunicating Akindynos. And a few weeks later, when a delegation of bishops arrived in the city headed by the patriarch of Jerusalem, yet another council was held, this time in Hagia

Sophia and attended by Anne, John V Palaiologos, and John VI Kantakouzenos. Three councils had now been held in the city within the space of just a few months to confirm the teaching of Palamas, the last of them confirming the decrees of all the previous ones since 1341.

One of Kantakouzenos's first tasks was to find another patriarch to replace Kalekas. Palamas was said to be the most popular candidate, according to the emperor's own *History*, primarily because of his political stance during the recent civil war. Another strong candidate was the eccentric hermit of Vatopedi, Sabas, whom also the emperor was known to admire. But in the end the bishops chose Isidore Boucheiras, the former bishop-elect of Monemvasia, who also was a friend of Palamas. Immediately after his consecration as patriarch, Isidore annulled the excommunication of Kantakouzenos which had been imposed by his predecessor and announced the election of thirty-two new bishops. This list included Gregory Palamas who was named archbishop of Thessaloniki, the second city of the empire.

These ecclesiastical appointments did not go unopposed. In Constantinople, a group of some twenty disaffected bishops held councils of their own, at one of which, in July 1347, they published a decree excommunicating both Isidore and Palamas. Having failed to bring them to heel, Isidore had the bishops deposed by a synodal decree that was countersigned by the patriarch of Jerusalem. Meanwhile in Thessaloniki, the rebel 'Zealots', who had controlled the city since 1342, refused admission to their new archbishop, not on doctrinal grounds, but because of his loyalty to Kantakouzenos.

Unable to take possession of his see, Gregory went instead to Mount Athos, where he had not been for eight years. Since his last visit, the Holy Mountain had in 1345 come under the rule of Serbia and on arrival there he encountered the Serbian ruler, Stefan Dušan, self-styled 'Emperor of the Serbs and Romans'. Dušan was there to gather support from the monks for his ambition to unite all Serbian and Byzantine territory under his own authority, and to this end he had made substantial donations to the monasteries. When he was offered similar blandishments by the Serb, no doubt in an attempt to gain possession of Thessaloniki, Gregory remained loyal to both his emperor and his hesychast principles, saying: 'We have absolutely no need of political power, land, revenues, rents, or wealth . . . We have long since learnt to live on little and to be content with bare necessities.'[8]

---

[8] Philotheos Kokkinos, *Encomion* of Palamas, *PG* 151. 615CD; cited in Meyendorff, *A Study of Gregory Palamas*, p. 91.

Having failed to surrender their city to Dušan in 1349, the Zealots fell from power and the moderates handed Thessaloniki over to Kantakouzenos. At the start of 1350 both emperors arrived in the city together with the new archbishop, and Gregory at last was able to take possession of his see. During his tenure he preached a gospel of peace and reconciliation, condemning the excesses of the Zealots but soothing the wounds caused by the social and political conflicts of the past decade.

Meanwhile in Constantinople, he continued to be the subject of attack from intellectuals, such as the learned Nikephoros Gregoras, and some of the bishops who had been deposed in 1347. Patriarch Isidore died in 1350 and was replaced by Kallistos, an Athonite hesychast, who had been a disciple of St Gregory of Sinai at Paroria and more recently a hieromonk at the Athonite skete of Magoula and abbot of Iviron. In 1351 Kantakouzenos and Kallistos convened a new council, more numerous and more solemn than any that had gone before. It took place in the palace of Blachernae in the presence of the whole Senate. Gregory Palamas was there, supported by twenty-five metropolitans and seven bishops. The anti-Palamites were represented by three metropolitans and an assortment of monks and humanists. The latter were given a fair hearing and the emperor was at pains to achieve consensus. The proceedings were spread over two weeks, at the end of which the bishops present were invited to adjudicate on the questions at issue. All acknowledged the unity of God and the basic distinction between the divine essence and divine energy, both being uncreated. The patriarch then called on the dissenters to recant, and when they declined, pronounced the metropolitans deposed and their supporters condemned. After a final session, held without the presence of the condemned opponents, at which the teachings of Gregory were put to the test for one last time, the emperor declared that the archbishop of Thessaloniki was fully Orthodox and his teaching entirely conformed with the tradition of the Fathers, and so it has remained to this day.

Despite the final vindication of his teaching, Gregory's troubles were not yet at an end. Fresh strife had broken out between Kantakouzenos and John V and the latter, now resident in Thessaloniki, blocked the archbishop's return to his see until his mother, Anne, arrived and overruled her son. Gregory was then able to apply himself diligently to his pastoral concerns and to administering his diocese. As the civil war between the emperors worsened, and Kantakouzenos agreed to the coronation of his son Matthew as co-emperor in 1353, which resulted in the deposition of Patriarch Kallistos and his replacement by Philotheos Kokkinos, Gregory was invited by John to intervene and attempt a reconciliation. Gregory was well placed to do this: he had always supported the claims of Kantakouzenos, but he also upheld the rights of the poorer people who backed John V, and he was the spiritual father of both Kallistos and Philotheos. Furthermore, his prime objective had always been the restoration of peace throughout the empire. Gregory was provided with an imperial warship to take him to Constantinople, but bad weather forced him to put in at Gallipoli, which he was surprised to find was now in Ottoman hands. He and his entourage were therefore taken prisoner and shipped to Asia Minor, where they were required to remain for almost a year.

Gregory has left a description of his captivity in letters that he wrote as well as an account of a theological debate in which he was forced to participate.[9] These documents reveal a constructive attitude towards the Turks, which contrasts with the uncompromising views of most of his contemporaries. He looked on his captivity as an opportunity to proclaim the gospel to the infidel, clearly placing his missionary duty above his loyalty to the empire, and his description of the life of the subject Christian population stresses the tolerance shown by the occupying power. This recognition of the tolerance of Islam towards Orthodox Christians was shared by many of the hesychast monks at this date as well as by the poorer classes in Byzantium and provides an interesting and foresightful preview of the actual state of affairs that was to follow the inevitable collapse of the empire a century later.

Gregory remained in Asia Minor, moving from place to place, until the spring of 1355 when the ransom that the Turks demanded for his release was paid by Kantakouzenos. The latter by then had abdicated the throne and entered the religious life as the monk Joasaph. John V was now sole emperor and Philotheos had been replaced on the patriarchal throne by Kallistos. John was interested in uniting with the Church of Rome and, since a papal legate happened to be visiting the city, detained Gregory in Constantinople to take part in an open debate with Gregoras. But divisions within Orthodoxy were not helpful to the main issue and Gregory was soon sent on his way back to Thessaloniki, armed with letters from John confirming his loyalty to the new regime in Constantinople. There he resumed his episcopal duties, preaching, visiting monasteries, and, according to Philotheos, performing healing miracles. And there, on 14 November 1359, at the age of sixty-three, after a long illness, he died.

---

[9] See G. Georgiades Arnakis, 'Gregory Palamas among the Turks and Documents of his Captivity as Historical Sources', *Speculum*, 26 (1951), 104–8.

Almost immediately after his death, a popular cult for Gregory sprang up
in Constantinople, in Thessaloniki, and on the Holy Mountain. Only nine
years later, by a decree of Patriarch Philotheos (now reinstated) and the
Synod, he was formally included in the calendar of saints of the Great
Church.

In the calendar of the Orthodox Church, St Gregory Palamas enjoys
a position of special prominence because he is commemorated not only on
14 November, the day of his death (in 1359), but also (since 1368) on
the second Sunday of Great Lent. The first Sunday celebrates the restoration of the holy icons at the end of the iconoclast controversy in 843 and is
therefore known as the 'Sunday of Orthodoxy' or the 'Triumph of
Orthodoxy'. The fact that St Gregory's feast follows on the second
Sunday implies that his teaching and his victory over his adversaries were
recognized as a continuation of the previous Sunday's celebration, as
nothing less than a second Triumph of Orthodoxy. Gregory's relics are
preserved in the metropolitan cathedral of Thessaloniki, which is named
after him, but it is no accident that the earliest known portrait of him is on
the Holy Mountain at the monastery of Vatopedi, which claims him as one
of its greatest saints.

The Legacy of St Gregory Palamas

Why does Gregory merit such a prominent place in the calendar of the
Church? He was by no means the only exponent of hesychasm on the Holy
Mountain at the time. Nor was he the most successful propagator of the
hesychastic tradition within Orthodox monasticism: that title belongs to
his namesake the Sinaite, as we shall see developed in the following
chapters. Gregory's principal achievement was far more fundamental: it
was nothing less than to underpin the doctrine of hesychasm with a secure
theological foundation and (eventually) to win universal recognition for
that foundation throughout the Orthodox Church as a whole.

Gregory had powerful supporters among both the aristocracy and the
clergy; his teaching was confirmed by a series of councils held at
Constantinople between 1341 and 1351, which, though not technically
ecumenical, were scarcely inferior in weight to the seven original councils;
and most importantly, he had the support of his fellow monks. Before the
Latin empire the monks had been largely pushed to one side by the clergy
of the Great Church who monopolized the major bishoprics and domi-
nated most theological discourse. Since the restoration of 1261 the position
had been reversed and monks now occupied most senior positions in the

hierarchy and played a leading role in opposing the reunion of the Churches. So strong were they that even before the meeting of the first council they were able to issue a doctrinal statement condemning their opponents and they were able to maintain the upper hand until they were finally vindicated by the events of 1351. The victory of Palamas may therefore be seen as partly the victory of the Holy Mountain, without which the rest of this book could not be written. But it is above all the victory of the man himself: a truly creative theologian of the first order who changed the theology of Orthodoxy for all time.

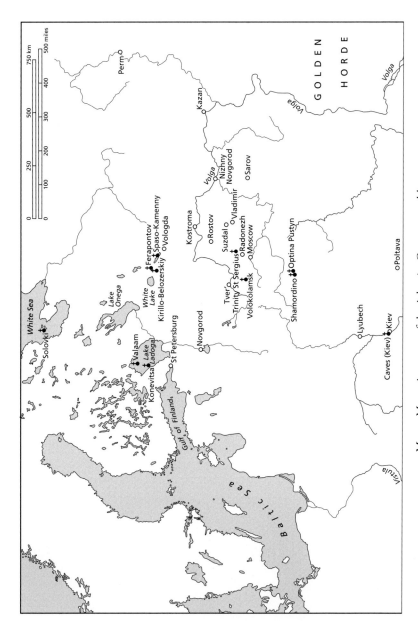

Map 5. Monastic centres of the Athonite Commonwealth.

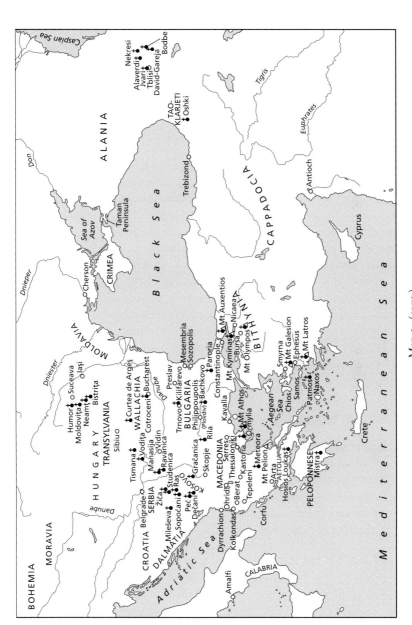

Map 5. (cont.)

CHAPTER 9

St Theodosius of Trnovo (c.1300–1363) and the Bulgarian School of Hesychasm

The victory of St Gregory Palamas and the formal recognition of his teaching as truly Orthodox stimulated an unprecedented international monastic revival in the late Byzantine period. Mount Athos retained its supremacy as the principal fount of monasticism, but pirate raids made it a dangerous place for monks who sought solitude away from the fortified monasteries. For this reason, other centres sprang up and for a while played a part in transmitting the doctrine of hesychasm across the Balkans and Eastern Europe. Such a centre was Paroria, founded by St Gregory of Sinai in 1330. By the end of the fourteenth century, the revival had spread from Thrace across Bulgaria, into Serbia and Wallachia, and up into Russia, while at the same time also travelling south into Thessaly. Almost all those who inspired this revival had received at least part of their training on the Holy Mountain. One of the first to provide such inspiration was St Theodosius of Trnovo.

St Theodosius and the Monastery of Kilifarevo

Theodosius was born near the Bulgarian capital at the end of the thirteenth century. At an early age he became a monk in a monastery near Vidin on the Danube in north-west Bulgaria. After the death of his spiritual father, he took to wandering from one monastery to the next until one day he heard news of the new foundation at Paroria in the far south-east of the country and of the arrival there of St Gregory of Sinai. Gregory had only recently been driven from the Holy Mountain of Athos by Turkish raids and had taken refuge in the Strandzha Mountains with a group of disciples. Theodosius hastened to join them and applied himself diligently to learning the practice of prayer of the heart and the techniques of hesychasm at Gregory's feet. The years that the Sinaite spent at Paroria from 1330 until his death in 1346 saw Gregory operating at his most charismatic and attracting disciples from all over south-east Europe. After his death, many of them scattered and returned to their homelands taking with them the fruits of his teaching. The brethren who remained at Paroria invited Theodosius to become their abbot, but he refused and together with his friend St Romylos of Vidin took to wandering again, first through Bulgaria and subsequently to Athos. But the Turks continued to make life difficult for them and once again they took to the road, initially making for Thessaloniki and then going via Veroia to Constantinople. Finally, Theodosius returned to his native Bulgaria and in 1350 with the generous assistance of Patriarch Kallistos I (1350–3 and 1355–63) of Constantinople and Tsar Ivan Alexander (1331–71) founded a monastery at Kilifarevo (Plate 20) in the foothills of the Balkan Mountains about 14 kilometres south of Trnovo.[1]

By this time Paroria had ceased to function, but Kilifarevo was founded on the same principles, and very soon there was a community of more than fifty monks who devoted themselves to practising mystical prayer, copying manuscripts, and translating hesychast texts into Slavonic. Theodosius himself translated the works of his elder, St Gregory of Sinai, and translations were also made of early patristic texts and the works of contemporary Byzantine theologians as well as lives of the saints, Byzantine chronicles, and accounts of ecumenical councils. The *typikon* of the monastery was that of St Catherine's monastery, introduced to Paroria by St Gregory of Sinai and brought from there by St Theodosius. And Bulgarian monks who travelled regularly between Kilifarevo and Athos brought back knowledge of Athonite techniques of hesychasm. The founder's reputation for holiness swiftly turned Kilifarevo into another international centre of hesychasm, and in his Life of Theodosius, Patriarch Kallistos, who had also been a disciple of Gregory of Sinai at Paroria, comments on the cosmopolitan character of the community: 'No sooner had he settled in the mountainous place called Kilifarevo than rumour flew all around, not only to the Bulgarian people, but also to the Serbs and the Hungarians and the Romanians and to those who live around Mesembria.'[2] This experience

---

[1] Unlike Paroria, the monastery of Kilifarevo survives, though moved to a lower site, close to the river Belitsa. There it maintains the traditions of hesychasm with a small but spirited community of nuns. The original monastery was destroyed by the Ottomans in the fourteenth century and again in the sixteenth, when it was assumed the lower monastery was built. But recent analysis of the two chapels (dedicated to St Theodosius of Trnovo and St John of Rila) at the eastern end of the katholikon has shown that they are in fact the remains of the east end of a large three-apse medieval church. We may tentatively conclude from this that the original monastery had two campuses, one upper and one lower, the latter perhaps created to house increasing numbers of monks attracted to the famous hesychast school.

[2] The Life of Theodosius, originally written in Greek, survives only in a Bulgarian copy, edited by V. N. Zlatarski in *Sbornik na Narodni Umotvoreniya, Nauka i Knižnina*, 20 (1904), 1–41; cited in Obolensky, *The Byzantine Commonwealth*, p. 391.

and that of his previous sojourn at Paroria bred in Theodosius and his disciples a strong belief in the pan-Orthodoxy of hesychasm as well as a shared loyalty to their Byzantine mentors.

Nor did his devotion to mystical prayer prevent Theodosius from taking an active interest in contemporary events in the world around him. His pan-Orthodox principles manifested themselves in two distinct ways. First, he played a leading part in suppressing heresy and in particular opposing a fresh outbreak of Bogomilism in Bulgaria.[3] Secondly, Theodosius strongly supported the primacy of Constantinople over the recently established patriarchate of Bulgaria, and when the primate of Bulgaria ceased the practice of commemorating the patriarch of Constantinople in the Liturgy, St Theodosius wrote a letter of support to his friend and fellow hesychast, Patriarch Kallistos. Kallistos responded with a letter to Theodosius and the community at Kilifarevo, strongly condemning the uncanonical actions of the Bulgarian primate. For twenty years there was tension between Constantinople and Trnovo until 1375 when the hesychast monk Euthymius, a disciple of Theodosius, became patriarch of Bulgaria. But for two decades the pan-Orthodox loyalty of the hesychasts had been able to withstand the forces of nationalism in Bulgaria and prevent a schism that could have created a permanent split in the structure of the Byzantine Commonwealth. As Anita Strezova has written,

> Through hesychasm . . . different parts of the Byzantine Empire were linked with each other and to its centre. In a way, hesychasm became a cultural tradition common to Greeks, Slavs and Romanians and assumed the role of an intermediary, analogous to the role played by the Cyrillo-Methodian movement of the 9th, 10th and 11th centuries.[4]

Theodosius himself may have found life in Kilifarevo more difficult after the spat between the patriarchs. For whatever reason, some years later he and a group of disciples left the monastery that he had founded and moved to Constantinople where Patriarch Kallistos found them accommodation in the monastery of St Mamas. There St Theodosius died on 27 November 1363. His last words, supposedly addressed to his disciples on his deathbed, are recorded in the Life written by the patriarch and constitute a summing up of all that they (or he) believed to be essential to hesychast teaching:

---

[3] See D. Obolensky, *The Bogomils: A Study of Balkan Neo-Manichaeism* (Cambridge: Cambridge University Press, 1948), p. 262.

[4] A. Strezova, *Hesychasm and Art: The Appearance of New Iconographic Trends in Byzantine and Slavic Lands in the 14th and 15th Centuries* (Canberra: ANU Press, 2014), p. 27.

First of all, hold fast to the holy faith of the Church of the Apostles and Councils, and to its unshakable precepts. Shun, as unfitting, the Bogomil and Messalian heresies, and after that those of Barlaam, Akindynos, Gregory and Athanasios. Believe those things which we have received from the beginning, without removing or adding anything, for this leads to blasphemy. This is what caused Akindynos to blaspheme, when he described Christ's glory, which at one time shone forth in a truly glorious and miraculous way, as something created. Likewise, keep the holy commandments. Hold fast to both these things; and a true Christian – by name, deed and repute – in addition roots out the love of self-will. Do not burden your life with possessions; practise fasting and self-denial, and so lull your passions. Subdue anger and all forms of bodily commotion, and [thus] drive away spiritual darkness. To speak briefly, this dries up all the moisture and sweetness of the flesh. He whose spiritual eye is clear sees himself, in the manner of the pious David, and overcomes the realms of evil, that is, the cunning inward thoughts of our hearts. Keep constantly before your eyes the remembrance of death and the Judgement of the Saviour, who will judge everyone and render to each according to his deeds. Have constantly and clearly before you the vision of God, as an activity of the mind; for this is a powerful weapon, unswerving against all opposing forces. Above all, hold fast to love, the supreme virtue, with all your strength, for this is the fulfilment of all blessings. Make all strangers welcome; do not make false accusations and avoid anger, rage, remembrance of wrongs and hatred; for these things darken the soul and estrange it from God.[5]

Theodosius died, as he lived, a humble hesychast, following the traditions of Athonite spirituality that he had learned at the feet of his elder, St Gregory of Sinai. Yet his legacy was momentous.

St Euthymius of Trnovo (*c*.1325–*c*.1400) and His Literary Reforms

The disciples of St Theodosius were numerous, influential, and drawn from a broad cross-section of the Balkans. Among the first was St Euthymius who was born at Trnovo in about 1325 to a noble family and was tonsured a monk at Kilifarevo soon after its foundation in 1350.[6] He became St Theodosius's closest disciple and accompanied him to Constantinople for his final years. After the death of his spiritual father,

---

[5] Life of Theodosius, pp. 33–4; cited in M. Heppell, 'The Hesychast Movement in Bulgaria: The Trnovo School and its Relations with Constantinople', *Eastern Churches Review*, 7 (1975), 15.

[6] On St Euthymius, see Obolensky, *The Byzantine Commonwealth*, pp. 434–42; D. Obolensky, 'Late Byzantine Culture and the Slavs: A Study in Acculturation', ch. 17 in *The Byzantine Inheritance of Eastern Europe* (London: Variorum, 1982), pp. 16–26; Maurice La Bauve Hébert, *Hesychasm, Word-Weaving, and Slavic Hagiography: The Literary School of Patriarch Euthymius* (Munich: Otto Sagner, 1992).

he remained for a while at the monastery of St Mamas and subsequently moved to Athos in about 1365. There he began as a monk of the Great Lavra and immersed himself in the practice of hesychasm as well as developing skills as a copyist of manuscripts and a writer, skills that he subsequently took with him to the Bulgarian monastery of Zographou (Plate 21).[7] The combination of his spiritual qualities, acquired from his close relationship with St Theodosius, and his intellectual abilities as a scribe and a scholar marked him out as the leading representative of the third generation of hesychasts in the school founded by St Gregory of Sinai.

By 1371 Euthymius had returned to Trnovo where he served as abbot of the monastery of the Holy Trinity, which had recently been founded just outside the city by Tsar Ivan Alexander. Here he established a scriptorium and literary school, which were to develop into a major centre of scholarship of international renown and influence. On the strength of his learning, he was elected patriarch of Trnovo in 1375 and remained in that position until Bulgaria was absorbed into the Ottoman Empire in 1393. Deprived of his throne, he then retired in exile to the monastery of Bachkovo in the foothills of the Rhodope Mountains where he ended his days around the turn of the century.[8]

Euthymius set ambitious targets for his literary reform. He firmly believed that not just the purity of Orthodoxy but the very basis of public education and morality depended on the accuracy and readability of the liturgical texts. In his opinion, the texts that were in current circulation were unacceptably defective in both respects. The translations from Greek originals contained many mistakes and inelegancies arising from misunderstanding or incompetence, and subsequent copying had further corrupted them. As a result, standards of writing were in decline, and the corrupt nature of the sacred texts left the door open to heresy. Several heretical movements were operating in Bulgaria at the time, not least that of the Bogomils, in opposing which we have already seen St Theodosius playing a leading part.

---

[7] On Athos, Euthymius seems to have preferred the eremitic life to the cenobitic and after a few months at the Lavra established himself in the tower of Selina, which lies between the monasteries of Zographou and Esphigmenou. See K. Pavlikianov, 'The Bulgarians on Mount Athos', in Speake and Ware, *Mount Athos: Microcosm of the Christian East*, p. 64.

[8] Bachkovo is still a functioning monastery, though all that remains of its eleventh-century Georgian foundation is the remarkable ossuary containing tombs of the founder's family and superb contemporary wall paintings. Georgian influence survived into the fourteenth century but by then the monastery was largely in Bulgarian hands. Endowments flowed from Bulgarian rulers including Tsar Ivan Alexander who is portrayed among the frescos in the entrance to the ossuary which he sponsored. See pp. 62–3.

Evidently Euthymius and his school were aiming to replace the whole corpus of Slavonic versions of the sacred books, including the Scriptures, with completely new translations from the Greek, and one of the reasons for this was their devotion to hesychasm. In spelling, punctuation, and grammar they were to take as their model the versions made nearly five centuries earlier by the disciples of Sts Cyril and Methodios and in syntax to follow closely the Greek originals. This archaizing emphasis on linguistic purity and adherence to Greek models was in line with the declared ambitions of the hesychasts to purify the religious life and support the primacy of the Byzantine Church in matters of faith and doctrine. It was no doubt also intended to result in a supranational form of Slavonic that would operate as a lingua franca for all Slavs. The patristic texts that were selected for retranslation into Slavonic included a good many of those that were especially favoured by the hesychasts, such as the works of St John Klimakos, St Symeon the New Theologian, St Gregory of Sinai, and St Gregory Palamas. With his own writings Euthymius set the style for hagiography and panegyric in Slavonic for the next century, a style that was ornate, rhetorical, and coloured by emotion. His models in form and content as well as style were the Lives of the saints composed by the hesychast patriarchs, Kallistos I and Philotheos Kokkinos.

Euthymius's linguistic reforms achieved widespread acceptance and were rapidly passed on to Serbia, Romania, and Russia. Bachkovo also became a centre of learning at this time, and Euthymius continued to promote his ideas while in retirement there. According to his pupil and encomiast, Gregory Tsamblak, his disciples were drawn 'not only from the Bulgarian peoples . . . but from all the northern peoples as far as the Ocean and from the west as far as Illyricum . . . He became their teacher in piety and they became instructors in their homelands.'[9] Gregory continues with a wonderfully melodramatic image of Euthymius as a second Moses:

> When he [Euthymius] had destroyed all the old [books], this second law-giver, descending from the top of the spiritual mountain and carrying in his hands [the books] (similar to the Tablets written by God) at which he had labored, delivered to the Church in truth a heavenly treasure – all new, all true, in accord with the Gospel, unshakable in the force of the dogmas, like the water of life for the souls of the pious, like a knife for the tongues of the heretics, like fire for their [heretics'] faces. And he cried out with Paul:

---

[9] P. Rusev et al. (eds), *Gregory Tsamblak, Pokhvalno slovo za Evtimii* (Sofia: B'lgarskata Akademiia na Naukite, 1971), pp. 196–7; cited by J. Shepard in Angold, *The Cambridge History of Christianity*, vol. 5: *Eastern Christianity*, p. 37.

'The old has passed away. Behold! Everything has become new' [2 Cor. 5:17].[10]

One of his disciples at Bachkovo himself had a pupil called Constantine of Kostenets who moved to Serbia where in about 1418 he wrote a popular treatise, *On Letters*. Constantine was a pedant and had little grasp of history, but his work does tell us something about the theory and practice of Euthymius's reforms. He professes himself to be appalled by the corrupt state of sacred texts in common use and proclaims that only in Trnovo and on Mount Athos are there Slavonic texts that are untainted by heresy. He calls for a rigorous code of practice to be applied by all scribes that would involve slavish adherence to Greek models in matters of spelling, grammar, and style and the most literal translation of Greek texts, even at the expense of clarity of meaning. Taken at their face value, such reforms would scarcely have resulted in the elegance and rhetorical effects that Euthymius was striving to achieve.

Euthymius's own writings were making their mark on Romanian scholars by the second quarter of the fifteenth century. Manuscripts of two of his biographies and three panegyrics were copied in the monastery of Neamț in Moldavia in 1438 and 1441, though it is not known how they came to be there. It is, however, known that his liturgical works reached Moldavia via the Bulgarian monastery of Zographou on Mount Athos.[11] Until the middle of the fifteenth century, little Slavonic literature circulated in the monasteries and courts of Moldavia and Wallachia that was not translated from the Greek and derived from the Balkan Slavs.

Meanwhile, the reforms had already spread as far as Russia. According to the Russian scholar A. I. Sobolevsky, a remarkable change may be observed in manuscripts in Church Slavonic used by the Russians between the mid fourteenth century and the mid fifteenth.[12] Both New Testament and other sacred texts display marked differences in terms of language, script, and spelling between manuscripts copied in the first and second of these periods. But manuscripts copied in the latter period display marked similarities to those originating from the Balkans during the century from 1350 to 1450. Also during that period, the number of patristic texts available to the Russians in translation almost doubled. All these changes

---

[10] Rusev et al., *Gregory Tsamblak*, pp. 196–7; cited by H. Goldblatt, *Orthography and Orthodoxy: Constantine Kostenecki's Treatise on the Letters* (Florence: Le Lettere, 1987), p. 33.

[11] On the Bulgarian monastic presence on Mount Athos in the fourteenth century, see Pavlikianov, 'The Bulgarians on Mount Athos', pp. 59–65.

[12] A. I. Sobolevsky, *Perevodnaya literatura Moskovskoy Rusi XIV–XVII vekov* (St Petersburg, 1903), pp. 1–14.

Sobolevsky attributes to the powerful literary influence of the Southern Slavs. Furthermore, the changes seem to have been accepted without the sort of violent reaction that greeted similar attempts of Patriarch Nikon to introduce liturgical texts and practices of the contemporary Greeks three centuries later. As Obolensky remarks, 'No doubt in 1400 religious nationalism in Russia was still in its infancy, and the Byzantines, who sponsored these textual emendations, still enjoyed a towering prestige.'[13]

That the reforms of Euthymius were able to travel so far and so fast within the Byzantine Commonwealth may be attributed to a number of factors. As we have already noted in the case of men such as St Gregory of Sinai, it was not uncommon for monks to move from place to place at regular intervals either in search of a spiritual father or teacher of hesychasm, or to disseminate the practice of prayer of the heart, or simply to avoid the consequences of their own worldly reputation. Most of the leading protagonists of the hesychast movement travelled widely and most shared a common background, having received at least part of their training on Mount Athos or at Paroria or Kilifarevo. The steady advance of the Ottomans across the Balkans following the battle of Kosovo in 1389 and the fall of Trnovo in 1393 no doubt gave added impetus to this movement, though since the monks' travels were within the same cultural sphere it should not be assumed that their reasons for moving were necessarily political.[14] At least as important as any political motivation were the strong personal links between them, especially the bond between spiritual father and disciple than which there is no more sacred and unbreakable relationship in Orthodox monasticism. As we shall see as we examine more of their careers, they operated primarily on the basis of their common membership of the so-called 'hesychast international'.[15] All of them maintained links, either directly or indirectly, with the religious and cultural powerhouse of Byzantium which despite its reduced political strength continued to provide the literary and spiritual models for the whole of Eastern Europe.

But, as Jonathan Shepard has written, 'to treat the imperial–ecclesiastical complex as sole pillars of a "commonwealth" would be to disregard "the Holy Mountain", at once landmark and generator of spiritual movement,

---

[13] Obolensky, 'Late Byzantine Culture and the Slavs', p. 18.
[14] Jonathan Shepard writes ('The Byzantine Commonwealth 1000–1550', p. 39) that 'to speak of a "hesychast movement" is misleading if it implies a hierarchical leadership directing a programme, or card-carrying members with agreed objectives.' But were the leaders of the Kollyvades, for example, any more hierarchical than the hesychasts? If we are happy to speak of a Kollyvades movement in the eighteenth century (see p. 222), why should we not speak of a hesychast movement in the fourteenth?
[15] On the term 'hesychast international' see p. 103, n. 17.

and known to fourteenth-century writers as "the workshop of virtue."' As he says, 'The "workshop of virtue" on Athos served as a kind of seminary or haven for advocates of the new rigorism; the bonds forged there or in their own foundations transcended existing institutional frameworks.'[16]

St Cyprian (*c.*1330–1406), Metropolitan of Kiev and All Russia

Another well-travelled disciple of St Theodosius was the monk Cyprian. 'His remarkable personality', writes John Meyendorff,

> dominates the ecclesiastical, cultural and political situation in Russia after 1370. Byzantino-Russian relations, relations with the Latin West, historio-graphy, hagiography and liturgical practice have all been marked by his personality and ideas, which – just as those of Philotheos Kokkinos and John Cantacuzenos – implied the unity of the Byzantine Orthodox Commonwealth and envisaged Russia, from the Carpathians to the Volga, as an inseparable part of it.[17]

We know very little about his early years, except that he became a close friend of St Euthymius. A letter survives, written by Euthymius, addressed 'to the monk Cyprian, who lives on the Holy Mountain of Athos', replying to a number of questions relating to discipline and liturgy which the monk had asked him. The letter is not dated, but most probably it was written before 1363 when the writer was still a monk at Kilifarevo. Cyprian was Bulgarian by birth and had almost certainly received his early training there before moving to Athos. It was no doubt on Athos that he acquired his lifelong devotion to the hesychast tradition and also his supranational breadth of outlook. By 1373 he was already described in a document as a close confidant of the Patriarch Philotheos, which suggests that some time in the early 1370s he had moved from the Mountain to Constantinople.

By the second half of the fourteenth century, the secular government of the empire had become so absorbed by its own internal divisions that it had more or less abandoned all pretensions to a foreign policy and handed over its diplomatic responsibilities to the patriarchate. The patriarchate had its own agenda which was to maintain and strengthen its authority over the Churches of Eastern Europe. But the secular authorities in Constantinople

---

[16] Shepard, 'The Byzantine Commonwealth 1000–1550', pp. 36–9.
[17] J. Meyendorff, *Byzantium and the Rise of Russia: A Study of Byzantino-Russian Relations in the Fourteenth Century* (Cambridge: Cambridge University Press, 1981), p. 199. On Cyprian see especially ibid., pp. 200–60, and Obolensky, *Six Byzantine Portraits*, pp. 173–200.

also liked to think that these same lands could be relied on to support the rump of the empire with money or troops or both. As the agent of this policy on behalf of both the Church and the empire, the patriarchate often appointed Slav monks who from their training could be relied upon to promote pan-Orthodox ideals based on the role of the ecumenical patriarch as spiritual leader of all the Orthodox Churches. Thus Cyprian, who with his training as a hesychast and his experience at court had clearly won the trust of the patriarch, in 1373 was appointed envoy to Kiev.

The appointment called for considerable diplomatic skills as there was tension between the two states that were in competition for dominance in the region, namely the grand duchy of Lithuania and the principality of Moscow. Kiev lay in the heart of what was now Lithuanian territory, but Moscow claimed to represent the political and cultural traditions of medieval Kievan Rus', as was symbolized by the title of the primate of the Russian Church who was known as the metropolitan of Kiev and All Russia but was now resident in Moscow. The Lithuanians naturally resented this situation and requested either that the metropolitan transfer his residence to Kiev or that a second metropolitanate be established to serve Lithuania. When Cyprian arrived in Kiev in the winter of 1373–4, the Lithuanians sent another embassy to Constantinople repeating their request for the establishment of a separate metropolitanate independent of Moscow. In response, Patriarch Philotheos hit on the solution of appointing Cyprian metropolitan of Kiev and Lithuania on the understanding that on the death of Alexiy, the incumbent metropolitan of Kiev and All Russia, Cyprian would assume responsibility for the entire Russian Church. Cyprian was duly consecrated in Constantinople on 2 December 1375.

Metropolitan Alexiy died on 12 February 1378, whereupon Cyprian set out for Moscow in accordance with the arrangement made by Philotheos. On his arrival however, he found that he was not made welcome but was arrested and expelled from the principality, apparently because he had gone first to Kiev and was regarded as a Lithuanian agent. He returned to Constantinople over land through Romania and Bulgaria. There followed a decade of anarchy in the Russian Church during which time Cyprian was shunted around between Constantinople, Moscow, and Kiev following successive regime changes in the respective capitals. While in Constantinople he lived in the Stoudios monastery, which was noted for its scholarly activities and its scriptorium where Byzantine and Slav monks worked together. In a postscript to a manuscript of St John Klimakos that he had copied, Cyprian wrote, 'On 24 April 1387 this book was completed in the Stoudite monastery by Cyprian, the humble metropolitan of Kiev and All Russia.'[18] Clearly, he still regarded himself as the legitimate holder of that see, though it was to be another three years before he was formally restored to it.

Fifteen years after his consecration, Cyprian finally entered Moscow via Kiev as metropolitan of All Russia early in 1390. At last he was able to initiate the scheme that he and Patriarch Philotheos had put together in the early 1370s by which the Churches of the South Slavs and the Russians would be tied more closely to the Constantinople patriarchate by the shared aspirations of senior clergy who as friends and disciples of each other owed a common devotion to both the traditions of hesychasm and the Church of Byzantium. The cornerstone of this scheme was the see now held by Cyprian, the metropolitanate of Kiev and All Russia, centred in Moscow. No doubt he played a part in securing a brief period of peaceful relations between Moscow and the Polish–Lithuanian federation which lasted until 1406. More significant for us is his role as the chief Byzantine representative in Russia. He was clearly instrumental in having commemoration of the emperor restored in church services throughout the land, a practice that Basil I, grand prince of Moscow, had forbidden. He also operated effectively as a fund raiser at a time when Constantinople was being besieged by the Turks from 1394 to 1402. Evidence of this survives in the form of a letter that is preserved in the patriarchal archives, dated 1400, in which Patriarch Matthew encourages Cyprian, as a 'Byzantinophile' (*philorromaios anthropos*), to undertake another campaign and assure his Russian flock that 'it is more meritorious to contribute money for the defence of Constantinople than to build churches, to give alms to the poor, or to redeem prisoners. For this holy city is the pride, the support, the sanctification, and the glory of Christians in the whole world.'[19]

Apart from his services as a Byzantinophile, Cyprian also contributed a great deal to the benefit of his adopted country. Russian collections include a number of manuscripts copied by him of translations into Slavonic of texts such as the works of St John Klimakos and pseudo-Dionysios and the Psalter. He himself made new translations into Slavonic of a number of sacred texts including the Liturgy of St John Chrysostom and did his best to make the liturgical practices of the Russian Church conform with those of Constantinople. He advanced the spread of

[18] This manuscript, formerly in the collection of the Trinity-St Sergius monastery, is now housed in the Russian State Library in Moscow (Fund No. 152).
[19] F. Miklosich and I Müller (eds), *Acta Patriarchatus Constantinopolitani*, 2 vols (Vienna, 1860–2), vol. 2, p. 361; cited in Obolensky, *Six Byzantine Portraits*, p. 197.

hesychasm in Russia by inserting into the official church Synodikon for the Sunday of Orthodoxy the new articles endorsing the teaching of Gregory Palamas. And he contributed to the compilation of the first Muscovite chronicle, which was completed after his death.

Cyprian had had a remarkable career during which he did his best to counter the forces of nationalism and separatism, to win support for the embattled empire, and to strengthen the spiritual unity of the Byzantine Commonwealth by uniting the Slav Churches in a restored loyalty to Constantinople. As a Bulgarian monk schooled on Athos, he remained true to his hesychast principles as he switched from being the confidant of the Byzantine patriarch to being his representative in Kiev, a casualty of the conflict between Lithuania and Moscow, and finally the acknowledged metropolitan of Kiev and All Russia. A typical product of the cosmopolitan culture prevailing across Eastern Europe at the time, he was in Obolensky's words, 'a man who, drawing his spiritual and intellectual inspiration from the hermitages of Athos and the example of his mentor, the Patriarch Philotheos, devoted the greater part of his active life to the task of keeping together the disparate fragments of the Byzantine commonwealth. He fought hard, and in the end achieved a large measure of success.'[20]

In retirement, he withdrew to his country house near Moscow where he had leisure to read, copy manuscripts, and pray. Russian chroniclers describe the place as being 'quiet, silent and free from noise, between two rivers . . . beside a pond, and there was much forest all round'. As his life drew to a close, he dictated a letter of farewell to both his friends and his enemies in which he begged for forgiveness and sent to all his 'peace and blessing and last embrace'. There he died on 16 September 1406 and the letter, as he requested, was read aloud as his body was lowered into its coffin and according to the chronicler many were the tears of the mourners as they heard it.[21]

Gregory Tsamblak (*c.*1365–1419), International Hesychast

Gregory Tsamblak grew up in Trnovo and became St Euthymius's star pupil. He belonged to a distinguished family with Byzantine connections, and it used to be assumed that he was the nephew of St Cyprian. This assumption was based on a reference in his funeral oration on Metropolitan Cyprian to the deceased as 'the brother of my father'.[22]

---

[20] Obolensky, *Six Byzantine Portraits*, p. 199.   [21] Ibid.
[22] English translation in M. Heppell, *The Ecclesiastical Career of Gregory Camblak* (London: n.p., 1979), pp. 109–20 (114).

Scholars now agree that this is most likely to be a reference to spiritual fatherhood rather than actual paternity, the 'brotherly' relationship being that between Cyprian and Euthymius.[23] Gregory received a good education, which included extended visits to Mount Athos and to Constantinople, though how long he stayed in either is uncertain. No doubt under the influence of the Trnovo school and its leading light Euthymius, he decided at an early age to become a monk. In his eulogy of Euthymius, written many years after the fall of Trnovo in 1393, Gregory described his master as 'a physician who healed spiritual fevers by his wisdom and most skilfully excised other passions and sins, right from the depth'.[24]

There are few other details of Gregory's early life, but by the start of the fifteenth century he was established in Constantinople, apparently in the service of Patriarch Matthew, and from now on his career is a paradigm of the fluidity of ecclesiastical life for those with the right connections in the last century of Byzantium. In 1401 he was dispatched by the patriarch on a mission to Moldavia, a country that had only recently achieved its independence from Hungary and acquired a ruling dynasty but owed ecclesiastical allegiance to Byzantium. The Church of Moldavia was now seeking a degree of autonomy. Constantinople was in principle sympathetic to the idea but needed to verify the credentials of the candidate selected to be its first metropolitan. Patriarch Matthew wrote to the people of Moldavia that in order to investigate this matter on the spot he was sending 'the most honourable among hieromonks, the spiritual father and monk close to my person, Gregory, and the highly honoured teacher of the Gospel, the deacon Manuel the Archon, beloved sons of our humility in the Holy Spirit'.[25] While he was in Suceava, Gregory preached a series of sermons in the cathedral, which established his special relationship with that church and his reputation as a preacher.

Nothing for sure is known about Gregory's career for the next few years before 1406 when he was summoned to Kiev by Metropolitan Cyprian, but it seems highly likely that he spent the intervening years in Serbia. Unlike Bulgaria, Serbia retained a degree of independence despite being defeated by the Ottomans at the battle of Kosovo in 1389. Prince Lazar was killed in the battle, but his son Stefan Lazarevic, who agreed to pay tribute to Sultan

---

[23] Obolensky, *Six Byzantine Portraits*, p. 175; Meyendorff, *Byzantium and the Rise of Russia*, p. 202.

[24] E. Kalužniacki (ed.), *Lobrede auf Euthymios*, in *Aus der panegyrischen Literatur der Südslaven* (Vienna, 1901; repr. London, 1971), p. 47; cited in Heppell, 'The Hesychast Movement in Bulgaria', p. 17.

[25] Cited in Heppell, *The Ecclesiastical Career of Gregory Camblak*, pp. 19–20.

Bayezid, was able to rule a virtually autonomous Serbia until his death in 1427. In fact, Stefan presided over a period of prosperity and a renaissance of Serbian culture in which he participated as a generous patron of the arts and literature. The so-called 'Morava school' of architecture and painting flourished, most notably in the monastery of Manasija (Plate 23), which was founded in 1407 and rapidly became a celebrated centre of literary activity.[26] Here one of the leading lights was Constantine of Kostenets whom we have already met as a pupil of Euthymius, and there were other Bulgarian exiles, such as Romylos of Vidin (whom we shall meet again below), who found a haven from political turmoil and opportunities for artistic and literary activity in Serbia. In such circumstances, it was no surprise that Stefan should have invited Gregory Tsamblak, already well known as a writer and a preacher, to come to Serbia.

During these years, roughly 1402–6, Gregory served as abbot of the monastery at Dečani in present-day Kosovo, which had been founded by King Stefan Uroš III (1321–31), subsequently known as Stefan Dečanski (Plate 24). In the course of his abbacy, he wrote a Life of the founder, which is not only of considerable historical interest but is also a characteristic example of the author's florid prose style. It includes a charming description of the monastery, which to this day remains the pearl of medieval Serbian monastic architecture as well as being a model of Orthodox spirituality amid very difficult circumstances.

> The monastery lies on a patch of high ground, refreshed by trees of all kinds, for it is a place that abounds in fruits and foliage; at the same time it is level and grassy. On all sides streams flow most sweetly, for a large stream gushes out there, and the place is watered by a swift river. This water gives pleasure to the eye before it delights the taste; and its taste makes it dissolve so pleasantly in the body that no one could have enough of such pure water. [The monastery] is surrounded on its western side by high hills, the slopes of which enclose it, providing healthful air on all sides. To the east there stretches a large plain, through which the same river flows. Such is this place, most suitable and admirable for the building of a monastery.[27]

In the summer of 1406 Abbot Gregory received a letter from Metropolitan Cyprian summoning him to Moscow. The letter has not survived, but presumably the already ailing metropolitan wished to discuss with his disciple the future administration of his Russian dioceses, and he

---

[26] See Ćurčić, *Architecture in the Balkans*, pp. 680–2.
[27] A. Davidov et al. (eds), *Žitie na Stefan Dečanski ot Grigorij Camblak* (Sofia, 1983); cited in Heppell, *The Ecclesiastical Career of Gregory Camblak*, p. 32.

may have suggested that he should travel by way of Kiev. At all events, before Gregory could reach Moscow, Cyprian had died. A successor had to be found, and in the meantime Gregory, who was not in the running, returned to Constantinople. In 1409 he was back in Kiev to deliver a eulogy on Cyprian, presumably at the invitation of the Lithuanian ruler, Vitovt. Meanwhile, a successor to Metropolitan Cyprian, a Greek by the name of Photios, had been appointed and consecrated in Constantinople in 1408 but did not reach Moscow until 1410. Despite his pious credentials, Photios seems not to have proved himself an effective administrator and to have gained a reputation for self-aggrandizement with respect to church property and revenues. By 1414 a powerful group of opponents of Photios had emerged and took their complaints to the court of Vitovt, where they were likely to be given a sympathetic hearing, exploiting the old rivalry between Kiev and Moscow. Vitovt's response was to summon a council of all the Orthodox bishops in his territory and invite them to choose a separate metropolitan of Kiev. The bishops demurred, but they did agree to write a letter, addressed to Vitovt, in which they complained that the metropolitan of Kiev and All Russia was their pastor only in name and that he took no notice of the Church in Kiev except to impose taxes on it and remove its treasures to Moscow.

On hearing of this letter, Photios made plans to depart for Constantinople in order to protest at Vitovt's wish to appoint a separate metropolitan of Lithuania. But he made the mistake of travelling via Kiev, where he was detained by Vitovt's supporters who blocked his route and forced him to return to Moscow. Meanwhile, Vitovt summoned a second council of bishops and invited them again to choose a metropolitan of Kiev who should then go to Constantinople to be consecrated, and this time, despite continuing reluctance to upset the status quo, they unanimously chose Gregory Tsamblak. The fact that he was their unanimous choice suggests that Gregory was a popular figure in Kiev and that he most probably had remained in the city after delivering his eulogy on Cyprian in 1409. After his election by the Lithuanian bishops, he set out for Constantinople, but the patriarch refused to consecrate him, no doubt on the grounds that he had no wish to divide the Russian metropolitanate. Thereupon Vitovt, abandoning Gregory, wrote to the patriarch, asking him to make his own choice for metropolitan of Lithuania, but this letter received no reply. In the absence of any guidance from Constantinople, Vitovt felt free to act alone. Once more he summoned his bishops and this time he asked them to consecrate Gregory as metropolitan of Kiev. With great reluctance they complied, protesting that it was uncanonical to have two metropolitans in one province. Realizing that his actions may have been irregular, Vitovt instructed the bishops to write a letter of justification. 'At the bidding of Vitovt', says the *Nikon Chronicle*, 'the bishops sat down with their metropolitan Gregory, whom they themselves had consecrated', and wrote a letter. Muriel Heppell summarizes its contents as follows:

> The bishops proceeded to justify their action by the following arguments: (i) a metropolitan can be canonically consecrated, by the laying on of hands, by two or three bishops; (ii) that this had happened previously in the Russian Church 'in the reign of Grand Prince Izjaslav'; and (iii) the Orthodox states of Bulgaria and Serbia both have an autocephalous ecclesiastical administration, in which the head of the Church is elected and consecrated by the bishops of that country ... Then they come to the core of their letter, in which they affirm that they are acting in accordance with the traditions of the Church and the principles of canon law; at the same time they affirm their loyalty to the patriarch of Constantinople ... Nevertheless they feel obliged to act independently of him, because the patriarch and the synod in Constantinople are not free to choose the metropolitans they want but have to obey the orders of the emperor; moreover the office of metropolitan of Kiev and All Russia is in effect put up for sale.[28]

There followed letters from both Vitovt and Photios in which each sought to justify his actions, the latter condemning the behaviour of the Lithuanian bishops and instructing the faithful to have nothing to do with them or with Gregory and his supporters. Finally, a letter from the patriarch announced that Gregory Tsamblak was excommunicated and warned Vitovt against continuing to support him. But this letter seems to have fallen on deaf ears, as does Photios's appeal to the people of Lithuania to reject Gregory as metropolitan. Vitovt strengthened his grip over Lithuania, Gregory was installed as metropolitan, and Kiev had more serious business to attend to in coping with an assault by the Tatars.

It may be assumed that Gregory served as metropolitan of Lithuania until his death, which probably occurred in 1419. During his reign his activities go unrecorded save for one last overseas journey, which was to visit the Council of Constance in 1418. The council had already been in progress for some four years, and its most urgent business concerned the crisis in the Western Church caused by the simultaneous existence of three rivals for the papacy, namely John XXIII, Gregory XII, and Benedict XIII. There was also some discussion of the so-called 'Wycliffite heresy' and the

[28] Heppell, *The Ecclesiastical Career of Gregory Camblak*, pp. 65–9.

inadequacies in the administration of the Western Church. The schism between Rome and Constantinople was also on the agenda, and this topic was actively promoted by a delegation of bishops from Poland and Lithuania. These bishops had large numbers of Orthodox on their door-step; and Vitovt in particular, who took the initiative in sending Gregory Tsamblak to Constance, ruled over a mixed population. Gregory arrived in Constance in February 1418 as part of a large delegation and created quite a stir. Within a few days of his arrival, he had an audience with the recently elected Pope Martin V for which he composed an eloquent address, which is unpublished but is preserved in the manuscript collection of Vilnius Public Library.[29]

The address opens with elaborate compliments to the assembled fathers, likening them to 'experienced pilots, guiding the ship of the Church to the tranquil harbour of reconciliation ... wise and skilful physicians, preserving the body of the Church from every kind of disease ... stars shining more brightly than the stars of heaven'. Having compared the leaders of both Churches with Moses and their flocks with the children of Israel, he pleads that 'the body of the Church, dismembered for so many years through the agency of the devil' might once more be made whole, though there is no suggestion of submission to the Pope. He urges the members of both Churches to practise greater humility and tolerance towards each other and he ends by emphasizing the need for a general council which would 'renew the honourable and blessed confession of the faith according to the first tradition of the fathers ... without departing in any respect from the dogmas handed down by those God-inspired fathers'.[30]

The address is a good example of Gregory's rhetorical prose style and, unlike the version that was actually delivered, demonstrates his cautious attitude to the proposed reunion of the Churches. But a very different text is preserved in the diary of Cardinal Fillastre, who was one of the principal participants in the council and whose diary is an important source for it.[31] It seems that Gregory's original text did not find favour with other delegates and, when it came to be translated into Latin prior to delivery, significant changes were made so that it read far more like a personal plea for the reunion of the Churches:

---

[29] Vilnius Public Library MS 105, ff. 41–4.
[30] Heppell, *The Ecclesiastical Career of Gregory Camblak*, pp. 91–2.
[31] The diary of Cardinal Fillastre is published in L. R. Loomis, *The Council of Constance*, ed. J. H. Mundy and K. M. Woody, Records of Civilization. Sources and Studies, 63 (New York and London: Columbia University Press, 1961), pp. 435–7.

So I, most blessed Father, who have long hoped for this sacred union, went to my most Christian lord, the king of Poland, and the lord duke Withold [Vitovt], his brother . . . The sincere devotion and faith of these most serene princes inspired me with a burning ardour for the holy faith of the Church and to diligent labour with all my strength to bring as many as I could to the same pious mind by preaching and admonition in the Ruthenian tongue. Among us, Holy Father, I have found many of pious mind, who long for the sacred union of the Church.[32]

The sermon purports to represent also the views of the emperor and patriarch of Constantinople who, it claims, 'also desire this sacred union'. And it ends with a recommendation that so important a matter should be discussed at a general council, to be convened by the Pope, and that 'scholars learned in the law be assembled on both sides, to pass judgement on matters of faith'.

Not surprisingly, the sermon in Latin was well received. 'The lord pope', writes Fillastre in his diary, 'replied praising the archbishop's desire and saying that he would consider how to carry it out, and a method of accomplishing it, and would fix a day for its purpose.' Nothing more is reported of Gregory at the Council of Constance, and it is to be assumed that shortly after this he departed. His visit to the council must have been a considerable disappointment, since he was unable to deliver the sermon that he had written, and he returned to find Kiev in the grip of an epidemic of plague to which, no doubt exhausted by his travels and demoralized by his experiences, he soon succumbed. The reference to his death in the *Nikon Chronicle* is followed by this brief tribute: 'In this year [1419] died Gregory Tsamblak, archbishop of Kiev, a very learned man, well read in books from his childhood. He left many writings of his own, and this was his legacy.'[33]

In the course of his career, Gregory had found himself involved in many of the most important movements in the Orthodox Church at the time: he first of all benefited from and participated in the cultural flowering of the Trnovo school in his native Bulgaria; he played a part in the establishment of an autocephalous Church in Moldavia; he was caught up in the complex problems associated with the administration of the unwieldy metropolitanate of Kiev and All Russia; and finally he made an appearance at the Council of Constance at which he tried to present the Byzantine attitude towards the proposed reunion of the Churches. It has to be said that his

[32] Heppell, *The Ecclesiastical Career of Gregory Camblak*, p. 88.
[33] Ibid., pp. 89, 106; *Nikon Chronicle, Polnoe Sobranie Russikix Letopisej*, 11 (St Petersburg, 1897; repr. Moscow, 1965), p. 235.

role in all these movements was to a large extent passive and was mostly directed by others, notably Metropolitan Cyprian or Prince Vitovt. Indeed, he might have been happier if he had remained as abbot of Dečani rather than accepting the summons to Kiev. We may conclude that he was born into a family where it was expected that he would take high office and play a part in making the world a better place; that he did his best to live up to these expectations, even though he was temperamentally unsuited to them; and that he left behind a body of writings which identify him as a man of sincere piety and learning, profoundly devoted to the hesychastic traditions of Orthodoxy.

St Romylos of Vidin (*c.*1300–*c.*1381), Link to Serbia

Another disciple of St Theodosius of Trnovo was St Romylos who was born around 1300 to a Greek father and a Bulgarian mother at Vidin in the north-west of Bulgaria. Like most parents they wanted their son to marry, but the young Romylos preferred to become a monk and ran away to the monastery of the Mother of God Hodegetria in the area of Zagora near Trnovo. He impressed his elder with his zeal and humility, but he silently hankered after the solitary life, and when he heard about the monastery being built at Paroria by St Gregory of Sinai, he set his heart on going there. 'From that time on then', we read in his Life, 'while Zagora held his body, the wilderness of Paroria possessed his soul. Just as the thirstiest deer seeks the fountainhead he thirsted, and he asked God that he might go to Paroria.'[34] With his elder's blessing he was at last allowed to leave Trnovo with a fellow monk called Ilarion and with joy they were received by St Gregory.

Perceiving the respective strengths of the two newcomers, St Gregory assigned lighter tasks to the weaker Ilarion but to the robust Romylos much heavier tasks were given. In particular, he was asked to care for an ill-tempered old monk who would eat nothing but fish. Even in the depths of winter, when the fish ponds were frozen hard, Romylos would break through the ice with a hammer and willingly jump into the freezing water to catch fish, thus proving himself a true spiritual athlete. In due course both the old monk and St Gregory passed away and Romylos, finding himself bereft of an elder, joined his friend Ilarion who was already

---

[34] M. Bartusis, K. Ben Nasser, A. Laiou, 'Days and Deeds of a Hesychast Saint: A Translation of the Greek Life of Saint Romylos', *Byzantine Studies/Etudes Byzantines*, 9: 1 (1982), 24–47, ch. 4. Available online at https://sourcebooks.fordham.edu/basis/romylos.asp.

serving another elder who was living in quietude far from the monastery. But soon they were afflicted by a severe famine and at the same time they were attacked by brigands, which combined to drive them out of Paroria, and the three of them made their way back to Zagora for safety. This happened three times. On the second occasion, they returned to Zagora, but the third time Romylos went with his companions in the early 1350s to Mount Athos where, 'finding many holy men who were living the same life [i.e. in hesychasm], especially those of his own race [i.e. Bulgarians], he led them to the path of salvation'.[35]

Romylos was evidently well known as a spiritual father and found himself in great demand among the Athonites who deprived him of the very isolation that he had come to seek. He was therefore forced to change his abode at regular intervals until he finally came to rest in the Athonite desert at a remote spot near the Great Lavra known as Melana. 'Here I, the unworthy Gregory', writes the author of his Life, 'having come from Zagora, found him building a cell for his dwelling place. There, bending my head, I submitted to him, since I had known him for a long time and he was dear to me in the Lord.'[36] But no sooner had they finished building their cell than they were beset by a great spiritual clamour. 'For one could see the monks of the Holy Mountain, like bees that run around dewy fields, absorbing both his holy words and his holy deeds. And as the magnet draws iron to itself, so did his words and his sweetest conversation attract men's souls.'[37] For some time the saint and his companion endured the clamour and responded to it with spiritual instruction and inspiring stories while at the same time practising fasting, vigilance, poverty, purity of the body, and incessant prayer. But eventually the clamour grew too great and once more Gregory was sent out in search of a retreat on the northern slopes of the Mountain where they might find solitude and respite from the tumult. Here, in a ravine above St Paul's monastery, Romylos at last found the leisure to write his only known literary work, *Rules Recommended for Proper Monastic Behaviour*, which survives in a single copy preserved in the monastery of Hilandar. This he must have completed before 1371, the year in which persistent Turkish attacks forced him to leave the Holy Mountain for good.[38]

The hermits had to leave Athos in a hurry and Romylos now travelled to Avlona, modern Vlora, on the Adriatic coast of Albania, then part of Greater Serbia. Here, according to his biographer, the people were like

---

[35] Ibid., ch. 12.   [36] Ibid.   [37] Ibid., ch. 15.
[38] See Pavlikianov, 'The Bulgarians on Mount Athos', pp. 68–9.

sheep without a shepherd, accustomed to brigandage and murder. The governors of the town welcomed him and called him equal to the apostles, but the saint did not find the place to his liking and appealed to another Athonite to advise him where he should go. The response was that it would be better for him not to return to the Holy Mountain but to go to another place where God would lead him. Accepting this advice, Romylos went with his disciples into Serbia and settled at the monastery of Ravanica (Plate 25), which was then being built on a grand scale by Prince Lazar, not far south of Manasija. He brought with him the ascetical and mystical traditions that he had inherited from his elders in Bulgaria and on Mount Athos and thus played a key part in bringing hesychasm to Serbia. Although he died shortly after his arrival at Ravanica, his disciples remained there and the monastery flourished as a centre of spirituality and culture, which it remains to this day.

By the end of the fourteenth century hesychasm was well established in monasteries throughout Bulgaria and Serbia. The principal channel for its dissemination had flowed through the monastery of Paroria, initiated by St Gregory of Sinai and supported by St Theodosius of Trnovo and his disciples, all of whom had received at least part of their monastic formation in the spiritual seminary on the Holy Mountain. This third generation after St Gregory of Sinai, all Bulgarians by birth and all of them Athonites, exemplified by St Euthymius of Trnovo, St Cyprian, metropolitan of Kiev and All Russia, the roving Gregory Tsamblak, and the hermit-monk St Romylos of Vidin, succeeded in taking their master's teaching to all corners of the Balkan peninsula and even to Russia. As products of that international and dynamic 'workshop of virtue', they all went back into the world as faithful ambassadors not only for hesychasm but for an entire cultural diaspora that we have now termed the Athonite Commonwealth.

Plate 22. The cathedral of St Sophia in Kiev, the metropolitan's church, noted for its fine eleventh-century mosaics.

Plate 23. The interior of the main church of the fortified monastery of Manasija in Serbia. Its magnificent frescos, dating from the early fifteenth century, represent the high point of the Morava school of painting.

Plate 24. A monk stands guard over a casket containing the relics of Stefan Dečanski (d.1331) in Dečani monastery, Kosovo.

Plate 25. The main church of the fortified monastery of Ravanica in Serbia where the relics of St Romylos are preserved alongside those of Prince Lazar (d.1389).

Plate 26. The main church of Moldoviţa monastery in Moldavia, a centre of hesychasm until the late eighteenth century. Its church is famed for the painting of its external walls, including a dramatic depiction of the siege of Constantinople in defiance of the inexorable Ottoman advance into Romania.

Plate 27. The main church of Bistriţa monastery in Moldavia, founded in 1402 by Voivode Alexander the Good. Most of its external painting was removed in the late sixteenth century.

Plate 28. The refectory (right) and defence tower (top) of Koutloumousiou monastery on Athos, originally built by Voivode Vladislav, for what was to become known as the 'lavra of Wallachia'.

Plate 29. The Trinity monastery of St Sergius near Moscow, the model for all subsequent religious foundations in medieval Russia. The cathedral of the Dormition, with its colourful domes, dates from the sixteenth century.

CHAPTER 10

St Nikodimos of Tismana (1320–1406): Transmitter of Hesychasm to Wallachia

Hesychasm came to Romania in the fourteenth century not only from the Bulgarian monasteries of Kilifarevo and Paroria but also direct from the Holy Mountain itself where the monastery of Koutloumousiou came very close to becoming a Wallachian house. Before that, there had been isolated hermits and a few clusters of monastic cells of which fragmentary remains survive, but until the formation of the states of Wallachia and Moldavia in the fourteenth century, the country was not yet equipped for the foundation of organized communities. With the establishment of the two metropolitanates, of Wallachia in 1359 and Moldavia in 1370, the direction of Romania's ecclesiastical allegiance was firmly set towards Byzantium, the local rulers (or voivodes) were keen to identify themselves as Orthodox sovereigns, and the metropolitans strove to increase links with the Mother Church in Constantinople, from which they had originated, and with Mount Athos, the heart of Orthodox monasticism.

The Arrival of Hesychasm in the Romanian Lands

The man credited with being the principal transmitter of hesychasm to the Danubian principalities, and hence the 'father' (or 're-organizer', as some prefer to say) of Romanian monasticism, was the monk Nikodimos. Details of his life are sketchy because of the paucity of contemporary sources: all that survives is three late Lives, all dating from the seventeenth or eighteenth centuries and preserved at his monastery of Tismana. From these and from the contemporary Life of his friend, the learned monk Isaiah of Hilandar, a tentative biography may be constructed. He was born around 1320 in Prilep, Macedonia, to a Greek father from Kastoria and a Serbian mother and received his monastic training on Mount Athos at the Serbian monastery of Hilandar. Hilandar at that time was a major centre for scholarly and literary activity. Its scriptorium was busy copying manuscripts not only of the Scriptures and service books but also of such important theological texts as the works of St John Chrysostom and St Theodore the Stoudite, many of which are still to be found in the monastery's library. Other monks were concerned with translating into Slavonic whatever texts were available, both those of contemporary Byzantine theologians such as Gregory Palamas and Gregory of Sinai and those classics of early Byzantine literature in which the leaders of the hesychast movement took a renewed interest. Among the latter, the works of pseudo-Dionysios the Areopagite were translated by monk Isaiah. Nikodimos therefore, as Isaiah's disciple, may be assumed to have gained a thorough grounding in hesychasm and the literature associated with it during his time at Hilandar. In due course, he rose to become abbot, and he gathered around him a large circle of disciples, not only from Serbia, but also Greeks, Romanians, and Bulgarians.

Exactly when Nikodimos left Hilandar is not known, but after many years on Athos he went north to Serbia, perhaps with a group of his own disciples, and founded there two monasteries, at Vratna and Monastirica near the Danube. His piety and his energy drew him to the attention of Prince Lazar (1371–89) who, according to some sources, invited him to become head of the Serbian Church, which had proclaimed its independence in 1346, or at least exarch for the Serbian monasteries on Mount Athos. But Nikodimos would not surrender his independence and his devotion to hesychastic principles in return for high office or ecclesiastical preferment and declined the offer.

At some point in the reign of Voivode Vladislav-Vlaïcu (1364–77) Nikodimos crossed the Danube, either for political reasons or driven by missionary zeal, and settled in Wallachia near Severin. Here, with the support of the voivode, in about 1370 he founded the monastery of Vodiţa. Under the spiritual protection of Patriarch Philotheos and Metropolitan Hyacinth of Hungro-Wallachia, this new foundation, dedicated to St Antony the Great, was peopled mostly by hermits already living in the vicinity; and archaeological investigations have shown that Vodiţa was built on the site of an earlier monastery. Nikodimos was named abbot, a position that he would hold until his death, and he determined that the monastery would follow the *typikon* of Hilandar. It was to adopt Athonite principles of hesychasm and be independent of any ecclesiastical or political authority in the region.

In 1375 Prince Lazar invited monk Isaiah, now abbot of St Panteleimonos monastery on Athos (to which position he had been appointed by Stefan Dušan), to lead a delegation to Constantinople to resolve the schism between the Serbian Church and the ecumenical patriarchate. Isaiah chose a team of hesychasts to go with him and asked his former disciple Nikodimos to serve as their interpreter. The embassy was well received by Emperor John V Palaiologos and Patriarch Philotheos, and after lengthy discussions the anathema was lifted and the head of the Serbian Church was hereafter given permission to use the title 'patriarch'. At the same time, Nikodimos was raised to the rank of archimandrite, which gave him the authority to consecrate churches.

After the death of Prince Vladislav in 1377 that part of Wallachia around Severin fell to Hungary, and so its monasteries found themselves under a foreign, Roman Catholic ruler. Vodiţa continued to function as an Orthodox house under Nikodimos, while he himself decided in 1384 to move to a more sheltered location, protected by forests and mountains, and founded a new monastery at Tismana. This monastery was built with the support of Voivode Radu I (1374–c.1384) and was further enriched with property by Voivode Mircea (1386–1418) so that it became one of the wealthiest foundations in the country. Its *typikon* was the same as that of Vodiţa and its autonomy was similarly guaranteed by royal decrees. Tismana became a renowned spiritual centre from which prayer of the heart spread throughout Wallachia. Nikodimos founded a number of other monasteries, but it is Tismana that is still venerated as the cradle of Romanian monasticism.

Nikodimos himself continued to shun ecclesiastical honour and preferred to withdraw to a cave that was created for him above the monastery of Tismana where he could devote himself to solitary prayer and fasting. Unfortunately, his own writings have not survived, but it is known that he corresponded with Patriarch Euthymius of Trnovo (1375–93). Two of the patriarch's replies to Nikodimos are extant and show that the latter was concerned with some fine points of theological scholarship and that relations between the two men were clearly very good. But the Romanian scholar Emil Turdeanu is no doubt right to set no great store by this relationship and to set Nikodimos apart from the Bulgarian tradition of the fourteenth century:

> Considered in its entirety, the work of Nikodimos represents an original synthesis between the hesychast movement imported from Mount Athos and the artistic and literary influences coming from Serbia. Contrary to the currents that supply the first literary school in Moldavia established at the monastery of Neamţ by the monk Gabriel (1424–49), it stands apart from the Bulgarian tradition of the fourteenth century. Nikodimos's relations

with Patriarch Euthymius of Trnovo merely assume the character of an episode without profound implications for the life of his foundations.[1]

In 1399 Nikodimos moved to Transylvania where he founded a monastery at Prislop and again he withdrew to a cave. It was during his time here that he copied (and signed) a manuscript of the Gospels in Slavonic, which is one of the greatest treasures of the National Museum of Romanian History in Bucharest. Not only is it written in a fine, clear hand, but it is ornamented with miniatures and decorative initials and encased in superbly embossed silver covers. The subscription reads, 'This holy Gospel book was written by the monk Nikodimos in the Hungarian land in the sixth year of his exile, which is the year 6913 since the creation of the world [i.e. 1405].' Transylvania at the time was occupied by the Hungarians, which accounts for his claim to be in 'exile'. It may be assumed that he learnt the art of calligraphy during his time on Mount Athos, and he may have copied other manuscripts over the years (though no others signed by him have survived). But why he should have chosen to undertake such a task in this otherwise dark period of his life, when his days were rapidly drawing to a close, is unclear. Turdeanu suggests that he may have needed to calm his religious ardour and console himself for his remoteness from the foundations to which he had devoted the better part of his life.[2] Or perhaps he simply wanted to leave behind a beautiful monument more durable than bronze.

In the following year, 1406, Nikodimos was back in his monastery at Tismana and summoned Abbot Agathon of Vodiţa, whom he appointed as his successor. He then retired to his cave to live out the remainder of his days in hesychastic seclusion and died there on 26 December 1406. His grave is still venerated in the narthex of the monastery's church. All his monastic foundations continued to follow the hesychast tradition for many years and together they operated as a bulwark safeguarding the Orthodox against Roman Catholic influences from Hungary. The language they used was Slavonic and most of the monks were drawn from Serbia or Hilandar.

The list of monasteries founded by Nikodimos traditionally included those at Topolniţa (not far from Vodiţa), Cosuştea-Crivelnic, Gura Motrului, and Vişina, all in Oltenia. Other monasteries that were founded

---

[1] E. Turdeanu, 'Les premiers écrivains religieux en Valachie: l'hégoumène Nicodème de Tismana et le moine Philothée', in Turdeanu (ed.), *Etudes de littérature roumaine et d'écrits slaves et grecs des principautés roumaines* (Leiden: Brill, 1985), pp. 15–49 (pp. 36–7). My translation.

[2] Ibid., p. 36. For an illustrated description of the manuscript (inv. no. 131507), see 'The Tetraevanghelion of Pious Nicodim', www.capodopere2019.ro/the-tetraevanghelion-of-pious-nicodim.html, accessed 15 December 2014.

either under his influence or by his disciples were those of Cozia, built by Voivode Mircea, Cotmeana in Argeş county, Snagov, Strugalea, Glavacioc, probably Dealu, and several sketes. Others of his disciples went to Moldavia where they founded a large number of monasteries including those of Neamţ, St Nicholas of Poiana Siretului, Moldoviţa (Plate 26), Bistriţa (Plate 27), Humor, Vîrşevăţ, and Bogotin. Metropolitan Serafim Joantă concludes his chapter on 'The Dawn of Hesychasm in the Romanian Countries in the 14th Century' with these words:

> A hesychast missionary in the spirit of St Gregory the Sinaite, whom he had known in his youth, St Nicodemus established his rule of life in the many communities founded by himself or his disciples in the three Romanian lands. Romanian monasticism thus owes to him its hesychastic orientation in the 14th century. The resulting cultural and spiritual blossoming was to continue, more or less without interruption, for the next three centuries.[3]

Koutloumousiou, the 'Lavra of Wallachia'

Nikodimos and his disciples were driven largely by the stream of spiritual guidance flowing from the Serbian monastery of Hilandar on Mount Athos. But there were other forces at work in the Romanian lands, notably those from the hesychast houses of Kilifarevo and Paroria, and also from the monastery of Koutloumousiou on Athos.

The origins of this monastery are obscure. A chrysobull that purports to be signed by Emperor Alexios I Komnenos (r.1081–1118), preserved at the monastery and claiming to be its founder's *typikon*, is in fact a forgery.[4] The first reliable reference to its existence is the mention of its abbot Isaias among the signatories of a document dating from 1169 in the archive of St Panteleimonos, on the basis of which a date for its foundation in the first half of the twelfth century seems reasonable. There is then a long silence in the records until the late thirteenth and early fourteenth centuries when it is mentioned again in documents as a low-ranking monastery with few monks and inadequate resources. Not until the time of Abbot Chariton (*c.* 1355–*c.*1381) does it emerge as a house of substance with estates in Macedonia and Wallachia and a brotherhood of forty monks. It was Chariton who won the support of Voivode Vladislav for the monastery, thus establishing a link with the rulers of Wallachia that was to endure for

---

[3] Metropolitan Serafim Joantă, *Treasures of Romanian Christianity: Hesychast Tradition and Culture*, trans. I. Bănică and C. Hâncianu Latiş (Whitby, ON: Cross Meridian, 2013), p. 72.
[4] See P. Lemerle (ed.), *Actes de Kutlumus*, 2nd edn (Paris: Editions P. Lethielleux, 1988), p. 1.

500 years. Vladislav wrote in a document preserved in the monastery's archives:

> I will encircle the monastery with walls and a reinforcing tower and build a church, a refectory, cells [Plate 28]; I will ransom lands and donate animals so that through this my lordship's parents and I should be commemorated ... as the Serbian, Bulgarian, Russian, and Georgian rulers are commemorated on the Holy Mountain.[5]

But Romanian support came at a price: Vladislav insisted that the monastery take a complement of Wallachian monks and allow them to adopt the idiorrhythmic system (i.e. setting their own rhythm) as opposed to the cenobitic way of life traditionally followed there.

It is our good fortune that three versions of Abbot Chariton's testament are preserved in the monastery's archives.[6] In the first of these, dated 1370, he explains that when he was appointed abbot he was charged by the then Protos of the Mountain and bishop of Ierissos to do all he could to improve and strengthen the monastery. To this end, he obtained some donations from prominent Byzantines, but to underwrite the costs of fortification he appealed to Voivode Vladislav, whose father Nicholas Alexander (Alexander Basarab, 1352–64) had already begun the construction of a great tower which had not yet risen above its foundations. 'He too', wrote Chariton,

> ought to imitate his father. This would assure him of remission of his sins, good health of soul and body, and an enviable reputation among emperors and rulers, for he would not be inferior to them in his munificence and his offerings to this most holy mountain, the eye, so to speak, of the whole civilized world. All this would be his if he should choose to build fortifications in this monastery of Koutloumousi.[7]

This much was achieved by dint of much hardship and suffering on the part of Chariton, in return for which the voivode received the title of *ktitor* (founder). In his capacity as *ktitor*, he asserted his right to import a number of Wallachians (Vlachs) as monks and demanded that they be permitted to live in the monastery according to the idiorrhythmic system to which they were accustomed. This was too much for Chariton and he refused to allow it, whereupon Vladislav convened a council of his most senior clergy who

---

[5] Ibid., no. 26; cited in C. Coman, 'Moldavians, Wallachians, and Romanians on Mount Athos', in Speake and Ware, *Mount Athos: Microcosm of the Christian East*, p. 122.
[6] *Actes de Kutlumus*, nos. 37, II B, and 98. English translations are published with commentary in Thomas and Constantinides Hero, *Byzantine Monastic Foundation Documents*, vol. 4, pp. 1408–32.
[7] Ibid., p. 1414.

accused Chariton of disobeying the founder. Unwilling to take sole responsibility for such a fundamental change to the monastery's constitution and subjected to abuse for his 'arrogance' by the members of the council, Chariton agreed to refer the matter to the elders of the Holy Mountain (i.e. the Holy Community) and to abide by their decision. Fearful lest he should forfeit future benefits from the founder, the elders offered Chariton the following advice:

> You do well not to go ahead and boldly try this experiment simply on your own initiative. But, be assured that even those whom God has put in charge of spiritual matters often have to make use of a certain economy to allow for changes in accord with various conditions, as indeed has been done in the other, larger monasteries on this holy mountain. Those who began this practice did not do so out of bad will, but because of the anomaly of the situation. They made concessions lest, by being too rigid, they might be deprived of what was more important. You too must do as the fathers. Such condescension is the only way in which you will gain what may be needed for the souls and the bodies of the brothers.[8]

On the strength of this advice, Chariton agreed to receive the Wallachians (who included some quite senior hierarchs such as the *proto-papas* of Hungro-Wallachia, Michael) and permitted them for the time being to continue their way of life on condition that the voivode confirmed his support for the monastery. He also composed a document for the voivode to sign whereby he (Vladislav) agreed to redeem the monastery's debts, to build a church of a size to accommodate its present and future brotherhood and a refectory of similar proportions, to supply enough goods, vines, and animals to enable the fathers to enjoy some respite from their labours, and to acknowledge that the Greek monks, both now and in the future, be accorded 'due honour and precedence' over the Wallachians. There was also a requirement that the abbot and his brothers should retain the right to choose his successor, that the choice be approved by the voivode in his capacity as *ktitor*, and the new abbot then be handed his pastoral staff by the Protos of the Mountain. Any change to the cenobitic status of the monastery was dependent on the voivode's agreement to the above.

Chariton's second testament was written a few months later in the same year, 1370. This time he emphasizes his opposition to the voivode's wish to change the monastery's way of life from cenobitic to idiorrhythmic:

---

[8] Ibid., p. 1416.

For the above-mentioned voivode, while attentive to the funds he was doling out, paid little heed to the strictness of our way of life. Some of the Vlachs who were coming here and being tonsured wanted to live in a relaxed, loose, and irregular manner, inasmuch as they are mountain folk and unaccustomed to monastic continence and discipline. It was his intention to alter and to transform the rule legislated and defined by our holy, God-bearing, immortalized fathers, and that rule of common life which had been so well elaborated and observed by those founders and holy fathers of mine ... But God from whom all good comes was on my side, and the *zupan* [the voivode's representative] did not succeed in shaking my resolve or in changing the position I adhered to regarding our paternal, or if you will, divine inheritance.[9]

The report of the council summoned by the voivode is similar to that in the earlier document but more detailed and distinctly more hurtful to Chariton who stresses the insults that he was subjected to and the hardships that he suffered in the course of his numerous journeys. Similar also is the response of the Athonite elders who commend the abbot as the true 'founder' of his monastery and again counsel him to exercise 'economy' in his dealings with one who 'comes from a lordly and more luxurious manner of living'. They go on to mention that one of the monks who recently joined them, the *protopapas* Michael, had been tonsured and 'enjoyed a softer way of life' but had still been unable to cope with the regime and had returned to his homeland. The document for the voivode's signature contains the same provisions as before but with some additions: that the Vlachs joining the monastery be able to support themselves from their own resources; that neither Greeks nor Vlachs disparage or sit in judgement on the other, but 'let each receive proper honor and reverence from his subordinates in food, drink, and seating, and, in corresponding manner, in what is due to him according to the years and labors of each one, as is done in the rest of the hagioritic monasteries, who are at peace with the brothers of other nationalities living in them'; that the monastery retain its name; and 'to this end I requested the pious voivode to issue a letter guaranteeing precedence in all things to the Romans'.[10]

The third version of the testament is dated July 1378, by which time Chariton has become metropolitan of Hungro-Wallachia, titular bishop of Amaseia, and Protos of Mount Athos. He is now in poor health and fears that his end is near, but his tone is much more relaxed than before. The Voivode Vladislav and his wife Anna are given posthumous credit for providing the funds with which the monastery has now been rebuilt

---

[9] Ibid., p. 1420.   [10] Ibid., p. 1423.

and beautified, though the contributions of Greeks, Serbs, and Bulgarians are also mentioned. Presumably because these works are now complete, there is no reference to any bad-tempered negotiations with the voivode's council or to demands for founder's rights over the monastery. Nor is there any reference to the change from the cenobitic to the idiorrhythmic system for the sake of the Wallachians, though Chariton is at pains to stress his own poverty and to commend the same to his brothers and successors. Any funds raised from the sale of his own vestments should be used to ransom those monks who have been captured by the Turks in raids that, despite the new fortifications, had become a serious threat to the monastery. He repeats the procedure for the selection of his successor but does not mention the need for the new abbot to be approved by the voivode. He signs in his capacity as bishop of Hungro-Wallachia and Protos. Chariton recovered from his illness sufficiently for him to attend the synod of Patriarch Neilos Kerameus in Constantinople in 1380, and he probably died the following year.

This document in its three different versions is of great significance as an illustration of how patronage was secured across national boundaries by an Athonite monastery. Both sides had an agenda to pursue and both were willing to drive a hard bargain and to endure considerable physical hardship and verbal abuse in order to achieve their respective goals. Both succeeded: the monastery secured financial backing that stood it in good stead for as long as the Orthodox Church was respected by the rulers of Romania; and the Romanians were able to infiltrate a monastery on the Holy Mountain for the first time, and had the satisfaction of hearing it referred to as the 'lavra of Wallachia', though in fact they never gained full control of it. The wily Chariton required Vladislav to sign a document which stated that Koutloumousiou was a Greek monastery, not a Romanian one, 'since threats and curses hang over him who dares upset the Greeks by claiming that the monastery ought to belong to the Romanians because of the lord's donations'.[11] Nevertheless the Romanians went on to provide financial support for almost every monastery at some point or other during the Tourkokratia and were among the Mountain's most generous benefactors. It is one of the seeming injustices of history that they never gained title to a monastery of their own, though they came close to it on more than one occasion, but they had certainly earned for

---

[11] P. Nasturel, 'The Links between the Romanian Countries and Mount Athos until the Middle of the Fifteenth Century', in G. Vasilescu and I. Monahul (eds), *Românii și Muntele Athos [Romanians and the Holy Mountain]*, 2 vols (Bucharest: Editura Lucman, 2007), vol. 1, pp. 460–1; cited in Coman, 'Moldavians, Wallachians, and Romanians on Mount Athos', p. 122.

themselves full membership of the Athonite Commonwealth, both contributing to it and benefiting from it at least as enthusiastically as any other
nation. What did that mean in practice?

Romanian Participation in the Athonite Commonwealth

The Romanians have performed a very distinctive role in the history of
Athos. Unlike the Serbs, Bulgarians, and Byzantines, they never aspired to
empire; unlike the Serbs, Bulgarians, and Russians, they were not Slavs;
unlike all these others, they never acquired a monastery of their own. And
yet it could be argued that they were, at least throughout the Tourkokratia,
the most generous benefactors that the Mountain had ever had. Without
Romanian support, it is likely that many of the monasteries would not have
survived into modern times. In a remarkable demonstration of the
Athonite Commonwealth in action, we find Romanians constantly present
and deeply involved in the affairs of the Mountain, and at the same time we
find Athonites making substantial contributions to the development of
cultural life in general and monastic organization in particular in Romania.

The assistance provided by the Romanians to the Mountain took
a variety of forms. Sometimes it was gifts of money or ecclesiastical
artefacts; sometimes they sponsored the construction, renovation, or decoration of churches or other buildings; sometimes it manifested itself in the
hospitality shown to Athonite monks in their cultural and monastic
activities in Romania; but perhaps most remarkably and most generously,
it took the form of the dedication of large numbers of actual monasteries
and their estates in Romania to the Athonite houses. As Fr Constantin
Coman has written,

> We are dealing with a phenomenon which is unique in its dimensions and
> hard to explain from a purely historical perspective. The voyevods of
> Wallachia and Moldavia, almost without exception, would regularly help
> all the Athonite monasteries. Their wives, the noblemen of the country, the
> Romanian hierarchs, and the people as well, all took part in this charitable
> activity both through the taxes that filled the state treasuries and directly.[12]

Among the most generous benefactors there is perhaps no better example than St Stefan the Great of Moldavia (1433–1504), who is warmly
remembered for the assistance that he gave to the monasteries of
Konstamonitou, Vatopedi (where he paid for the construction of the

[12] Ibid., p. 123.

quay in 1496), and Grigoriou (which he rebuilt after it had been destroyed by pirates). But he reserved his greatest generosity for the Bulgarian monastery of Zographou. Here he built the port tower (which still stands), cells for the monks, and the refectory, and later he paid for the restoration of the entire monastery and the decoration of the katholikon. He was no doubt gratified to be described by monk Isaiah of Hilandar in 1489 as the 'founder' of Zographou, which he made 'a lavra of the Moldavian principality', the equivalent of what Koutloumousiou represented for Wallachia, and before his death he was careful to endow the monastery with an annual income of 100 Hungarian gold coins

> so that he, his wife, and their two children, Alexander and Helen, would be commemorated at the Prothesis; so that he should have a paraklisis sung on Saturday evenings and a Liturgy on Tuesdays as long as he was alive, and after he died he would be commemorated by tradition and then he would have a Panikhida sung in the evening and a Liturgy in the morning once a year.[13]

Another monastery that listed a Romanian *ktitor* in the fifteenth century was Philotheou, whose original foundation dated from the year 1141.[14] After generous donations from St Sava in the early thirteenth century and the Palaiologos family in the fourteenth, who were also recognized as *ktitores* by the monastery, the Wallachian voivode known as Vlad the monk sometime between 1487 and 1492 issued a chrysobull granting it an annual stipend of 4,000 aspra in return for the standard forms of commemoration during church services. But it seems that the monastery decided against continuing the relationship, perhaps because Vlad (like Vladislav at Koutloumousiou) had insisted on exercising founder's rights and demanded that it convert to the idiorrhythmic system. The brotherhood at the time contained a mixture of Greeks and Bulgarians under the direction of alternating Greek and Bulgarian abbots. By 1505, when the Greek elder Dionysios became abbot, the Bulgarians were in the ascendancy. In an attempt to rehellenize the monastery and return it to cenobitic rule, he recruited monks from Constantinople. This resulted in ugly scenes of violence in the course of which Dionysios was driven out of the monastery. The house remained idiorrhythmic, but the hellenization of the brotherhood seems to have been successful and the relationship with Wallachia was terminated.

---

[13] Ibid., p. 130.
[14] See Robert Allison, 'Founders and Refounders of Philotheou Monastery on Mt Athos', in M. Mullett (ed.), *Founders and Refounders of Byzantine Monasteries* (Belfast: Belfast Byzantine Enterprises, 2007), pp. 465–524.

It is clear from these examples, of Koutloumousiou, Zographou, and Philotheou, that the Romanian voivodes had an 'agenda' when making their donations. Their generosity, however, and that of their successors was not diminished by their failure to achieve the goal of a monastery of their own; on the contrary, despite these setbacks, it seems to have been exercised with even greater determination. Neagoe Basarab, for example, voivode of Wallachia (1512–21), in an attempt to demonstrate his legitimacy as the successor to the Byzantine emperors, summoned to the consecration of the cathedral in his monastery Curtea de Argeş on 15 August 1517 not only the abbots of all the monasteries on Mount Athos but also high-ranking representatives of the entire Orthodox world, patriarchs and hierarchs from every jurisdiction. The assembled flock were witnesses to the canonization of Niphon II, twice patriarch of Constantinople (1486–9 and 1497–8) and former metropolitan of Hungro-Wallachia (1503–5), an event that conferred not only political legitimacy on the ruler but also religious legitimacy on the ecclesiastical authorities of the country. Neagoe Basarab went on to support nearly all the monasteries on Athos: he completely rebuilt the Lavra and endowed it with a substantial annual income; he did the same for Dionysiou, which had been St Niphon's monastery and to which he now sent the saint's holy relics; at Koutloumousiou he built the church of St Nicholas, the refectory, the cellar, and the port; and he made similar gifts to Vatopedi (the chapel of the Holy Belt and the great cellar), Pantokrator (the high walls), Xeropotamou (the refectory and the cellar), Zographou (3,000 aspra per year), St Paul's (the defence tower), and Iviron (an aqueduct). For this he was given the title 'the great founder of the whole Mountain' by St Niphon's biographer, Gavriil Preotul.[15] He was also named as a founder of the churches in Constantinople, Sinai, Jerusalem, and Serbia. What motivated him to exercise such unbounded generosity?

From an early age Neagoe Basarab had been deeply influenced by monastic spirituality and as a young man he spent long periods at the monastery of Bistriţa. Here he became the spiritual child of the former patriarch and Athonite hesychast Niphon, under whose influence the future voivode grew up with the aim of becoming a sort of hesychast-monarch. His two greatest gifts to posterity, of the vast number of works achieved in his short reign (he died at the age of forty), were the monastery of Curtea de Argeş (his 'stone cathedral') and his theological reflections

---

[15] See E. Babus, I. Moldoveanu, and A. Marinescu (eds), *The Romanian Principalities and the Holy Places along the Centuries* (Bucharest: Sophia, 2007), p. 57.

entitled *The Teachings of Neagoe Basarab to His Son Theodosius* (his 'literary cathedral'). This remarkable work, written in Slavonic in the last years of his life, has been described as a masterly synthesis of medieval Romanian culture and the first product of universal value in the literature. Its publication brought its author the reputation of a legislator who had codified the political and religious thinking of his time and has given rise to such accolades as a 'patriarch of the Romanian voivodes', a 'Marcus Aurelius of Wallachia', and a 'prince-philosopher, excellent stylist, profound thinker, a lucid writer and moralist'.[16] The first part of the work is specifically addressed to the author's son and those who will succeed him and takes the form of a guide to behaviour to ensure a virtuous and successful reign. The second part is directed to society as a whole, some parts explicitly for 'patriarchs, bishops, boyars, abbots, rich, and poor'. The whole work is firmly grounded in Scripture and patristic texts and is imbued with hesychast principles, indicating a high level of spiritual experience, no doubt learned at the feet of Niphon. For example, he writes:

> The first thing is silence. It makes confusion cease, and this produces repentance and compunction. Compunction gives birth to fear, and fear to humility. Humility thinks of the things to come, and this procures the love that makes the soul converse with the angels. Then the man knows that he is not far from God.[17]

As Metropolitan Serafim suggests, such passages are worthy of inclusion in a philokalic collection.

Alexander Lăpuşneanu, voivode of Moldavia (1552–68), was another generous benefactor, responsible for rebuilding the monastery of Dochiariou and decorating its church. In giving permission for the work, the sultan stated that 'the buildings of the monastery were founded by the voivodes of Moldova-Wallachia, and the renovations made to the monastery's ruins at various times were also the Romanian voivodes' work.'[18] Other monasteries to benefit from his charity included Karakalou and Xeropotamou (whose churches he decorated), Vatopedi (for which he bought a warehouse costing 1,060 gold pieces and made an annual grant of 300 gold pieces), and Dionysiou, where he built the infirmary and the south wing and enlarged the refectory. His wife, Ruxandra, redeemed the dependencies of Zographou from Macedonia for 52,000 aspra, and after his death donated 2,700 gold pieces to Dochiariou.

[16] Joantă, *Treasures of Romanian Christianity*, pp. 120–1.   [17] Ibid., p. 128.
[18] Coman, 'Moldavians, Wallachians, and Romanians on Mount Athos', p. 124.

The Dedicated Monasteries

From the middle of the sixteenth century onwards, the most important way in which the Romanians showed their support for the Mountain was by dedicating monasteries to Athonite houses. A dedicated monastery ceased to come under the jurisdiction of the local bishop and was thereafter administered by the monastery to which it was dedicated. Its income, often exempt from state taxation, was used in the first place for the upkeep of that monastery, but any surplus was passed to the monastery to which it was dedicated. The dedication usually included whatever property the monastery owned, such as its land, forests, lakes, farms, warehouses, stables, animals, carts, and tools. The first such dedication, according to Ioan Moldoveanu, occurred in about 1500 when the monastery of Robaia-Zdrelea in Oltenia was dedicated by the brothers Craioveşi to Xenophontos. In all, as many as 125 monasteries in Romania were placed under the authority of the Holy Mountain. Their archives are still in the process of being investigated, but according to the most recent list, 23 Romanian monasteries were dedicated to Vatopedi, 15 to Esphigmenou, 13 to Iviron, 9 to the Protaton, 7 to Zographou, 6 to Simonopetra, 4 to St Paul's. Only two monasteries, Philotheou and Pantokrator, are absent from the list.

By 1863, when Prince Alexander Cuza put an end to the practice by confiscating all monastic estates, the dedicated monasteries and their dependencies owned between 700,000 and 1 million hectares, roughly a quarter of all Romania's land.[19] This, of course, had profound consequences for the economy of the country as a whole which, thanks to the expansion of trade and improvements in agriculture and in communications, began to show real signs of growth in the nineteenth century. The income of the monasteries also grew and the position of the dedicated monasteries in particular became more and more anomalous: 'The situation can best be described as that of a state within a state', writes the Italian scholar Antonio D'Alessandri; 'in fact hundreds of thousands of Romanians lived in monastery villages and worked for the well-being and the wealth of institutions outside of their own country . . . Most of the best land . . . did not contribute at all to the public coffers.'[20]

Two of Romania's greatest royal monasteries, that of Cotroceni in Bucharest and the Three Holy Hierarchs in Iaşi, were dedicated in their

---

[19] Ibid., p. 127.
[20] A. D'Alessandri, 'Orthodox Monasticism and the Development of the Modern Romanian State', in I. A. Murzaku (ed.), *Monasticism in Eastern Europe and the Former Soviet Republics* (London and New York: Routledge, 2016), pp. 173–89 (177).

entirety to the Holy Mountain. The income went in the first instance to the Protaton and was subsequently shared between the twenty ruling monasteries. Cotroceni had been built by Şerban Cantacuzino in 1682 and was the richest of all the monasteries to be dedicated to Mount Athos with its four *metochia* and extensive landholdings. It has been estimated that by 1828 its annual income was the equivalent of 33 kilos of gold. The Three Holy Hierarchs was built by Prince Basil Lupu in 1639 and dedicated by him to the Holy Mountain. It acquired numerous estates, forests, orchards, and vineyards from which by 1828 it drew an annual income of about 27 kilos of gold.

Of the Athonite monasteries, Vatopedi was the one most favoured by Romanian benefactors and, thanks to the work of Florin Marinescu on the monastery's Romanian archive, many of the dedications have been published.[21] The monastery of St Demetrios in Galaţi, for example, was built by Basil Lupu around 1640, probably to mark the arrival in Moldavia of the relics of St Paraskevi, and was bequeathed by him to Vatopedi. The monastery of Golia in Iaşi was first built as a church about 1564 by the Grand Logothete Ioannis Golia and his wife Anna. In 1606 after Golia's death, his widow Anna donated the church to Vatopedi, and it was probably the Vatopedi fathers who transformed the church into a monastery. Many of its abbots were monks of Vatopedi and under their leadership the monastery acquired so many gifts of land and property that by 1828 its estates covered an area of 10,000 hectares. The monastery continues to flourish to this day and maintains good relations with Vatopedi. The monastery of Precista at Galaţi was founded in 1641 by a local merchant called Theodore. Its fortified church was completed in 1647 with some assistance from Abbot Ignatios of Vatopedi and was immediately dedicated to the Athonite monastery. At its foundation it was endowed with estates, farms, vineyards, mills, beehives, and even a boat, and in subsequent centuries its landholdings were greatly increased. It continues to flourish as a monastery today.

Monastic wealth and monastic estates on such a scale are open to abuse and in many cases the dedicated monasteries with their foreign abbots grew to be more interested in material revenue than spiritual exchange. But when operating at their best, they acted as channels for Athonite values and disseminators of hesychast teaching. Many of them housed libraries containing important manuscripts, some started printing presses, and others

---

[21] See Florin Marinescu, 'The Metochia in Romania', in *The Holy and Great Monastery of Vatopaidi: Tradition – History – Art*, 2 vols (Mount Athos: Monastery of Vatopaidi, 1998), vol. i, pp. 89–96.

opened schools, not just primary schools, but also high schools in which students were taught mathematics, theology, and poetry as well as the Romanian, Greek, and Slavonic languages. Thanks largely to the monasteries, the Romanian principalities enjoyed a notable cultural flowering and maintained close relations with the Orthodox East. Had the monasteries simply become dens of profligacy, they would not have continued to attract the degree of support that they did right up until the time that their estates were secularized in the nineteenth century. It is worth noting also that these exchanges operated in both directions, and it has been suggested that the Romanian art of Moldavia exercised a greater influence on Athonite art than Athonite art exercised on Romanian art.[22] Even today, long after the termination of formal ties, spiritual links with the Holy Mountain are maintained. Athonite abbots regularly make visits to their former dependencies, and Romanian monks and novices are turning in increasing numbers to the monasteries and sketes of Mount Athos, none more so than Vatopedi where the Romanians form the largest ethnic minority.

[22] Joantă, *Treasures of Romanian Christianity*, p. 114.

CHAPTER 11

St Sergius of Radonezh (1314–1392) and St Nil Sorsky (c.1433–1508): Revivers of Russian Monasticism

The 'Flight into the Desert'

In 1237–40 Russia was invaded by the Mongols and many of the 200 or so monasteries that had been founded in the previous 250 years were sacked or destroyed. The monks of the Caves monastery in Kiev retreated to the comparative safety of their subterranean labyrinth, but the inhabitants of other religious houses, especially those in or near towns, were less fortunate. Once the initial onslaught was over, however, the attitude of the Mongol rulers to the Russian Orthodox Church and its institutions was marked by tolerance and protection, and by the second quarter of the fourteenth century monasteries began to grow in size and even multiply in number. The rule of the Kipchak Horde was cruel, and many people turned to the religious life as a means of escape from the misery of their day-to-day existence. Some fled to the relative security of the cloisters in order to escape death or capture in the endless civil wars and power struggles that tore Russia apart in the half-century from 1275 to 1325. Others sought refuge or a cure from the regular outbreaks of plague that struck the Russian population in the fourteenth century in the only place where medical care, however rudimentary, might be available. Others wished to avoid conscription into the Mongol army, or punitive taxation, or whatever worldly cares beset them, or – more positively – were attracted by the reputation of a particular abbot. For whatever reason they came, people knew that once they were inside the walls of a monastery, they would be protected from external interference.

'The growth of the monastic fraternity', writes John Fennell,

> led to the increase in the number of monasteries. Monasteries begat monasteries. Monks would leave their communities, sometimes singly, sometimes in groups, sometimes as the result of a dispute with the abbot, through dissatisfaction at the strictness – or the laxity – of the rule. Sometimes monks left simply to find peace in hermitages of their own making. At the

same time princes and wealthy laymen, anxious to leave a memorial to their
names or to found a house where their kin could be buried and prayed for in
perpetuity, used their wealth to create ever new communities on their lands.[1]

This new monastic movement, like its predecessor, owed its spirituality
and its organization to Byzantine principles, but in other respects it
differed from the earlier Russian model. In their search for safety, solitude,
and silence, its leaders plunged deeper and deeper into the boundless tracts
of virgin forest that lay to the north of Moscow beyond the Volga, up to
Lake Ladoga, and on to the desolate shores of the White Sea where
conditions were extremely harsh. Even here the 'Transvolga hermits', as
they became known, were rarely left alone for long but were soon joined by
disciples, eager to sit at the feet of a charismatic elder. Groups of cells
formed themselves into small communities, or *lavras*, which in turn grew
into cenobitic monasteries. Trees were felled, crops were sown, villages
were created, and peasants from the surrounding area were settled.
The original hermit became the often-reluctant abbot of a substantial
coenobium which owned estates either donated by the state or given by
wealthy landowners. Then one of the monks would take off on his own,
with the blessing of the abbot, and found a new hermitage deeper into the
forest and the whole process would start all over again. This movement,
dubbed the 'flight into the desert' by contemporary writers, led to the
golden age of Russian monasticism, which saw numerous new monasteries
being founded in northern Russia during the fourteenth and fifteenth
centuries.

St Sergius and His Trinity Monastery

This was the environment into which Varfolomey Kirillovich, later known
as St Sergius of Radonezh, was born around 1314 in Rostov, the second son
of a noble family of boyars. St Sergius's future disciple and biographer
Epiphanius the Wise tells how the family fell on hard times and were forced
to surrender their estates when the people of Rostov were made subject to
Moscow. Then Kirill took his wife and three sons and settled in the village
of Radonezh, some 70 kilometres north-west of Moscow. The young
Varfolomey hankered after the religious life, but dutifully remained at
home to care for his ageing parents while his two brothers married. By the
time his parents died, Stephen, his elder brother, was also a widower and
had become a monk. Liberated at last from his filial duties, Varfolomey

---

[1] Fennell, *A History of the Russian Church to 1448*, p. 206.

asked Stephen to join him and search for a suitable spot for a hermitage. Stephen agreed and together they roamed the forest until they found the ideal place in a thicket near a stream. Here they constructed a shelter for themselves and also built a chapel which they dedicated to the Holy Trinity. But the life in this desert place was not easy, the bare necessities of life were hard to find, no one brought them food, and they were surrounded by a trackless forest on every side. This was more than Stephen could endure and he returned to Moscow where he settled in the monastery of the Theophany, where Alexiy, the future metropolitan, was living.[2]

Soon after his brother's departure, around 1342, Varfolomey was tonsured a monk with the name of Sergius, but he remained alone in the forest, enduring the trials of the wilderness, fighting wild beasts as well as satanic demons, even making friends with a bear, and all the while reading the Scriptures and training his mind to concentrate on prayer. After two years of this extreme austerity and physical hardship, Sergius was joined by a number of like-minded brethren who had moved into the forest in search of solitude. These men became his first disciples and Sergius gradually assumed the role of *starets* or spiritual father. In about 1354, at the insistence of his disciples, he was ordained a priest and accepted the role of abbot. Some time later, he received a delegation from Patriarch Philotheos of Constantinople (1353–4/5, 1364–76) who complimented him on his efforts but, wary perhaps of the idiorrhythmic system that was beginning to infiltrate the monasteries on Mount Athos, urged him to impose a cenobitic lifestyle. After some hesitation Sergius agreed, and by adopting the Stoudite rule the Trinity monastery became the model for all subsequent religious foundations in medieval Russia. Thus was born the Trinity monastery of St Sergius, which within the lifetime of its founder became the greatest monastery in the land (Plate 29). As Bishop Kallistos put it, 'What the Monastery of the Caves was to Kievan Russia, the Monastery of the Holy Trinity was to Muscovy.'[3]

At the time of the monastery's construction, however, the brethren still had to endure many hardships and privations. As St Epiphanius relates, sometimes there was no bread, sometimes no wine, or incense, or wax for candles. But Sergius led by example and shared every hardship with his fellow monks. He ground the grain and baked the bread and cooked the food. He carried water from the spring in buckets, placing a jug of it in each

---

[2] St Epiphanius, 'The Life of St Sergius', in Fedotov, *A Treasury of Russian Spirituality*, pp. 59–60.
[3] Ware, *The Orthodox Church*, p. 81.

cell. He made clothes and shoes for others, while his own clothes were so shabby that often visitors failed to recognize him. He performed miracles and, what is especially revealing, he saw visions that are highly reminiscent of the contemporary teaching of St Gregory Palamas on the uncreated light:

> One night the saint, who in accordance with his ordinary rule, was watching and praying for the brethren, heard a voice say: 'Sergius.' He started, and opened the window of his cell. And he saw a wondrous vision: a great light appeared in the heavens, illumining the night, so that it became brighter than day. And again there was a voice saying: 'Sergius. You pray for your children, and the Lord has heard your prayer. Look attentively, then, and you shall see a multitude of monks, assembled in the name of the holy, life-giving Trinity, to become your flock and be instructed by you.' The saint looked and beheld a multitude of beautiful birds, fluttering not only over the monastery, but all around it. And the voice said: 'Your disciples will be as many as the birds you see, and their number will not diminish after you, if they will follow in your steps.'[4]

On another occasion the saint was praying before the icon of the Mother of God when he became aware that he was about to see a wondrous vision and a voice was heard, saying: 'The Pure One is coming.'

> Hearing these words, the saint left his cell and hurried into the vestibule. Thereupon a great light, brighter than the sun, descended upon him, and he beheld the Most Pure Mother of God, accompanied by the two Apostles, Peter and Paul, radiant with an ineffable glory. Unable to bear the blinding light of that dawn, he fell with his face to the ground. The Most Pure Mother of God then touched him with her hands, saying: 'Fear nothing, elect of God. I have come to visit you. Your prayer concerning your disciples and this monastery has been heard. Therefore let nothing trouble you; from this day forth, this monastery shall have everything in abundance. And not only during your life, but also after your death, I shall be constantly with the monastery, bestowing in profusion all that is necessary, providing for it and protecting it.'[5]

It is tempting to conclude that these episodes provide evidence of the spread of hesychasm to Russia by the middle of the fourteenth century, facilitated by Sergius's close connections with Constantinople.[6] Further evidence is provided by the contents of the monastery's library, which in the fourteenth and fifteenth centuries included Slavonic translations of many of the basic texts of hesychast spirituality.

---

[4] Fedotov, *A Treasury of Russian Spirituality*, pp. 72–3. [5] Ibid., pp. 79–80.
[6] See Gabriel Bunge, *The Rublev Trinity: The Icon of the Trinity by the Monk-Painter Andrei Rublev*, trans. A. Louth (Crestwood, NY: St Vladimir's Seminary Press, 2007), p. 75.

The austerity of the regime at St Sergius's monastery did not suit all the brethren and a group of them staged a rebellion. Rather than stay in a divided house, the saint moved away into the desert and established a new hermitage near the river Kerzhak. But he was soon joined by some of his former brethren who followed him in twos and threes, and with the blessing of Metropolitan Alexiy he built a church and founded a new monastery there. Meanwhile, some of the monks at the monastery of the Holy Trinity, unable to bear the absence of their elder, asked the metropolitan to recall him. He did so, and out of obedience to his superior the saint returned and was welcomed back by the brotherhood amid scenes of great rejoicing.

Some years later, when the Russian people were greatly alarmed by the threat of an attack by the Tatar hordes, the Grand Prince Dimitri Donskoy, who had great faith in Sergius, came to the saint to ask his advice. Sergius gave the prince his blessing and encouraged him to march against the infidel: 'with God's help you shall defeat them and return unhurt to your native land, and you shall merit great praise.' The prince replied: 'If God lends me His help, I shall found a monastery in the name of the Most Pure Mother of God.' God helped the great and victorious Dimitri, the Tartars were duly defeated at the battle of Kulikovo on 8 September 1380, and this battle marked the beginning of deliverance from the Tatar yoke. Prince Dimitri returned joyfully to his native land and, true to his word, visited Sergius in order to make a generous donation to the Trinity monastery and take steps to found a monastery dedicated to the Mother of God.[7] This monastery, with Sergius's help, was in due course founded at Stronym on the Dubenka river and dedicated to the Dormition. There was at this time an explosion of monastic foundations and, if the sources are to be believed, Sergius was involved in a large proportion of them. These included the Vysotsky monastery in Serpukhov, as well as other monasteries in Pereslavi, Vladimir, and Nizhny Novgorod, all of which adopted the cenobitic rule.

Metropolitan Alexiy had also been associated with the foundation of many monasteries, including the cenobitic Chudov monastery in the Moscow kremlin in 1365. He remained in close contact with Constantinople and he was responsible for implementing the use of the Stoudite rule in these Russian houses. Adoption of the cenobitic lifestyle meant that monasteries were well placed to share resources and to acquire estates, to organize an efficient division of labour to make the best use of

---

[7] Fedotov, *A Treasury of Russian Spirituality*, pp. 77–8.

their property, and to establish an efficient network of subsidiary houses. This was to have serious implications for the future of Russian monasticism, though there is no evidence that the Trinity monastery acquired any landed property during Sergius's lifetime.

Having worked together for many years as leaders of the monastic movement, Metropolitan Alexiy and St Sergius came to have a great admiration for each other. Finding a successor to the metropolitan was not easy at a time when the political situation in Russia required that attention be paid not only to the Mongol khan (whose Horde was itself in turmoil) but also to the Orthodox rulers of Lithuania, who wanted a metropolitan who would assist them to check Roman Catholic influence from Poland. As we have seen,[8] in 1375 Patriarch Philotheos consecrated St Cyprian as metropolitan of Kiev on the understanding that, on Alexiy's death, he would be elevated to oversee all Russia. Meanwhile, Alexiy himself summoned Sergius and invited him to accept the chains of office. Sergius declined the offer, protesting his monastic humility. Alexiy called on Sergius to observe his vow of obedience, but the abbot was not to be moved, whereupon the metropolitan, accepting the saint's resolution, sent him back to his monastery. Metropolitan Alexiy died, aged eighty-five, on 12 February 1378. Four months later Cyprian set out from Kiev to assume the office that he had been promised, but it was to be another twelve years before he was able to enter Moscow as metropolitan of All Russia.

Despite his refusal to accept ecclesiastical preferment, Sergius did not remain totally aloof from public life. After baptizing Prince Dimitri's newborn son Peter in July 1385, the saint was asked by the prince later that year to travel to the neighbouring principality of Ryazan' and try to persuade its Prince Oleg to make peace with Moscow. Oleg's forces were threatening the borders of Muscovy and Dimitri realized that Sergius was perhaps the only man who could bring about a reconciliation between them. The episode is vividly described by the Trinity chronicle:

> That autumn during Advent the venerable elder Abbot Sergius went by himself to Riazan' to Grand Prince Oleg regarding peace. Previously many others had gone to him but none of them were able to pacify him. The venerable elder though with gentle words, a quiet voice and affectionate speeches by grace given to him spoke for a long time with him in a way beneficial to his soul and about peace and love. By this Prince Oleg saw his truculence become tenderness and submitted, became humble and most

affected in his soul and so shamed before the holy man [that he] concluded an eternal peace with Grand Prince [Dimitri].[9]

Duly reconciled with Oleg, Prince Dimitri died on 19 May 1389, and the next day Sergius was among the mourners at his funeral in the kremlin church of the Archangel Michael. Dimitri had seen to it that his son, Vasily (1389–1425), would be safely installed as his successor. Cyprian was at last enthroned as metropolitan, having achieved a rapprochement between Moscow and Lithuania which, like the reconciliation of Oleg with Dimitri brokered by Sergius, boded well for the future. Sergius was now enjoying unprecedented prestige and influence, but he too sensed that his days were numbered and he therefore entrusted the care of his Trinity monastery to his disciple Savva before he died in 1392. The opening of the encomium for Sergius in the Trinity chronicle (on which, see p. 169) runs as follows:

> That autumn in the month of September on the 25th day, the feast day of the venerable saint Ephrosinia [of Alexandria] the venerable Abbot Sergius, that holy elder, so estimable, unimpeachable and benevolent, gentle, humble, plainspoken, whose life surpasseth anything one can say or write, died. Formerly no one like him existed in our land who was pleasing to God and [whom] tsars and princes deemed honorable, [who] drew praise from a patriarch, in whose life unbeliever tsars and princes marveled so that they sent him gifts; [who] was universally beloved for his saintly life, who was the shepherd not only of his flock but [was] the teacher and mentor of our entire Russian land; [who was] a guide to the blind, [who helped] the lame to walk, [who was] to the sick a healer; to the hungry and thirsty a provider, [who] clothed the naked, [who] gave solace to the miserable, [and] to all Christians was the beacon without whose prayers we sinners would not receive God's mercy, to the glory of God forever, amen.[10]

Widely regarded as Russia's greatest national saint, Sergius has been described as a 'Builder of Russia', which he was in three distinct ways.[11] Politically, he favoured the ascendancy of Muscovy and its resistance to the Tatars, and there is no doubt that the diffusion of the monasteries contributed to the spread of Muscovite hegemony. Geographically, he did more than anyone else to inspire the 'flight into the desert' and the

---

[9] M. D. Priselkov (ed.), *Troitskaia letopis': Rekonstruktsiia teksta* (Moscow–Leningrad, 1950), p. 429; cited in D. B. Miller, *Saint Sergius of Radonezh, His Trinity Monastery, and the Formation of the Russian Identity* (DeKalb, IL: Northern Illinois University Press, 2010), p. 38. The Trinity chronicle itself is lost, but its text can be reconstructed on the basis of other surviving chronicles.

[10] *Troitskaia letopis'*, pp. 440–1; cited in Miller, *Saint Sergius of Radonezh*, pp. 39–40.

[11] N. Zernov, *St Sergius, Builder of Russia, with the Life, Acts and Miracles of the Holy Abbot Sergius of Radonezh* (London: SPCK, 1939).

movement of monks into the untracked forests. Spiritually, by means of his own experience of mystical prayer, he enhanced the inner life of the Russian Church. It was largely his success in achieving a balance between the social and spiritual aspects of monasticism that opened the door to the golden age of Russian spirituality that ran from 1350 to 1550.

The Cult of St Sergius

Alone of all the monastic subjects of this book, Sergius was not an Athonite, and yet to exclude him from the commonwealth would have been absurd. Russia had few masters of spirituality at the time when he began his monastic career, so he must have been largely an autodidact, and yet his way of life from the start was redolent of Palamite hesychasm. In company with his near contemporaries Kirill of Beloozero and Stefan of Perm', he looked not only to the Desert Fathers and other early practitioners of monasticism, but also to contemporary exponents on Mount Athos, in Constantinople, and in other centres of spiritual excellence. And if they were unable to obtain instruction from living elders, they searched for recently compiled manuals of monastic practice, accurate translations of liturgical texts, and other spiritual works emanating from the 'workshop of virtue' with whose luminaries they eagerly entered into correspondence. As abbot of the Trinity monastery, Sergius was in regular contact with Constantinople and frequently sought the patriarch's advice. His standing was also such that he in turn was consulted on a wide range of issues, even by the Grand Prince Dimitri who asked him to baptize his son and sought his blessing before attempting to resist the Tatars at Kulikovo in 1380. And his co-operation and that of the grand prince was sought by Byzantine envoys in 1377 when they were pushing for Cyprian to be adopted as the successor to Metropolitan Alexiy. In short, secular and ecclesiastical matters were inextricably intertwined throughout the Orthodox world and, despite its rapidly dwindling temporal power, the ultimate authority in both remained Byzantium. The terms on which Russia maintained its membership of the (Byzantine) commonwealth are summarized by Jonathan Shepard:

> This was not merely an empire of the mind, a metaphor akin to the city
> extolled as a model for well-ordered communities in the works of Sergii of
> Radonezh and other monastic writers, for membership of the common-
> wealth had always been quintessentially voluntary and was inevitably so
> after 1204. Acceptance of the Constantinopolitan patriarch's profession of
> faith and the Byzantine-authorised forms of worship – virtually the only

stable denominators of adherence to the Byzantine order – did not rule out a variety of other cultural identities or political allegiances. The weaker the empire was in material terms, the easier it became for individuals living far beyond its territorial remains, often under uncongenial regimes, to conceive of the emperor's mission as a last best hope for mankind, which might against all rational expectations be fulfilled.[12]

At the time of his death in 1392, no one thought of Sergius as a saint. No doubt his tomb was venerated by those who had known him in life, just as today the tomb of a recently deceased elder on Mount Athos is often placed in a prominent position so that it can serve as a reminder of his teaching and a focus for cherishing his memory. But in 1408 the Trinity monastery was attacked and razed to the ground by a Tatar raid and ironically this destruction was the catalyst for initiating the cult of St Sergius. When rebuilding the monastery, Sergius's former disciple Abbot Nikon (who had succeeded Savva in 1398) decided to raise a wooden church over his tomb and invited a member of the brotherhood to recite an encomium over it. In it the author, who is presumed to be Epiphanius, says that he has recently visited Athos as well as Constantinople and Jerusalem, a pilgrimage that will have deepened his understanding of the conventions of hagiography. Following the traditions of the genre, Epiphanius lavishes praise on Sergius and devotes twenty pages to an extravagant elaboration of the content of the opening paragraph on his death, quoted above. Still the encomium says nothing about miracles that might have been worked by Sergius, though it does mention that by means of prayer he cured many who were sick and describes him as 'adorned in the manner of a monk, but even more [he looked] like an angel'. The fathers who listened to the encomium were presumably left to draw their own conclusions.[13]

As if that were not sufficient, Andrey Rublev (1370–1430), the most famous iconographer of the time (if not of all time), painted his celebrated icon of the Holy Trinity for this little wooden church (Plate 30). Now safely housed in the anodyne environment of the Tretyakov Gallery in Moscow, it is surely the best-known icon in the world and needs no description here. What does need to be imagined is the electrifying effect that its appearance on the iconostasis of this small dark church would have had on the assembled brotherhood. Rublev was himself a monk and his work was deeply permeated by contemporary currents of hesychast

---

[12] Shepard, 'The Byzantine Commonwealth 1000–1550', p. 45.
[13] Miller, *Saint Sergius of Radonezh*, pp. 42–4.

spirituality. Anita Strezova, who has made a close study of his icon and its relation to hesychasm, thinks that Rublev may have been influenced by an earlier icon of the Holy Trinity that takes pride of place in the katholikon of the monastery of Vatopedi:

> The spread of hesychasm and the interchange between the Byzantine and Russian traditions reflected in the art of Mt Athos, resulted in paintings reflecting an intermingling of Russian and Byzantine style. Rublev painted his icon under the direct influence of Byzantine icons from Athos, where the cult of the Trinity existed before the 15th century. The icon of the *Trinity* from the Monastery of Vatopedi on Mt Athos . . . attests to this fact. It is possible that the Vatopedi icon served as a prototype, due to the close associations between the monastic communities of the Trinity Sergius Lavra, and those of Mt Athos, beginning in the time of Sergius and Metropolitan Cyprian. The icon of the *Trinity* from the Monastery of Vatopedi, painted at the end of the 14th century, also attests to the widespread representation of the new hesychast iconography of the Holy Trinity.[14]

Of course, the fact that an icon is on Athos now does not necessarily mean that it has always been there. According to tradition, the Vatopedi Trinity and its companion, the Virgin Hodegetria, which both date from the last quarter of the fourteenth century, came from the church of Hagia Sophia in Thessaloniki and were only brought to Vatopedi when that church was turned into a mosque in 1523/4.[15]

In this newly painted icon by Rublev, dazzling with its brilliant palette of colours, the three figures of the Holy Trinity are bathed in the uncreated light of God in which Christ appeared to the apostles on Mount Tabor at the time of his Transfiguration. If the fathers' thoughts did not turn straight to the writings of St Gregory Palamas, they would surely at least have recalled the visions of light that Sergius had himself experienced and described to them while he was their abbot. As David Miller writes,

> Even if only few of those present had knowledge of recent models for the icon in eastern iconography, here where their master lay buried, they gazed on a new symbol of hope, made wondrous by the quiet power exuded by its figures. Rublev offered the image and its promise in open denial of the misery and fear that washed over the land in the wake of Edigei's Mongol raiders.[16]

---

[14] Strezova, *Hesychasm and Art*, pp. 173–219 (209).

[15] See N. Tsigaridas and K. Loverdou-Tsigarida, *Holy and Great Monastery of Vatopaidi: Byzantine Icons and Revetments* (Mount Athos: Holy and Great Monastery of Vatopaidi, 2007), pp. 174–81.

[16] Miller, *Saint Sergius of Radonezh*, p. 45.

For Dimitri Obolensky this icon represents the culmination of everything that is implied in his understanding of the Byzantine Commonwealth, for he ends the final chapter of his book with these words:

> Never before or since did the Byzantine tradition reach such mature perfection on Russian soil as in the figures of the three angels, symbolizing the triune God, seated in total stillness round the eucharistic table, expressing in a subtle rhythm the idea of harmony and mutual love. It is with good reason that this masterpiece of medieval Russian painting has been called 'a Greek hymn upon a Slavonic tongue'.[17]

In 1422, thirty years after Sergius's death, the foundations were laid of a new church to be built of stone and dedicated to the Holy Trinity. To it Abbot Nikon translated the relics of his beloved predecessor, proclaiming him at the same time to be a saint. Rublev's icon was prominently displayed immediately to the right of the royal doors and it soon became the palladium of the monastery. Evidence of this is provided in the many representations of Sergius's vision of the Mother of God in which the icon always occupies a central position symbolizing the house that she has placed under her personal protection. The church of the Holy Trinity stands to this day as the spiritual heart of the monastery, if not of the whole of Russia, to which witness is borne by the never-ending queue of silent pilgrims patiently waiting their turn to venerate the saint's relics, which are contained in a magnificent silver casket to the right of the iconostasis. Still in the monastery's treasury is the remarkably well-preserved, full-length shroud depicting the saint that dates from about 1424 and was presumably woven as a cover for his tomb. Finally, Monk Pakhomy the Serb, rewriting Epiphanius's Life of Sergius in the 1430s, compared the abbot's vision of the Mother of God and her promise to protect the monastery to that experienced by St Athanasios of Athos at a similar moment of crisis. The copy of the Life of Athanasios that was available to Pakhomy in the library of the Trinity monastery is dated 1431 and inscribed: 'this book was copied at the holy mountain of Athos ... in the laura of the great Athanasius ... by the most sinful and humble monk Afanasii the Russian', who presumably also translated it from the Greek. Knowing that St Athanasios was commemorated on 5 July, it must therefore have been Pakhomy who first dated the translation of Sergius's relics to that same date, thus marking him out to be a saint in the image of Athanasios of

---

[17] Obolensky, *The Byzantine Commonwealth*, p. 464, quoting C. R. Morey, *Medieval Art* (New York: W. W. Norton & Co., 1942), p. 167.

Athos and at the same time confirming his honorary membership of the
Athonite Commonwealth.[18]

The Successors of St Sergius

The Trinity monastery set the pattern for a large number of new monastic
foundations in northern Russia in the fourteenth and fifteenth centuries.
Following Sergius's own example, many of his disciples and associates set
off alone into the forest to identify a site suitable for their own hermitages.
Once established, they attracted others who settled in cells around them
and formed small communities, which in turn developed into monasteries.
But the forest was not to everyone's taste and others moved into nearby
towns such as Zvenigorod, Serpukhov, Kolomna, and especially Moscow,
where again they laid the beginnings of monasteries. It has been estimated
that during this period as many as twenty-seven forest hermitages and eight
town monasteries were founded by monks from the Trinity monastery and
its offshoots.

The Simonov monastery in Moscow was founded in 1370 by monk
Feodor, a nephew and disciple of Sergius, who became its first abbot.
In 1388 Abbot Feodor was made bishop of Rostov, and Kirill (d.1427),
a humble monk deeply devoted to ascetic pursuits, was appointed to
succeed him, much against his will. In 1392 Kirill left the monastery and
together with a fellow monk called Ferapont travelled north for about 500
kilometres until he came to the region of the White Lake. Here at
Beloozero he founded a hermitage where he was soon joined by both
local people and by more monks from the Simonov monastery, and in
due course the hermitage became the Kirillo-Belozersky monastery, one of
the greatest religious houses in northern Russia (Plate 31). Kirill adopted
a very strict attitude to the rule, which he imposed with severity, but recent
research has suggested that the community that he formed was initially
a lavra and not a coenobium.[19] According to Monk Pakhomy the Serb,
who visited the monastery and (in about 1462) wrote a Life of Kirill, monks
were not allowed wine in the refectory or drinking water in their cells; nor
were they permitted to ask visitors for alms. Kirill himself, who was
glorified as a saint only some twenty years after his death, was strongly
opposed to monasteries acquiring landed property. Once when he was

---

[18] Miller, *Saint Sergius of Radonezh*, p. 55.
[19] See R. Romanchuk, *Byzantine Hermeneutics and Pedagogy in the Russian North: Monks and Masters at the Kirillo-Belozerskii Monastery 1397–1501* (Toronto, Buffalo, London: University of Toronto Press, 2007), pp. 95–104.

offered the gift of a village by a wealthy boyar, the saint declined the offer, saying to himself:

> If we shall own villages, there will come from them only noise and cares for the brethren, and our silence will be interrupted; we shall have settlers and contractors. Would it not be better for us to live without villages? For the soul of one brother is more precious than all possessions.[20]

Meanwhile, Ferapont found the conditions at Beloozero too harsh and established a hermitage of his own nearby, which in turn grew into a major foundation, the Ferapontov monastery, which attracted numerous hermits to the region (Plate 32).

Many more hermits settled further south in the dense forests around Vologda and Kostroma, some of them living in complete isolation. St Paul, for example, a former disciple of St Sergius, apparently spent several years living in the hollow of a lime tree before building himself a hermitage near the confluence of the rivers Obnora and Nurma, in which he could devote himself to prayer and fasting. Not far away another ascetic was living, St Sergius of Nurma, who had been tonsured and ordained priest on Mount Athos. He too had sought wisdom at the feet of his namesake of Radonezh who had sent him into the forest to settle. Here he was joined by a large number of brethren for whom he built a church dedicated to the Transfiguration and founded a cenobitic monastery. The two elders became close friends and St Paul chose the Athonite Sergius (as he was known) to be his spiritual father. Gradually more ascetics began to gather around St Paul. Reluctant to give up his solitude, he finally yielded and agreed to found a monastery but on condition that one of his disciples would serve as abbot and he himself could withdraw to his former hermitage. According to his Life, he died in 1429 at the age of 112.[21]

A number of religious houses were founded in the area of Lake Kubena, which lies to the south-east of Beloozero, including the Spaso-Kamenny monastery. Its first abbot was an Athonite called Dionisy who arrived during the reign of Dimitri Donskoy (1359–89) bringing a strict Athonite rule with him. Several of his disciples founded subsidiary houses in the area. St Dionisy Glushitsky (d.1437), for example, revived an old monastery beside the lake and also founded a hermitage on the river Glushitsa from which as many as seven *metochia* were established in the neighbourhood.

[20] The Life of St Cyril of Belozersk, in Fr Seraphim (Rose) and Fr Herman (Podmoshensky) (trans.), *The Northern Thebaid: Monastic Saints of the Russian North* (Platina, CA: St Herman of Alaska Brotherhood, 2004), p. 64.

[21] The Life of St Paul of Obnora, in Rose and Podmoshensky, *The Northern Thebaid*, p. 47.

Others, even more intrepid, setting out from the Kirillo-Belozersky monastery, travelled further and further north. Aleksandr Oshevensky (d.1479), for example, founded the Oshevensky monastery near Kargopol' in the province of Archangel.

In 1427 another ascetic, Savvaty by name, received a blessing from Kirill to leave Beloozero and trek to the monastery of Valaam, which stands on an island in the middle of Lake Ladoga (Plate 34). The origins of Valaam are obscure, but it is not far from the Konevitsa monastery, which is also on an island in Lake Ladoga and was founded in the fourteenth century by Arseny who had visited Athos and brought Athonite spirituality to the place. Valaam also claims to have received its cenobitic rule direct from Athos, and it seems that there was a web of connections between Athos and northern Russia at the end of the fourteenth century. Savvaty spent no more than two years at Valaam, but he quickly gained a reputation for extreme asceticism and was sought out by the younger brethren for his spiritual guidance. Fearful that his life was becoming too easy in the monastery, he set out again in search of solitude, looking for somewhere to settle as a hermit. Travelling north to the shore of the White Sea, not far short of the Arctic Circle, he asked the local people about the island of Solovki which stood opposite. They told him that it was suitable for habitation in that it had plenty of fresh water as well as timber for building and good fishing, but it was uninhabited because of the difficulties of communication, since it took two days to reach it by boat even in calm weather and the passage was possible only from June to August. Such a place was inhospitable to the local people but well suited for ascetic labours, characteristics that the region shared with the far-away deserts of Egypt and of Athos, hence its sobriquets the 'Northern Thebaid' and the 'Athos of the north'.[22]

Near the shore, Savvaty encountered another younger hermit named Herman who was living nearby. The two of them decided to settle together on Solovki where they built a hermitage and lived for six years, barely surviving on a diet of berries, mushrooms, and fish. From time to time Herman sailed back to the mainland to obtain provisions and, when he was away on one such trip in 1435, the older monk died. Bereft of his spiritual father, Herman went in search of another companion as he knew that he could not live alone on Solovki. Eventually he found someone, a younger man called Zosima, whose looks reminded him of Savvaty. Together they decided to return to Solovki and this time try to build a cenobitic

[22] The Life of St Sabbatius of Solovki, in Rose and Podmoshensky, *The Northern Thebaid*, pp. 72–85.

monastery rather than just a hermitage. Their holy way of life attracted others to join them, and in due course a brotherhood emerged and after forty years of toil Zosima found himself abbot of an established monastery. The house prospered and was granted estates by wealthy landowners. The brotherhood soon numbered 200, mostly drawn from neighbouring towns and villages, and in the course of its history it produced a whole army of saints whose Lives may be read in the Solovki *Paterikon* of 1873.[23] In 1471 word reached Zosima that Savvaty was buried in the Kirillo-Belozersky monastery. Realizing that he must be a saint, Zosima immediately travelled south in order to recover the body and bring it back to Solovki where it was reburied with due honour beside the altar. Seven years later Zosima himself died and the two saints are revered to this day as joint founders of the monastery (Plate 33).

St Nil Sorsky

Cenobitic monasticism on Athonite principles had now spread all the way from Moscow to the White Sea. All of European Russia was now included in the Athonite Commonwealth, but only one or two of the elders named above were themselves Athonites. All of them knew of the Holy Mountain and held its traditions and its spirituality in great respect. Their libraries contained books that had been copied there, but very few of them had actually been there. The dynamic thrust, the 'flight into the desert', was so far largely northbound. Nil Sorsky would buck the trend.

Details of Nil's early life are sketchy since he wrote little and no contemporary biography survives.[24] Even his baptismal name is unknown, Nil being his monastic name, but it seems likely that he was born to a well-to-do Muscovite family in about 1433. At least he and his brother (who later became a diplomat) were given a good education, and at an early age Nil entered the Kirillo-Belozersky monastery near the White Lake as a novice some time in the early 1450s. By this time the monastery was well established as a cenobitic community – 'much more recognizably Byzantine and Athonite' – with a secondary school attached (possibly the only one in Russia at the time) and a well-stocked library, and it was enjoying a period

[23] Ibid., p. 86. See also Roy R. Robson, *Solovki: The Story of Russia Told through its most Remarkable Islands* (New Haven, CT, and London: Yale University Press, 2004), pp. 6–25, and J. B. Spock, 'Monasticism in Russia's Far North in the Pre-Petrine Era', in Murzaku, *Monasticism in Eastern Europe and the Former Soviet Republics*, pp. 285–307.

[24] See G. A. Maloney, *Russian Hesychasm: The Spirituality of Nil Sorskij* (The Hague/Paris: Mouton, 1973), pp. 33–47, and Romanchuk, *Byzantine Hermeneutics*, pp. 192–204.

of growth under the strong leadership of Abbot Kassian (r. 1448–70).[25] Despite the forcefully expressed wishes of the founder, the house had grown wealthy and had acquired extensive landholdings, tax concessions, and generous donations from lay benefactors in return for promises of commemoration in perpetuity. Such wealth was in due course to ignite an internal debate that would spread far beyond the walls of the monastery and engulf the whole country in a controversy about the legitimacy of monastic estates. The monastery was also in the process of becoming a centre of learning with a scriptorium engaged in copying and editing works of Byzantine hagiography and theology as well as secular works such as histories and chronicles. If Nil found himself developing his skills here, it would have given him an opportunity to extend his knowledge of the classic texts of hesychast prayer and spirituality. It would also have brought him into contact with other learned men, perhaps including Monk Pakhomy the Serb who visited the monastery in order to collect information for the Life he was writing of St Kirill.[26]

Who his spiritual mentors were is not known, though Paisy Yaroslavov (d.1501), subsequently abbot of the Trinity monastery, may have been one of them. The nineteenth-century Life of Nil, preserved in the *Paterikon* of the Trinity monastery, asserts that he was, though doubt has been cast on this by others in the light of Paisy's support for the landholding monasteries, which Nil would have opposed.[27] It seems also that Nil acquired a disciple named Innokenty, and the two of them probably sometime in the 1470s travelled south to Mount Athos, 'in search of the true sources of Orthodox monastic life', as the Life puts it. They may also have visited Constantinople and (rather less likely) Palestine to broaden their experience of monasticism, but they seem to have spent longest on the Holy Mountain, steeping themselves in its hesychast traditions and acquiring first-hand understanding of mystical prayer at the feet of an instructor. Exactly where on Athos they went is not known, though the Life suggests they may have spent time at the Russian monastery of Xylourgou, near the present skete of the Prophet Elijah, and that Nil studied all forms of monastic asceticism, especially the 'skete life' which was new to him.

---

[25] Romanchuk, *Byzantine Hermeneutics*, p. 128.

[26] The Kirillo-Belozersky monastery survives and remains one of the largest monasteries in Russia today. But most of its (very grand) buildings serve as a museum and the brotherhood (which at the time of writing consists of seven monks and three novices) is confined to a secluded priory.

[27] The Life of St Nilus of Sora, in Rose and Podmoshensky, *The Northern Thebaid*, p. 89, and T. Allan Smith, 'Nil Sorskii', in Augustine Casiday (ed.), *The Orthodox Christian World* (London and New York: Routledge, 2012), p. 304; see also D. Goldfrank (trans., ed.), *Nil Sorsky: The Authentic Writings* (Kalamazoo, MI: Cistercian Publications, 2008), pp. 33–61.

Plate 30. Andrey Rublev's celebrated icon of the Holy Trinity was originally painted
for the Trinity monastery of St Sergius. At a synod in 1551 the Russian Church
established it as the canonical model for all subsequent depictions of the Trinity.
Tretyakov Gallery, Moscow.

Plate 31. Walls and towers of the Kirillo-Belozersky monastery in northern Russia, founded in 1397 by St Sergius's disciple Kirill.

Plate 32. The entrance to the cathedral of the Ferapontov monastery in northern Russia, founded in 1398 by Kirill's former companion Ferapont. Its frescos, by the renowned artist Dionisy, date from 1495–6.

Plate 33. An icon of Sts Savvaty and Zosima standing either side of the monastery of Solovki which they founded on a remote island in the White Sea close to the Arctic Circle. It became a notorious prison camp in the twentieth century. Icon Museum, Vologda.

Most importantly, he strove everywhere to enter into the meaning and spirit of the so-called *mental monastic work*, the inward self-trial and practice of the Jesus Prayer, applying everything to his own spiritual life. He attentively studied and applied in experience the teachings of the Divinely-wise Holy Fathers; Sts Anthony the Great, Ephraim and Isaac of Syria, Barsanuphius, John of the Ladder, Abba Dorotheus, Maximus the Confessor, Hesychius, Simeon the New Theologian, Peter Damascene, and Gregory, Nilus, and Philotheus of Sinai.[28]

As a result of his experiences on Athos, Nil determined to return to Russia and to introduce the practice of monks living together not in monasteries but in small groups gathered in obedience to an elder. This middle path, sometimes referred to as the 'royal way', represents a way of life that is halfway between that of a cenobitic brotherhood and that of a solitary hermit, and is the way preferred on Athos by such masters of hesychast practice as St Gregory Palamas and St Gregory of Sinai.

On his return to the White Lake, Nil put this scheme into practice and first built himself a small timber cell close to the monastery. But this proximity to the main house did not give him the seclusion he needed, and he soon moved to a site beside the river Sora (hence his name Sorsky), about 15 kilometres away. The place he chose for his skete is described in the Life as desolate, swampy, and surrounded by forest, but here he and Innokenty built a cell in which they could live a simple life practising stillness and unceasing prayer. In due course, they were joined by other like-minded monks and together they built a chapel dedicated to the Meeting of the Lord and another in honour of St Ephraim the Syrian, but the community remained small and never numbered more than a dozen. The brethren would come together for a vigil service in preparation for the Divine Liturgy on Sunday and on feast days, but for the rest of the week each monk would remain alone in his own cell, devoting himself to prayer and stillness and doing whatever manual work was necessary for his material needs. The *Skete Typikon*, which Nil adapted from that of the Kirillo-Belozersky monastery, describes the daily routine that was prescribed for monks of the skete. Kirill had made provision in his rule for illiterate monks, who were told to say the Jesus Prayer when they did not know the psalms set for the day. Nil omitted that concession, though he did prescribe it for those unable to be in church:

---

[28] Rose and Podmoshensky, *The Northern Thebaid*, p. 90. See also Romanchuk, *Byzantine Hermeneutics*, pp. 193–4.

> And again, if someone is unable to sing, and it happens to such a one to be
> somewhere by necessity without a church, or without brothers able to sing,
> then he shall sing the Trisagion and the prayer, holding the prayer rope in
> his hand – as has been said above, each according to his strength.[29]

Despite his retreat from the world, Nil gained a reputation for spiritual wisdom that spread beyond the confines of the forest, and in 1490 he was asked by Metropolitan Gennady of Novgorod to attend a council convened to formulate measures to be taken against the Judaizing heretics. Together with Iosif Volotsky, abbot of Volokolamsk monastery, Nil took a strong line in defence of Orthodoxy, though he advocated clemency when it was suggested that the heretics be burnt. In 1503, according to some traditions, Nil attended another council, this one convened to discuss the tendentious issue of monastic landholdings, and this time Nil found himself bitterly opposed to Abbot Iosif. Both Sergius and Kirill had striven to preserve a balance between the social and the spiritual aspects of monasticism in their respective monasteries and had resisted the temptation to accept donations of villages and estates. However, since their time not only the Trinity and the Belozersky but all the major monasteries in northern Russia had become extremely wealthy, and by the end of the fifteenth century a third of the land in Russia was owned by the monks. Both Nil and Iosif delivered passionate speeches from opposite sides at the council. Most of those present came from the large monasteries and supported Iosif, and they were known as the Possessors; but there were others, mostly the 'Transvolga hermits', who agreed with Nil, and they were called the Non-Possessors. The Possessors defended their position on the grounds that monks had a duty to care for the sick and to provide hospitality and teaching; to carry out these tasks efficiently they needed an income and for that they needed land. The Non-Possessors on the other hand believed that a monk's first duty was to pray and to demonstrate his care for others by means of prayer; to do this properly he needed to be detached from the world and such detachment could only be achieved by adhering strictly to the vow of poverty. They maintained that monks who owned land and employed serfs, albeit on behalf of their monasteries and not for their own benefit, inevitably became embroiled in secular affairs and could not but operate in a worldly fashion. Nil was outnumbered by Iosif and his supporters,

---

[29] Goldfrank, *Nil Sorsky*, p. 265. The prayer rope is a circle or chaplet, usually made of wool or twine, that is used to accompany the recitation of the Jesus Prayer. It is primarily an aid to concentration. No Orthodox monastic is ever seen without one.

but there was continuing tension between the opposing parties for many years. The Possessors were victorious for the moment, but their victory had unforeseen consequences in the subsequent secularization of the Church in the seventeenth and eighteenth centuries. Meanwhile, the spirit of Nil, though driven underground, continued to smoulder like charcoal, and his writings were to resurface in the nineteenth century when they exercised considerable influence on the spiritual revival that was initiated by St Nikodimos of the Holy Mountain, St Paisy Velichkovsky, and the elders of Optino.

Though a large number of spurious texts have been attributed to him, Nil's authentic writings were few. Of the latter, by far the most substantial is his *Ustav* (or *Typikon*), which fills 100 pages in its printed English translation[30] and comprises spiritual guidance intended for all monks rather than rules directed specifically at his skete monks. It contains eleven discourses, which may be divided into three parts: part 1 (discourses 1–4) is concerned with the struggle for stillness and against the passions and proclaims hesychasm to be the only correct path for monks; part 2 (discourses 5–6) is a treatise on the eight principal passions (pride, despondency, lust, gluttony, anger, vainglory, sadness, and avarice); part 3 (discourses 7–11) stresses the need for remembrance of death, for tears, and for detachment from the world. His debt to his sources is apparent from the calculations made by David Goldfrank, his most recent translator. In the *Ustav*, 9.6 per cent of the text is taken from St Isaac the Syrian, 9.1 per cent from St Gregory of Sinai, and 7.8 per cent from St John Klimakos. Not surprisingly, his debt to the Sinaite is especially apparent in what he has to say about prayer of the heart and stillness of the intellect, when he exhorts the monk to

> speak diligently, be you standing, sitting, or lying down, and confine your intellect within your heart and hold your respiration as much as you can, so that you do not breathe often ... And if you cannot pray in stillness of the heart, without urges, but see them multiplying in your intellect, do not be faint-hearted over this, but still persevere in praying. And the blessed Gregory the Sinaite, knowing full well that it is impossible for us, the passionate, to defeat wicked urges, said this: No neophyte restrains his intellect and drives off urges, if God does not restrain him and drive away the urges ... And, instead of armament, summon the Lord Jesus often and assiduously, and they shall flee, as if invisibly seared by the fire of the divine name.[31]

[30] Ibid., pp. 124–227.   [31] Ibid., pp. 139–40.

In a much shorter work, the *Predanie* (or *Tradition*), Nil writes about the requirement to know, heed, and practise the traditions, by which he means the wisdom handed down by the spiritual masters of the past. Thus, 'If any brother, through sloth or negligence, falls away from his traditions in some wise, he should confess this to the superior and the latter, as is proper, shall correct the transgression.' Similarly, 'It is improper for us to have excess goods . . . That is an obvious monk, who need not give alms . . . St Isaac writes: non-possession is superior to such giving. The monk's alms are to aid a brother with a word at a time of need and to console the afflicted with spiritual discretion.'[32] But his most outspoken criticism of the Possessors is contained in his discourse on pride in the *Ustav*:

> And to have the title of the finest monastery in a place and a multitude of brothers – this is the pride of the worldly, the Fathers said – or, according to the prevailing custom now, from the acquisition of villages, and accumulation of many properties, and from success in worldly reputation – what can we say about this? . . . their glory is shame.[33]

Apart from occasional forays into the outside world to attend councils and defend his way of life, Nil remained at his skete, enjoying the seclusion of the forest, copying texts of the Fathers, and practising hesychasm until his death in 1508 at the age of seventy-five. Before he died, he compiled a *Testament* in which he asked that his body remain unburied:

> After my death, cast my body into the desert for the animals and birds to devour, for it has so foully sinned against God that it is unworthy of burial. And if they do not do this, let them dig a hole at the place where we live and bury me without any consideration. I have striven with all my might throughout my life to receive neither honour nor praise in the monastery; let it be so after my death.[34]

Nil's wishes were followed by his brethren and they buried his body in a simple grave near the church of the skete. The skete survived into the mid eighteenth century, but it remained one of the poorest in the whole of Russia and its brotherhood was always small, just as its founder had intended. Also out of respect for his wishes, St Nil was not officially canonized by the Church until 1903, but rather he was glorified by the will of the faithful. He continues to be revered as one of the greatest saints and one of the most respected spiritual guides of all Russia. Fr George Maloney summarizes Nil's place in the Russian spiritual tradition thus:

[32] Ibid., pp. 117–19. [33] Ibid., pp. 186–7.
[34] Hieromonk Makarios, *The Synaxarion*, vol. 5 (2005), p. 80.

As he repeated so often, he was a mere channel through which passed the riches of the Holy Fathers to Russian monasticism and hence to the Russian people. In his humility he never felt himself as an original writer or spiritual director. He was gathering 'crumbs' that fell from the table of the Holy Fathers and he was passing them on to those who cared to profit from his teaching. But perhaps in this lies his true greatness, that Nil, in so doing, passed on the rich heritage of the early Fathers of the Church who formed for both the East and the West the one common ancient monastic tradition plus the Fathers of the later hesychastic mysticism.[35]

---

[35] Maloney, *Russian Hesychasm*, p. 47.

CHAPTER 12

St Maximos the Greek (c.1470–1556): Enlightener of Russia

The debate about monastic landownership was still smouldering when in 1522 Abbot Daniil of Volokolamsk, leader of the so-called Possessors, was appointed bishop of Moscow and primate of the entire Russian Church. When St Maximos, known as 'the Greek', was asked by Daniil to translate a book that supported monastic ownership of estates among other controversial matters, he declined. This was no doubt unwise, but Maximos, though he was a foreigner and an Athonite to boot, was outspoken in his criticism of anything that contradicted his understanding of the truth. Whenever he encountered corruption, be it in the social circles that he moved in or in the texts that he was asked to translate, he was programmed by his academic education and his monastic formation to eradicate it. For his pains, he was rewarded with a sentence of life imprisonment.[1]

From Arta to Italy (*c.1470–c.1505*)

Michael Trivolis, who was later to be known as the monk Maximos, was born in Arta in about 1470 to a prosperous Greek family of Peloponnesian origin. At the time Arta still retained the trappings of a Byzantine metropolis, having survived until 1449 as the capital of the despotate of Epirus, which had come into existence in the wake of the Fourth Crusade in 1204. But for much of the fifteenth century the dominant power in the region was Venice, and though the city adhered to Byzantine traditions of faith and language, culturally it looked more to Italy than to either Thessaloniki or Constantinople. The principal church, for example, dedicated to

---

[1] On Maximos's life, see especially J. V. Haney, *From Italy to Muscovy: The Life and Works of Maxim the Greek* (Munich: Fink, 1973); D. Obolensky, 'Maximos the Greek', in *Six Byzantine Portraits*, pp. 201–19; D. J. Geanakoplos, 'The Post-Byzantine Athonite Monk Maximos "the Greek": Reformer of Orthodoxy in Sixteenth Century Russia', *Greek Orthodox Theological Review*, 33 (1988), 445–68; and most recently A.-E. N. Tachiaos, 'The Greek Monk Maximus Trivolis between Eastern and Western Religious Tradition', *Studi Slavistici*, 7 (2010), 327–37.

Panagia Parigoritissa, conceals its inner cruciform plan so successfully that, seen from the west, it could easily be taken for a three-storey central Italian *palazzo*. Venetian influence was even more apparent in Corfu, where the family moved to when Michael was about ten. Both cities would have provided him with perfectly adequate primary and secondary schooling, and in Corfu he studied philosophy and rhetoric under the learned John Moschos. But to obtain the best higher education available, it was necessary for him to travel to Italy, where he settled first in Florence and later in Venice, both cities renowned at the time as centres of Greek scholarship.

Michael spent about three years in Florence (*c.*1492–5) where his academic mentors were the Greek scholar Janus Laskaris (1445–1535) and the Platonist philosopher Marsilio Ficino (1433–99). Laskaris shared refugee status with Michael, having fled with his family from Asia Minor following the ill-starred Council of Ferrara–Florence (1438–9), but was now established as one of the most respected scholars in Renaissance Florence. He found employment at the court of Lorenzo de' Medici where he taught Greek and for whom he made two journeys to the east to collect Greek manuscripts, the second of which (1491) took him to Athos. He came back with more than 200 manuscripts, 74 of them from Athos.[2] Michael supported himself by copying manuscripts for Laskaris, including a text of the *Geoponica*, a popular farming encyclopaedia compiled in the tenth century, which is signed by Michael and preserved in the Bibliothèque Nationale in Paris. Laskaris introduced Michael to many of the leading scholars of the day, including Ficino, Giovanni Pico della Mirandola, Angelo Poliziano, and possibly Michelangelo. Ficino also enjoyed the patronage of the Medicis and was appointed by Cosimo to be the head of his Platonic Academy and also tutor to his grandson Lorenzo. Ficino was one of the greatest philosophers in Florence and argued in his *Theologia Platonica* that Plato's philosophy provided a secular proof of the validity of Christian doctrine. His was the first translation of Plato to be done into Latin; it was printed in 1484 in an edition of over 1,000 copies, which sold out within a few years. Laskaris and Ficino were probably the two most influential scholars in Florence at the time, and the young Trivolis was fortunate to number them among his instructors.

He also came under the spiritual influence of the Dominican friar, preacher, and prophet Girolamo Savonarola (1452–98), whose sermons he listened to, even if he did not meet him in person. Savonarola was

---

[2] See G. Speake, 'Janus Lascaris' Visit to Mount Athos', *Greek, Roman, and Byzantine Studies*, 34: 3 (1993), 325–30.

outspoken in his denunciation of clerical corruption and was renowned also for his love of poverty and his courage in the face of adversity, characteristics that may have appealed to the impressionable Michael.

Meanwhile, after visiting a number of other Italian cities (Bologna, Padua, and Milan) and possibly even Paris (whose university he described in some detail in his later writings, though there is no evidence that he actually went there), Michael settled in Venice from 1496 to 1498. At the end of his book on relations between Venice and Byzantium, Donald Nicol quotes the Latinizing Cardinal Bessarion's description of the city as 'like another Byzantium'. It was at this time the greatest centre of Greek scholarship not just in Italy but in the whole Western world, and here Michael will have encountered many of the most eminent scholars of the day.[3] That is why in 1495 Aldus Manutius (1449–1515) chose Venice as the place to establish his Aldine press with the specific aim of preserving the texts of ancient Greek literature. Nicol goes on, 'Venice alone had the raw material in the form of Greek manuscripts, a rich and leisured class who could afford the money to buy and the time to read the classics in print, and above all the native Greek copyists, editors and typesetters.'[4] For at least three months Michael was a member of this team, a training that he would put to good use later in his career.

In 1498 Michael went to live in Mirandola, Pico's family home, though the famous humanist of that name was now dead. Here for the first time since leaving Greece he studied the Church Fathers with Pico's nephew, Gianfrancesco (1470–1533). The two of them will have been shocked by the execution of Savonarola on 23 May 1498. They may have worked together on some of Gianfrancesco's early works, such as the *De Imaginatione* (1500), the *De Rerum Praenotione* (1501), and the *Theoremata de Fide et Ordine Credendi* (1502), which are partly translations from the Greek. In his philosophical treatises, Gianfrancesco attempts to rethink and restate Christian doctrine in the full light of the newly discovered philosophers of Greece and Rome. One positive outcome of their collaboration was Michael's return to Christianity following a period of uncertainty.[5]

In 1502 he renounced his past life and entered the Dominican priory of San Marco in Florence, where Savonarola had been prior until his death

---

[3] D. M. Nicol, *Byzantium and Venice* (Cambridge: Cambridge University Press, 1988), p. 419. See also D. J. Geanakoplos, *Greek Scholars in Venice: Studies in the Dissemination of Greek Learning from Byzantium to Western Europe* (Cambridge, MA: Harvard University Press, 1962); and N. G. Wilson, *From Byzantium to Italy: Greek Studies in the Renaissance* (London: Duckworth, 1992).

[4] Nicol, *Byzantium and Venice*, p. 420.

[5] See Tachiaos, 'The Greek Monk Maximus Trivolis', pp. 330–1.

four years earlier. But as Jack Haney writes, we should not necessarily assume that he was renouncing his Orthodox upbringing:

> Michael's return to the faith should not be interpreted as a victory for the Latin Church. The Church itself attracted him, but it was the Church of the Greek fathers, not the Church of Pope Alexander VI. His conversion was to Christianity and not to Catholicism.[6]

This was Michael's first experience of life as a friar and he cannot have found it easy. The brotherhood was bitterly divided over its opinion of their recently departed leader, Savonarola. The resulting turmoil and internal conflict made life impossible for the novice Michael and after just two years he decided to leave on the grounds of ill health. By April 1504 he was writing from Florence to a friend that he had abandoned the religious life and he compared his current distressed state to that of a ship tossed by the waves in mid-ocean.

From Italy to Athos (*c.*1505–1516)

After his brief flirtation with the Dominicans, and after some twelve years away from home, Michael decided in 1505 or 1506 to return to his native Greece. Whether he spent any time with his family in Corfu is not known, for he is next heard of as monk Maximos at the monastery of Vatopedi on Mount Athos (Plate 35). It appears from later writings that he had developed serious reservations about certain doctrines of the Western Church, especially the double procession of the Holy Spirit entailed by the insertion of the *Filioque* into the Creed. He was also disturbed by the behaviour of the popes, not so much their claim to universal primacy as what he saw as their arrogant attempts to extend their own temporal power. Relations between Rome and Constantinople had deteriorated since the discredited Council of Florence in 1439, and though there was still a good deal of tolerance and even intercommunion in places such as Corfu and Venice where Greeks and Latins rubbed shoulders on a daily basis, attitudes were becoming entrenched. Maximos's criticisms were restrained and courteous, but he found himself in a monastery where no quarter was given to the Latin Church.

The move to Athos may have been partly inspired by what he had heard from his teacher Janus Laskaris. As for the choice of monastery, again Laskaris will have described to him the rich contents of Vatopedi's library,

---

[6] Haney, *From Italy to Muscovy*, p. 26.

which included the collections of the emperors Andronikos II and John VI Kantakouzenos, and this may well have influenced his decision.[7] Whatever his reasons were, it was certainly a happy choice and for the rest of his life Maximos was to regard Vatopedi as his spiritual home. This time he must have found it relatively easy to adapt to his monastic environment and have been happy with it, for he spent ten years at Vatopedi, though it has been suggested that he may in due course have rebelled against the strictures of cenobitic obedience and moved outside the walls of the monastery to live in a nearby skete or cell.[8]

It was the Russian scholar Elie Denissoff who first identified the Greek émigré Michael Trivolis with the monk Maximos the Greek and, thanks to this identification, was able to suggest that his life took the form of a diptych, of which Italy and Russia are the two leaves and Athos is the hinge.[9] Since the role of Athos is therefore pivotal in his life, it is frustrating that this period is not better documented, but we may be sure that he took every opportunity to spend time in the library of the monastery and familiarize himself with Byzantine texts, both spiritual and secular. Among the Church Fathers, he seems to have studied most closely St John of Damascus, whom he later described as having achieved 'the summit of philosophy and theology', and St Gregory Nazianzen.[10] In addition to the Fathers, he will have had access to Aristotle and Augustine. Of secular works, he made greatest use of the *Suda*, a general encyclopaedia that dates from probably the late tenth century.

Another aspect of Athonite society that no doubt appealed to Maximos was its cosmopolitan nature. As we have seen, the revival of hesychasm in the late Byzantine period attracted large numbers of men from Russia, Serbia, Bulgaria, and Romania and the Mountain became a flourishing centre for the copying and collation of manuscripts and the translation of Byzantine texts into Slavonic. Slavs were especially numerous in the monasteries of Zographou, Hilandar, and St Panteleimonos, but Vatopedi, which had a brotherhood of some 300 monks, also had a large contingent. Despite the fall of the empire, this spirit of international co-operation and exchange continued into the sixteenth century and will have

---

[7] Tachiaos, 'The Greek Monk Maximus Trivolis', p. 332.

[8] Geanakoplos, 'The Post-Byzantine Athonite Monk Maximos "the Greek"', p. 448.

[9] E. Denissoff, *Maxime le Grec et l'Occident: Contribution à l'histoire de la pensée religieuse et philosophique de Michel Trivolis* (Paris: Brouwer, 1943). Hence the title of Obolensky's 1981 Raleigh Lecture on History, 'Italy, Mount Athos, and Muscovy: The Three Worlds of Maximos the Greek (c.1470–1556)', published in the *Proceedings of the British Academy*, 67 (1981), 143–61, which preceded its publication in his book, *Six Byzantine Portraits*, by seven years.

[10] Obolensky, 'Maximos the Greek', p. 206.

made its mark on Maximos and provided some preparation for his future life in Russia. He may even have taken the opportunity to learn a Slavic language, though this is far from certain.

Clearly, the authorities at the monastery were not unduly concerned by Maximos's previous involvement in the humanist schools of Renaissance Italy, nor was he required to repudiate his attachment to Plato, though this may have been viewed with some suspicion in a monastery that had nurtured the hesychast teachings of St Gregory Palamas who did not think that monks should study Plato. But it seems that he did renounce some of Plato's theories, such as the belief in the coeternity of God and the world, and his views on the relationship of faith to knowledge were found to be impeccably Orthodox.[11] That the elders were satisfied with this, and were also impressed by his intellectual abilities, is demonstrated by their trusting him to travel in the outside world to collect alms for the monastery and to preach the Orthodox faith. One such trip may have been to Wallachia to accompany the body of the former patriarch Niphon II (1486–9, 1497–8) who was on Athos from 1505 until his death in 1508. Maximos wrote three epitaphs for him at the time. Six or seven years later, when the Voivode Ivan Neagoe IV Basarab sent a delegation to Athos to bring back Niphon's body to his native Wallachia, it is possible that Maximos went with it. Missions between Athos and Moscow were also quite common at the time, not only for the monks to gather alms but also for diplomatic reasons, so it was no cause for surprise that a Russian envoy from Grand Prince Vasily III arrived on the Mountain on 31 March 1516 carrying a sum of money to be given to the monasteries in return for prayers on behalf of the Russian royal family and also a letter addressed to the Protos.

The letter was very specific. It asked the monks to send to Moscow 'the elder Savvas from Vatopedi monastery as a literary translator for a time and when he will have served us, then we, if God grant it, having favoured him, will release him again to you'. Until the mid fifteenth century, the Russian Church had been subject to the patriarchate of Constantinople, and over time its library had acquired a large collection of Greek manuscripts that had come mostly as gifts from Byzantium. But by the early sixteenth century there were very few people in Moscow who could read them and there was a great need for a scholar who knew Greek to come and translate them into Slavonic. The monk Savvas had clearly gained a reputation as a translator, hence this request. The abbot of Vatopedi replied that Sava was

---

[11] Haney, *From Italy to Muscovy*, pp. 138–52.

unable to accept the invitation because of his age, but instead he offered to send another monk:

> our most worthy brother Maxim, who is from our holy cloister of Vatopedi, experienced in the divine scripture and capable of interpreting all sorts of books, both church and those called Hellenic [i.e. secular], because from his youth he has grown up in them and has been instructed virtuously, and not like others, only by having read them.[12]

The abbot was sending Maximos not just as a translator but as a scholar who was familiar with both secular and patristic literature. He may also have had in mind Maximos's humanist past, which would be of value to the Russians who were having to deal with an influx of ideas and practices from the West. And he would also have expected him to raise funds for the monastery. On his way north, Maximos broke his journey in Constantinople where we may be sure that the patriarch took the opportunity to brief him on the two most pressing issues of the day: the wish to restore his authority over the Russian Church and his hope that Moscow might provide aid for the Greek subjects of the Ottoman Empire. It was therefore with a mixed bag of obligations and aspirations that Maximos set out on a journey that for reasons that are unclear was to take him the best part of two years.

From Athos to Moscow (1516–1525)

On this stage of the journey, Maxim (if we may now change to use the Russian form of his name) was accompanied by a metropolitan, representing the patriarch of Constantinople, and two monks, the Greek Neophytos and the Bulgarian Lavrentii. They arrived in Moscow in March 1518 and were received with great honour. It is to be hoped that Lavrentii will have taught Maxim at least some Slavonic, since his first assignment was to translate as many as twenty-four patristic commentaries on the Psalms and he did not yet know any Russian. Many years later, we are told by one of his disciples that he had mastered Russian, Serbian, Bulgarian, and Church Slavonic in addition to Latin and Greek, but for the moment he was ill equipped for the task. His method of working was first to translate the texts into Latin, which his Russian collaborators then translated into Slavonic. This was far from ideal and inevitably mistakes were made for which he would pay dearly in the future. There are a few errors of substance, there

---

[12] *Akty istoricheskie, sobrannye i izdannye Arkheograficheskoyu Kommissieyu* (St Petersburg, 1841), vol. 1, no. 122, p. 176; cited in Haney, *From Italy to Muscovy*, pp. 32–3.

are some grammatical mistakes, and there are some infelicities of language; but a number of earlier errors are corrected, enhancing the overall value of the work.

Muscovite society in the first half of the sixteenth century was deeply divided, and debate raged over a wide variety of issues: should the sovereign have a monopoly of power or should it be shared with the aristocracy? What was the appropriate relationship between Church and state? What role should the monasteries play? And was it right that heretics be burnt at the stake? As we saw in Chapter 11, the Transvolga hermits, as the Non-Possessors were known, had suffered a major defeat at the councils held in 1503 and 1504 when Grand Prince Ivan III had been forced to abandon his scheme to secularize the Church's lands. Heretics (mostly Judaizers) had been burnt or hanged, and the Possessors or Iosifians, as the followers of Abbot Iosif of Volokolamsk were known, were in the ascendant. But Metropolitan Gennady of Novgorod had been arrested for simony in 1504 and in 1511–12 Vasily III, who had succeeded his father as grand prince in 1505, revived the plan to restrict the property rights of the Church. When Iosif warned him of the threat to the state from a resurgence of heretics, Vasily chose to follow the line that had been taken by Nil Sorsky and adopted a more lenient approach. Iosif himself died in 1515 and, though his followers continued to be a forceful group, the successors of Nil Sorsky under the able leadership of Vassian Patrikeev regained some influence.

Vassian was a strong character who came from a princely family and had served as a general and a diplomat. But he had been disgraced by Ivan III in 1499 and was forcibly tonsured. Returning to Moscow in 1509, he rose to a position of some influence over the grand prince at the expense of Iosif and succeeded in engineering the deposition of Metropolitan Simon and his replacement by Barlaam, who was known to be a sympathizer of the Transvolga hermits. In 1515 Vassian began a new edition of the *Nomocanon*, the ecclesiastical code of canon law, which he arranged thematically instead of the previous chronological order. His intention was no doubt to demonstrate that monasteries with large estates were contravening canon law. When Maxim arrived in Moscow in 1518, Vassian had just completed his work and the two men became close friends. Coming from Athos, Maxim naturally supported the Non-Possessors and offered his knowledge of Greek to assist his friend. Vassian was particularly exercised about the meaning of the word *proasteion*, which according to the *Nomocanon*, monasteries were allowed to own. In ancient Greek, this word means 'the space immediately in front of [*pro*] or round a town [*astu*], a suburb'. Russians had previously translated it as 'villages with resident peasants', which is clearly a distortion that conveniently suited the Possessors. Maxim told Vassian that the word meant 'ploughed field and orchards', which is more accurate, though not a literal translation, and which appeared to support the view of the Non-Possessors. Vassian accepted Maxim's suggestion and incorporated it into his edition.[13]

Vassian was also a writer and had composed a number of works on topical matters such as monastic organization and the punishment of heretics. His tone was somewhat polemical, and this may have rubbed off on Maxim who adopted a similarly sharp tongue when he came to write his dialogue on the 'Dispute of the Lover of Possessions with the Non-Possessor'. But no such polemic appears in the description of monastic organization on Mount Athos that Maxim wrote in a letter to Vassian. In this short work, 'On the Way of Life on the Holy Mountain', Maxim is careful to avoid any mention of monastic landownership and specifically (and surely somewhat disingenuously) says that usually no laymen worked for the monasteries on Athos, though there were occasional hired labourers. He describes the differences between the cenobitic and the idiorrhythmic monasteries and the sketes but does not hide his preference for the cenobitic houses in which all property is held in common and monks labour for their own sustenance. In both types, he says, the abbot enjoys absolute power but is required to work alongside the rest of the brotherhood in all monastic labour. His remarks are more or less accurate as far as they go but are perhaps more conspicuous for what they leave unsaid. His own monastery, Vatopedi, despite some losses of property to the Ottomans, remained one of the wealthiest on the Holy Mountain, owning extensive estates in other parts of Greece, and in the course of the sixteenth century it turned from the cenobitic to the idiorrhythmic system. Maxim could not but be aware of the ongoing dispute between the Iosifians and the Non-Possessors, and yet he makes no mention of the situation of the larger monasteries in Russia, which had become immensely wealthy from their possession of enormous estates and their exploitation of peasant labour. His silence would not be lost on the Iosifians; his friendship with Vassian would also be noted with disapproval.

In the autumn of 1519, when he had finished his translations of the Psalter and its patristic commentaries, Maxim expected to be allowed to return to Athos with his fellow monks, as had been agreed before his

---

[13] N. A. Kazakova, *Vassian Patrikeev i ego sochineniya* (Moscow–Leningrad, 1960), p. 62; Obolensky, 'Maximos the Greek', p. 213; Haney, *From Italy to Muscovy*, pp. 47–8.

departure. In September, monks Neophytos and Lavrentii were indeed sent home, but Maxim remained in Moscow, perhaps because he had agreed to undertake another translation, this time of some commentaries on the Acts of the Apostles, but perhaps because he was refused permission to return. Whatever the reason, he was later to lament the fact that he was detained in Moscow against his will and against canon law. Not but what he continued with his work, first translating the commentaries on Acts, and then moving on to commentaries on the epistles of James, Peter, John, and Jude, which took him until March 1521. He also translated a Life of the Mother of God and some discourses of Symeon Metaphrastes, and he devoted some time to correcting the texts of the liturgical books, which he found to be full of errors. 'It became obvious to him', writes Dimitri Obolensky,

> that the howlers committed by early translators, compounded by scribal errors, had led to mistranslations which at best were absurd, and at worst heretical. Some of the most glaring he corrected himself, unaware of the trouble he was storing up for the future.[14]

If Maxim was restrained in his public utterances, his friend Vassian went to the opposite extreme in declaring:

> All our books are false ones, and were written by the devil and not by the Holy Spirit. Until Maxim we used these books to blaspheme God, and not to glorify or pray to him. Now, through Maxim, we have come to know God.[15]

Such remarks were calculated to provoke a response. In 1522 Vasily decided to replace Barlaam as metropolitan of Moscow with Daniil, who had succeeded Iosif as abbot of Volokolamsk. At a stroke, the pendulum now swung in favour of the Possessors and Vassian lost what influence he had at court. Maxim still enjoyed a close relationship with the grand prince, but his position was weakened by the deposition of Barlaam and he found relations with Daniil at best difficult. Maxim did not confine his activities to his translations but also engaged in writing of his own on a wide range of mostly theological topics and he corresponded with a great many of the leading residents of the city. They included the grand prince and his advisers, various other princes and members of the aristocracy, visiting foreign scholars and diplomats, scribes, churchmen of all

[14] Obolensky, 'Maximos the Greek', p. 211.
[15] V. S. Ikonnikov, *Maksim Grek i ego vremya*, 2nd edn (Kiev, 1915), p. 409; cited in Obolensky, 'Maximos the Greek', p. 213.

persuasions, and intellectuals. Not all of them were impressed by his academic prowess and his popularity at court, and he was outspoken in his criticism of certain aspects of Muscovite society, particularly what he saw as malpractices among the clergy. This did not endear him to Metropolitan Daniil, at whom some of Maxim's sharpest barbs were no doubt directed. For example, his grandly titled 'Discourse Extremely Elevating for the Soul of Him Who Heeds It. Wherein the Mind Speaks to the Soul. Also about Extortion', which takes the form of a diatribe that the mind addresses to the soul, contains an extended catalogue of sins that the metropolitan could scarcely fail to recognize as being attributed to him. On the subject of property:

> Do not be deceived by the accursed and pernicious thoughts of those who advise you that you must have possessions – gold and estates – for use in your old age for your frequent illnesses . . . Thus the soul, having become inflated with pride because of its many estates, little by little ejects from its heart the fear of God, and thus deprived of it, no longer is careful about lies, or swearing, or theft; it covets, is spiteful, extols itself mightily, and is overjoyed at ruinous quarrels, feeding like a leech on blood, always finding the sins of others, never sensing its own . . . You, accursed one, drinking without pity of the blood of the poor by means of extortion and other unjust affairs, obtain for yourself by these means all that pleases you, when and how you wish, riding about the towns on thoroughbred horses with a host of servants.[16]

Whether such attacks were aimed at Metropolitan Daniil in person or at senior clergy in general can only be conjectured, but it is worth noting that when Maxim was later charged with slandering the metropolitan he did not deny it.

It was in 1524 that Metropolitan Daniil asked Maxim to translate the *Religious History* of Theodoret of Cyrrhus, which was considered by some (including Maxim) to be heretical and also contained support for the Iosifian view of monastic landholding.[17] Maxim refused, more than once, and claimed later that publication of such heretical texts would be harmful to readers who lacked the mental capacity to interpret them and would only serve to spread the heresies contained in them. Maxim also expressed his disapproval of the grand prince's divorce and second marriage, thereby acquiring enemies for himself both princely and ecclesiastical. Having provoked the wrath of both Metropolitan Daniil and Grand Prince

[16] Maksim Grek, *Sochineniya*, vol. 2 (Kazan, 1860), pp. 39–44; cited in Haney, *From Italy to Muscovy*, pp. 62–3.

[17] See p. 182.

Vasily, Maxim was arrested in the winter of 1524/5 on charges of heresy (for making changes to the liturgical books), treason (for allegedly entering into relations with the Sublime Porte), and sorcery (against the grand prince). His trial took place in May 1525 before an ecclesiastical court over which the metropolitan and the grand prince presided.

Detention in Moscow (1525–1556)

Given the nature of the charges and the constitution of the court, it was a foregone conclusion that Maxim would be found guilty. He was condemned to solitary confinement in the monastery of Volokolamsk where he was excommunicated, put in chains, and deprived of the means to read and write. Six years later a second trial took place, partly to silence the prisoner's protestations of his innocence, and again he was found guilty. The sentence was the same as before, except that he was now moved to a prison in Tver' where gradually some of the terms of his confinement were relaxed.

The exact nature of the charges laid against Maxim is confused, largely because the account of them conflates the two trials, but the text of a near-contemporary pamphlet, which is based on a record of the trials, survives and provides a good deal of information. There were essentially six charges. The first was of heresy, based on the very flimsy evidence of grammatical errors and linguistic infelicities that occurred in his translations and in the corrections he made to the liturgical texts. These resulted from his poor command of Russian, which he freely admitted, and the cumbersome method of working that he had been forced to adopt. The charge was blatantly unjust. Even more absurd was the second charge, that he had practised sorcery against the grand prince and had been converted to 'Judaism' in Italy. This was no more than an attempt further to blacken his character in the eyes of the court. Similarly far-fetched was the third charge, that Maxim had criticized the grand prince, apparently for cowardice in fleeing from Moscow at the time when the Crimean Tatars threatened to invade in 1521. Maxim denied the charge and there seems to be no evidence to support it. A fourth charge, that he had entered into treasonable relations with the Turkish government, seems also to be unproven. Maxim was accused of having sent letters and gifts to the Turkish pasha in Athens, encouraging him to exercise his influence with the sultan in promoting a war between Turkey and Russia. But no such letters were produced at the trial; and though Maxim may have been indiscreet in his dealings with members of the court in suggesting that it was highly likely that one day Turkey would invade Russia, as a Greek it must have been his fervent desire that one day Russia would invade Turkey and free the Balkan Christians from the Turkish yoke.

The remaining two charges, that Maxim had stated that the secession of the Russian Church from Constantinople was uncanonical and that he had impugned the Russian monasteries for their ownership of land and serfs, were much less controversial and were largely true. For almost a century, the Russian Church had been electing its own bishops without reference to the patriarch in Constantinople. Maxim had never concealed his disapproval of this, which had no doubt been impressed on him by the patriarch before his departure, and he was quite outspoken in what he wrote on the subject:

> Then your Reverence ought to know that the bishops consecrate rulers in their kingdoms, they crown and confirm them and rulers do not appoint the bishops. Because of this rulers with reverence and love kiss the hands of the bishops as having been consecrated to God on high, and bow their head before them just like other people, receiving their blessing with the sign of the cross. Thus it follows that the episcopacy is greater than the royal power of earthly kings, for 'without all contradiction the less is blessed of the better' (Hebrews 7:7).[18]

This can only have struck Daniil and Vasily as aimed at them personally. Nor did Maxim pull his punches in the matter of landholding by the monasteries, a subject on which he had written frequently and with strong feelings. On numerous occasions, he attacked the Russian monasteries for their accumulation of wealth, their exploitation of peasants, and their corrupt financial practices. This was the most hotly debated issue of the day; the Non-Possessors still commanded a good deal of support; and Metropolitan Daniil must have felt extremely uncomfortable in the presence of this articulate, well-read, and influential Athonite monk. It was no doubt this last charge that ultimately sealed Maxim's fate and influenced the severity of his sentence.

Maxim was subjected to incredibly harsh treatment at Volokolamsk, which was one of the Possessors' monasteries whose conspicuous wealth he had singled out for especial contumely. He disobeyed the injunction that he should not write letters from his cell, and to Metropolitan Makary of Novgorod he wrote that whenever as an Athonite monk he had gone out asking for alms, he 'never was put in chains or incarcerated in a dungeon or

---

[18] Maksim Grek, *Sochineniya*, vol. 3, 2nd edn (Kazan, 1897), p. 127; cited in Haney, *From Italy to Muscovy*, p. 76.

devastated by hunger, cold and smoke, which happened here'. Prince Andrey Kurbsky, with whom he became acquainted in later years, also described the conditions in which he was held: 'He had endured much – long-lasting and grievous chains and long-lasting imprisonment in the direst prisons – and in his innocence he had suffered other kinds of torments because of the envy of Metropolitan Daniil, that most proud and fierce man, and at the hands of those evil monks who are called Iosifians.' As Haney remarks, there is no reason to believe that either statement was an exaggeration.[19]

At the second trial, in 1531, the charges were no doubt very similar to those at the first, with the added fury of Metropolitan Daniil that the defendant had refused to repent of those sins of which he had been found guilty six years earlier. As before, Maxim protested his innocence and claimed that all those who testified against him were guilty of perjury, but once again he was found guilty. This time he was banished to the Otroch monastery in Tver', but from the start the terms of his confinement were a little less harsh than they had been at Volokolamsk. He was still chained and banned from receiving Holy Communion, but he was allowed to receive visitors and he was given access to his books and the means to write. Vassian Patrikeev was also tried and convicted of heresy soon after Maxim. He was imprisoned at Volokolamsk, and it is possible that Maxim's move to Tver' was intended partly to keep the two friends apart. The condemnation of both Maxim and the once influential Vassian in the same year gave a clear signal that the power of the Non-Possessors was now in decline.

Despite the change of scene and minor adjustments to the regime, Maxim's sentence was the same as before. The local bishop of Tver', Akakij, was a Iosifian and Daniil no doubt assumed that he would take a firm line with his new prisoner, but in fact Akakij developed a lasting friendship with Maxim and a high regard for his learning. He often turned to him for advice and did whatever he could to lighten his friend's burdens as long as he was in Tver'. Maxim wrote letters to a wide circle of acquaintances on a variety of topics, and of those who might be able to influence the decision he begged again and again for permission to return to Mount Athos, but the request fell on consistently deaf ears. The Russian nobleman Ivan Bersen'-Beklemishev had told him even before his trial that he would never be allowed to return because 'you are an intelligent person and you have found out our good and our bad here, and if you returned

---

[19] Haney, *From Italy to Muscovy*, p. 78.

there, you would tell all.'[20] In the mid 1540s the patriarchs of Constantinople and Alexandria asked the new Russian ruler Ivan IV (known as 'the Terrible', who in 1547 was the first to take the title of Tsar of All the Russias) to release him, but without success. And in 1548 Maxim wrote to Metropolitan Makary for permission to return to Holy Communion and to make the journey to Athos. He may have agreed to the former request, but all Maxim's requests to be allowed to go home were refused by the authorities, most probably because he knew too much about their practices.

At last in 1551, when he was more than eighty years old and had spent twenty-six years in prison, Maxim was released on the orders of the tsar himself and was given permission to live in the Trinity monastery of St Sergius near Moscow. This was also the year in which the tsar convened a synod of the Russian Church, known as the *Stoglav* or One Hundred Chapters, which was an attempt to curb abuse and indiscipline in all areas of religious life. It discussed the ritual practices that had evolved in Russia and that did not conform with those of the Greek Church, and it somehow contrived to rule that they were all correct, an outcome that was deplored by many Orthodox believers and drew a sharp rebuke from the monks of Athos. It is unlikely that Maxim played any part in the council, though it is possible that he influenced its decision to institute an ecclesiastical censorship prior to the foundation of a printing press. It is only to be expected that with his experience of printing in Venice Maxim would take an interest in, and indeed encourage, the start of printing in Muscovy. But after that he lived out the remainder of his days at the Trinity monastery, reading, writing, and teaching, in as much as his failing eyesight would allow, until his death, at the age of eighty-six, on 21 January 1556 (Plate 36).

Maxim's Legacy

In purely material terms, Maxim's legacy was immense. He was the author or translator of as many as 365 works, of which 163 remain unpublished. He wrote on a wide range of topics, which embraced secular philosophy, statecraft, and social issues, but his chief concern was with theology: not without reason did Steven Runciman call him 'the father of later Russian theology'.[21] He corresponded with all the leading figures in Moscow of his

---

[20] Ibid., p. 65.
[21] S. Runciman, *The Great Church in Captivity: A Study of the Patriarchate of Constantinople from the Eve of the Turkish Conquest to the Greek War of Independence* (Cambridge: Cambridge University Press, 1968), p. 327.

day, but his stinging attacks on those whose behaviour did not meet acceptable standards and his determination to root out corruption made him more enemies than friends. His work on patristics, his polemics against the Western Church and against Latin scholasticism, and his own contributions on matters of dogma, liturgy, and canon law made him the most celebrated and influential scholar in Russia. But his work had a much greater impact on future generations than it did on his contemporaries, and it is no doubt true, as Haney suggests, that 'Muscovy was not yet ready for him'.[22] Within a few years of his death he was being hailed by those who took issue with the official Church as a saint, a martyr, and 'enlightener of Russia'; icons were painted of him, and several hagiographies were written. But it was to take another century before his canonization was approved by Patriarch Nikon (1652–66), celebrated for his remark, 'I am Russian, but my faith and religion are Greek'; and it was not until 1988 that Maxim's name was formally added to the calendar of saints.

Dimitri Obolensky, who had championed the cause of Maxim and was personally instrumental in his eventual canonization, concludes his portrait with a balanced assessment:

> Maximos, though not a creative thinker, was at least a sound and wide-ranging scholar, with an excellent training in ancient philosophy and textual criticism; though he played an important role in the controversies that shook sixteenth-century Muscovite society, his learning was, with a few notable exceptions, above its head; and he lived in a cosmopolitan world where the Byzantine heritage, the late medieval Italo-Greek connections, and the traditional links between Russia, Mount Athos, and Constantinople were still to some extent living realities. He was one of the last of his kind.[23]

To this we may add that Maxim was an Athonite to the very core of his being. To the end of his life he remained devoted to the monastery of Vatopedi, he longed to be allowed to return to it, and he regarded himself as perpetually in obedience to its abbot, even though it was forty years since he had set eyes on him. More to the point, it was primarily as an Athonite that he was regarded by his Russian contemporaries. They went to Athos as the only place where they knew they would find a scholar fit for the job in hand, which was to provide them with accurate translations into Slavonic of the sacred texts and liturgical books. And it was primarily as an Athonite, a representative of the spiritual model of Orthodox belief and practice, that they heard him respond so vehemently to the abuses as he saw them in current Russian monastic practices.

---

[22] Haney, *From Italy to Muscovy*, p. 90.   [23] Obolensky, 'Maximos the Greek', p. 219.

It was not until 1997 that the final denouement of the drama was to be played out. In July of that year Abbot Ephraim of Vatopedi travelled to Moscow to be presented with a portion of the relics of Maxim by Patriarch Alexiy II. After concelebrating the Divine Liturgy with the patriarch in the church of the Intercession (St Basil's) in Red Square, the abbot returned to Athos with the relics and placed them in the katholikon of the Annunciation at Vatopedi. This joyful event, by which some of the physical remains of Maxim were at last laid to rest in his spiritual home some 480 years after he had left it, was seen as symbolic of the increasingly close relationship between Vatopedi and the rest of the Orthodox world. It might also be said to be symbolic of the way in which for half a millennium the Athonite Commonwealth has operated for mutual enlightenment and spiritual advantage.

Five years before he himself was to be the victim of unjust incarceration in 2011–12, in the course of which he acquired numerous spiritual children from among his fellow prisoners, Abbot Ephraim published a prescient paper on 'St Maximos of Vatopaidi' (as he is known in the monastery) in which he discusses the sources of spiritual strength that will have enabled the saint to survive his ordeal:

> Saint Maximos suffered all of his ordeals with patience and without resent-ment. Never did he reproach those who had caused him to undergo such great sufferings, nor did he ever depart from the bounds of spiritual nobility and meekness. This he achieved through humility. Emulating other holy Fathers, while protesting against his condemnation as a heretic and a blasphemer, he nevertheless accepted his trials as if they had been permitted by God on account of his sins . . . Living in seclusion and silence, he prayed unceasingly, with wordless groanings of the heart, noetically calling from the depths of his heart upon the Name of his sweetest Bridegroom, Jesus Christ.[24]

In other words, the abbot is suggesting that the saint was sustained throughout his ordeal by the spiritual forces of hesychasm that he would have imbibed in the course of his ten-year sojourn at Vatopedi, forces that it is to be hoped similarly sustained the abbot during his own (happily much shorter but none the less shockingly traumatic) imprisonment.

---

[24] Archimandrite Ephraim, 'An Indomitable Herald of Patristic Tradition', *Pemptousia*, 20 (April–July 2006), 114–21.

CHAPTER 13

St Kosmas the Aetolian (1714–1779): Teacher of the Greek Nation, Apostle to the Albanians

'Do you have a school here, here in your village, to teach your children?'

'We don't, O saint of God.'

'You must all get together and establish a good school. Appoint a committee to govern it, appoint a teacher to teach all the children, rich and poor. Because it is in school that we learn who God is; who is the Holy Trinity; who are the angels, demons; and what is paradise, hell, virtue, evil; what is the soul, body, etc. Without a school we walk in darkness. The school leads to the monastery. If there were no school, how would I have learned to teach you?

'I studied about priests and about unbelievers, heretics, and atheists. I searched the depths of wisdom, but all the faiths are false. I learned this to be true, that only the faith of the Orthodox Christians is good and is sacred: to believe and to be baptized in the name of the Father, and of the Son, and of the Holy Spirit.

'In conclusion, I tell you this. Rejoice that you are Orthodox Christians and weep for the impious and heretics who walk in darkness.'[1]

'The Prophet Moses studied for forty years to learn his letters in order to understand where he walked. You too should study, my brethren; learn as much as you can. And if you fathers haven't, educate your children to learn Greek because our Church uses Greek. And if you don't learn Greek, my brethren, you can't understand what our Church confesses. It is better, my brother, for you to have a Greek school in your village rather than fountains and rivers, for when your child becomes educated, he is then a human being. The school opens churches; the school opens monasteries.'[2]

---

[1] From 'The Life of St Kosmas Aitolos together with an English Translation of his Teaching and Letters', translated by N. M. Vaporis, First Teaching, 'The Importance of Schooling'. Available at http://annunciationscranton.org/files/PDF/Apostle-to-the-Poor.pdf.

[2] Ibid., Fifth Teaching, 'The Importance of Education'.

Early Years and Elementary Education

In the sphere of education Fr Kosmas, whose baptismal name was Konstas, was a late starter. He was born in 1714 in the village of Megadendron, which is 30 kilometres west of Arta in the province of Aetolia. His parents, who originally came from Epirus, were weavers and the young Kosmas worked with them until he was twenty years old. During that time, he received no formal education apart from what he learnt from his brother, Chrysanthos (d.1785). Dissatisfied with this situation and frustrated by his inability to understand the Bible readings in church which he loved to hear, he left home and travelled some 250 kilometres south-east to the village of Segditsa near Amphissa where he was able to attend a school. Later he moved to another school, at Lompotina (now Ano Hora), which is about 50 kilometres west of Amphissa. There he seems to have made good progress and after four years he was appointed an assistant teacher in the same school, while at the same time giving frequent sermons in the local church. But then he moved again, this time back to Aetolia to a village near Vragiana, which is about 40 kilometres east of Arta, where his brother Chrysanthos was headmaster.[3] There he was able to study Greek, theology, and even medicine, all of which (including the last) would stand him in good stead for his future ministry in remote mountainous regions. We have no information on how long he remained at Vragiana or indeed about his life for the following decade. He is next heard of on Mount Athos where at the age of thirty-five he enrolled as a student at the academy that had recently been founded near the monastery of Vatopedi.

The popular belief that the Ottomans deprived the Greeks of the opportunities of education by forbidding the operation of schools has recently been challenged by the Greek historians John Koliopoulos and Thanos Veremis. They have suggested that the visual 'evidence' of this myth comes from a painting by the nineteenth-century artist Nikolaos Ghyzis entitled *Hidden School*, which depicts a 'secret' schoolroom in which a priest is teaching a few children to read by candlelight. 'Evidence that lay schools of high quality operated in seventeenth- and eighteenth-century Greece, catering also for the needs of clerics, and the argument that these were not greatly inferior to educational establishments in most other European countries have not been enough to demolish the

---

[3] Chrysanthos was a distinguished teacher who was to teach for a time at the patriarchal academy in Constantinople before becoming director of the school on Naxos.

"hidden school" myth', they write.[4] Education, they claim, 'flourished in commercial and administrative centres', though they go on to say that education under the Turks was always associated with the Orthodox Church, which needed schools for the training of its senior clergy, and that 'the lay schools of later years grew out of these early church schools'.[5] The fact that in the first half of the eighteenth century Kosmas had had to travel such great distances in order to provide himself with even an elementary education scarcely supports these remarks, and we should rather conclude that such schools that did exist, even if they were not 'hidden', were few and far between.

Athos and the Enlightenment

The foundation of the Athonite academy (or Athonias) in 1748 has been described by Paschalis Kitromilides, doyen of studies of Greece and the Enlightenment, as 'undoubtedly the most important initiative of the Church in the field of education during the eighteenth century'.[6] The ecclesiastical school in Patmos, founded as recently as 1713, was already in decline, and there was a need for a new school to provide religious and philosophical training for the Orthodox subjects of the Ottoman Empire. The newly elected patriarch of Constantinople, Cyril V (1748–51, 1752–7), and the Holy Synod gave it their blessing, but the initiative came from the monastery of Vatopedi, which under its abbot Meletios was the leading monastery on the Mountain. The intention was that the school should become the chief centre of higher education for all Greek-speaking people and should produce suitably qualified leaders for the Church and for the Orthodox world as a whole. Handsome buildings were erected at Vatopedi's expense on high ground overlooking the monastery, and monk Neophytos of Kafsokalyvia, perhaps the most learned man on the Mountain at the time, was appointed its first director in 1749. The school was to operate as a fully fledged university, open not only to the monks of Vatopedi, but to all monks who had the blessing of their abbot, and to any Orthodox priest or layman who wished to study there. As for its

---

[4] J. S. Koliopoulos and T. M. Veremis, *Greece: The Modern Sequel, from 1821 to the Present* (London: Hurst, 2002), p. 157.
[5] Ibid., pp. 159–60.
[6] P. M. Kitromilides, 'Initiatives of the Great Church in the mid Eighteenth Century', ch. 5 in his *An Orthodox Commonwealth*, p. 5. See also his 'Athos and the Enlightenment', in Bryer and Cunningham, *Mount Athos and Byzantine Monasticism*, pp. 257–72 = ch. 7 in *An Orthodox Commonwealth*.

curriculum, according to its charter the school was to provide a complete course in classical learning: in short, it was to operate as a vehicle for the revival of Hellenism. Kosmas was among its first cohort of pupils.

Much later Fr Kosmas explained how he came to be a teacher:

> If, my brethren, it were possible for me to climb up into the sky, to be able to shout with a great voice, to preach to the entire world that only our Christ is the Son and Word of God, true God and the life of all, I would have done it. But because I can't do such a big thing, I do this small thing: I walk from place to place and teach my brethren as I can, not as a teacher but as a brother. Only Christ is a teacher. How I was moved to do this, my brethren, I'll tell you. Leaving my homeland fifty years ago, I travelled to many places, forts, towns, villages, and especially to Constantinople. I stayed the longest on the Holy Mountain, seventeen years, where I wept over my sins. Among the countless gifts which my Lord has granted me, he made me worthy to acquire a little Greek learning and I became a monk.[7]

He does not tell us how long he spent as a student at the academy, but it is likely that he left shortly before the arrival of its most famous director, Evgenios Voulgaris (1716–1806), in 1753. At that point he entered the monastery of Philotheou as a novice and was in due course tonsured a monk and shortly thereafter ordained to the priesthood. From the time of his youth he had wanted to be a missionary and to preach the word of God to the people of Greece. He had also benefited from having the best education currently available in Greece and he was anxious to share this with others. But Athonite monasteries like to do things in their own time and the recently tonsured Fr Kosmas will have been asked to possess himself in patience until his elder deemed him ready to go back into the world. All the same, the number of years that he states he spent on Athos must be cumulative, not consecutive.

The eighteenth century was a low point for the Orthodox Church, especially in the poor, mountainous areas such as Aetolia, far from the centres of cultural and economic activity. The Ottomans had been in control for 300 years and there seemed no prospect of any change to the political status quo. Taxation was oppressive and was harsher for Christians than for Muslims. Local administrators were notoriously corrupt and frequently levied extortionate taxes of their own. The forms of oppression and discrimination to which Christians were subjected not surprisingly led many to accept conversion to Islam, though it was by no means uncommon for Christians to subscribe outwardly to the religion of their

---

[7] 'The Life of St Kosmas Aitolos', First Teaching.

conquerors while secretly adhering to the beliefs and practices of their ancestors.

In spite of this depressed state of affairs, or perhaps even because of it, the Holy Mountain, not for the first time, responded with a remarkable spiritual revival. The same thing had happened in the mid fourteenth century at the time of the hesychast controversy: as the political situation of the empire grew more and more hopeless, so the intellectual revival on the Mountain demonstrated the capacity of the monks to rise to a challenge and produce inspired and inspiring thinkers. As we shall see in the next three chapters, something comparable occurred in the mid eighteenth century. As if to counter the prevailing mood of despair and the rapidly increasing rate of conversion of the people from Christianity to Islam, a number of charismatic figures emerged, first of all as monks, and subsequently as missionaries, teachers, writers, thinkers, and apostles to the Orthodox, not only in Greece but throughout the Balkans and Russia. From an age of darkness, the Mountain moved to an era of enlightenment. Fr Kosmas was one of its leading lights.

The Mission of Kaisarios Dapontes

In 1760, after about seven years in the monastery of Philotheou, Kosmas was ready to begin his ministry. He had before him the example of Kaisarios Dapontes (1714–84), who had set out on his mission just three years earlier, though there is no reason to suppose that the two men ever met.[8] Kaisarios, whose baptismal name was Constantine, was born on Skopelos where he was educated at the local school, which was run by a monk of Iviron. At the age of seventeen, his father sent him to Constantinople where he moved in Phanariot circles and in due course he joined the retinue of Constantine Mavrocordatos, who was voivode of Moldavia and of Wallachia for several periods between 1732 and 1769. Dapontes followed the prince to Iași and to Bucharest and remained in the principalities until 1746, living the life of a wealthy and worldly courtier and, by his own admission, committing many sins. He also made enemies and on his return to Constantinople in 1747 he was imprisoned for nearly two years which, as he says, was just punishment for his misdemeanours. Soon after his release in 1749 he married, but two years later was widowed. In 1753, repenting of his sinful existence, he decided to renounce the world

[8] On Dapontes, see P. M. Kitromilides, '"Balkan Mentality": History, Legend, Imagination', ch. 1 in his *An Orthodox Commonwealth*, pp. 172–6.

and become a monk. He retired to the island of Piperi, which is near his beloved Skopelos and which was uninhabited except for about ten monks who had established a skete there. Tonsured as Kaisarios, he spent three years there in total solitude, spending all his time writing in his cell. He poured out thousands of lines of verse, comprising his autobiographical narrative, *Garden of the Graces*, which is perhaps better described as his confessions.

After a year at the monastery of the Annunciation on Skopelos, in May 1757 Kaisarios went to Athos and found a home in the monastery of Xeropotamou. Here by chance the brotherhood was on the point of dispatching a mission to Wallachia to raise funds for the rebuilding of their church which was in a sorry state. The newly arrived Fr Kaisarios was clearly the perfect man for the job, given his intimate knowledge of the principality and close acquaintance with the local elite, including Prince Constantine Mavrocordatos, his former patron. Kaisarios accepted the challenge and before the end of the month he had left Athos on a tour that was to encompass a large slice of the Balkans over the next eight years, carrying with him the monastery's most sacred relic, a large piece of the True Cross. From Athos he sailed along the north Aegean coast to Ainos in Thrace and from there continued over land via Adrianople into central Bulgaria. From Trnovo he crossed the Danube into Wallachia and was given a rapturous reception in Bucharest where the faithful flocked to venerate the precious relic. After seven months in Wallachia, he travelled north into Moldavia and entered Iași just before Easter 1758. After two years in Romania, Kaisarios returned to Constantinople in August 1760 and stayed there for four years, during which time the cross performed a number of miracles and greatly enriched the Athonite's purse. From the capital Kaisarios set out in July 1764, island-hopping across the Aegean, calling at Chios, Samos, Psara, Euboea, and his native Skopelos, and finally returning to Athos in September 1765. He brought back 100 purses of gold – more than enough for the rebuilding of the church – and many precious treasures for its decoration.

Kaisarios spent the remainder of his life at Xeropotamou producing a remarkable number of books on a wide variety of topics. His religious publications include such titles as *Discourse of our Holy Father Cyril of Alexandria on the Departure of the Soul and the Second Coming of Christ*, *Pearls of the Three Hierarchs, or Admonitory Discourses, Translated into Simple Language*, and an *Explanation of the Divine Liturgy*. Secular works included the *Historical Catalogue* and a chronicle of the contemporary Balkan wars entitled the *Dacian Ephemerides*. Many of his books were published during his lifetime and were much admired by his contemporaries, such as the *Mirror of Women* (1766) and the *Spiritual Table* (1770); others were published after his death, such as the *Garden of the Graces* (1881); others remain unpublished. Kitromilides sums up Dapontes's *oeuvre* in the context of Orthodoxy:

> Dapontes approached the world of Balkan Orthodoxy with energetic optimism and euphoria and provides us with a pervasively extrovert interpretation of it ... the picture we are offered emerges from the world of the archipelago and is bathed in Aegean sunlight, though this does not imply a limitation of the horizons of the Orthodox vision, which continued to look towards the major Orthodox power of the North, of whom it now had specific political expectations. Dapontes was the great poet of the Greek eighteenth century, and gives expression to the Orthodox vision not merely as a system of religious belief and a form of worship, but as the principal element in the social existence of the Christian peoples of the Ottoman empire ... Of the many places he visited, Dapontes singles out Samos for special praise, because of its natural beauty, fertility, and its products, especially its excellent wine, but also for another factor that sets the island apart:
>
> > Here nobody else resides, no other race, per Dio
> > No Jew, no Turk, God forbid, no other race
> > Neither Armenian nor Franc nor Lutheran,
> > Pure Orthodoxy everywhere. [*Garden of the Graces*, pp. 136–7][9]

I have written at some length about Dapontes in order to show that, although their missions were very different, Kosmas was by no means unique at this time in being sent back into the world to make the best use of his talents on behalf of his monastery and to pursue his own avocations. In each of their cases, the Holy Mountain attracted a talented man to its precinct, appreciated that he had skills that should be given a free rein, and enabled him to spend long periods of time in other parts of the Balkans as an ambassador for Athos. Even in the darkest days of the Tourkokratia, the Athonite Commonwealth continued to function as a versatile vehicle of Orthodoxy.

Fr Kosmas's Ministry

Fr Kosmas was eager to begin the task to which he believed he was called, but rather than follow his own will, we are told that he sought confirmation

[9] P. M. Kitromilides, 'Orthodox Identities in a World of Ottoman Power', ch. 3 in his *An Orthodox Commonwealth*, pp. 5–6.

that it was also God's will by randomly opening a page of the Holy Bible. The book fell open at 1 Corinthians 10:24: 'Let no man seek his own, but every man another's.' Thus reassured, and having taken the advice of his elders at the monastery, he set out for Constantinople in order to obtain the blessing of the patriarch, Seraphim II (1757–61). The patriarch provided him with a written permit (or *firman*), which entitled him to travel and preach anywhere in the Greek world without hindrance from either Turkish officials or local bishops. He also took the opportunity to call on his brother Chrysanthos, who was then on the staff of the patriarchal academy and was able to give him some lessons in rhetoric. But what concerned Kosmas most was the widespread ignorance of his compatriots in matters of religion and the speed with which they were abandoning Orthodoxy and embracing Islam. The principal motive for his mission was his desire to counter this by sharing his knowledge of the Scriptures and of the Fathers and of Athonite spirituality with the people of Greece and the Balkans.

He began his ministry by visiting the churches in and around Constantinople. He was evidently a charismatic preacher. Wherever he went, he attracted large crowds of people eager to hear his message. His extensive journeys and the impact that he made on his audiences are described in some detail in the Life written by his disciple Sapphiros Christodoulidis, which is included in the *New Martyrologion*. Sapphiros writes:

> Wherever this thrice-blessed man went, people listened with great contrition and devoutness to his grace-imbued and sweet words, and there resulted great improvement in their ways and great benefit to their souls ... Aided by Divine grace, he tamed the fierce, rendered brigands gentle, made the pitiless and unmerciful compassionate and merciful, the impious pious, instructed those who were ignorant in divine things and made them attend the church services, and briefly he brought the sinners to great repentance and correction, so that everybody was saying that in our times there has appeared a new Apostle.[10]

From Constantinople he travelled round the central parts of Greece – Naupactus, Mesolongion, Pelion, and Thessaly – and then back to Constantinople. Then he returned to Athos for a while, before setting out again and receiving permission from Patriarch Sophronios II (1774–80) to travel round the Cyclades and bring consolation to the people who were

---

[10] *Neon Martyrologion* (Venice, 1799), pp. 202–3; cited in C. Cavarnos, *The Holy Mountain*, 2nd edn (Belmont, MA: Institute for Byzantine and Modern Greek Studies, 1977), p. 58.

depressed by the outcome of the recent Orlov revolt against the Turks (1770). After another brief visit to the Holy Mountain, no doubt in order to recharge his spiritual batteries, he felt compelled to leave again, this time travelling throughout Macedonia and the Ionian islands – Cephalonia, Zakynthos, and Corfu – and from there to Epirus and through the whole of Albania.

He preached a simple message, using vernacular Greek so that everyone could understand him; and wherever he went, he urged the people to establish schools that would promote the study of Orthodox Christianity and knowledge of the Greek language that was used in the Bible and the writings of the Fathers, saying: 'My beloved children in Christ, bravely and fearlessly preserve our holy faith and the language of our Fathers, because both of these characterize our most beloved homeland, and without them our nation is destroyed.'[11] He was aware of the many pressures, both economic, social, and religious, that made conversion to Islam seem attractive to the Orthodox and he did his best to argue against them. He lived a life of abject poverty, though he succeeded in attracting some wealthy patrons who supported his mission by contributing ecclesiastical objects such as prayer ropes, crosses, head coverings, candles, prayer books, and other items for the use of the poor. He would ask the local priest to prepare the people for his visit by hearing their confessions, holding a vigil service, and encouraging them to fast. On arrival, Fr Kosmas usually asked for the sacrament of Holy Unction to be administered and then he would preach, preferably out of doors because of the crowds. After his sermon, there would be a distribution of *antidoron* (blessed bread) and *kollyva* (boiled wheat, as eaten at memorial services), which would ensure forgiveness of both the living and the dead. At the place where he preached, he would ask the people to set up a wooden cross, and he himself would stand beside it on a footstool. After he left, the cross would remain standing at the site as a reminder of his visit. Many of these crosses are still standing in remote parts of Greece today, and some have been renewed and marked with inscriptions to record the event.

Kosmas's teaching ranged widely over all aspects of Christianity: the incarnation, cross, and resurrection of Christ, understanding of the Trinity, explanations of the parables, the creation and the institution of the sabbath, the loss of paradise, lives of the saints, the value of fasting and

[11] N. M. Vaporis, *Father Kosmas, the Apostle of the Poor: The Life of St Kosmas Aitolos together with an English Translation of his Teaching and Letters* (Brookline, MA: Holy Cross Orthodox Press, 1977), p. 146.

forgiveness, confession and the sacraments, death and the last judgement, even the painting of Easter eggs: 'This world is like an egg', he explained.

> And just as the yolk is in the centre of the egg, so is the earth made by God to stand without touching any other place. And just as the egg white surrounds the yolk, so does the air the earth. And just as the shell encloses everything, so does the sky the earth. The sun, the moon, and the stars are attached to the sky. The earth is round and wherever the sun goes it becomes day; night is the shadow of the earth. Here it is night, somewhere else dawn. And just as there are people here on earth, there are some under the earth. This is why the holy Fathers have ruled that we should colour our eggs red for Easter: because the egg symbolizes the world, while the red colour symbolizes the blood of our Christ which he spilled on the Cross to sanctify the whole world. We too should rejoice and be glad a thousand times, because Christ has spilled his blood and purchased us from the hands of the devil. But we should also weep and mourn because our sins crucified the Son of God, our Christ.[12]

In particular, it is notable that Kosmas advocated use of the Jesus Prayer and that this formed a regular part of his teaching. At a time when traditions of hesychasm are thought to have more or less died out on the Holy Mountain, Fr Kosmas was instructing the common people to pray continually. Could it be that Philotheou, a strict monastery (then as now), had managed to preserve spiritual traditions that had been lost elsewhere on the Mountain?

> Now I tell you to do this. Let all of you take a prayer rope. Let it have thirty knots, and pray. Say: 'Lord Jesus Christ, Son and Logos of the living God, through the intercessions of the Theotokos and of all your saints, have mercy upon me, a sinner and an unworthy servant.' What does one see in the 'Lord Jesus Christ', my brethren? The Holy Trinity, our God, the incarnate dispensation of our Christ and all of the saints. With the Cross and the 'Lord Jesus Christ' they went to paradise. And whoever says this prayer and makes the sign of the Cross, whether man or woman, he blesses the sky, the earth, and the sea. With the sign of the Cross and with the prayer 'Lord Jesus Christ' all illnesses are cured. With the Cross and the prayer 'Lord Jesus Christ' the Apostles raised the dead and cured every illness. With the Cross and the prayer 'Lord Jesus Christ' a person is blessed and goes to paradise to rejoice and be glad as angels.[13]

[12] From 'The Life of St Kosmas Aitolos together with an English Translation of his Teaching and Letters', First Teaching, 'The Eggs of Easter'.
[13] Ibid., Eighth Teaching, 'The Jesus Prayer and the Sign of the Cross'.

But the subject that Kosmas comes back to time and again in his teaching is the crucial need to establish schools, Greek schools, for the education and enlightenment of the young, because 'school enlightens people and they are able to open their minds and learn the mysteries of our faith'.

> Why, o holy priests and honourable elders, don't you counsel our blessed brethren to establish and build a school in each village, so that the children will receive an education to learn what is good and what is evil? Because I too learned, my brethren, the alphabet in school with the help of our Christ. I also learned a little ancient Greek and a lot of other things: Hebrew, Turkish, French, and something from all the nations with the grace of our Christ. I read a lot and I found all secular knowledge to be false, all inventions and seeds of the devil ... This is why you must establish Greek schools, so that people will be enlightened because by reading Greek I found that it enlightens and illuminates the mind of the student as the sun illuminates the earth. Then it is clear and we can see far. In this same way the mind can see the future, all that is good and evil and it is protected from every kind of evil and sin. Schools open the way to the church. We learn what God is, what the Holy Trinity is, what an angel is, what virtues, demons, and hell are. We learn everything in school.[14]

We may note that Kosmas stresses the need for *Greek* schools in particular and the need to learn the *Greek* language. Some scholars have interpreted this as evidence of the pious preacher attempting to make a (somewhat premature) political contribution towards the arousal of Greek national consciousness, but as Kitromilides has pointed out, this is to misjudge his motives. Kosmas advocates the study of Greek in order to promote a wider understanding of the Christian faith and to ensure the continuation of Greek cultural identity. He is indeed asking his audience to use their knowledge of Greek as a means to draw distinctions. But those distinctions are not between Greek and Turk, or Greek and Albanian, or Greek and Slav; they are rather between Orthodoxy and Islam, Orthodoxy and Judaism, Orthodoxy and Roman Catholicism. Kitromilides concludes his survey of the initiatives of the Great Church in the mid eighteenth century with these words:

> The activities [of the Church] in the sectors of education [in the hands of Voulgaris], pastoral care [in the hands of Kosmas] and administration [in the hands of Patriarch Samuel I] ... appear to aim at safeguarding the Orthodox community as a whole, and do not seem to issue from any nationalist motives or from expediencies of secular power politics. For this

---

[14] Ibid., Eighth Teaching, 'Education and Faith'.

reason, the systematic effort that has been made in Greek historiography to elevate Kosmas the Aetolian to this status of 'awakener of the nation' and to dub him a 'national apostle' of the political interests of Hellenism in the Balkans is not only a misinterpretation but also a suppression of the significance of the Church's solicitude for the weal of Orthodoxy.[15]

The Greeks labelled Kosmas 'Isapostolos', equal to the apostles, and it is entirely proper to think of him as playing a leading role in the religious enlightenment that flowed from Athos in the second half of the eighteenth century. But far from being a 'national awakener', he was revered by Muslims and Christians alike for his moving sermons, his pious way of life, and the miracles that frequently resulted from his visits. In fact, he belonged to the tradition that regarded subjugation to the Turks as a punishment sent by God for the sins of the Greeks: 'And why did God bring the Turks and not some other race? For our good, because the other nations would have caused detriment to our Faith.'[16] This was the view of the Kollyvades and, as we shall see in Chapter 15, of Nikodimos of the Holy Mountain, who with reference to Roman Catholic proselytism wrote, 'Divine Providence has set a guardian over us', that 'guardian' being none other than the Ottoman Empire.[17] Far from lending their support to rebellions against Turkish oppression, many traditionalist Orthodox believed that it was wiser for Greeks to stay with the devil they knew. Thirty years later, this same line of thought would manifest itself in the declaration of Patriarch Anthimos of Jerusalem, stirring great resentment among the pro-nationalist intellectuals in the decades before 1821: 'Our Lord . . . raised out of nothing this powerful Empire of the Ottomans in the place of our Roman [Byzantine] Empire which had begun, in certain ways, to deviate from the beliefs of the Orthodox faith, and He raised up the Empire of the Ottomans higher than any other Kingdom so as to show without doubt that it came about by Divine Will.'[18] With reference to this statement, the historian Richard Clogg remarks: 'The argument advanced by the Patriarch Anthimos of Jerusalem in 1798 that Christians should not challenge the established order because the Ottoman Empire had been raised up by God to protect Orthodoxy from the taint of the heretical,

[15] Kitromilides, 'Initiatives of the Great Church', p. 6.
[16] C. Cavarnos, St Cosmas Aitolos, 3rd edn (Belmont, MA: Institute for Byzantine and Modern Greek Studies, 1985), p. 23.
[17] Hieromonk Agapios and Monk Nikodimos, The Rudder, trans. D. Cummings (Chicago, IL: 1957), p. 73.
[18] Anthimos, patriarch of Jerusalem, Didaskalia Patriki (1798), cited in R. Clogg, A Concise History of Greece (Cambridge: Cambridge University Press, 1992), p. 13.

Catholic West was by no means untypical of the views of the hierarchy at large.'[19] Indeed, the same view was being argued by Fr Kosmas in the 1760s.

Martyrdom in Albania

In addition to carrying his written permit from the patriarch wherever he went, Kosmas always took the precaution of asking permission to preach of both the area bishop and the local Turkish aga. But once he had obtained it, he did not pull his punches in references to the Antichrist, the end of the world, and (despite his belief in the Ottomans as the guardians of Orthodoxy) the liberation of Greece, which he prophesied would happen within three generations. It is scarcely surprising therefore that he aroused the suspicions of the Turkish authorities who jumped to the conclusion that he and his associates were somehow linked with the declared aim of the Russian government to free the Orthodox peoples of south-eastern Europe from Ottoman rule. One day, when preaching in the Albanian village of Kolkondas (Kolikontasi in Greek) near the town of Fier, he was arrested by agents of the local pasha. Realizing that his life's work was about to be crowned with the ultimate accolade of martyrdom, he gave thanks to Christ for counting him worthy to receive such an honour. The next day, 24 August 1779, he was duly hanged from a tree beside the road to Berat. 'Thus', writes Christodoulidis, 'the thrice-blessed Kosmas, that great benefactor of men, became worthy of receiving, at the age of sixty-five, a double crown from the Lord, one as a Peer of the Apostles and the other as a holy Martyr.'[20]

His corpse was thrown naked into the river by his executioners, weighted down with a stone round his neck. For three days, his companions searched in vain with their nets until a priest from the local monastery of the Presentation of the Theotokos, fortified with prayer, discovered the body floating upright on the surface as if the saint were still alive. Rescued from the water, he was clad in his monastic habit and given due burial in the priest's monastery. His tomb acquired fame as the site of numerous miracles, and in 1813 Ali Pasha of Tepeleni, for whom the saint had predicted a glittering career thirty years earlier, erected a church and a monastery at the site in his honour. He was immediately venerated as a saint by the people, who regarded him as a new apostle and a 'prince

---

[19] Ibid. See also R. Clogg (ed. and trans.), *The Movements for Greek Independence 1770–1821: A Collection of Documents* (London: Macmillan, 1976), pp. 56–62.
[20] Cavarnos, *St Cosmas Aitolos*, p. 45.

among the new martyrs', though he was not officially canonized by the patriarchate of Constantinople until 1961. His relics, which survived the era of iconoclastic atheism under communism, were returned to the Church of Albania in 1998 and are now the object of fervent veneration by the faithful.

Unlike the relics, the monastery succumbed to the iconoclastic regime and the flood waters of the river, but it has since been completely rebuilt with loving care and funds provided by Archbishop Anastasios of Albania. On 24 August 2014 the saint's memory was celebrated in majestic style in the monastery that bears his name with a Synodical Divine Liturgy concelebrated by His Beatitude Archbishop Anastasios and all the members of the Holy Synod of the Church of Albania. In his address, the archbishop spoke about the difficult conditions in which the saint had conducted his ministry, which had resulted in the halting of the massive wave of Islamization and the rescue of Orthodoxy in those parts, 'a beautiful reality for which today's Christians owe so much to the saint'.[21] Parallels can be drawn between the dark times that preceded Fr Kosmas's ministry in the eighteenth century and the even darker decades that preceded the reconstruction of the monastery in the twenty-first. Both the relics and the monastery serve as tangible symbols of the restoration of the faith in the land of Albania, just as a further – Albanian – link may now be added to the chain of the Athonite Commonwealth.

---

[21] See http://orthodoxalbania.org/old/index.php/eng/news/2373-magnificent-festival-in-kolkondas-for-the-feast-of-saint-cosmas, accessed 27 November 2015.

CHAPTER 14

St Paisy Velichkovsky (1722–1794): Reviver of Hesychasm

As we have already noted, in the second half of the eighteenth century the Holy Mountain witnessed a remarkable spiritual revival, not so different from the one that had occurred in the fourteenth century. It focused on three particular concerns: a return to the early Church Fathers and to reading patristic literature; a revival of hesychasm, and in particular the practice of the Jesus Prayer; and finally an emphasis on the institution of the spiritual father (*geron* in Greek, *starets* in Russian). Since the early sixteenth century, when St Maximos spent an intellectually fruitful and spiritually rewarding decade at Vatopedi, the tradition of hesychasm had worn very thin and very nearly died out on the Mountain. Similarly in Russia, monasticism as a whole was for practical purposes eclipsed by the reforms of Peter the Great (1682–1725), but there is a strong possibility that the teachings of Nil Sorsky and the Non-Possessors somehow migrated to the Romanian principalities of Moldavia and Wallachia. These two slender hesychastic threads were still in existence when a man 'sent from God', as it were, appeared and was inspired with a determination to join them together.

Paisy was born, he tells us, in 'the glorious Ukrainian city of Poltava', about 250 kilometres east of Kiev.[1] He came from a long line of Orthodox clerics and his family seems to have been well connected. His father, archpriest of Poltava, died when Paisy was only four and he was raised by his mother, who was later to take the veil herself. When he was twelve, his mother petitioned the metropolitan of Kiev that her son be named his father's successor, a petition that was granted. But the young Paisy already had other ideas: from a very early age he immersed himself in reading, not

---

[1] Paisy's partial autobiography survives, covering his early years to 1746, and is available in English: J. M. E. Featherstone (trans.). *The Life of Paisij Velyčkovs'kyi* (Cambridge, MA: Ukrainian Research Institute of Harvard University, 1989), p. 4. See also J. A. McGuckin, 'The Life and Mission of St Paisius Velichkovsky, 1722–1794: An Early Modern Master of the Orthodox Spiritual Life', *Spiritus*, 9: 2 (2009), 157–73.

only Holy Scripture, but also lives of the saints and writings of the Fathers, and, he writes, 'there began to grow in my soul a longing for withdrawal from the world and assumption of the holy monastic habit.'[2]

Paisy was sent away to school in Kiev, where he seems to have devoted much of his time to visiting the local monasteries, including the great monastery of the Caves. One day he chanced upon a Divine Liturgy being celebrated in Moldavian (i.e. Romanian) by the metropolitan of Moldavia. He found himself instantly attracted to that language and that nation and formed a strong desire to travel to foreign parts in order to become a monk. Having completed his studies and taken leave of his mother, he began a series of wanderings from monastery to monastery, first of all in Ukraine and subsequently in Moldavia. His account is full of adventure and makes good reading, but frustratingly it breaks off at the very point when he is about to depart for Mount Athos. This provokes a series of questions that we may try to answer. What drew him to the Holy Mountain? What condition was the Mountain in when he arrived there and what impact did he make on it? Why (after a stay of seventeen years) did he decide to leave? And, most significantly, what did he take away with him when he left Athos?

Arrival on Mount Athos

After the abrupt termination of Paisy's autobiography, the description of his life is continued by Fr Mitrofan, an elderly monk of the monastery of Neamţ in Moldavia. Mitrofan is not as readable as Paisy, but his account is accurate and attractively personal. He tells us that Paisy and his companion Tryfon travelled by sea from Galaţi via Constantinople to Athos where they landed at the harbour of the Great Lavra on the eve of the feast of St Athanasios (5 July). The year was 1746 and Paisy was aged twenty-four. After celebrating the feast, they decided to go to Pantokrator, eight hours' walk up the coast, where there were known to be Russian-speaking monks. But they took no precautions against the Athonite sun, which can be fierce in July; both were seriously afflicted with sunstroke; and though they succeeded in reaching Pantokrator, on the third day Tryfon died. Paisy survived and, having recovered his strength, set out on a quest to find a spiritual father.

Why did Paisy go to Athos? He scarcely mentions the Holy Mountain in his autobiography except to say (with approval) that the holy offices at a certain hermitage were performed 'according to the rule of the holy

---

[2] Featherstone, *The Life of Paisij Velyčkovs'kyj*, p. 5.

mount of Athos' and (with awe) that a certain hieromonk 'had been on the holy mount of Athos'.[3] But Athos obviously stood out, even at this relatively low point in its history, as a beacon of pan-Orthodoxy where the highest monastic standards were upheld, where charismatic elders of all tongues were to be found,[4] and where libraries were believed to contain unknown treasures of spiritual wisdom. Paisy by his own admission enjoyed travelling and was never one to shirk adventure. Having got as far as Moldavia, where many of the monasteries he visited had close links with Athos,[5] it was only natural that he should wish to continue his journey to the spiritual heart of Orthodox monasticism.

Paisy toured the monasteries and hermitages in search of a spiritual father, but he failed to find one, 'for few of our Rus' brethren there knew holy Scripture', according to the Life.[6] Precise statistics are hard to come by, but another Ukrainian, Vassily Barsky (1702–47), visited the Mountain as a pilgrim in 1725 and again in 1744, leaving copious accounts of both journeys. When he visited the Russian monastery of St Panteleimonos in 1725, he found just four monks, two Russians and two Bulgarians; on his second visit, in 1744, he noted that the monastery was now in Greek hands, that it was idiorrhythmic, and that its buildings were in a serious state of disrepair.[7] He observed Russian monks 'wandering hither and thither about the hills, living by manual labour, eating scraps and being despised by all', though he suggested that they only had themselves to blame for this sorry state of affairs: 'for in Russia, where all labour is carried out by dedicated Christians, the monks live in great ease and comfort'.[8] Spiritual life on the Holy Mountain had clearly reached a pretty low ebb, especially for the Slavs, but when the author of the Life writes that 'all the holy monasteries, sketes and cells are filled with Turks', this is surely an anachronism.[9] There is no evidence for a Turkish military presence on

---

[3] Ibid., pp. 70, 80.

[4] On the cosmopolitan make-up of Athos, see Obolensky, *Six Byzantine Portraits*, p. 125: 'The Byzantines, aware of the reality of this supranational bond, called these different ethnic communities of Athos not "nations" (*ethni*) but "tongues" (*glossai*).'

[5] See Chapter 10, pp. 154–60. [6] Featherstone, *The Life of Paisij Velyčkovs'kyj*, p. 99.

[7] Fennell, *The Russians on Athos*, p. 58.

[8] V. G. Barsky, *His Journeys to the Holy Mountain 1725–1726, 1744–1745*, ed. P. Mylonas (Thessaloniki: Agioritiki Estia/Benaki Museum, 2009), pp. 490–1 (in Greek). See also R. Gothóni, *Tales and Truth: Pilgrimage on Mount Athos Past and Present* (Helsinki: Helsinki University Press, 1994), pp. 73–80.

[9] Fr Seraphim Rose (trans.), *Blessed Paisius Velichkovsky: The Man behind the Philokalia* (Platina, CA: St Herman of Alaska Brotherhood, 1976), pp. 58–61. This edition includes later additions to the Life of Paisy which are not present in Mitrofan's text. This is one of them. On the somewhat confused history of the text of this Life, see the Introduction to the 2nd edition (1993), p. 12, and McGuckin, 'The Life and Mission of St Paisius Velichkovsky', p. 159 and n. 8. For convenience we shall continue to refer to the author as Fr Mitrofan.

Athos until the outbreak of the Greek War of Independence in 1821 when
a Turkish garrison of 3,000 troops did indeed enter the peninsula and
proceeded to occupy all the monasteries.[10]

For two-and-a-half years Paisy enjoyed complete ascetic solitude, eating
almost nothing, sleeping on a bare board, rejoicing in his poverty. He
practised profound humility, constant self-reproach, gratitude for everything, contrition of the heart, tears which ran in streams, ceaseless prayer of
the heart. He borrowed books from the monastery of Hilandar. His only
regret was the absence of a spiritual father to whom he could offer
obedience.

An Athonite Brotherhood

There is a long tradition on Athos of hermits shunning disciples but in due
course, as their fame spreads, being pursued by adherents until eventually
they become spiritual fathers to a whole brotherhood. This happened, for
example, to St Euthymios the Younger as long ago as the ninth century; it
happened to St Maximos of Kafsokalyvia in the fourteenth century; in
more recent times, it happened to Elder Joseph the Hesychast (d.1959); and
so it happened to Paisy. One day a certain Wallachian named Bessarion
came to Paisy and begged him to receive him in obedience. Paisy refused.
But Bessarion persisted with tears and finally Paisy was moved to accept
him, but as a companion, an equal, not as a disciple. They rejoiced in
a common pledge of obedience to each other, and in place of a spiritual
father they had the writings of the holy Fathers.

This blessed state was not to last for long. Soon they found themselves
attracting others from the Danubian principalities and Ukraine who had
left the world and wished to live such a life together. For a long time Paisy
refused their requests, protesting his own unworthiness. But eventually,
against his will, he was persuaded to start accepting them and gradually
a group of disciples formed in obedience to him. Before the age of thirty,
then, Paisy, who had failed to find a spiritual father for himself, found
himself already a spiritual father to others.

As the brotherhood grew, they needed more spacious accommodation.
First they were able to buy the cell of Sts Constantine and Helena, which is
close to the monastery of Pantokrator and has a church. But when his
disciples numbered twelve, Paisy was granted a charter by the monastery to
convert another of its dependencies, the cell of the Prophet Elijah, into

---

[10] Speake, *Mount Athos: Renewal in Paradise*, p. 127.

a skete (Plate 37). In less than five years, by 1762, Paisy governed a brotherhood of sixty.[11] At this point he was asked by the Holy Community, the governing body of Mount Athos, to take charge of the monastery of Simonopetra, which was burdened with debts and more or less deserted. Paisy arrived there on 15 April 1762 with thirty-five monks, 'and he entered our monastery', according to the codex of the monastery, 'to dwell here for good, to guard it and to rule it [as] general master, and he was not able to, but rather left it and departed to Moldavia; and on his departure, the monastery was closed up and the Great Mese [the Holy Community] had authority over it'.[12] Paisy was no match for the monastery's Turkish creditors who demanded the repayment of the huge sums that were owing to them. He left the Mountain in 1763, never to return.

Paisy's Legacy to Mount Athos

What impact did Paisy make on the Holy Mountain? It is clear that during the time he spent on Athos his fame spread throughout the Mountain and beyond and he acquired spiritual children of many tongues. His disciples begged him to accept the priesthood and, as before, he protested his unworthiness. But the elders of the Mountain knew differently and told him that he would be guilty of disobedience if he refused. 'For they knew', writes Mitrofan, 'that he was worthy and able to bring many souls to the Lord through his instruction, to enlighten with his teaching those who sat in the darkness of ignorance, to invigorate the enfeebled cenobitic life, and to plant in it the tree of life – thrice-blessed obedience, the soul, as it were, of the cenobitic life.'[13]

At the time of Paisy's stay on Athos, every monastery followed the idiorrhythmic system and had done so since the end of the sixteenth century. This system, which allowed monks greater freedom of action and helped the monasteries to cope with the increasing economic difficulties of the Tourkokratia, may have been a necessary evil, but there is no doubt that it contributed to a moral and spiritual decline that was all too evident by the middle of the eighteenth century. Paisy on the other hand insisted on strict adherence to the cenobitic rule. 'Now he shone yet more brightly', writes Mitrofan after his move to the Prophet Elijah skete, 'and

[11] Fennell, *The Russians on Athos*, p. 62.
[12] G. Smyrnakis, *To Agion Oros* (Athens: 1903; repr. Mount Athos: 1988), p. 591. Cited in S. Papadopoulos (ed.), *Simonopetra: Mount Athos* (Athens: Hellenic Industrial Development Bank, 1991), p. 24.
[13] Featherstone, *The Life of Paisij Velyčkovs'kyj*, p. 101.

illumined all the Holy Mountain through his renewal of the cenobitic monastic life and his institution in it of the chiefest virtue, thrice-blessed obedience.'[14] From the start, the Prophet Elijah skete was a coenobium, guided by the principles of work, obedience, and prayer.

The skete was poor and its grant of land was small, but at least it was self-sufficient. In addition to building their own cells, the monks carved wooden spoons, from the sale of which they derived a small income. And while the brotherhood rested, Paisy copied books and studied. In the words of his biographer, he was 'an example of the virtuous life to all on the Holy Mountain, and a new restorer of the cenobitic monastic life which had fallen into desuetude, he was an instructor and teacher of divine obedience, a true leader to salvation for those in obedience to him, a new miracle'.[15] As for prayer, Paisy was an ardent advocate of the Jesus Prayer and he has been called 'the reviver of the hesychast movement'.[16] Hesychasm had been practised widely on the Mountain in the fourteenth century but had largely died out by the eighteenth. Paisy learnt about it from the elders of Wallachia before he ever went to Athos. We read in his Life,

> As for the nature of vision, and true silence of the mind, and heedfulness to prayer performed by the mind in the heart – these he not only came to understand, but in part also came to enjoy in actuality their Divine power ever moving in the heart . . . And there, strengthened by the doing of God's commandments among those skete ascetics, and by diligent attention to moral virtue and unceasing mental prayer, he made his heart a fragrance of Christ; which, being watered by many tears, with God's cooperation, grew and blossomed.[17]

By his own example, Paisy inspired large numbers of disciples. They were especially attracted, we are told, by the good order in his church, by the services sung antiphonally in Romanian and Slavonic, by the humility and reverence shown by chanters and readers alike, and by the whole brotherhood's standing in church 'with fear of God'; they were struck by the dignified manner in which the services were conducted, by the obedience and humility of the fathers in their work, and by the peace and love that they felt for each other; and they were impressed by their reverent and loving obedience to their elder, and by his fatherly guidance of them, the care with which he assigned tasks, and his loving compassion for their infirmities of soul and body. Even allowing for the eulogistic conventions of the hagiographical genre, it is clear that Paisy set new standards for

---

[14] Ibid., p. 145. [15] Ibid., p. 104. [16] Papadopoulos, *Simonopetra*, p. 24.
[17] Rose, *Blessed Paisius Velichkovsky*, p. 54.

spiritual fatherhood that had widespread and lasting influence on the Mountain and beyond.

The Search for Patristic Texts

We have noted Paisy's love of books and devotion to the Fathers of the Church from an early age. It was partly the famed contents of the libraries that drew him to Athos in the first place; and once there he was borrowing books from the monastery of Hilandar, and making copies of his own of whatever he could lay his hands on. But how did he know that such books existed on the Mountain and how did he know what to look for? Clearly this was not knowledge gained on Athos since the monks there were quite ignorant of these books. Nor is it likely that he was told about them during his period of study in Kiev where the teaching was heavily influenced by Western traditions. Most probably it was during his stay in Moldavia, and most probably Metropolitan Kallistos is right to identify the individual with St Basil, spiritual father of Poiana Mărului (1692–1767), with whom Paisy clearly formed a close bond.[18] As Paisy wrote himself,

> This pious servant of God far surpassed everyone in his understanding of divine Scripture and the teaching of the holy fathers, in spiritual discernment, and in his thorough knowledge of the sacred canons of the holy Church and interpretation of them in accordance with the commentaries of Zonaras, Theodore Balsamon, and others. The fame of his teaching and pious direction toward the path of salvation went out everywhere.[19]

Most significantly, Basil also wrote introductions to the works of Hesychios, Philotheos, and Gregory of Sinai that were to appear in the anthology of spiritual texts known as the *Philokalia*.[20]

In due course, Basil visited Paisy on Athos in 1750 and tonsured him as a monk. Basil was extremely well read in the hesychastic tradition and peppered his own writings with quotations from the 'philokalic' authors. It is therefore highly likely that it was from Basil that Paisy first heard about the Greek texts in the 'philokalic' tradition which he was later to search for on the Holy Mountain, and so it seems that the hesychastic tradition was

[18] Ware, 'St Nikodimos and the *Philokalia*', in Conomos and Speake, *Mount Athos the Sacred Bridge*, pp. 104–5. On Elder Basil, who was canonized in 2003, see also D. Raccanello, *Elder Basil of Poiana Mărului (1692–1767)* (Liberty, TN: St John of Kronstadt Press, 1996).
[19] Featherstone, *The Life of Paisij Velyčkovs'kyj*, pp. 75–6.
[20] Raccanello, *Elder Basil of Poiana Mărului (1692–1767)*, pp. 43–85. Hesychios of Sinai was the author of a work of uncertain date entitled *On Watchfulness and Holiness*.

better preserved in Moldavia in the early eighteenth century than it was on Mount Athos.

Many years later in an important letter to Archimandrite Theodosy of the St Sophrony hermitage in Russia, Paisy explained that the reason for his collecting, correcting, and translating so many works of the Fathers was to ensure that the instruction he gave to his own disciples was based on correct interpretation of Scripture such as could only be found in the teachings of the Fathers, the Apostolic Canons, and the canons of the ecumenical councils:

> And first of all, I began diligently to acquire, by God's help and with not a little labor and expense, the patristic books which teach of obedience and sobriety, of heedfulness and prayer. Some of them I copied out with my own hand, and others I bought with the coins which we had acquired from the labor of our hands.[21]

He began to copy the works of St Hesychios of Vatos, Presbyter of Jerusalem, of St Philotheos of Sinai, of St Theodore of Edessa, and of St Isaac the Syrian. He soon realized, however, that the Slavonic texts he was using were hopelessly corrupt and that the only way to be sure of obtaining an accurate text was to turn to the Greek originals, but he was unable to find them.

> Then I went to the Great skete of the Lavra, St Anne's, and to Kapsokalyvia, and to the skete of Vatopedi, St Demetrius', and to other lavras and monasteries, everywhere asking learned people, and the eldest and most experienced confessors and venerable monks, for the patristic books by name; nowhere, however, was I able to obtain such books, but from everyone I received the same set answer, that 'not only have we not known such books up to now, but we have never even heard of the names of such Saints.'[22]

Shocked by this response from Athonite monks of all people, Paisy did not give up but continued his search, praying for divine mercy. One day as he was walking round the southern tip of the peninsula with two fathers from the Great Lavra, he reached the skete of St Basil, recently established by monks from Cappadocia. Invited into a cell by 'a monk of reverent appearance', he noticed an open book lying on a little table by the window, which the monk, who was a calligrapher, was copying. To his unutterable delight he recognized it as the book of St Peter of Damascus. Paisy asked the monk if he had other such books, to which he replied that he had St

---

[21] Rose, *Blessed Paisius Velichkovsky*, p. 78.   [22] Ibid, p. 81.

Antony the Great, St Gregory of Sinai (but not all), St Philotheos, St Hesychios, St Diadochos, St Thalassios, St Symeon the New Theologian's homily on prayer, St Nikephoros the Monk's homily on prayer, the book of St Isaiah, and other such books, 'but only 22 chapters of St Niketas Stethatos'. Paisy asked the monk why he had not been able to find such books for himself in the monasteries and why everyone he asked had denied all knowledge of them. The monk explained that it was no doubt because the books were written in the purest form of Greek, which very few Greeks nowadays understood, and so they had fallen out of use. But the monks of St Basil's had heard about them before they left Cappadocia; they had acquired a knowledge of ancient Greek; and having found such books in some monasteries, they were now copying them, using them, and trying to put their teaching into practice. Overjoyed at this discovery, Paisy then negotiated with another monk of the skete to have copies made for himself:

> And thus, for the two years and a little more before our departure from the Holy Mountain, this calligrapher, setting to work, copied for me a certain part of the much-desired books, as much as God gave him help; and we, having received them with all joy as a gift of God sent to us from Heaven, departed from the Holy Mountain of Athos.[23]

At last Paisy had found what he came to Athos to seek. We may even surmise that this was his chief reason for going to Athos, that he knew exactly what he was looking for, and once he had found it he had no reason to remain any longer on the Mountain. Without more ado, he returned north to Moldavia with a large contingent of disciples where he continued the task of translating the works of the Fathers into Slavonic and Moldavian for the enlightenment of his spiritual children. As Mitrofan writes,

> For God in His providence had taken His servant, our blessed father, to the Holy Mountain of Athos in order to show him there the true path of the monastic life, that he might become an example of virtue to all and introduce the cenobitic life, and then return here to confirm and enlighten and instruct many in a life of virtue by his words and deeds.[24]

The Kollyvades and the *Philokalia*

In 1754, when Paisy was first searching on Athos for patristic texts in ancient Greek, a disturbance arose in the skete of St Anne over the wish

---

[23] Ibid., p. 85.   [24] Featherstone, *The Life of Paisij Velyčkovs'kyj*, p. 106.

of some of the monks there to celebrate memorial services on Sundays after the Divine Liturgy instead of on Saturdays, as was the Athonite tradition. The dispute was broadened to include other issues such as that of frequent communion and developed into a major controversy which came to divide the Mountain, the supporters of the traditional position being known as Kollyvades (from *kollyva*, the concoction of boiled wheat and sugar that is eaten after memorial services). The leaders of the Kollyvades movement, who included St Makarios Notaras (1731–1805), formerly archbishop of Corinth, and St Nikodimos of the Holy Mountain (1749–1809), took the view that it was necessary to return to the authentic springs of Orthodox tradition in order to combat the spiritual decline that had set in even in the monasteries of Mount Athos under the influence of the Western Enlightenment. This involved a rediscovery of patristic theology and Orthodox liturgical life, aspirations with which Paisy was happy to be associated. They were attacked especially for their advocacy of frequent communion, not only by other monks but even by the ecumenical patriarchate, and it was not until 1819 that a council in Constantinople settled the dispute by affirming that, if properly prepared, the faithful may receive the sacrament at every celebration of the Divine Liturgy.[25]

One of the most important achievements of this movement, of which more will be said in the next chapter, was the publication in Venice in 1782 of the *Philokalia*, a voluminous anthology of ascetic and mystical writings dating from the fourth century to the fifteenth, and the following year its companion volume the *Evergetinos*. The editors of the *Philokalia* were St Makarios and St Nikodimos of the Holy Mountain, but the selection of the material to be included was made by Makarios, and it was Makarios who raised the funds to pay for the printing of both books as well as the treatise *On Continual Communion*. On what principles Makarios selected the texts for inclusion is an open question, though C. Papoulides has written, 'It is not accidental that almost all the Greek texts which Paisy was interested in are again found in the *Philokalia*. These texts were no longer in use among the Greeks.'[26] Paisy himself tells us that Makarios came to Athos and scoured the libraries of the monasteries for patristic texts:

---

[25] On the Kollyvades and their advocacy of frequent communion, see Hieromonk Patapios and Archbishop Chrysostomos, *Manna from Athos: The Issue of Frequent Communion on the Holy Mountain in the Late Eighteenth and Early Nineteenth Centuries* (Oxford: Peter Lang, 2006), pp. 27–43.

[26] C. Papoulides, 'Le Starets Paisij Velitchkovskij (1722–1794)', *Theologia*, 39 (1968), 8–10.

Above all, in the library of the most glorious and great monastery of Vatopedi he acquired a priceless treasure, a book on the union of the mind with God, gathered from all the Saints by great zealots in ancient times, and other books on prayer which until then we had not heard of. Having copied these out in several years by means of many skilled calligraphers and at no little expense, and having read them himself, comparing them with the originals, and having corrected them most surely and added the lives of all the holy writers of these books at the beginning of their books, he departed from the Holy Mountain of Athos with unutterable joy, having obtained a heavenly treasure upon earth.[27]

To this he added a further thirty-six patristic works, from which it seems that his selection was guided not so much by his own judgement as by a tradition that had long existed on Athos. Of this tradition, Metropolitan Kallistos has written:

> There seem to have been earlier 'philokalic' collections, circulating in manuscript, of which Makarios made use and with which Paisii was also familiar. In that case, the selection of material in the *Philokalia* is perhaps not due simply to the personal judgement of Makarios, or to the joint decision of Makarios and Nikodimos: it may reflect an established programme of spiritual formation, pursued more or less widely by Athonite monks in the later Byzantine and post-Byzantine era.[28]

On his return to Moldavia, Paisy found himself at the head of an ever-increasing flock of monks as he moved from one monastery to the next, eventually settling in 1779 at Neamţ (Plate 38). Here he continued his work of editing the Greek texts of the Fathers, and he made a translation of the *Philokalia* into Slavonic, which was finally published in Moscow in 1793 under the title of the *Dobrotolyubie* (which literally means 'love of good' and is simply a calque of the Greek *philokalia*). This publication signalled the beginning of the rapid dissemination of the *Philokalia* from its original Athonite cradle throughout the Slav Orthodox world. As a result of Paisy's dominating presence and spiritual eminence, Paschalis Kitromilides writes,

> Neamţ Monastery became a beacon that radiated the 'Philokalic' tradition of Orthodox mysticism to monasteries in the Ukraine and the Volga region. As Orthodoxy spread across Siberia along with Russian imperial expansion into those regions, the heritage of the *Philokalia* was transmitted from its new great centre at Optino monastery, to monasteries across northern Asia and from there it crossed the Beringian straits into Alaska and found new hearths of reception in Russian monasteries in the Aleutian islands.

---

[27] Rose, *Blessed Paisius Velichkovsky*, pp. 180–3.
[28] K. Ware, 'The Spirituality of the *Philokalia*', *Sobornost*, 13: 1 (1991), 6–24 (11).

The phenomenal spread of Philokalic spirituality to the North and East is captured graphically in a truly impressive chart of the transmission of Paisij Veličkovskij's teaching that adorns his cell in Neamț monastery. No fewer than 177 monastic foundations are listed on the chart and 212 names of persons who acted as agents in the process of spiritual transmission.[29]

Paisy's entry in the *Synaxarion* ends with these words:

> Saint Paisius fell asleep in peace on 15 November 1794, one year after the publication of the *Philokalia* in Slavonic, based largely on translations that he and his disciples had made many years before. These translations, and the influence of the Saint through the activity of his disciples in Russia, led to a widespread spiritual renewal, and to the restoration of traditional monastic life there which lasted until the Revolution of 1917.[30]

Paisy's Legacy to Russia

'In the midst of all their activities', asks Fr Mitrofan when discussing Paisy's legacy, 'where precisely was the *heart* of Paisius' monks? It was in the desert, in the love for the silent inward activity in secluded forested mountains.'[31] Throughout his life, the saint had maintained contact with many contemporary desert-dwellers who lived under his guidance in the forests of Moldavia. After his death, many of his Russian disciples returned to their homeland, bearing with them this ideal of the desert which they promoted vigorously. They included such elders as Feofan who travelled north as far as the Arctic desert of Solovki; Feodor and Kleop who together with the future Leonid of Optino toiled in the monastic desert around Valaam; another Kleop who suffered persecution and through his ceaseless wandering inspired many other disciples including the celebrated desert fathers Vasilisk and Zosima of Siberia; and another Feofan who with the future founders of Optino monastery, Moisey and Antony, and Dorofey pursued the ascetic life in the dense forests of Roslavl. These last-mentioned monks inherited many of Paisy's patristic manuscripts, which they copied and recopied in their remote desert huts and which in due course formed the kernel of the library of patristic texts to be published by the elders of Optino. These books were much in demand and circulated widely, contributing to the dissemination of the hesychast ideal and the

---

[29] P. M. Kitromilides, '*Philokalia*'s First Journey', ch. 8 in his *An Orthodox Commonwealth*, p. 344.
[30] Hieromonk Makarios, *The Synaxarion*, vol. 2 (1999), pp. 153–4.
[31] Rose, *Blessed Paisius Velichkovsky*, pp. 249–50.

monastic renewal that continued in Russia, Mount Athos, and the Holy Land until the Revolution of 1917.

Many monasteries played a part in this renewal, but there was one that served as the undisputed centre for the whole movement. Optina Pustyn (Pustynya means 'desert' in Russian) is located in the region of Kaluga about 130 kilometres south-west of Moscow. According to oral tradition, it was originally founded in the fifteenth century but suffered destruction more than once before its restoration was initiated in the 1790s by Metropolitan Platon of Moscow and Kaluga (1775–1812). At the turn of the century, it was in the care of Abbot Avraam (1796–1813), whose teacher had himself been a disciple of Paisy and who had himself possessed a copy of the *Dobrotolyubie.* But it was under the long-reigning Abbot Moisey (1825–62), one of the desert fathers from the forest of Roslavl, that the monastery first attained a position of wealth and influence. In 1821, with the blessing of Platon's successor, Metropolitan Filaret, Fr Moisey (four years before he became abbot) with his younger brother Antony founded the skete or hermitage of St John the Forerunner, which was designed to cater for the current revival in eremitic monasticism. When Moisey became abbot of the main monastery in 1825, Antony was elected prior of the skete. The hermitage became a centre for the practice of hesychasm and spiritual guidance (*starchestvo*) under a succession of elders who brought renown to the monastery. By 1865 the whole place was flourishing with over a hundred monks in the monastery and another thirty in the hermitage.

In addition to spiritual guidance, the monastery acquired a reputation for the editing and publication of patristic texts and other spiritual literature. This was another activity inherited as part of Paisy's legacy, which extended the influence of the elders way beyond their immediate geographical location. The monks began in the 1840s by producing books written in Church Slavonic, but by the 1860s all their publications were in Russian in order to reach a wider readership.[32] The literary activities of the monks combined with the spiritual reputation of the elders made the monastery a focal point of pilgrimage for Russia's most celebrated writers of the time. Fyodor Dostoevsky, Nikolai Gogol, Leo Tolstoy, Ivan Kireevsky, Vladimir Soloviev, and Konstantin Leontiev are all recorded as visitors, many of them on a regular basis.

---

[32] An annotated bibliography of the monastery's publications appears in L. J. Stanton, *The Optina Pustyn Monastery in the Russian Literary Imagination: Iconic Vision in Works by Dostoevsky, Gogol, Tolstoy, and Others* (New York: Peter Lang, 1995), pp. 265–76.

But it was for its remarkable succession of spiritual elders that Optino gained its greatest renown. Abbot Moisey, though not an elder himself, was sufficiently pragmatic and magnanimous to see the need for a spiritual haven in which eldership could flourish. During his abbacy two highly influential elders, Leonid (1768–1841) and Makary (1788–1860), joined the community at Optino and they, together with *Starets* Amvrosy (1821–91), represent a golden age spanning the years from 1821 to 1891. The first two were both trained by former disciples of Paisy; Amvrosy was a disciple of Leonid. Leonid's spiritual children were mostly monastics and peasants and he appealed to women of all classes. His cell was just outside the precinct of the skete, which enabled him to receive women without causing offence to the brotherhood. Makary by contrast had wide contacts with intellectuals whose discipleship enabled the elders to address issues of contemporary concern in the areas of politics, culture, and ideas. Amvrosy was bedridden for much of his life, but this did not prevent him from receiving a stream of visitors in need of counsel or from founding a women's monastery in nearby Shamordino. The intelligentsia in particular swarmed to receive his inspired guidance.

Writers as Disciples of the Elders

By the 1840s Optino was established as a centre of *starchestvo*. Elder Leonid had died in 1841 and was succeeded by Makary whose noble birth and educated background enabled him to mix easily with Russia's new breed of questioning intellectuals. One of the first to seek him out was the philosopher Ivan Kireevsky (1806–56) who with Aleksey Khomyakov was co-founder of the Slavophile movement. Kireevsky had developed an interest in monasticism and monastic literature, particularly of the patristic period, which he regarded as the forgotten heart of Russia's spiritual tradition, and this drew him into a literary partnership with Makary. In the late 1840s and early 1850s Kireevsky made regular visits to Optino in connection with the monastery's publishing programme of translations from the Church Fathers. He was very well connected with all the intellectual circles of the time, and through him many came to think of Optino as the embodiment of Russia's ancient spiritual tradition, the very heart of the 'Russian idea'. In his book about the intellectual standing of the monastery, Stanton describes the attraction that the elder's lifestyle presented:

> What Makarii had found was a detachment from the things of the world that enabled him to enjoy continuous and intimate relations with the Holy

Spirit; and as a consequence of those relations, the Russian soil on which Makarii walked and the cell in which he received visitors, prayed, and slept were rendered holy and thus whole. If there was a spot where a wholistic [*sic*] and perichoretic Russian idea could be sprung from the soil it was here at Makarii's home, Optina Pustyn ... The Optina skete seemed to blend with the forest around it; the monastery was full of flowers and beehives. The elders, some tucked away in deep woods [and] hermitages even beyond the skete, were in such free and intimate relations with both heaven and earth that, in letter and legend, they became one with nature; after the model of St Serafim of Sarov, even the bears and wolves were their intimate companions.[33]

Nikolai Gogol (1809–52) visited Optino at least twice towards the end of his life. He seems to have struck a particularly close rapport with one of the younger monks, Fr Porfiry Grigorov, who was a great admirer of Pushkin's poetry and who valued Gogol as a writer, but this association was cut short by the monk's death in 1851. After that Gogol's relations with the fathers became more strained as he sent them desperate pleas for prayer for himself. Elder Makary grew fond of him and the two exchanged letters, but even the sympathetic elder was unable to save Gogol from his self-destructive tendencies, and his perceptive criticism of some of Gogol's more crackpot writing was more than the writer could bear. After his visit in September 1851, Gogol had no more contact with Optino. He returned to Moscow in utter misery and starved himself to death.

Fyodor Dostoevsky (1821–81) had a much more constructive relationship with the elders and made extensive use of Fr Kliment Zedergol'm's Life of Elder Leonid (1876) in writing his novel *The Brothers Karamazov*. Zedergol'm himself was a learned and educated intellectual, a protégé of Kireevsky, and in due course a monk of the Optino monastery where he was able to pursue his literary interests as a translator of patristic texts into Russian, a writer of elders' lives, and as secretary to Elder Amvrosy. In his Life of Elder Leonid, he tells the story of a distinguished academic's visit to the monastery, which is reminiscent of the stories told of St Sergius of Radonezh:

> One day the rector of Seminary 'N' arrived at Optina Pustyn. When it was suggested that he have a talk with Father Leonid, he said, 'Why would I speak with him, that peasant?' Nevertheless, he went to the elder. When he entered [Leonid's] cell, Father Leonid repeated his words, 'Why would you speak with a peasant like me?' In spite of such an impudent greeting, the rector spoke pleasantly with Father Leonid for two hours, and afterwards

---

[33] Ibid., pp. 97–8.

said of the elder, 'What is [all] our learning? His learning is hard-earned and blessed.'[34]

Zedergol'm was already dead before Dostoevsky made his only documented visit to Optino, shortly after the death of his three-year-old son Aleksei, in June 1878. The grief-stricken father had several meetings with Elder Amvrosy and used his impressions of the elder, the monastery, and the hermitage as background material for *The Brothers Karamazov*, which he had just started writing. His debt to Zedergol'm's Life of Elder Leonid, however, is especially apparent in the following two pairs of quotations. In the first Zedergol'm describes the origins of the institution of eldership and its transition to Russia:

> The elders' way of guidance has been recognized as the most reliable and fitting of any that were known in the Christian Church in all the ages of Christianity by all the great hermits, fathers, and teachers of the Church. Elderhood flowered in the ancient Egyptian and Palestinian cenobitic communities, was later planted on Mount Athos, and was brought from the East to Russia. But in the last centuries, with the general decline of faith and spiritual struggle, it had begun gradually to be forgotten, so that many even began to reject it. Even in the time of Nil Sorskii, the elders' way was odious to many, and at the end of the previous century it had become almost completely forgotten. A great contribution to the reestablishment in Russia of this form of monastic life founded on the teachings of the Holy Fathers was made by the great and renowned elder and archimandrite of monasteries in Moldavia, Paisii Velichkovskii. With a great amount of labour, he collected on Mount Athos, and translated from the Greek language into Slavonic, works of ascetic writers containing teaching on the monastic life generally, and on the spiritual relationship with elders in particular. Additionally, at the Niamets Monastery and other Moldavian monasteries subordinate to it he presented these teachings and put them into practice. One of archimandrite Paisii's disciples, the skhima-monk Feodor, who lived in Moldavia about twenty years, passed this order of monastic life to Father Leonid, and it was planted at Optina Pustyn by him and his disciple the skhima-monk Father Makarii.[35]

In *Karamazov* Dostoevsky models the *Starets* Zosima on his own meetings with Elder Amvrosy, but his explanation of the origins of elderhood is taken direct from Zedergol'm's Life of Leonid:

---

[34] Cited in ibid., p. 159.
[35] K. Zedergol'm, *Elder Leonid of Optina* (Platina, CA: St Herman of Alaska Brotherhood, 1976), pp. 35–6.

This elder was, as I have explained above, the elder Zossima; but I have first to say a few words here about what 'elders' are in our monasteries ... competent experts assert that elders and the institution of elders made an appearance in our country and in our monasteries quite recently, not more than a hundred years ago, while in the Orthodox East, and especially in Sinai and on Mount Athos, they have existed for over a thousand years. It is said that the institution of elders ... was revived in our country towards the end of the last century by one of the great ascetics (as he was called) Paissy Velichkovsky and his disciples, but today, even after a hundred years, they are to be found only in a very few monasteries, and are sometimes even persecuted as an unheard-of innovation in Russia. It flourished especially in Russia in the famous Kozelsky monastery. When and how it was introduced into our monastery I cannot say, but there has already been a third succession of elders there. Zossima was one of the last ...[36]

The novelist goes on to describe the role of the elder in the life of the disciple:

What then is an elder? An elder is a man who takes your soul and your will into his soul and his will. Having chosen your elder, you renounce your will and yield it to him in complete submission and complete self-abnegation. This novitiate, this terrible discipline is accepted voluntarily by the man who consecrates himself to this life in the hope that after a long novitiate he will attain to such a degree of self-mastery and self-conquest that at last he will, after a life of obedience, achieve complete freedom, that is to say, freedom from himself, and so escape the fate of those who have lived their whole lives without finding themselves in themselves ... The elder's disciples must always be ready to make confession to him, and there must be an indissoluble bond between the elder and his followers.[37]

As an example of the indestructibility of this bond, the narrator recalls the following story, which has a singular relevance to our theme in this book:

Here is something that happened quite recently: a Russian monk of our own day, who was seeking salvation on Mount Athos, was suddenly told by his elder to leave Athos, which he had grown to love greatly as a holy place and a haven of rest, and go first to Jerusalem to worship at the Holy Places, and then return to the north of Siberia. 'Your place is there and not here', the elder told him. Cast down with grief, the astonished monk went to the Oecumenical Patriarch at Constantinople and begged him to release him from his vow of obedience. But the Oecumenical Patriarch replied that not only was he unable to release him, but that there was not, and could not be,

[36] Fyodor Dostoevsky, *The Brothers Karamazov*, trans. D. Magarshack (Harmondsworth: Penguin, 1958), vol. 1, p. 27.
[37] Ibid., p. 28.

on earth a power which could release him from his vow, once exacted by an elder, except the elder who had exacted it from him.[38]

Here again we find that the novelist is indebted to Zedergol'm who tells a very similar story in the Life of Elder Leonid:

> St Feodor the Studite writes, 'an elder told his disciple several times to perform a certain task, but the latter kept putting it off. Disapproving of this, the elder in his displeasure imposed on the disciple a censure, not to eat bread until he had performed the assigned task. When the disciple went to perform what had been ordered, the elder died. After his death the disciple wished to receive a dispensation from the censure that had been imposed on him. But no one was found in that desert region who ventured to resolve that quandary. At last the disciple turned with his request to the Patriarch of Constantinople Germanus, who gathered the other bishops for the consideration of this matter. But neither the Patriarch nor the assembled council found it possible to dispense the censure of the elder about whom it is even uncertain whether or not he was under holy orders. Thus the disciple was required until his death to eat food solely of [uncooked] vegetables.'[39]

The adaptation and integration of these passages from the Life of Elder Leonid into the novel is striking and, as Stanton remarks, demonstrates Dostoevsky's use of the Life 'as a vehicle to appropriate the entire literary and devotional tradition of hesychasm and elderhood (as received by the monks at Optino) into the structure of his novel'.[40]

Karamazov is a work that defies description. At one stage during its composition, Dostoevsky gave it the title 'The Life of a Great Sinner', and Elder Amvrosy is said to have remarked about the writer after one of their meetings, 'there is one who repents'.[41] Its genre has troubled many critics, but it is surely verging on blasphemy to describe it as 'Scripture rather than novel or tragedy, saga or chronicle', as one translator has.[42] It is true that Dostoevsky believed that the solution to Russia's troubles lay in the Orthodox Church and hoped that his writing would show the way to it. But ultimately, we have to side with the conclusion of an earlier translator, David Magarshack: 'It is in the universal human drama that [*Karamazov*'s] greatness lies, and not in Dostoevsky's ill-contrived attempt to transform Russia into a huge monastery.'[43]

---

[38] Ibid., pp. 28–9.   [39] Zedergol'm, *Elder Leonid of Optina*, pp. 32–3.

[40] Stanton, *The Optina Pustyn Monastery*, p. 175.

[41] J. B. Dunlop, *Staretz Amvrosy* (London and Oxford: Mowbrays, 1975), p. 59.

[42] Fyodor Dostoevsky, *The Brothers Karamazov*, ed. and trans. H. Bloom (New York: Chelsea House, 1988), p. 1.

[43] Dostoevsky, *The Brothers Karamazov*, trans. D. Magarshack, vol. 1, p. xxiii.

Leo Tolstoy (1828–1910), a man more renowned for his pride than for asceticism, first met Elder Amvrosy in 1877 and was said to be 'impressed by his wisdom'. He came again four years later, dressed as a peasant, and is said to have remarked after their meeting, 'That Fr Amvrosy is a completely holy man. I talked with him and somehow my soul felt light and gay. When one talks with such a man one feels the nearness of God.'[44] He visited again at least three more times, in 1890, 1896, and shortly before his death in 1910. Exactly why he came to the monastery so often is unclear. His home was not far away; but his relations with the elders, as with religion as a whole, were equivocal to say the least. His sister, who had become a nun at Shamordino, tried to give an answer to the question when writing to a friend after his death:

> You are asking me what my brother sought in Optina? A father confessor or a sage living in solitude with God and his conscience who would have understood my brother and lightened somewhat the burden of his great sorrow? No, I do not think he sought either the one or the other. His sorrow was too complicated; he simply wanted to find peace and live for a time in quiet, spiritual surroundings. I do not think he wanted to return to the Orthodox faith.[45]

The work that tells us most about Tolstoy's regard for Optino is his posthumously published story 'Father Sergius' (1911) in which the hero, who begins life as a prince and an army officer, subsequently joins a monastery whose abbot had been a disciple of Elder Amvrosy. His reason for doing so is said to be a wish to show 'contempt for all that seemed most important to others and had seemed so to him while he was in the service, and he now ascended a height from which he could look down on those he had formerly envied'.[46] After twenty years in the monastery, and an unfortunate episode with a visiting merchant's daughter, he leaves and in fulfilment of a long-held ambition takes to the road as a wandering pilgrim. The story ends in Siberia where he has found work as the paid serf of a wealthy peasant. The hero, and perhaps the writer, is most at home in the natural world which is beautifully described in a number of lyrical passages.

The image of a holy man wandering in an antelapsarian paradise was familiar from the writings of the Desert Fathers and also from its more recent Russian revival in the nineteenth-century classic of Orthodox spirituality, *The Way of a Pilgrim*, first printed at Kazan' in 1881. This

---

[44] Cited in Dunlop, *Staretz Amvrosy*, pp. 60–1.
[45] Letter to Charles Salomon, cited in Stanton, *The Optina Pustyn Monastery*, p. 215.
[46] Cited in Stanton, *The Optina Pustyn Monastery*, p. 217.

anonymous story, in which the hero's most treasured (and almost sole) possession is his copy of the *Philokalia* and whose chief source of consolation is the Jesus Prayer, emerged directly from the tradition of St Paisy and the Optino monastery. There have been suggestions that its author was possibly Elder Amvrosy himself and certainly it was a tradition with which Tolstoy was thoroughly familiar.[47] But recently it has been shown to be a reworking of earlier material, edited into its current form by St Theophan the Recluse who was himself the Russian translator of the *Dobrotolyubie*.[48]

In this passage, which comes near the end, the pilgrim describes his feelings of intense joy as he wanders:

> I went along without hurrying for about a month with a deep sense of the way in which good lives teach us and spur us on to copy them. I read *The Philokalia* a great deal, and there made sure of everything I had told the blind man of prayer. His example kindled in me zeal and thankfulness and love for God. The Prayer of my heart gave me such consolation that I felt there was no happier person on earth than I, and I doubted if there could be greater and fuller happiness in the kingdom of Heaven. Not only did I feel this in my own soul, but the whole outside world also seemed to me full of charm and delight. Everything drew me to love and thank God; people, trees, plants, animals. I saw them all as my kinsfolk, I found on all of them the magic of the Name of Jesus. Sometimes I felt as light as though I had no body and was floating happily through the air instead of walking. Sometimes when I withdrew into myself I saw clearly all my internal organs, and was filled with wonder at the wisdom with which the human body is made. Sometimes I felt as joyful as if I had been made Tsar. And at all such times of happiness, I wished that God would let death come to me quickly, and let me pour out my heart in thankfulness at His feet in the world of spirits.[49]

The Way of a Pilgrim has been immensely influential throughout the Orthodox world and beyond. No doubt Fr Sergius (and perhaps his creator too) was among those influenced by it. It is directly linked with the Athonite tradition of spirituality: even its manuscript was first found, by the abbot of St Michael's monastery, Kazan', in the library of St Panteleimonos monastery on Athos. And the location of the pilgrim's travels is of no particular significance: he might just as well have been wandering from one monastery to another or one skete to another on the Holy Mountain as from one holy place to another across the widely scattered districts of Russia and Siberia.

[47] See Stanton, *The Optina Pustyn Monastery*, p. 228, n. 35.
[48] See A. Louth, *Modern Orthodox Thinkers: From the* Philokalia *to the Present* (London: SPCK, 2015), p. 12.
[49] *The Way of a Pilgrim*, trans. R. M. French, 2nd edn (London: SPCK, 1995), pp. 105–6.

Thanks to Paisy and the spiritual tradition that he inspired, the whole of Russia and Siberia, even if they were not one huge monastery, were now permanent members of the Athonite Commonwealth. And if there was a temporary lapse of membership in 1923, when Optino was closed, it was fully renewed in 1987, when the monastery was returned to the Russian Orthodox Church. In fact, we may say that with the revival of monasticism in Russia and Romania since the fall of communism Paisy's legacy is alive and well to this day. If the Prophet Elijah skete on Mount Athos ceased to be a Russian house in 1992,[50] the monasteries of Moldavia flourish as never before, as do those houses founded by his disciples across the breadth of Russia. As Fr Georges Florovsky has written, 'Paisy lived in the past, in traditions, and in Tradition. Yet he proved to be the prophet and harbinger of things to come. The return to sources revealed new roads and meant the acquisition of new horizons.'[51]

---

[50] See Speake, *Mount Athos: Renewal in Paradise*, pp. 165–6. It has since been colonized by Greek monks and remains a thriving coenobium.

[51] G. Florovsky, *Ways of Russian Theology. Collected Works*, vol. 5 (Belmont, MA: Institute for Byzantine and Modern Greek Studies, 1979), p. 161. On the resurgence of Orthodoxy in Russia since the end of communism, see J. P. Burgess, *Holy Rus': The Rebirth of Orthodoxy in the New Russia* (New Haven, CT, and London: Yale University Press, 2017).

CHAPTER 15

St Nikodimos of the Holy Mountain (1749–1809): Editor of the Philokalia

This book is primarily concerned with holy men who have been drawn to Athos from all parts of Eastern Europe, have absorbed its way of life and its spirituality, and have then returned, either whence they came or to some other part of the Orthodox world, taking with them the monastic fruits that they have gathered in the garden of the Mother of God. There are two exceptions to this pattern. St Athanasios qualified for inclusion because he was really the initiator of the whole process: it was he who established the first coenobium, attracted the first wave of immigrant monks from all over the Byzantine Empire and beyond, and turned the Mountain into a 'city'. The other exception is St Nikodimos. He moved to Athos at the age of twenty-six and remained there for the rest of his life. He did not himself return to the world, as all the others have done, but he is included for what he created when he was there. His principal gift to the world has perhaps had a greater influence on Orthodox spirituality than the missions of all our other characters put together; and the *Philokalia* was only one of no fewer than 109 works listed by Constantine Cavarnos as flowing from his pen.[1] If Athanasios turned the Mountain into a city, then Nikodimos turned himself into 'an encyclopedia of the Athonite learning of his time'.[2]

Nikodimos, whose baptismal name was Nicholas, was born on the island of Naxos in 1749. His parents were sufficiently prosperous to give their children a good education, and his younger brother became a doctor. The young Nikodimos attended the school on Naxos where he was a pupil of Archimandrite Chrysanthos (the brother of St Kosmas the Aetolian), whom we encountered in Chapter 13. Chrysanthos was a distinguished teacher in his own right, but he also shared his brother's beliefs and concerns for the Greek people which he imparted to his pupils.

---

[1] C. Cavarnos, *St Nicodemos the Hagiorite*, 2nd edn (Belmont, MA: Institute for Byzantine and Modern Greek Studies, 1979), pp. 96–114. See also Elia Citterio, 'Nicodemo Agiorita', in C. G. and V. Conticello (eds), *La Théologie byzantine et sa tradition*, vol. 2, pp. 905–97.

[2] M. Gedeon, *O Athos* (Constantinople, 1885), p. 216.

Nikodimos therefore grew up in the spiritual and intellectual atmosphere that St Kosmas was creating as he travelled around Greece on his missionary journeys. On leaving the school in Naxos, he continued his studies at the Evangelical School in Smyrna where the curriculum embraced both secular and religious topics and foreign languages including Latin, French, and Italian. After five years at this school (1765–70), during which time he so impressed his teachers with his learning and his photographic memory that he was invited to join the teaching staff, he returned to Naxos where he took up a post as secretary and assistant to Anthimos Vardis, metropolitan of Paros and Naxos. During these years on Naxos, Nikodimos met a number of monks from Athos. They put him in touch with Makarios Notaras (1731–1805), the former bishop of Corinth, whom he visited on the nearby island of Hydra, a meeting that was to have a significant impact on his future life. Makarios had been elected bishop of Corinth in 1764, while still a layman, and devoted himself to raising the spiritual and educational levels of the clergy. But under suspicion of collaborating with the Russians after the outbreak of the Russo-Turkish war (1768–74), he was unable to return to his see and led a peripatetic existence, wandering from island to island in the Aegean and staying in small hermitages on the Holy Mountain. The monks from Athos whom Nikodimos met on Naxos had in fact been expelled from the Mountain for being members of the so-called Kollyvades movement, which had its origins on Athos in the second half of the eighteenth century. So who were these Kollyvades and why had they been expelled from the Mountain?

Athos, the Kollyvades, and the *Philokalia*

The name 'Kollyvades', as noted in the last chapter, is derived from *kollyva*, which is a concoction of boiled wheat and sugar which is distributed to those attending memorial services for the dead. Such services are traditionally held on Saturdays, but when in 1754 the monks of St Anne's skete on Athos decided that it would be more convenient to hold them on Sunday, after the end of the Divine Liturgy, there was uproar. The leading opponent of this innovation, which he regarded as contrary to ancient tradition, was Deacon Neophytos of Kafsokalyvia (1713–84), but he was soon joined by others, and as a group they were known as the Kollyvades. Other leading members of the group included Athanasios Parios (1721–1813) and Makarios Notaras. It developed into a full-scale protest movement, and their cause was broadened to embrace the safeguarding of all aspects of Orthodox faith and life, both inner prayer and external observance.

In particular, they adhered to the teachings and practices of hesychasm and held in high regard the writings of such authors as St Symeon the New Theologian, St Gregory of Sinai, and St Gregory Palamas. They believed that Orthodoxy was being threatened by secularizing trends that had reached the Greek intelligentsia emanating from the Western European Enlightenment. The only hope for the Greek Church and the Greek people, they maintained, was to recover the theology and spirituality of the Fathers and to rediscover the authentic sources of patristic and Byzantine tradition.

The views of the Kollyvades were not shared by all their contemporaries and the ensuing controversy divided Athos. Feelings ran high, protests were not always peaceful, opinions on both sides were subject to distortion, some monks were beaten up, and others were banished from the Mountain. The patriarch of Constantinople was drawn into the argument and attempted without success to reach a compromise by means of a succession of conciliatory letters. In 1776 the anti-Kollyvades temporarily won the patriarchate to their side: Patriarch Sophronios II publicly condemned the movement and demanded that Athanasios Parios be unfrocked. This never in fact happened, the Kollyvades remained true to their beliefs and were eventually vindicated, but some of them were compelled temporarily to leave the Mountain.

This was the context in which Nikodimos met St Makarios on Hydra and the other Kollyvades on Naxos. He was particularly impressed by one Silvestros, an Athonite originally from Caesarea in Asia Minor, who was a practising hesychast with a deep understanding of the mystical writers of Byzantium. Silvestros introduced Nikodimos to the theory and practice of inner prayer and other aspects of Athonite spirituality and gave him a letter of introduction to the fathers of the Holy Mountain. Armed with this, Nikodimos left for Athos at the age of twenty-six and went first to the monastery of Dionysiou where he was tonsured a monk. He soon made an impression on the fathers of the monastery with his exceptional gifts of piety and learning, and he was appointed a reader. As Paisy Velichkovsky had found, standards of spirituality on the Holy Mountain had degenerated in the course of the eighteenth century, but Dionysiou seems to have been an exception (as it was to be again in the mid twentieth century). According to the Life of St Nikodimos compiled sixty years ago by Fr Gerasimos of Little St Anne,

> he found there many holy men adorned with every virtue, with piety and the gifts of spiritual endeavor. Among these was *Gerontas* Macarios with his

father Avramios and others leading a life of spiritual struggle with devout-
ness and holiness. Admiring their inner excellences, he settled in this holy
and venerable coenobitic monastery.[3]

It seems therefore that Nikodimos found there a spiritual father and that he
settled easily into the cenobitic life of the monastery. But he was not
destined to remain there for long.

In 1777 Makarios Notaras, the reformer and scholar whom Nikodimos
had met a few years earlier on Hydra, arrived on the Mountain.
Establishing himself in a *kelli* in Karyes, he sent for Nikodimos and the
two men began a collaboration that was to bear abundant fruit. Both were
also now leading members of the Kollyvades movement, whose objects
have been summarized by Metropolitan Kallistos:

> Their programme had two main aspects, sacramental and educational.
> On the sacramental side, they attempted to promote a eucharistic revival,
> commending – contrary to the normal Orthodox practice of the time –
> 'continual communion', that is to say, frequent and if possible daily
> reception of the sacrament. For this they were fiercely attacked, both on
> Mount Athos and at Constantinople, but their standpoint was eventually
> endorsed by the ecumenical patriarchate. Makarios and Nikodimos in
> particular were firm supporters of frequent communion, both in their
> personal practice and in their writings. On the educational side, the
> Kollyvades sought to publish and distribute editions of the Fathers, the
> lives of the saints and the liturgical texts, thus combatting the prevailing
> ignorance within the Greek Church under the Ottomans and recalling to
> their contemporaries the true but neglected foundations of Orthodox life.
> In this major programme of editing and publishing, no works were more
> important to the Kollyvades than the *Philokalia* and its companion
> volume the *Evergetinos*.[4]

Makarios immediately invited Nikodimos to correct and edit the texts of
these works and also the volume *On Frequent Communion*, all of which
were already in existence in manuscript. Nikodimos's role in producing
these books was therefore a secondary one, as we noted in the last chapter,
since Makarios had already selected the texts that were to be included.
Nikodimos remained in Karyes for the next five years, working on the task
that he had been given, and when the texts were ready, Makarios took them

[3] Fr Gerasimos, *Akolouthia of Our Holy and God-inspired Father and Teacher Nicodemos the Hagiorite*
(Mount Athos, 1955), abridged and translated in Cavarnos, *St Nicodemos the Hagiorite*, pp. 72–3. This
Life is based on that written by the monk Euthymios, a spiritual brother of Nikodimos, which was
published in the journal *Gregorios Palamas* (1920), 636–41, and (1921), 210–18.
[4] Ware, 'The Spirituality of the *Philokalia*', p. 10. See also his 'St Nikodimos and the *Philokalia*',
pp. 69–121.

to Smyrna in order to raise funds for their publication. He was evidently successful: the *Philokalia* was published in Venice in 1782 with no mention of the editors' names on the title page, though there is acknowledgement of John Mavrogordato as the sponsor; the other two books appeared in the following year.

If Nikodimos's role on the *Philokalia* was for the most part that of amanuensis, he at least had the satisfaction of contributing the introduction to the work.[5] In this, he outlines the importance of the book and its main theme, which is to be a guide to inner prayer. Inner prayer, or prayer of the heart, he says, is not the preserve of monks alone but may be practised by laymen and women too, but it needs 'scientific guidance'. The object of the *Philokalia* is to provide such guidance. The book, he writes, is 'the treasury of inner wakefulness, the safeguard of the mind, the secret school of mental prayer, the instrument of deification'.[6] The ideal of deification (*theosis*) is in fact a unifying thread not only in the introduction but throughout the book as a whole. 'Such then', writes Bishop Kallistos, 'is the purpose for which humans were created, and such is the supreme end of the spiritual life.'[7] And how is this to be achieved? Nikodimos answers that it is necessary for us first to rediscover the grace of baptism:

> The Spirit . . . revealed to the Fathers a method that is truly wonderful and altogether scientific, whereby grace can be rediscovered. This was to pray continually to our Lord Jesus Christ the Son of God; not simply to pray with the intellect and the lips alone . . . but to turn the whole intellect towards the inner self, which is a marvellous experience; and so inwardly, within the very depths of the heart, to invoke the all-holy Name of the Lord, and to implore mercy from Him, concentrating our attention solely on the bare words of the prayer.[8]

By this method, according to Nikodimos, we are enabled to eschew the passions, regain the grace of the Spirit that was bestowed on us at baptism, and achieve the ultimate goal which is *theosis*. The path is summarized by Bishop Kallistos under five headings:

(i)   to pray *without ceasing*;
(ii) to pray in the *depths of the heart*;
(iii) during prayer to *exclude all images and thoughts*;
(iv) to invoke the *Holy Name of Jesus*;

---

[5] This introduction is not included in the translation by Palmer, Sherrard, and Ware.
[6] *Philokalia*, vol. 1 (Athens: Astir-Papadimitriou, 1957), p. xxiii.
[7] Ware, 'The Spirituality of the *Philokalia*', p. 15.   [8] *Philokalia*, vol. 1, p. xx.

(v) to use, if so desired, the *physical technique* (head bowed on chest; control of the breathing; inner exploration).[9]

This is not to say that use of the Jesus Prayer is the sole object of 'philokalic' spirituality, but it is another of the unifying threads running through the whole work.

Nikodimos also goes to some lengths to insist that the *Philokalia* is a work intended for all. Although it is made up of texts written mostly by monks and intended for a largely monastic readership, and although the language is almost entirely the original Byzantine Greek that would be unintelligible to the majority of contemporary readers, the title page states that it is 'for the general benefit of the Orthodox' and in his introduction Nikodimos writes that the book is aimed at 'all who share the Orthodox calling, laity and monks alike'.[10] Similarly, in a prefatory note that he added before an excerpt from the Life of St Gregory Palamas by Philotheos Kokkinos, he wrote: 'Let no one think, my brother Christians, that only clergy and monks need to pray at all times without interruption, and not lay people. No, no! As Christians, we are all of us without exception under an obligation to devote ourselves unceasingly to prayer.'[11]

Nikodimos was himself aware that he was taking a risk in making mystical texts available to the general reader, and he writes in his introduction, 'someone may object that it is not right to publish certain of the texts included in this volume, since they will sound strange to the ears of the majority, and may actually prove dangerous.'[12] Paisy Velichkovsky had similar concerns and for a long time refused to allow his Slavonic translations to appear in print in case they should bewilder readers who lacked the necessary spiritual guidance; only in the last year of his life was he finally persuaded by Metropolitan Gavriil of St Petersburg that they should be published. Undeterred by any such qualms, Makarios and Nikodimos went ahead with their publication, saying:

> Even if occasionally some people go slightly astray, what is surprising in that? For the most part this happens to them because of their conceit ... But, trusting rather in Him who said, 'I am the way and the truth' (John 14:6), let us embark on the task [of inner prayer] with all humility and in a spirit of mourning ... Draw near, all of you who share the Orthodox calling, laity and monks alike, who are eager to discover the kingdom of God that is within you, the treasure hidden in the field of the heart, which is the sweet Lord Jesus.[13]

---

[9] Ware, 'The Spirituality of the *Philokalia*', p. 15 (italics in the original).
[10] *Philokalia*, vol. 1, p. xxiv.   [11] Ibid., vol. 5, p. 107.   [12] Ibid., vol. 1, p. xxiii.   [13] Ibid.

Reception of the *Philokalia*

The first edition of the *Philokalia* in Greek was published in Venice in 1782 in a weighty and large folio volume of 1,223 pages. It was no doubt a limited edition with a high cover price and was not likely to be a bestseller. It did not make much of an impact at a time when the Greek response to the Enlightenment centred rather on the polemical writings of another member of the Kollyvades movement, Athanasios of Paros. His writings provoked an equally sharp counterattack, which dismissed the spiritual movement from which the *Philokalia* had sprung as 'fundamentalist obscurantism, that was designed to legitimize Ottoman despotism and keep the Greek people in chains'.[14] At the time the Kollyvades were more influential through the preaching and teaching of men like St Kosmas the Aetolian than through their writing. The *Philokalia* was not reissued in Greek until 1893, the third edition had to wait until 1957, and there was no translation into modern Greek until the 1960s.

Meanwhile in the Slav world, it was a very different story. We have already noted the spectacular consequences of the publication in 1793 of Paisy Velichkovsky's Slavonic translation under the title *Dobrotolyubie*. Another edition followed in 1822, but the greatest impact was made by the publication of a five-volume translation into Russian by St Theophan the Recluse (1815–94), based on the original Greek edition. The first volume of this edition appeared in 1877 and was reissued no fewer than four times between 1883 and 1913. Available for the first time in the vernacular, this was the edition that finally brought the *Philokalia* to a wide readership throughout Russia. It remains the standard Russian translation and has exerted very great influence, not only in Russia, but throughout the Slavic-speaking world. This influence was further extended by the popularity of the nineteenth-century spiritual classic, *The Way of a Pilgrim*, in which the *Philokalia* takes centre stage.

Not surprisingly, given Paisy's long sojourn at Neamţ, a similarly influential philokalic tradition may be observed in the monasteries of Moldavia and Wallachia to which it was carried by Paisy's disciples. And in Transylvania Fr Dumitru Stăniloae (1903–93), rector of the Theological Academy at Sibiu, devoted his life to producing a Romanian version of the *Philokalia* which includes most of the same authors as the Greek version but goes back to the original texts and in many cases provides longer

[14] Kitromilides, '*Philokalia*'s First Journey', p. 343.

Plate 34. A skete belonging to the Russian monastery of Valaam, founded in the fourteenth century on an island in Lake Ladoga. Monks from here took Orthodoxy across Siberia to Alaska in the late eighteenth century.

Plate 35. The tenth-century katholikon of the monastery of Vatopedi on Athos where St Maximos the Greek lived for ten years (c.1505–16).

Plate 36. A casket containing the relics of St Maximos the Greek in the Trinity monastery of St Sergius where he died in 1556.

Plate 37. The main church of the Prophet Elijah skete on Athos, founded by Paisy Velichkovsky in 1757. It ceased to be a Russian house in 1992.

Plate 38. The main church of Neamț monastery in Moldavia, Romania, where Paisy Velichkovsky died in 1794. From here Athonite spirituality was transmitted throughout the monasteries of Ukraine and Russia.

Plate 39. The Byzantine tower of Prosphori at Ouranoupolis near the border of Athos where Sydney and Joice Loch kept open house for monks and pilgrims alike for much of the twentieth century.

Plate 40. Archimandrite Sophrony (1896–1993), a spiritual child of St Silouan of Athos, was founder of the monastery of St John the Baptist at Tolleshunt Knights in Essex. Photo © Monastery of St John the Baptist, Tolleshunt Knights.

Plate 41. The monastery of St Antony the Great at St Laurent-en-Royans in the Dauphiné, one of several Athonite dependencies founded by Fr Placide in France.

extracts from them. The first four volumes of this edition were published between 1946 and 1948 and the remaining twelve (after a break imposed by the communist takeover) between 1976 and 1991. In addition to the texts, Fr Dumitru provided concise commentaries which, in line with Nikodimos's emphasis on the need for guidance, are designed to fulfil that role in the absence of a spiritual father.

In the West, a number of translations and abridgements have appeared in English, French, German, Italian, and Spanish. A selection in English, entitled *Writings from the* Philokalia *on Prayer of the Heart,* translated by E. Kadloubovsky and Gerald Palmer and based on the *Dobrotolyubie,* appeared in 1951 and achieved unexpected commercial success. (According to Bishop Kallistos, it was only accepted for publication at the insistence of T. S. Eliot who was editorial director of Faber & Faber at the time.) It was reprinted twice in the 1950s, twice in the 1960s, and no fewer than five times in the 1970s. A more comprehensive approach was adopted by Gerald Palmer, Philip Sherrard, and Kallistos Ware who embarked on an English translation of the *Philokalia,* based on the original Greek version and respecting the integrity of the edition of Makarios and Nikodimos. This edition, begun in 1979 and projected in five volumes, is as yet incomplete. 'In this way', writes Metropolitan Kallistos,

> through numerous translations into Western languages, the influence of the *Philokalia* has extended far beyond the Orthodox Church. Its contemporary readers belong not only to other Christian communions but also to non-Christian faiths, while an appreciable number – as the English translators have learnt from the correspondence that they receive – are 'seekers' not as yet connected with any religious group ... simply persons with a sincere concern for the life of the spirit.[15]

Writing in 1991, the bishop continues:

> It is surely astonishing ... that a collection of spiritual texts, originally intended for Greeks living under Ottoman rule, should have achieved its main impact two centuries later in the secularised and post-Christian West, among the children of that very 'Enlightenment' which St Makarios and St Nikodimos viewed with such misgiving. There are certain books which seem to have been composed not so much for their own age as for subsequent generations. Little noticed at the time of their original publication, they only attain their full influence two or more centuries afterwards, acting in this manner as a spiritual 'time-bomb'. The *Philokalia* is precisely such

---

[15] Ware, 'The Spirituality of the *Philokalia*', p. 21.

a book. It is not so much the late eighteenth as the late twentieth century that is the true 'age of the *Philokalia*'.[16]

Nikodimos's Other Writings

Having completed his work on the *Philokalia*, Nikodimos turned to its companion volume, the *Evergetinos*, which he had also been asked to prepare for publication. This was another massive compendium, put together in the eleventh century by Abbot Paul (d.1054) of the Evergetis monastery in Constantinople, and containing the lives and sayings of the Desert Fathers and extracts from many other patristic works. Once again, Nikodimos's role was to edit and correct the texts, and also to add an introduction. If his introduction to the *Philokalia* concentrates on the mystical teachings of the Fathers, that to the *Evergetinos* emphasizes their ethical precepts. Contrasting the natural sciences as pursued by Enlightenment thinkers with the moral philosophy favoured by the Fathers, he writes, 'Men study the heavens, the earth, and all other things to discover their harmonious relationships and order, but extremely few inquire how to order *themselves* harmoniously through the acquisition of true virtue.'[17] The task of the Fathers is to withdraw to a place of undisturbed silence where they can, first of all, research the nature and causes of the passions and, secondly, acquire a scientific knowledge of the virtues, their goal being to eradicate the former and cultivate the latter. Like its companion volume, the *Evergetinos* gives the texts in the original patristic Greek and was intended to be read not only by monks but also by those living in the world. The first edition was published in Venice in 1783.

The third work that Nikodimos was asked to edit was concerned with a much more topical issue: the treatise *On Frequent Communion*. This has been shown to be the original work of monk Neophytos of Kafsokalyvia, though some have attributed it to St Makarios.[18] An earlier version had already been published anonymously in Venice in 1777; extensively reworked and enlarged by Makarios and Nikodimos, it was now reissued in 1783. The text of the treatise is divided into three parts: the first part is a commentary on the Lord's Prayer; the second explains why the practice of frequent communion is beneficial and indeed necessary for Orthodox

---

[16] Ibid., pp. 21–2.
[17] *Evergetinos*, vol. 1 (Athens, 1957), p. 14; cited in Cavarnos, *St Nicodemos the Hagiorite*, p. 19. *Evergetinos* is now available in English translation in 4 vols (Etna, CA: Center for Traditionalist Orthodox Studies, 1988–2008).
[18] See Hieromonk Patapios and Archbishop Chrysostomos, *Manna from Athos*, pp. 48–9.

believers; and the third part refutes the objections of those who do not agree with frequent communion. Its publication provoked a storm of protest among those opposed to the Kollyvades movement on Athos who wrote an inflammatory letter to the patriarch of Constantinople. This resulted in the book being banned on the grounds of its being contrary to the canons and provoking dissent. But in 1789 a new patriarch overturned his predecessor's decision and declared the book to be canonical, and recommended it to all Christians; and this view received further backing from a decree issued by Patriarch Gregory V in 1819. Thus it was from the Kollyvades movement that support for the practice of frequent communion spread from Athos to the whole Orthodox world where it was slow to catch on but has now become central to the spiritual renewal taking place in the Church today.[19]

Having completed the tasks that were initially assigned to him by Makarios, Nikodimos continued with his literary activities without interruption for the rest of his life. His output of editions, translations, and original works is formidable, and he became the most prolific and most important Greek theologian of the eighteenth century. As the Romanian monk Ioan of Neamț exclaimed, writing in 1807, 'who could recount all his labours and all his works of love?'[20]

For a while Nikodimos remained in Karyes at the cell of St George, commonly known as the monastery of Skourtaioi. The monks saw to all his everyday requirements, leaving him free to concentrate on his writing. At one point he decided that he would like to visit the celebrated hesychast Paisy Velichkovsky and set out by sea for Romania. But within a matter of days his ship encountered a violent storm and was almost lost. Taking this as a sign of God's will, he returned to Athos and, after a brief return visit to Karyes, he moved to the skete of Kapsala where he was better able to practise hesychasm under the guidance of his elder, Arsenios the Peloponnesian, whom he had first met on Naxos. In search of even greater seclusion, he and Arsenios spent the year 1782 on the deserted island of Skyropoulos, to the east of Euboea, where he wrote that he lived 'the life of a worker and labourer: digging, sowing, harvesting, and every day doing all the other things by which the toilsome life in barren islands is characterized'.[21] The following year he returned to the Holy Mountain where he settled in a cell near the monastery of Pantokrator with a disciple named John and was tonsured to the Great Schema. There his lifestyle was

---

[19] See Ware, 'St Nikodimos and the *Philokalia*', pp. 82–3.   [20] Cited ibid., p. 88.
[21] Cavarnos, *St Nicodemos the Hagiorite*, pp. 79–80.

remarkable for its simplicity. His diet consisted of boiled rice, honey
diluted with water, olives, beans, and bread. He dressed in rags, having
only one cassock, and always wore sandals. He spoke of himself as 'a
monster', 'a dead dog', 'a nonentity', 'unwise', 'uneducated', and yet his
visitors included patriarchs, metropolitans, prominent laymen such as
John Kapodistrias (1776–1831, later to be Greece's first president),
Orthodox and non-Orthodox alike, all seeking his advice and spiritual
guidance, and he was said to be generous to all. As his spiritual brother
Euthymios would say, he was prepared to explain the Scriptures to anyone,
and then he would put his head on one side and silently say the Jesus
Prayer. Often he would say, 'Fathers, let us go to a barren island so that we
may get rid of this world.'[22]

The most important of Nikodimos's original works is his *Handbook of
Spiritual Counsel*, which he wrote during the year he spent in self-imposed
exile on the island of Skyropoulos. This means that he wrote it without
access to any books, and yet it is full of quotations from and references to
the Scriptures and the Fathers. It was written at the request of his cousin,
Bishop Ierotheos of Euripos, and it pulls no punches in its warnings to the
clergy in general and bishops in particular. The author emphasizes the need
to guard the senses and the imagination, the mind, and the heart, but at the
same time he says that there is a good side to the senses, when the beauty of
the world around us lifts our mind to God the Creator, and a good side to
the imagination, when it helps us to meditate on Christ's passion and
resurrection. He writes with confidence and self-assurance:

> This manual of spiritual counsel ... teaches the mind not only to
> meditate upon divine matters, but also to do the virtues commanded
> by God. It teaches not only to examine the things of God and his divine
> perfections, but also to love God with our whole heart and through love
> to keep his commandments and to imitate his perfections. Knowledge,
> alone, makes one vain, but love edifies. Knowledge comes from nature,
> while love comes from faith. The former is simply knowledge and,
> therefore, uncertain; the latter is experience and union with God and,
> therefore, certain and true. Knowledge belongs to the philosophers and to
> those outside; faith belongs to the Christians and the faithful. Or to put it
> another way: the philosophers can possess knowledge but they are incap-
> able of faith.[23]

At the same time, he writes out of deep humility and love:

[22] G. S. Bebis, Introduction to P. A. Chamberas (trans.), *Nicodemos of the Holy Mountain: A Handbook
of Spiritual Counsel* (Mahwah, NJ: Paulist Press, 1989), pp. 14–15.
[23] Ibid., p. 231.

But, alas, what am I to do? I have become like a flintstone and you as a fiery iron. You knocked hard once, you knocked harder two and three times, seeking from him who needs advice to receive letters of counsel. What was I to do with such requests? I drew out these few sparks from the cold stone of my understanding for my own sake, as St Mark noted: 'A man is presented to his neighbor according to what he is, and it is God who will act on the hearer according to what he has believed.' It is therefore up to you from here on to take these few sparks and to light the fire of zeal and commitment in your heart . . .[24]

In the body of the work, Nikodimos analyses the various ways in which the five senses – vision, hearing, smell, taste, touch – must be protected against external temptations and dangers. 'All these ideas', writes George Bebis in his introduction to the English translation,

are relevant to our times, which stress so persistently and incorrectly the senses and their satisfaction in our daily life. Our senses are attracted by the sirens of consumerism, quick sensual satisfaction, and false materialistic promises. Under these continuous attacks our senses lose their orientation, and instead of becoming instruments for our salvation, they become organs for our spiritual and physical destruction. St Nicodemos realizes the failings of our fallen nature and warns us of the tremendous destructive power our senses can hold over us.[25]

Never has the Holy Mountain spoken so pertinently to us today.

In 1784, two years after the publication of the *Philokalia*, St Makarios returned to Athos and encouraged Nikodimos to undertake an edition of the writings of St Symeon the New Theologian (949–1022), one of the Fathers most favoured by the hesychasts. Working with another monk by the name of Dionysios Zagoraios, who translated the texts into modern Greek, Nikodimos collected the works, whose manuscripts were scattered in the various libraries of the Holy Mountain, and published them in one large volume in 1790. Once again, Nikodimos wrote an introduction, in which he described Symeon as 'an earthly Angel, a heavenly Man, the splendour of the Fathers, the dignity of the Priests, the true rule of monastic life, the glory of the Ascetics, the sweetest joy of the whole world'.[26] He also wrote an encomium for the saint, to be sung on his feast day, 12 October, in which he describes the life of St Symeon. This life he commends to us as

---

[24] Ibid., p. 232.   [25] Ibid., pp. 49–50.
[26] *Tou Hosiou Symeon tou Neou Theologou ta Heuriskomena*, 2nd edn (Syros, 1886), p. v; cited in Cavarnos, *St Nicodemos the Hagiorite*, p. 27.

the depository of virtues, the healing of the passions, the restoration of the divine grace, the trumpet of deification, the guidance of perfection, the height of theology, the depth of economy, the width of creation, the length of providence, the heirloom of the ascetic philosophy, the school of the mental prayer, the treasury of the mystical dogmas.[27]

It would be tedious to list all the many works of St Nikodimos, but we may single out his edition of the correspondence of the sixth-century Desert Fathers St Barsanouphios and St John of Gaza. This he prepared at the request of certain Athonite monks around 1797, but it did not appear in print until 1816. In his introduction, Nikodimos describes the authors as men of exceptional spiritual attainments and their book as not just a product of human wisdom but divinely inspired; and he commends it to all, 'for it is most profitable for bishops and priests, rulers and judges, and especially for monks, both hesychasts and those who live in monasteries; and briefly, for beginners, for those who are making progress, and for the perfect'.[28] Also worthy of mention would be his three-volume edition of the collected works of St Gregory Palamas, which he was urged to prepare by the prominent Kollyvades, Athanasios of Paros and Leontios, metropolitan of Helioupolis. Nikodimos devoted a great deal of care to this, assembling manuscripts from all over Athos and other parts of Greece, but tragically the final manuscript was seized by the Austrian authorities when it was sent to Vienna for printing and was mixed up with a batch of supposedly revolutionary pamphlets.[29] All that survived was Nikodimos's introduction, which was published in Constantinople in 1883. This misfortune was a devastating blow to him and a great loss to his potential readers. As a result, most of Palamas's theological works remained unpublished for a further 150 years.

In addition to his work on the Fathers, Nikodimos published in 1799 the *New Martyrologium*, a collection of the lives of eighty-five Orthodox New Martyrs who had died between 1492 and 1794, and a substantial collection of lives of the saints, *Synaxaristis*, which appeared posthumously in three volumes between 1817 and 1819. The latter proved popular with readers, has been reprinted four times, and formed the basis of many subsequent collections including that produced most recently in French by Hieromonk Makarios of Simonopetra and subsequently translated into

---

[27] *Akolouthia kai Engkomion tou Osiou kai Theophorou Patros emon Symeon tou Neou Theologou* (Athens, 1975), pp. 112–13; cited in Bebis, Introduction, p. 40.
[28] Cavarnos, *St Nicodemos the Hagiorite*, p. 49.   [29] Ibid., p. 83.

English.[30] There also appeared numerous commentaries on the Scriptures, on the liturgical texts, and on the canons of the Church; works of hymnography, various tracts, funeral orations, letters, and discourses on a variety of topics.

All the above-mentioned works belong in the mainstream tradition of Orthodox theology. A surprising addition to Nikodimos's *oeuvre* is his reworking of a number of Roman Catholic texts dating from the Counter-Reformation. The best known of these, *Unseen Warfare*, is an adaptation of a work by the Italian priest Lorenzo Scupoli (*c.*1530–1610) entitled *Combattimento Spirituale* (*Spiritual Combat*). The theme of this book is the 'warfare' against the passions and against impure thoughts and how it may be won by means of constant vigilance, mental prayer, and Holy Communion. Nikodimos has considerably altered the text, removing certain passages and expanding others, to ensure that it contains nothing that might offend an Orthodox reader, and he gives no clue to its original authorship, though he does make clear that it is not his own work. It achieved considerable popularity and has been reprinted several times as well as being translated into Russian and English. Nikodimos also produced a Greek version of the *Spiritual Exercises* of Ignatius Loyola, for which he used the expanded text of the Jesuit scholar Giampetro Pinamonti (1632–1703). These and other examples show that Nikodimos kept an open mind with regard to scholarship from the West. As he himself wrote, 'We must hate and detest the misbeliefs and unlawful customs of the Latins and others who are heterodox; but if they have anything sound and confirmed by the canons of the Holy Synods, this we must not hate.'[31]

In 1809 at the age of sixty, exhausted by long years of intellectual endeavour, Nikodimos breathed his last at dawn on 14 July, surrounded by friends at the monastery of the Skourtaioi near Karyes, where his relics are preserved to this day. News of his death was greeted with great sorrow throughout the Orthodox world, and almost immediately he was raised to the rank of a saint in the popular consciousness. He was officially canonized by the ecumenical patriarchate in 1955 with his feast day falling on 14 July, the date of his death. His entry in the *Synaxarion* for that day ends with these words: 'although this star's light was put out, its rays did not stop illumining the Church, and his books remain an inexhaustible

---

[30] Hieromonk Makarios of Simonos Petra, *The Synaxarion: The Lives of the Saints of the Orthodox Church*, trans. from French by C. Hookway and others, 7 vols (Ormylia: Holy Convent of the Annunciation of Our Lady, 1998–2008).

[31] *Heortodromion* (Venice, 1836), p. 584; cited in Cavarnos, *St Nicodemos the Hagiorite*, p. 31.

source of teaching, consolation and exhortation to the fullness of life in Christ.'[32]

By way of a summary of Nikodimos's relationship with Mount Athos, I cannot do better than quote a paragraph written by Bishop Kallistos who has devoted so much of his life to studying the works of this saint:

> Two things inspired St Nikodimos of the Holy Mountain throughout his years on Athos. The first was a love of *hesychia*, of stillness and solitude. He found constant inspiration in Christ's statement, 'The Kingdom of God is within you' (Luke 17:21) – words that he quoted in the introduction to the *Philokalia* – and he devoted himself unreservedly to the quest for this inner Kingdom. Doubtless it was this longing for stillness that led him to live in the remote hermitages of the Athonite desert rather than in one of the large cenobitic houses. In the second place, however, he was not only a solitary but also, like St Kosmas the Aetolian, a missionary. He sought to preach the faith not through apostolic journeys but through his writings. With good reason he is shown in engravings and icons holding a pen, with a bottle of ink at his elbow. In this way his life was marked equally by silence and by words: by words that came out of silence, and by a silence more eloquent than any words. He would have agreed, I think, with the saying, 'Words are the part of silence that can be spoken.'[33]

---

[32] Hieromonk Makarios, *The Synaxarion*, vol. 6, p. 153.
[33] Ware, 'St Nikodimos and the *Philokalia*', p. 93.

CHAPTER 16

Athos and the West

The Motor-Boat Age

Until quite recently (by which I mean the last fifty years or so), it would have been extremely unusual, if not unheard of, to encounter a monk on Mount Athos who came from the West. Western travellers – usually well-heeled academics such as John Covel (1638–1722), diplomats such as Paul Ricaut (1628–1700), or clergymen such as Richard Pococke (1704–65) or Joseph Dacre Carlyle (1759–1804) – occasionally ventured on to the Mountain and wrote accounts displaying varying degrees of accuracy and based on varying powers of observation, which they published for their own gratification or that of their patrons, but they were rare birds before at least the nineteenth century. Even then, most travellers from the West came with an agenda of their own which usually meant that they were not particularly interested in the spiritual activities of the monks. William Martin Leake (1777–1860), for example, was a military surveyor and antiquarian topographer whose visit to Athos in October–November 1806 was motivated exclusively by his desire to examine the military capabilities of the peninsula for the war against Napoleon. Robert Curzon (1810–73), fourteenth Baron Zouche, a wealthy aristocrat and dilettante, was inspired to make his visit to the Mountain in 1837 by the desire to scour the libraries for hitherto unknown manuscripts of lost classical texts (in which he was almost entirely unsuccessful, though he did rescue a number of important manuscripts that might not otherwise have survived much longer). The artist Edward Lear (1812–88) spent three weeks on Athos in 1856 and produced magnificent drawings of all the monasteries but made no attempt to conceal his revulsion from the monastic regime.[1]

---

[1] On early Western travellers to Mount Athos, see della Dora, *Imagining Mount Athos*, esp. pp. 124–61.

It is not until Athelstan Riley (1858–1945), budding diplomat and staunch Anglican, that any traveller from the West begins to look like a pilgrim. Riley's book, *Athos, or the Mountain of the Monks*, published in 1887, is a perceptive and highly readable account of the pilgrimage that he made to the Mountain in 1883 and records the following remark made at the summit of Athos to the author by the archbishop of Kavalla: '"We are all *hadjis* now", said he, using the Turkish word for a pilgrim. And, indeed, a visit to the Holy Mountain, including the ascent of the peak, is looked upon by the orthodox world as a pilgrimage second only to that of a visit to the Holy Land.'[2] F. W. Hasluck (1878–1920), an archaeologist and former Fellow of King's College, Cambridge, also writes a serious book about monastic Athos, *Athos and its Monasteries*, published posthumously by his widow in 1924. He intends it to serve 'as an introduction to Athos for the general reader' and the tone (serious but seriously romantic) is set by the first sentence: 'Much of the difficulty and not a little of the romance of a pilgrimage to Athos has vanished with the coming of steam.'[3] Richard M. Dawkins (1871–1955), Professor of Modern and Byzantine Greek at Oxford, concentrates on the legends and traditions of the Mountain in his book *The Monks of Athos*, published in 1936. As a scholar, he objectively dissociates himself from the standard run of Athonite pilgrim, whom he has carefully observed over the course of four extended visits, but writes perceptively:

> The orthodox pilgrim to Athos, very shrewd as he may be in the affairs of this world, is towards his religion a man of simple mind. He does not see Athos with the eyes of the Frank, which are held by the beauty of the woods and the hills; to him such things hardly count. Nor has he the feelings of the scholar or of the historian of art or of any of the curious and inquisitive tourists and travellers from the west, who from time to time come to enjoy the hospitality of the monks, and to see so many things which can hardly be seen in any other place.[4]

Finally, the Athonite pilgrim *par excellence*, Sydney Loch (1889–1954), pours all his knowledge and love of the Mountain into his delightful book, *Athos the Holy Mountain*, also published posthumously by his widow in 1957. Loch never became Orthodox, and yet he seems to be on the most familiar terms with every monk he meets and to know every stone of the paths that he treads. He has an 'unfair advantage' over all the other

---

[2] A. Riley, *Athos, or the Mountain of the Monks* (London: Longmans Green, 1887), p. 213.
[3] F. W. Hasluck, *Athos and its Monasteries* (London: Kegan Paul, Trench, Trubner, 1924), pp. v, 3.
[4] R. M. Dawkins, *The Monks of Athos* (London: George Allen & Unwin, 1936), p. 377.

travellers from the West in that his home was the tower of Prosphori in Ouranoupolis where monks and pilgrims alike regularly paused for refreshment and hospitality (Plate 39). Loch is in some ways the last of the old breed of pilgrim and the first of the new. Leaving the village in 1939, he did not return to Greece until after World War II nor to the tower until 1950. The following year, he makes his first return visit to the Mountain where his first impression is one of reassuring continuity: 'My previous visit had been before the war, but so unchanged was the scene, so great the sudden quiet, that I felt I was waking from some dream and that everything was still at the day when Marko's octopus boat had settled me on the beach below ten or twelve years ago.'[5] But when he reaches Simonopetra and joins Fr Barlaam and a 'bony' Fr Athanasios on the highest of the balconies, he looks out to sea and, noticing the faint smoke of a distant steamer bound for Kavalla, reflects nostalgically and prophetically on the changes that are after all taking place:

> The coastal steamers of years ago were so unassuming. The miniature St George nosed along the coast, stopping off Prosphori on Thursdays ... A second small steamer took her place ... Then road communication opened up with Salonika.
> 'And now the age of motor-boats', Barlaam complained, chiming his thoughts with mine, and fading out a dream.
> Was it that? Was the Mountain suffering from the motor-boat age, and all it represented?
> It was no longer secure in the old sense of the word from the outside world. Society no longer had sympathy with the monastic way of life. The modern man demanded speed, noise, change.
> The tourist was ousting the pilgrim of the past, who arrived after difficulty, in the mood to venerate. The sightseer now caught a bus across the mountains, or came in his own car to Erissos, and ran up and down either coast of the Mountain in a motor-boat. With him came the post, newspapers, and his own sceptical mind prepared to smile at what he found there, rather than regard a little enviously a single-mindedness beyond his own duplication. The Communists had heaped anti-religious argument and ridicule on humble old men without education or wits sufficiently nimble to reply to them. All this led to something intelligent monks constantly underline, that the ailing community could only be restored to health by men of education, conviction, and good will taking the habit. Newcomers with gifts of leadership and purpose must be found to take the age-old vows of stability, obedience, poverty, and chastity. But in this motor-boat age is it

---

[5] S. Loch, *Athos: The Holy Mountain* (London: Lutterworth, 1957), p. 231.

possible to find numbers of men whose fullest way of self-expression in the world is to be found by withdrawing from it?[6]

The story of the renewal that rescued the ailing community and restored it to health in the second half of the twentieth century has already been told, and the motor-boat age has indeed become the age of 'speed, noise, change'. Men of education, conviction, and good will and with gifts of leadership emerged, hesychasts from the remotest parts of the Athonite desert were coaxed into the monasteries together with their groups of disciples, and the Virgin's garden bloomed once again in ways that Loch could only have dreamt of. Buildings that lay derelict for years have now been restored to accommodate the influx of new monks. Guesthouses teem with unprecedented numbers of pilgrims from every continent. Churches resound from dusk until dawn with the melodious chanting of disciplined choirs.

The architects of this renewal were charismatic elders, living a hesychastic life in desert hermitages, who either by means of their writings or more often simply by word of mouth attracted groups of disciples eager to hear for themselves the new spiritual teaching. These were mostly young men, many of them university graduates, with inquiring minds, ready to exchange the shallow materialism of the secular world for a more purposeful existence in service to God. Modern communications allowed news of the teaching offered by these elders to travel greater distances than would have been possible in former times. As a result, recruits came from further afield than before – not just the traditional Orthodox heartlands, but from Western Europe, North America, Scandinavia, and Australia. Some had an Orthodox background, such as Greek-Americans or Greek-Australians, but others did not and were simply seekers. No concessions were made for these 'outsiders', and the course they had to follow was equally tough for all. Some inevitably dropped out, but many stayed, and the consequence is that the renewed monasteries have welcomed to their vacant cells a truly international intake of new monks. Suddenly, as never before, there were monks from Birmingham, Ottawa, Melbourne, New York City, Helsinki, and Paris. In monasteries where nothing but Greek had been spoken for centuries, it was not unusual to come across monks chatting to each other in English! The global village had come to Athos, not just in the shape of pilgrims, but as novices and monks.

---

[6] Ibid., pp. 242–3.

Athos Comes to England

But the arrival of Westerners on Athos did not signify an extension of the Athonite Commonwealth to the West. For that we need to turn in the first instance to the Russians and the diaspora that ensued from the Revolution of 1917. The leading role in this ground-breaking movement belongs to Archimandrite Sophrony (1896–1993).

Fr Sophrony was born Sergey Semyonovich Sakharov on 22 September 1896 in Moscow to a pious middle-class family. As a child he was both devout and studious and he had a fascination for oriental (Indian) mysticism, but the subject that he enjoyed most was painting. He studied at the Academy of Arts (1915–17) and also at the Moscow School of Painting, Sculpture, and Architecture (1920–1), and he displayed an outstanding talent as an artist. By focusing his attention on his creative work, Fr Sophrony to a large extent isolated himself from the intellectual currents in contemporary Moscow, yet he could not but be affected by the climate of instability and turmoil that characterized post-revolutionary Russia. In 1922–3 dissidents were given an opportunity to escape on board the so-called 'philosophers' ships', which carried hundreds of non-Marxist intellectuals to safety. They included such scholars as Nikolai Berdyaev (1874–1948), Sergei Bulgakov (1871–1944), and Nicholas Lossky (1870–1965) and his son Vladimir (1903–58). Fr Sophrony left shortly before them, in 1921, in order to pursue his career as an artist in the West, and he arrived in Paris in 1922. He exhibited at the fashionable salons of the day, and soon his work drew the attention of the French media. At the same time, however, he was searching for spiritual fulfilment and he was frustrated by his inability to find it in art. This came to a head at Easter 1924 when for three days he experienced a powerful vision of the uncreated light. This led him to decide to return to Christianity and even to begin to lose interest in his art.

Paris in the early 1920s was home to an enormous and dynamic community of tens of thousands of Russian refugees. They included a large number of intellectuals, philosophers, and theologians, who had been deported by sea and who initiated not only an academic renaissance but also a religious one. Orthodoxy flourished as never before in the West, and the centre for its study was the newly founded Institut St-Serge at 93 rue de Crimée. As Nicholas Zernov writes, 'The Institute became the main intellectual centre of the

Russian Church and an equally important point of contact between
Eastern Orthodoxy and Western Christians.[7] It recruited some very
distinguished scholars to its faculty including Sergei Bulgakov (who
became its first rector), Symeon Frank, and Georges Florovsky, and in
1924 Fr Sophrony enrolled as one of its first students. During this
period, he was much influenced by both Bulgakov (who was his
spiritual father as well as his teacher) and Berdyaev (whose understanding of man as *microtheos* appealed to him), but he soon realized
that academic theology did not fulfil his need for spiritual development any more than art had and the following year he left for Mount
Athos.

Sophrony spent twenty-two years on Athos (1925–47), initially as
a novice at the Russian monastery of St Panteleimonos. The monastery
was going through an extremely difficult period, suffering the repercus-
sions of World War I, the heresy of the Glorifiers of the Name,[8] the
Revolution of 1917, and the Civil War of 1919–21. Having so recently
been by far the wealthiest brotherhood on the Mountain, in just twelve
years they had been reduced to penury. Their supply of monks and
pilgrims was cut by both Greek and Russian authorities, and Sophrony
was among very few to obtain entry. Nevertheless, his stay in the monastery
clearly provided him with what he was seeking. Years later, in his inspira-
tional book *On Prayer*, he wrote about this period of his life with
a disarming frankness:

> There, on the Holy Mountain, I found the circumstances I needed – long
> church services, for the most part at night; simple tasks that demanded no
> intellectual exertion; the opportunity to live under obedience without
> having to think how the abbot and his associates, the monastery elders,
> regulated the cloister. Free from all worldly cares, I could pray without
> interruption, day and night. Little time was left for reading, half an hour or
> less in the twenty-four hours. But the Lord was with me; and I could not tear
> myself away from Him even for a moment.[9]

Looking back over half a century or more, he was able to identify his
turning-point when he suddenly discovered God within himself under the
name 'I Am'.

[7] N. Zernov, *Russian Religious Renaissance of the Twentieth Century* (London: Darton, Longman &
Todd, 1963), p. 231.
[8] This unfortunate episode resulted in the deportation of 833 Russian monks from Athos in 1913. See
Speake, *Mount Athos: Renewal in Paradise*, pp. 138–40.
[9] Archimandrite Sophrony (Sakharov), *On Prayer*, trans. R. Edmonds (Crestwood, NY: St Vladimir's
Seminary Press, 1996), pp. 72–3.

My entire way of thinking was changed: I saw everything differently . . . Art itself, which up to then had been the most important factor in my life as the means to knowledge of the world through contemplation of its visible aspect and wonder before its mysterious beauty, seemed to me to be limited and of little use in my search for absolute being. The old things collapsed – much that had seemed noble and great in the past now appeared naïve or, more often, 'an abomination' – to be replaced by unbridled prayer which bore me into other spheres of Being. Prayer, not without a struggle, broke my former bonds, with painting especially, and continued for months before I was given the possibility of leaving the world and going to the Holy Mountain. There, in that blessed place, prayer took possession of me to an even greater degree.[10]

Despite its difficulties, the monastery of St Panteleimonos still housed a very large brotherhood. Having reached a peak of almost 2,000 monks before the outbreak of World War 1, it had fallen to 561 according to a census of 1928, and this figure included those living in the sketes and cells: a huge reduction in just fifteen years, but still one of the largest brotherhoods on the Mountain (only the Lavra had more with 786). It was scarcely surprising therefore that it took Sophrony a few years to identify his spiritual father. In the meantime, he relied on his own mystical experience and profound repentance to see him through the rigours of life as a junior monk in such a huge cenobitic community. But by 1930 he had made contact with Elder Silouan (1866–1938; canonized in 1988) who for the next eight years was to be his mentor and spiritual guide. Silouan was a simple man of humble origins and almost no formal education, and yet he left behind a body of meditations which are poetic in their style and seriously profound in their spiritual vision. These have been edited by Sophrony and translated into many languages and are read widely throughout the Orthodox world today. It is the existence of men like Silouan, uneducated and largely illiterate but bearers of the deepest spiritual wisdom, emerging at a time when the spiritual life of the Mountain was in steep decline, that demonstrates the resilience of Athos. In his book entitled *Saint Silouan the Athonite*, Fr Sophrony presents an account of the life, personality, and teaching of the *starets* who inspired him to become one of the leading ambassadors of Athos in the twentieth century:

Hesychasm requires great self-denial and is the most arduous of ascetic practices. The resolution to accept such suffering in order the better to observe the commandments attracts Divine grace if the effort is made in a spirit of humility.

[10] Ibid., pp. 82–3.

Whatever the means he employs, the proud man will never attain to
genuine union with God. Just by wishing it, man cannot unite the mind
with the deep heart, and even if the mind does somehow penetrate into the
heart, it will see only itself, its own created beauty – splendid undoubtedly,
having been created in the Divine image – but God Himself will not be
found.

This is why the Blessed Staretz in his striving after humility seized on the
fiery weapon given him by God:

'Keep thy mind in hell, and despair not.'

Here was no subtle intellectual talking, but a 'simple' and 'ignorant' man
who many a time was found worthy of pure contemplation of God, and had,
indeed, grounds for saying, 'If you pray purely, you are a theologian.' Or,
'There are many on earth who believe but very few who *know* God.'[11]

After the death of his elder, and following his advice, Fr Sophrony
received a blessing to move out of the monastery of St Panteleimonos
and took up residence first at Karoulia, in the 'desert' of Athos, and
subsequently in a remote cave below St Paul's monastery. Here he
remained throughout World War II, and during these years he was
ordained to the priesthood and became a confessor and spiritual guide
to many of the Mountain's ascetics: 'Until I settled in the "desert" I did
not really know the life of the Holy Mountain as a whole. It was only
when I became spiritual counsellor to four monasteries and a great
number of hermitages and isolated hermits that the hidden kernel of
this astonishing place was opened up to me.'[12] This was no doubt an
extremely fulfilling period of his life, and yet in 1947 he chose to leave
the Mountain and return to Paris. Several reasons have been suggested
for this move. First, as a result of the intensity of his prayer for the world
(he would spend nights prostrate on the floor of his cave), added to the
damp conditions of his environment (where the winter rains would
drench his bed), his health began to break down. Secondly, as
a foreigner in post-war Greece, he may have faced political difficulties.
But most likely is his need to carry out the injunction of his elder to
publish his writings, if, as Silouan had put it, 'you think they could be
useful'. Paris was the cultural centre of the Russians in exile and would
provide a better platform for publishing than was available to him on
Athos. It would also offer him a chance to complete his studies at the
Institut St-Serge, though in fact his application was rejected because of

[11] Archimandrite Sophrony (Sakharov), *Saint Silouan the Athonite*, trans. R. Edmonds (Tolleshunt
Knights: Stavropegic Monastery of St John the Baptist, 1991), p. 143.
[12] Archimandrite Sophrony (Sakharov), *Wisdom from Mount Athos: The Writings of Staretz Silouan
1866–1938*, trans. R. Edmonds (London and Oxford: Mowbray, 1974), p. 10.

his sympathy with the Moscow patriarchate, which was anathema to the majority of dissident intellectuals.[13]

Abandoning the idea of further studies, Fr Sophrony settled in the Parisian suburb of Sainte-Geneviève-des-Bois where for twelve years (1947–59) he operated as a parish priest and father confessor. He resumed contact with the Russian theologians of the Paris School, notably Vladimir Lossky, and in opposition to much of their theological theory came to appreciate the place of his own monastic experience in the context of Russian ascetic and philosophical tradition. He began to publish, producing his first book, *Staretz Silouan*, in Russian in 1952. This book, which outlines the theological thinking of the elder, made an immediate impact, was in due course translated into more than twenty languages, and brought fame to its author.[14] As his reputation grew, more and more people came to him for spiritual guidance, and by 1958 a permanent community of people seeking the ascetic life had gathered around him. Meanwhile, his contacts with England were growing, his book had been well received by the British press, and, responding to a vocation to bring his teaching to the British people, in 1959 he decided to move across the Channel with a group of disciples. With the help of local people, he was able to buy a property at Tolleshunt Knights in Essex and this formed the nucleus of the monastery of St John the Baptist, initially under the jurisdiction of Metropolitan Antony of Sourozh and subsequently (from 1964) subject to the ecumenical patriarchate which granted it stavropegic status (Plate 40).

Fr Sophrony dedicated himself to this monastery for the rest of his life until his death in 1993 at the age of ninety-six. Fr Nikolai Sakharov, who is both the founder's great nephew and a monk of the monastery, has written about Sophrony's aims for the community:

> In his monastery Fr Sophrony attempted to restore the deepest principles of monastic life, so as to avoid distorted conceptions of the cenobitic life and its purpose. His main concern was primarily *inner asceticism*: inner perfection is more valuable than perfect outward conformity. The monastery does not have a written code of monastic rules, regulating fasting and hours of sleep. His teaching was largely focused on cultivation of the mind and the heart. While he was far from indifferent to everyday details and mundane tasks, he

---

[13] See N. V. Sakharov, *I Love, Therefore I Am: The Theological Legacy of Archimandrite Sophrony* (Crestwood, NY: St Vladimir's Seminary Press, 2002), pp. 28–30.

[14] Selections from it first appeared in English under the title *The Undistorted Image: Staretz Silouan, 1866–1938* (London: Faith Press, 1958). A fuller, revised edition appeared in two volumes as *The Monk of Athos* and *Wisdom from Mount Athos*, trans. R. Edmonds (London and Oxford: Mowbray, 1973–4). These were later combined in one volume, *Saint Silouan the Athonite* (1991).

tended to integrate them within the wider spectrum of his theological framework.[15]

Unusually, for practical reasons (since the elder could not oversee more than one monastery), the community includes both monks and nuns and is pan-Orthodox in character. A great emphasis is placed on use of the Jesus Prayer. This too has practical advantages for a small multinational community where use of one language would exclude others from fully participating in the liturgy. It also follows the tradition of Athonite sketes, where the daily services are often performed not with books but with prayer ropes, of Paisy Velichkovsky's monastery, and Fr Sophrony's own practice during his life in the desert.

From this monastery Fr Sophrony continued his programme of publishing, both revised versions of Silouan's teaching and his own original works. He interacted with the theological community in Britain, delivering papers at conferences including the second Patristics Conference at Oxford in 1962. And of course he gave regular talks to his own monastic community in Essex, collections of which have now been published. The monastery flourished, and the community grew, numbering twenty-five monks and nuns representing twelve different nationalities at the time of the elder's death. (It has since grown to almost forty.) As an obituarist wrote at the time, 'We are profoundly blessed in England – more than many of us realize – that this great and holy teacher should have settled in our land bringing with him such wealth of spiritual insight.'[16] His tomb, in a simple crypt in the monastery's grounds, is venerated daily by a stream of pilgrims; and a visit to the monastery is automatically included in the itinerary of every Orthodox hierarch visiting the UK from abroad. The buildings are of modest proportions, but they are adorned, both inside and out, with colourful mosaics and frescos in the founder's style. The atmosphere and spirit of the place is profoundly Athonite, as is confirmed by the awe in which it is held on the Mountain itself. The first question asked of any British pilgrim on Athos is invariably, 'Have you been to Essex?'

Athos Comes to North America

The spirit of St Paisy Velichkovsky was first brought to the American continent at the end of the eighteenth century by St Herman of Alaska (c.1756–1836). Herman was born near Moscow and began his monastic life at

---

[15] Sakharov, *I Love, Therefore I Am*, p. 34 (italics in the original).
[16] *Orthodox Outlook*, 7: 3 (1993), issue 49, p. 13.

the age of sixteen when he entered the St Sergius Lavra (or according to another tradition, the monastery of Sarov) as a novice and was later tonsured a monk at the monastery of Valaam on Lake Ladoga. There he became a disciple of Abbot Nazary, who had revived the monastery in the tradition of Paisy, and with the abbot's blessing Herman withdrew into the forest as a hermit. The Russian colony in Alaska had been in existence for about fifty years when in 1793 the Russian-American fur-trading company asked for a priest to be sent to minister to the native population, many of whom had become Orthodox Christians. Empress Catherine II responded to the appeal by asking Metropolitan Gavriil of St Petersburg to recruit a team of missionaries. Gavriil delegated the task to Abbot Nazary who chose ten monks from Valaam, including Herman. The journey across Siberia, and then from island to island across the Bering Strait, was a hazardous undertaking that took the best part of a year, but the missionaries arrived safely on Kodiak island in September 1794. Conditions were not easy, and the monks were shocked by the insolent behaviour of the Russian settlers towards the native Aleuts, but in less than a year about 7,000 baptisms had been performed and the monks began to build a church and a monastery. The monks tried to defend the native population, but within a few years they became disillusioned and abandoned the mission, leaving Herman in sole charge. Herman operated a mission school and was much loved by the local people, but he longed for the ascetic life. In 1811 he moved to the nearby uninhabited Spruce island where he built a hermitage which he named New Valaam. He had brought with him a copy of the Slavonic *Philokalia* and he lived a solitary and hesychastic existence, practising the Jesus Prayer. He received many visitors and even established an orphanage for children of the Aleuts, to whom he was a father. The spirit of Paisy died with Herman on Spruce island on 15 November 1836, and since they both died on the same date, they are commemorated together. But the spirit of Herman remains very much alive to this day for the Christians of Alaska and for the Orthodox Church in America, whose patron saint he became when he was canonized in 1970.

In 1987 a relic of St Herman was presented to the women's monastery at Ormylia in Chalkidiki. This event, which was the occasion for great rejoicing and profoundly experienced festivities, was seen as a true homecoming, completing the circle, as it were. The Aleuts felt it as proof of their own link to Athos and, through Athos, to the perpetual springs of the Orthodox tradition. Elder Aimilianos, abbot of Simonopetra, the parent monastery of Ormylia, preached two sermons to honour the occasion, in the second of which he said St Herman has truly 'reached out and united the very ends of the inhabited earth'.

He lived in a Russian monastery from the age of sixteen, and was there some twenty-two years as a monk. The monastery was the one called 'Valaam', to which two Athonite saints, Sergius and Herman, had been sent and which they built up and nursed as a brotherhood, and indeed they made it a place of miracles ... They were men who carried with and in themselves the whole Athonite spirit, the life of the Mountain and the spirituality of the *Philokalia* ...

Saint Herman, beloved, is not just an Alaskan saint, but a native of Mount Athos. He is a fruit of the Holy Mountain. His fathers were Athonites. Saint Herman, I repeat, is a most sweet and wonder-working fruit of the Holy Mountain of Athos.[17]

There have been a number of attempts to revive the Paisian tradition in North America, not least on Spruce island, where Archimandrite Gerasim (1888–1968) from St Tikhon's monastery in Kaluga followed the ascetic life for a while. Holy Trinity, Jordanville, and the New Diviyevo convent in New York also may lay some claim to being founded in the same tradition. But to trace the roots of a most remarkable recent turn of events in America, we must return briefly to Mount Athos.

During the 1950s a particularly dynamic brotherhood gathered around the renowned desert father Elder Joseph the Hesychast (1898–1959; also known as the Cave Dweller) who after many years in the desert had now settled at New Skete. Here he acquired fame as a teacher and spiritual father and became one of the principal architects of the renewal that took place on the Holy Mountain in the second half of the twentieth century. The story of this renewal has been told elsewhere.[18] Bishop Kallistos has described its spiritual roots in his Foreword to the elder's Life by his disciple Elder Joseph of Vatopedi:

> This renewal can best be characterized as Philokalic and Palamite. It has been deeply influenced by the collection of Orthodox ascetical and mystical texts known as the *Philokalia*, in which a central place is assigned to prayer of the heart and to the invocation of the name of Jesus; and it has taken as its special mentor the fourteenth-century Byzantine theologian St Gregory Palamas, himself an Athonite monk, who taught that the true fulfilment of inner prayer is the experience of the divine and uncreated light of Tabor, the light which shone from Christ at His Transfiguration. This Philokalic and Palamite orientation is a direct development from the teaching, simple

---

[17] Elder Aimilianos, 'Second Sermon in Honor of Saint Herman of Alaska', in Hieromonk Alexander (Golitzin) (ed., trans.), *The Living Witness of the Holy Mountain: Contemporary Voices from Mount Athos* (South Canaan, PA: St Tikhon's Seminary Press, 1996), pp. 246–59 (pp. 258, 248, 247).

[18] See Speake, *Mount Athos: Renewal in Paradise*, pp. 154–60.

yet profound, which Joseph the Hesychast gave to his small circle of immediate disciples.[19]

This 'small circle of immediate disciples', bursting out from the desert like a tornado, has created not ripples but waves that have washed over no fewer than six Athonite monasteries as they were revived by the elder's spiritual children. Among them was Fr Ephraim (Moraitis), who was born in Volos in 1927, moved to Athos in 1947, and became a disciple of Elder Joseph. The following year, he was tonsured and was later ordained priest. After the elder's death in 1959, Ephraim continued to live the ascetic life until 1973 when with a group of his own disciples he moved to the almost abandoned monastery of Philotheou and became its abbot. Fr Ephraim was so successful in reviving Philotheou and expanding its brotherhood that by the end of the 1970s it could afford to dispatch colonies of monks to revive yet three more monasteries, Xeropotamou, Konstamonitou, and (a few years later) Karakalou.

Only Elder Aimilianos could have described a saint as being 'like a kind of dishcloth, in that he soaks up and then flows with streams of divine grace. He gathers the fruits of the Spirit and brings them all together in himself. He becomes like a treasure chest.'[20] The description is entirely applicable to Abbot Ephraim of Philotheou. He acquired spiritual children in unparalleled numbers, soaking them up and then letting them flow out, and they came from all over the world. All the monasteries that he revived on Athos remain to this day under his spiritual guidance, as do several other monasteries in Greece. When he fell ill in 1979 and needed surgery, his spiritual children in Canada invited him to go there for his treatment. He accepted, and during the month that he spent there he met members of the Greek community and saw for himself the ways in which their spiritual life had declined. They had grown forgetful of their religious observances: they confessed infrequently, they received Holy Communion without due preparation, and they ignored the canons of the Church. Fr Ephraim saw a need for his intervention and made further visits across the Atlantic.

First, he concentrated on Canada, visiting Toronto, Vancouver, and Montreal. Then he was asked to go the United States. But by this stage he was spending so much time away from the Holy Mountain that the Holy Community felt obliged to ask him to decide between the two: either Athos or America. After much prayer, the elder opted for the latter and moved permanently to the United States in order to care for the people and

---

[19] Bishop Kallistos of Diokleia, Foreword to Elder Joseph, *Elder Joseph the Hesychast*, pp. 19–20.
[20] Elder Aimilianos, 'Second Sermon in Honor of Saint Herman', p. 247.

revive the spiritual life of the Greek communities there. For some of his followers (or would-be followers), his teachings appeared to veer too far towards a traditional, if not fundamentalist, Orthodoxy and at first he had some difficulty with jurisdictions. But after a brief spell under the Russian Church in Exile (ROCOR), he was accepted by the Greek Orthodox Archdiocese of America (Constantinople Patriarchate) and given permission to found monasteries in Canada and the United States. Between 1993 and 2005 he founded no fewer than seventeen monasteries, ten of them for women, seven for men. The first seven were all for women, two of them in Canada.

In 1995 Elder Ephraim established the first men's monastery, dedicated to St Antony the Great, 12 kilometres south of Florence, Arizona. The founding brotherhood consisted of six Athonite monks and together they set about creating a monastic oasis in the middle of the Sonoran Desert. The buildings are quite substantial and consist of a main church or katholikon, dedicated to St Antony and St Nektarios of Pentapolis, a refectory, living quarters for the monks, and a guesthouse for pilgrims. In addition, there are chapels dedicated to St Seraphim of Sarov, St Demetrios of Thessaloniki, St John the Baptist, St George, St Nicholas of Myra, and St Panteleimon. The extensive surrounding territory has been put to productive use and includes a vegetable garden, an olive grove, a vineyard, and citrus orchard, while the area immediately around the monastery has been laid to lawns, flowering plants, paths, and fountains. Architectural features such as turrets and domes, coloured tiles, external crosses, icons, and an ornate phiale create a quasi-Athonite atmosphere, but the vegetation, the water features, and the palm trees and cacti are reminders that this is a desert oasis. The monastery is strictly cenobitic, the common language is Greek, and the *typikon* is Athonite. This is the main monastery of the group and Elder Ephraim has his residence here.

In the Prologue to the English edition of Elder Ephraim's book, *Counsels from the Holy Mountain*, Metropolitan Hierotheos of Nafpaktos and St Vlasios writes:

> It is significant that the spiritual words contained in this book, which emanate from the vigils and stillness of the Holy Mountain, are presented to America where, on the one hand, a great disillusionment with the rationalistic and sensualistic atmosphere prevails, and on the other hand, a search for authentic life is being observed ... *Papa*-Ephraim (as we call him here in Greece), in the words of St Symeon the New Theologian, 'received fire', and he has imparted this fire to many

monks of the Holy Mountain and in turn to the Church in America that has great need of it.[21]

Indeed, Athos has come to stay in Arizona.

Athos Comes to France

So far, we have examined how in recent years Athonite monasticism has been brought, first, to England and, secondly, to North America by Athonite monks who themselves had originated in the Orthodox heartlands. In the first instance, Fr Sophrony, a Russian by birth, initially left his fatherland in the wake of the 1917 Revolution to join the Russian immigrant community in Paris but soon felt a calling to become a monk on Mount Athos. There he was inspired by St Silouan first to move into the desert as a hermit and, only after his health broke down, to go back to Paris from where he led a mission to England. In the second instance, Fr Ephraim, a native of Greece, was drawn at an early age to join the embryonic brotherhood being formed by Elder Joseph the Hesychast at New Skete. Inspired by his teaching, and only after a long spell as a hermit himself, he moved into the monastery of Philotheou with a group of disciples and with great speed and love revived it. Discovering a talent for recruiting novices and reviving monasteries, and forced to choose between a newly renewed Athos and a United States seriously in need of renewal, he chose the latter and with a group of disciples founded not one but seventeen monasteries scattered across the continent. So far, Athos has been drawing in men from its traditional recruiting ground, as Dimitri Obolensky described. Now, in the case of France, it drew a Frank,[22] 'ex partibus infidelium', as it were, and charged him with the task of taking Athonite spirituality back to his fatherland. This was something quite unprecedented in the history of Orthodox monasticism. How did it come about?

Fr Placide Deseille (d.2018) was born in Paris in 1926 into a devout Roman Catholic family and was brought up in the liturgical and patristic traditions of the Church.[23] He tells us that he was very much influenced in his youth

---

[21] See Elder Ephraim, *Counsels from the Holy Mountain: Selected from the Letters and Homilies of Elder Ephraim* (Florence, AZ: St Anthony's Greek Orthodox Monastery, 1999), p. xv.

[22] The standard (somewhat derogatory) Byzantine term for anyone from the West, still current in monastic parlance on the Holy Mountain today.

[23] See his brief but heart-searching spiritual autobiography: Fr Placide Deseille, 'Stages of a Pilgrimage', in Golitzin, *The Living Witness of the Holy Mountain*, pp. 63–98, to which this section is greatly indebted.

by three women in his family, his grandmother and two paternal aunts, who inspired him with a deep respect for tradition and also a love of monasticism, notably the works of Dom Marmion and the great abbeys of Beuron, Maredsous, and Solesmes. At the age of twelve he read a magazine article about the monasteries of Meteora which made him think that there might exist a tradition in those parts that was even more ancient and more authentic than that represented by the great Benedictine abbeys that his grandmother was always telling him about. Even then he longed to become a monk at Great Meteora, but he realized that it was not remotely possible.

During World War II he had the chance to visit a number of monasteries in France, notably the abbey of Wisques in the Pas-de-Calais and also Solesmes, for which he retained a strong affection. But in 1942, at the age of sixteen, he was received as a postulant at the Cistercian abbey of Bellefontaine in Anjou. Among the Cistercian Trappists, he says, he felt 'closer to the living sources of monasticism, closer to the Gospel as the Desert Fathers had wished to live it'.[24] Indeed, he was taught the meaning of the Rule of St Benedict by relating it to its sources, the Desert Fathers, St Pachomios, and St Basil the Great, and his later monastic education required him to read as deeply in the Fathers of the Eastern Church as in the Western. The more he read of the former, the more he warmed to them, though his devotion to them was not shared by his spiritual fathers who rebuked him for it. He was entirely happy at the monastery, but he acknowledges that he did feel a certain disparity between their observance of the Rule and the liturgy on the one hand and their theology and spirituality on the other, the former displaying continuity from an ancient tradition, the latter characterized by modern dogma. He felt a need to return to the teaching of the early Fathers and already suspected that this tradition had been better preserved by the Orthodox Church.

In 1952 Fr Placide was ordained to the priesthood and soon after that was given the title of professor of dogmatic theology and put in charge of the spiritual formation of the younger monks in the monastery. He visited Paris more than once on monastery business and took advantage of the opportunity to meet Fr Kiprian Kern, who was professor of patristics at the Institut St-Serge, and also Vladimir Lossky, whose recently published book, *Mystical Theology of the Eastern Church*, had greatly impressed him. Fr Kiprian introduced him to the writings of St Gregory of Nyssa, St Maximos the Confessor, and St Gregory Palamas and to many of the doctrines of the Orthodox tradition, but he never proposed that he should

---

[24] Ibid., p. 65.

think of joining the Orthodox Church. At that stage he was simply concerned to find in the Eastern tradition a better understanding of his own tradition, just as experience of the Orthodox liturgy, to which he was now for the first time exposed, increased his awareness of the comparable, if more deeply hidden, richness of the Latin rite.

In 1958 he was sent to Rome to pursue his studies in theology where he immersed himself in not only the literary treasures of the libraries but also the stone monuments to the early Church. At the same time, he became involved with the editors of the series entitled 'Sources Chrétiennes', which he was asked to expand with the addition of some volumes of medieval Cistercian texts. But rather than restrict the series to Cistercian spirituality, Fr Placide wanted to broaden its scope to embrace a much wider monastic and patristic tradition. The Abbot General of the Cistercian Order, who had formerly been abbot of Bellefontaine, accepted this suggestion, and Fr Placide on his return to France found himself rewarded with this editorial responsibility together with various other book projects in addition to his teaching load. His ambition was to produce a series of Eastern monastic texts alongside the Western texts in 'Sources Chrétiennes', but the first volume of the series 'Eastern Spirituality', devoted to the sayings of the Desert Fathers, did not appear until 1966, by which time he had left Bellefontaine.

Meanwhile, in 1960 he was invited by the patriarchal vicar for the Greek Catholics in Egypt to visit that country in order to experience something of Coptic monasticism, which was then enjoying a revival that is still evident today. From his base at the monastery of Deir el-Syriani, he was able to visit the other monasteries of the Wadi Natrun, the ancient desert of Scetis, which deeply impressed him with their ancient spirituality and direct link with the Desert Fathers who had always been so dear to him. The revival had been brought about largely by a charismatic elder, Matthew the Poor, who had been living in a cave since 1935 and had come back into the monastery with a group of young disciples. A few elderly monks from the previous regime continued to live an idiorrhythmic life in the monastery, but all the newcomers, most of whom were university graduates, followed a strictly cenobitic way of life. This included common worship, common tasks, such as gardening, printing, and translating patristic texts into Arabic, as well as use of the Jesus Prayer. For the first time, Fr Placide came across a way of life that was almost identical to what he was later to find on Mount Athos.

Fr Placide initially had high hopes that the Second Vatican Council (1962–5) would bring about a renewal of the organization and observances of the Catholic Church through a return to the spirit and teaching of the Fathers. However, in the event it brought him deep disappointment. He began to realize that his continuing devotion to what he saw as the truth in the doctrines of the Fathers and the early Church was no longer compatible with his remaining in the monastery, and he began to wonder if the Uniate practice of following the Orthodox tradition and using the Eastern rite within the context of the Roman Catholic Church might be the key to bringing back the body of the Church to the spirit of the Fathers. Rejecting the idea of the Byzantine tradition as exercising an 'oriental' or 'eastern' allure, Fr Placide rather aligned his thinking with that of the French Dominican theologian, Marie-Joseph Le Guillou, who wrote of the Byzantine liturgy:

> It has done nothing more nor less than closely incorporate into liturgical life all the great theology elaborated by the Fathers and Councils before the ninth century. In it the Church, triumphant over heresies, sings her thanksgiving, the great doxology of the Trinitarian and Christological theology of St Athanasios, the Cappadocians, St John Chrysostom, St Cyril of Alexandria, and St Maximos the Confessor. Through it shines the spirituality of the great monastic movements, from the Desert Fathers, from Evagrios, Cassian, and the monks of Sinai, to those of Studion and, later, of Mount Athos ... In it, in a word, the whole world, transfigured by the presence of divine glory, reveals itself in a truly eschatological dimension.[25]

This was the spirit in which on 14 September 1966 Fr Placide, together with another monk from Bellefontaine who had gone through a similar spiritual transformation, founded the monastery of the Transfiguration at Aubazine in Corrèze in south-west France. Others joined them and for ten years they tried to adhere to the liturgical and spiritual traditions of Orthodoxy while remaining inside the Roman Catholic Church. They built a wooden church, a service block (kitchen, refectory, library, etc), a workshop, and separate wooden cabins for the monks to live in. Despite living in separate cells, which the elder later admitted was probably a mistake, they led a cenobitic existence in utter simplicity and great poverty which fulfilled their aims for the monastery. After some years, however, they began to find that this halfway house between Roman Catholicism and Orthodoxy was not entirely satisfactory. They were in touch with Orthodox monasteries and also with other Uniate communities, and they came to realize that the position of the latter with regard to the Catholic Church was no better than marginal. At the same time, the

---

[25] M.-J. Le Guillou, *L'Esprit de l'Orthodoxie grecque et russe* (Paris: Fayard, 1961), p. 47.

Roman Church since Vatican II was continuing to change, and it became apparent that the Church that they had so recently left behind no longer existed.

For some time, Fr Placide had been interested in an argument put forward by a number of Catholic theologians who were well disposed towards Orthodoxy, including the former Lutheran minister Louis Bouyer who had converted to Catholicism in 1939. Their view was that, despite appearances to the contrary, the Catholic Church and the Orthodox Church had never ceased to be one Church: 'They are two local Churches, or rather, two groups of local Churches, each fulfilling the fullness of the Church of Christ in a different though equivalent way. The quarrel between them is age-old and based on misunderstandings, but they are not really separate and have never ceased to comprise, together, the one, visible Church of Christ.'[26] They argued that the Orthodox Church has preserved certain aspects of the Church's original tradition better than the Catholic Church, but that the Catholic Church has developed other aspects of church life better than the Orthodox, such as missionary activities and a sense of universality, and has learnt to adapt itself better to the modern world. If full communion between them were to be restored, it would enhance them both and, furthermore, would enable the Roman Church to set aside some of the problems that had arisen since Vatican II.

Attractive though this notion was, Fr Placide and his associates slowly began to realize that it was an illusion. Two Churches that had been in schism for more than a thousand years on grounds of such fundamental dogmatic difference could not both represent the Church of Christ. 'It was only very gradually', he writes, 'that I came to the conclusion that the Orthodox Church is the Church of Christ in her fullness, and that the Roman Catholic Church is a member separated from her.'[27] Towards the end of 1976 he and his two brothers at Aubazine became certain that they could not delay any longer and that they had to make preparations for being received into the Orthodox Church. They decided that it would cause less offence to the Catholic hierarchy in France if they were to go abroad for this purpose, a view that was accepted by their area bishop, who was initially supportive. But the bishop subsequently gave them notice to quit their premises at Aubazine and informed both Catholic and Orthodox authorities that he was doing so. Soon after this they left for the monastery of Simonopetra on Mount Athos where they knew from past experience they could be sure of a sympathetic welcome.

[26] Deseille, 'Stages of a Pilgrimage', p. 81.   [27] Ibid., p. 82.

Elder Aimilianos had only been on Athos for a very few years when Fr Placide arrived with his associates, but already the abbot's warm-hearted personality was well known as was the spiritual vigour of his young brotherhood. It was decided that the newcomers should be received by baptism. The issue of rebaptism of converts has aroused controversy for centuries, but the position of the Athonites is very clear:

> Athos is a country where only monks live, who by virtue of their calling must strive to live out as best they can all the demands of Christian life and the Church's Tradition. They engage in no pastoral activity, nor do they seek to proselytize, that is, to draw people to Orthodoxy by making things easier for them. It is therefore normal for them to abide by *akribeia* [precision], though without blaming those who, finding themselves in different circumstances, have recourse to economy. Athos's vocation is *akribeia* in all spheres. It is normal for the non-Orthodox who become monks there to be received by baptism.[28]

Fr Placide makes it clear that the Athonites imposed no conditions on them. They were free to be received into Orthodoxy elsewhere by other means. But since they had chosen to become Athonite monks, they had no alternative but to be received in the only way that was acceptable to their future brothers, and so they asked to be received by baptism. This event took place on 19 June 1977; and on 26 February 1978 they were tonsured as monks of Simonopetra.

They discussed with Elder Aimilianos whether they should remain on the Holy Mountain or return to France, and it was his decision that they should return and operate as monks in their own country. Accepting his decision, they returned to France and established two new monasteries, the monastery of St Antony the Great, for men, at St Laurent-en-Royans in the Dauphiné, and the monastery of the Transfiguration, for women, at Martel on the Quercy plateau. Both were *metochia* (dependencies) of Simonopetra. In due course, the monastery of the Transfiguration moved from its original site to Terrasson in the Dordogne where it has an active community of six nuns under the spiritual care of Fr Elie. The monastery of St Antony the Great, of which Fr Placide was abbot, was initially housed in a converted house and barn on a small piece of land surrounded by steep, rocky cliffs. But as the brotherhood increased, they needed a proper church, which, thanks to the generous donations of local Orthodox and friends of the monastery, they were able to build. A magnificent church in the Byzantine style, dedicated to St Silouan the

---

[28] Ibid., p. 89.

Athonite, is the result, which has been beautifully decorated with frescos by a distinguished iconographer from Moscow, who gave his services free of charge (Plate 41). Meanwhile, from 1981 female vocations materialized, and it was necessary to establish a women's monastery in the vicinity. For this purpose, Fr Placide founded the monastery of the Protection of the Mother of God, but it soon became too small for the size of the community and in 1991 it moved to Solan, near Avignon, in the Gard region. Here the sisters acquired a large agricultural domain and, in addition to constructing a substantial monastery complete with a fine church, they began to practise organic farming and have developed a successful winery.

There are now therefore three *metochia* of Simonopetra in France, all of which maintain the spiritual traditions of their parent monastery. They follow a cenobitic lifestyle and an Athonite *typikon*, but the liturgy is celebrated in French with Byzantine-style chant. But unlike their brothers on the Holy Mountain, who live in a world apart, these communities are all very much of this world and form part of a diaspora that owes allegiance to a multiplicity of jurisdictions. Fr Placide has summarized their situation and the opportunity that it offers in words that, *mutatis mutandis*, are equally applicable to all the religious communities throughout the world that have their origins and inspiration on the Holy Mountain:

> Our position as Athonite monks in France has the advantage of placing us outside certain jurisdictional antagonisms. For centuries Athos has had a 'pan-Orthodox' vocation: monks from very different nationalities mingle together there and share a common experience of belonging to the 'Garden of the Mother of God'. We would like our presence in France to be such a unifying factor, a cause of spiritual convergence among Orthodox of differing origins ...
>
> We are Orthodox monks, called to live the tradition of the Holy Mountain in the land of France. We know that the mission of the monk 'is not to accomplish something by his own resources, but to bear witness throughout his life that death has been overcome. And this he does only by burying himself in the earth, like a seed'.[29]

---

[29] Ibid., pp. 92–3, quoting Archimandrite Vasileios, abbot of Stavronikita, in *Contacts*, 89: 1 (1975), 101.

Epilogue

In the course of this book, we have observed Athonite 'seeds' being planted in the soil of numerous countries throughout the Orthodox world and beyond. Dimitri Obolensky's thesis has been put to the test and proved to be accurate. Men have indeed been drawn to Athos from all over Eastern Europe seeking a monastic training, or a spiritual father, or the wisdom of a charismatic elder. In time, many of them have returned, either to their homeland or to another part of the Orthodox world, taking with them the fruits of their labours and learning, planting seeds in distant lands from which Athonite corn has sprung up and matured. The Slav monasteries have played a significant role in this movement, but it has not been confined to them, and over the years every monastery has been involved. It is a movement that has ebbed and flowed. At times there have been serial incursions from outside, at other times there have been mass excursions from within, and in between there have been long periods when apparently nothing very much happened, though this is no doubt partly due to the fact that monks do not advertise their business very much but simply keep a low profile and get on with what they have to do.

There was obviously an extraordinary initial burst in the tenth century. The foundation of the Great Lavra in 963 symbolized the arrival of cenobitic monasticism on the Mountain. And thanks to the determination, energy, and excellent networking abilities of the founder, Athos became not just a city but an international melting-pot, a pan-Orthodox centre of spirituality, a beacon of light which drew men from all corners of the empire and even beyond. St Athanasios was a native of Trebizond where he would have grown up with Georgians on his doorstep, so it is no surprise to find them among the first to follow him. Amalfitans too had their own quarter in Constantinople where they would have rubbed shoulders with agents of the monasteries doing business in the city. Athanasios was determined that no one should be excluded on grounds of race or creed, so he happily admitted Benedictine monks who used a Latin rite, and it was the Georgians who encouraged them to establish a monastery of their own. Within Athanasios's lifetime there were at least half a dozen new monasteries on Athos, each with a sizeable complement of monks; arrangements had been made for the eremitical life to continue alongside the cenobitic; constitutions had been drawn up for the administration of each monastery which remain the basis of those still in force today; and the Mountain was gaining a reputation as a dynamic centre for the religious life that was at least the equal of any of the other holy mountains already in existence.

The Byzantines were past masters at the exercise of what is sometimes called 'soft power', and it was soft power that was the basis of what we now know as the Byzantine Commonwealth. Soft power, based on literary, cultural, and religious influence, enabled Byzantium to gain a hold over the whole of Eastern Europe and to retain it long after its political power had waned. Byzantium represented a venerable and august civilization to which all the younger states that emerged around it aspired. They adopted its systems of administration, its royal titles, its forms of art and architecture, and they adopted its religion. As soon as this new beacon of religious excellence made its presence felt, what could be more natural than for all the members of the Byzantine Commonwealth to wish to join it? One by one, therefore, the member states sent contingents of monks to Athos with a view to establishing there a monastery of their own. After the Georgians and the Amalfitans, the Rus' from Kiev were next with their monastery of Xylourgou, first recorded in a document of 1016. By the end of the twelfth century, the Bulgarians and the Serbs had acquired monastic houses of their own at Zographou and Hilandar respectively. And in the fourteenth century the Romanians took control of Koutloumousiou, though it never officially ceased to be a Greek monastery. By this time Athos was firmly established as the chief spiritual centre for the entire Orthodox world.

Meanwhile, the alternating current of this monastic movement began to operate also in the opposite direction, and for a variety of reasons, not always voluntarily, monks left the Mountain and returned either to their homeland or to some other part of Eastern Europe bearing Athonite seeds. Thus St Antony of Kiev was instructed by his Athonite abbot to return to Rus' with the blessing of the Holy Mountain so that many other monks might spring from his example. Similarly St Sava, having successfully founded the monastery of Hilandar with his father, St Symeon, returned to his homeland to become abbot of Studenica and in due course archbishop of the newly independent Church of Serbia. Gregory of Sinai, after many years of travelling, found a spiritual home at last on Athos, only to be driven from it by Turkish raiders and forced to take refuge in the mountains of Bulgaria. There he founded a monastery that proved to be the channel for the spread of Athonite spirituality throughout the Balkans. Russian monasticism had been all but extinguished by the Mongols when it was revived by St Sergius of Radonezh and his contemporaries in the fourteenth century who looked to Athos and the hesychast doctrines of Gregory Palamas as models of spiritual excellence and good practice. St Maximos the Greek, when invited to Moscow to translate the classics of patristic texts into a language that the Russians could understand, took with him a fund of deep learning and high ideals that were to cost him his freedom but eventually led to his recognition as a martyr and a saint.

It is noticeable that the peaks of Athonite spirituality, while operating as ambassadors for Byzantine and post-Byzantine soft power, were also responding to troughs in the political world around them. Thus in the fourteenth century, when the empire was crumbling, riven by civil war, stricken by plague, and politically on its knees, there was a cultural flowering, sometimes known as the Palaiologan renaissance, which bore fruit not only in magnificent art and architecture but also in intellectual and spiritual debate. Athos was at the heart of this debate in which the monks gave their full support to their protégé, Gregory Palamas. Palamas's victory was a victory for the Holy Mountain, on the strength of which Palamite theology and the practice of hesychasm spread like wildfire throughout the Balkans and became the basis on which the Athonite Commonwealth stood thereafter.

Similarly in the eighteenth century, when Eastern Europe had been subject to the Ottomans for 300 years or more and there seemed little prospect of any change, there sprang up a movement for the revival of traditional Orthodox practices and the renewal of education among the Greeks. This movement also had its origins on Athos and did much to ensure that Orthodoxy survived as the prime ingredient of Greek culture when it was threatened by currents of Western Enlightenment. At the same time, a conscious effort was made on Athos to draw together the remaining threads of hesychasm and ensure their survival by means of a return to patristic literature. This resulted in the compilation of an anthology of mystical and ascetic texts known as the *Philokalia*, which was first published in Greek in 1782. Subsequently translated into Slavonic, and then Russian and many other languages, this book was responsible for a remarkable spiritual revival that began in Moldavia and then spread to monasteries throughout Russia.

The twentieth century also was an extremely difficult time politically for all the countries of Eastern Europe. All of them were engulfed in war or revolution or tyranny of one form or another for almost the entire century. As if in sympathy with this disorder, the Holy Mountain responded with another remarkable spiritual revival. In the second half of the century, when all appeared to be on the brink of disaster, a group of charismatic elders emerged, not in the monasteries, but outside in the sketes and cells of the desert, where so many luminaries had operated in the past. Once again, there were men who had received their monastic formation either on the Mountain or in some cases elsewhere who were willing and able to revive the apparently moribund monasteries. Others were ready to depart with the fruits of their labours and plant seeds in other lands, but the traditional route, north into the Balkans and Russia, was barred to them by the Iron Curtain. Instead they had to find another outlet for their gifts, and so they chose (or rather had no choice but were compelled) to turn to the West. For the first time the countries of Western Europe and North America were blessed to receive Athonite elders and Athonite wisdom.

Now in the twenty-first century an interesting situation has arisen. The Iron Curtain has been lifted and the traditional routes are open once more. Freedom of religious worship means that the peoples of Eastern Europe are at last free to practise the religion of their choice, and the opening of borders has removed any remaining restrictions of movement. As a result, churches and monasteries, especially in Russia and Romania, but also to some extent in Serbia and Bulgaria, have reopened their doors and are receiving unprecedented crowds of believers. In Russia, for example, since 1991 the number of parishes has grown from 7,000 to 33,000 in 2015, and over the same period the number of monasteries has increased from fewer than 30 to more than 800. The same phenomenon, slightly retarded, is taking place on the Holy Mountain: the monastic houses, especially those of the Russians and the Romanians, but also to a lesser extent those of the Serbs and Bulgarians, are once again filling up with monks. The St Panteleimonos monastery, for example, which in 1986 had a brotherhood of twenty-three monks, by 2013 had grown to eighty, one of the largest on the Mountain. Its guest accommodation has been refurbished and it can now house up to 500 pilgrims as it celebrates the millennium of the Russian presence on Athos in 2016. Similarly, each of the Romanian sketes has a brotherhood of fifty monks, whereas in former times Prodromou had never had more than twenty and in 1977 Lakkou was down to just one. As for pilgrims, there are now probably as many Slavs as there are Greeks. These changes open up interesting possibilities for the future role of Athos. Could we see a return to the situation that obtained at the start of the twentieth century when Greek monks were actually in a minority on the Mountain? Whatever happens next, it is clear that Athos is once again open to all men who wish to enter, and the Athonite Commonwealth has become a global phenomenon. The garden of the Mother of God provides enough seeds not only to regenerate its own neglected groves and abandoned orchards but to export to spiritual deserts and godforsaken cities that are thirsting and ready to receive them anywhere in the world.

Glossary

Antidoron: bread that has been blessed by a priest and is then distributed to the faithful, most commonly after a celebration of the Divine Liturgy.

Archimandrite: an honorific title given to a celibate priest or abbot in the Orthodox Church.

Bogomils: a heretical dualist sect founded in tenth-century Bulgaria, which subsequently spread throughout the Balkans. Its adherents believed that the material world was the creation of the devil and opposed most of the tenets of the Byzantine Church.

Cenobitic monasticism: the monastic system by which monks live a common life in spiritual obedience to an abbot, worshipping and eating together, and contributing any wealth they may have to the common purse; cf. *idiorrhythmic monasticism.*

Chrysobull: a document or charter bearing the emperor's gold seal.

Ecumenical councils: a series of six councils held between 325 and 681, which represented (at least in theory) the entire episcopate of the Byzantine Church and defined the basic doctrines of the Christian faith. A seventh council in 843, known as the Triumph of Orthodoxy, established the orthodoxy of the use of icons.

Ecumenical Patriarch: courtesy title for the archbishop of Constantinople indicating that he holds a special place as *primus inter pares* among all the Orthodox patriarchs.

Elder (Greek *geron*; Russian *starets*): the term most commonly used for a spiritual guide or director.

Evergetinos: an anthology of edifying monastic sayings, compiled in the eighteenth century as a companion volume to the *Philokalia* (q.v.).

Filioque: a Latin phrase, meaning 'and from the Son', inserted into the Creed by the Western Church in the sixth century with reference to the procession of the Holy Spirit ('who proceeds from the Father . . .').

Geron: see Elder.

Hegoumenos: the abbot of a cenobitic monastery.

Hesychasm: a spiritual tradition developed by St John Klimakos (seventh century) for whom *hesychia* ('stillness', 'tranquillity') was a state of inner silence and vigilance, closely associated with the name of Jesus and the repetition of short prayers; cf. *Jesus Prayer*.

Holy Community: the democratically elected parliament of Mount Athos to which each of the ruling monasteries sends an elected representative to serve for a year.

Iconoclasm: a religious movement of the eighth and ninth centuries that opposed the veneration of icons and relics in Orthodox worship.

Iconostasis: the screen that divides the nave from the chancel in an Orthodox church and is usually embellished with icons.

Idiorrhythmic monasticism: the monastic system by which monks were permitted to set their own 'rhythm', were not bound by vows of poverty or obedience to an abbot, and lived in separate apartments, often with their own servants and their own worldly goods, neither eating together nor contributing to a common purse; cf. *cenobitic monasticism*.

Jesus Prayer: a short prayer, focusing on the name of Jesus, commended by the hesychasts for constant repetition, most commonly taking the form: 'Lord Jesus Christ, Son of God, have mercy on me.'

Judaizers: adherents of a heresy that arose in late fifteenth-century Russia and was critical of the clergy, iconoclastic, and anti-Trinitarian; its connection with Judaism is obscure.

Katholikon: the main church of a monastery.

Kollyvades: a religious movement, originating on Mount Athos in the eighteenth century, which insisted that a regeneration of the Greek nation could only be brought about by a return to the true roots of Orthodox Christianity.

Ktitor: a founder of a monastery; also used to refer to a major benefactor.

Lavra: originally a group of monastic cells in which the monks would live as hermits during the week and come together at weekends to attend the services and share meals. The term was later applied to much larger cenobitic monasteries, e.g. the Great Lavra on Mount Athos and the Caves monastery in Kiev.

Messalians: a heretical sect, originating in the Middle East, who claimed that they could perceive God's essence with their senses.

Metochion: a dependency of a ruling monastery.

Non-Possessors: opponents of the trend in sixteenth-century Russia for monasteries to become major landowners; sometimes known as the 'Transvolga hermits'; cf. *Possessors*.

Paterikon: an archive or collection of literary material relating to the history of a monastery.

Phanariots: originally the Greek Christian inhabitants of the Phanar district in Constantinople, they formed a social and political elite under the Ottomans and rose to prominent positions in the administration, especially in the Danubian provinces.

Phiale: a covered basin or fountain in which water is blessed for ritual purposes in a monastery.

Philokalia: an anthology of ascetical texts, compiled in the eighteenth century by St Makarios of Corinth and St Nikodimos of the Holy Mountain.

Possessors: supporters of the trend in sixteenth-century Russia for monasteries to become major landowners, led by Abbot Iosif of Volokolamsk.

Prayer of the heart: see Jesus Prayer.

Protos hesychastes: the 'first hesychast', subsequently shortened to Protos ('first'), as the primate of Athos is still known.

Rason: a loose-fitting, black gown with billowing sleeves, part of the monastic habit.

Schema: the monastic habit: the small *schema* is the first grade; the Great *Schema* (or great habit) denotes the highest rank to which a monk may be promoted.

Skete: a monastic village or group of cells, gathered around a central church, dependent upon a ruling monastery.

Starets: see Elder.

Synaxarion: a compendium of biographies of the saints of the Orthodox Church.

Synodikon: a monastery's archive or collection of statutes; also a room designed for meetings of the brotherhood.

Talanto: a wooden plank used instead of a bell and struck rhythmically with a mallet to summon the fathers to prayer.

Typikon: a rule or charter by which a monastery or group of monasteries is governed.

Uniates: Christians who acknowledge the supremacy of the Pope but continue to follow certain Orthodox practices such as allowing married clergy and use of the Byzantine Liturgy; also known as Greek Catholics.

Voivode: a Romanian term for the local rulers of Wallachia and Moldavia.

Zealots: the leaders of an uprising who seized power in Thessaloniki from 1342 to 1349.

Select Bibliography

I. Primary Sources

Athanasius, *The Life of Antony and the Letter to Marcellinus*, trans. R. C. Gregg (New York: Paulist Press, 1980).

Cross, S. H. and O. P. Sherbowitz-Wetzor (eds and trans.), *The Russian Primary Chronicle* (Cambridge, MA: Medieval Academy of America, 1953).

Goldfrank, D. (ed. and trans.), *Nil Sorsky: The Authentic Writings* (Kalamazoo, MI: Cistercian Publications, 2008).

Grdzelidze, T. (trans.), *Georgian Monks on Mount Athos: Two Eleventh-Century Lives of the Hegoumenoi of Iviron* (London: Bennett & Bloom, 2009).

Greenfield, P. H. and A.-M. Talbot (eds and trans.), *Holy Men of Mount Athos* (Cambridge, MA, and London: Harvard University Press, 2016).

John Climacus, *The Ladder of Divine Ascent*, trans. C. Luibheid and N. Russell (Mahwah, NJ: Paulist Press, 1982).

John of Damascus, *Three Treatises on the Divine Images*, trans. A. Louth (Crestwood, NY: St Vladimir's Seminary Press, 2003).

Makarios of Simonos Petra, Hieromonk, *The Synaxarion: The Lives of the Saints of the Orthodox Church*, trans. C. Hookway et al., 7 vols (Ormylia: Holy Convent of the Annunciation of Our Lady, 1998–2008).

Noret, J. (ed.), *Vitae duae antiquae Sancti Athanasii Athonitae* (Turnhout: Brepols, 1982).

Palmer, G. E. H., P. Sherrard, and K. Ware (trans.), *The Philokalia: The Complete Text Compiled by St Nikodimos of the Holy Mountain and St Makarios of Corinth*, 4 vols of 5 (London: Faber & Faber, 1979–95).

Thomas, J. and A. Constantinides Hero (eds), *Byzantine Monastic Foundation Documents: A Complete Translation of the Surviving Founders' Typika and Testaments*, 5 vols (Washington, DC: Dumbarton Oaks, 2001).

Veilleux, A. (trans.), *Pachomian Koinonia* (Kalamazoo, MI: Cistercian Publications, 1981).

Ward, B. (trans.), *The Sayings of the Desert Fathers: The Alphabetical Collection*, new edn. (Kalamazoo, MI: Cistercian Publications, 1984).

2. Secondary Sources

Angold, M. (ed.), *The Cambridge History of Eastern Christianity, vol. 5: Eastern Christianity* (Cambridge: Cambridge University Press, 2006).

Balfour, D., 'Gregory the Sinaite: Life and Spiritual Profile', *Theologia*, 53: 1 (1982), 30–62.

Bryer, A., and M. Cunningham (eds), *Mount Athos and Byzantine Monasticism* (Aldershot: Variorum, 1996).

Bunge, G., *The Rublev Trinity: The Icon of the Trinity by the Monk-Painter Andrei Rublev*, trans. Andrew Louth (Crestwood, NY: St Vladimir's Seminary Press, 2007).

Burgess, J. P., *Holy Rus': The Rebirth of Orthodoxy in the New Russia* (New Haven, CT, and London: Yale University Press, 2017).

Casey, R. P., 'Early Russian Monasticism', *Orientalia Christiana Periodica*, 19 (1953), 372–423.

Casiday, A. (ed.), *The Orthodox Christian World* (London and New York: Routledge, 2012).

Cavarnos, C., *St Cosmas Aitolos*, 3rd edn (Belmont, MA: Institute for Byzantine and Modern Greek Studies, 1985).

St Nicodemos the Hagiorite, 2nd edn (Belmont, MA: Institute for Byzantine and Modern Greek Studies, 1979).

Chamberas, P. A. (trans.), *Nicodemos of the Holy Mountain: A Handbook of Spiritual Counsel* (Mahwah, NJ: Paulist Press, 1989).

Charanis, P., 'The Monastic Properties and the State in the Byzantine Empire', *Dumbarton Oaks Papers*, 4 (1948), 53–118.

Conomos, D. and G. Speake (eds), *Mount Athos the Sacred Bridge: The Spirituality of the Holy Mountain* (Oxford: Peter Lang, 2005).

Conticello, C. G. and V. (eds), *La Théologie byzantine et sa tradition*, vol. 2 (Turnhout: Brepols, 2002).

Ćurčić, S., *Architecture in the Balkans: From Diocletian to Süleyman the Magnificent* (New Haven and London: Yale University Press, 2010).

della Dora, V., *Imagining Mount Athos: Visions of a Holy Place from Homer to World War II* (Charlottesville and London: University of Virginia Press, 2011),

Dunlop, J. B., *Staretz Amvrosy* (London and Oxford: Mowbrays, 1975).

Ephraim, Elder, *Counsels from the Holy Mountain: Selected from the Letters and Homilies of Elder Ephraim* (Florence, AZ: St Anthony's Greek Orthodox Monastery, 1999).

Featherstone, J. M. E. (trans.), *The Life of Paisij Velyčkovs'kyj* (Cambridge, MA: Ukrainian Research Institute of Harvard University, 1989).

Fedotov, G. P., *The Russian Religious Mind (I): Kievan Christianity, the 10th to the 13th Centuries* (Cambridge, MA: Harvard University Press, 1946).

Fedotov, G. P. (ed.), *A Treasury of Russian Spirituality* (London: Sheed & Ward, 1950).

Fennell, J., *A History of the Russian Church to 1448* (London: Routledge, 1995).

Fennell, N., *The Russians on Athos* (Oxford: Peter Lang, 2001).

Franklin, S. and J. Shepard, *The Emergence of Rus, 750–1200* (London: Longman, 1996).

Geanakoplos, D. J., 'The Post-Byzantine Athonite Monk Maximus "the Greek": Reformer of Orthodoxy in Sixteenth-Century Russia', *Greek Orthodox Theological Review*, 33 (1988), 445–68.

Golitzin, Hieromonk Alexander (ed., trans.), *The Living Witness of the Holy Mountain: Contemporary Voices from Mount Athos* (South Canaan, PA: St Tikhon's Seminary Press, 1996).

Gothóni, R. and G. Speake (eds), *The Monastic Magnet: Roads to and from Mount Athos* (Oxford: Peter Lang, 2008).

Haney, J., *From Italy to Muscovy: The Life and Works of Maxim the Greek* (Munich: Fink, 1973).

Hébert, M. L., *Hesychasm, Word-Weaving, and Slavic Hagiography: The Literary School of Patriarch Euthymius* (Munich: Otto Sagner, 1992).

Heppell, M., *The Ecclesiastical Career of Gregory Camblak* (London: n.p., 1979).

'The Hesychast Movement in Bulgaria: The Turnovo School and its Relations with Constantinople', *Eastern Churches Review*, 7 (1975), 9–20.

Joantă, Metropolitan Serafim, *Treasures of Romanian Christianity: Hesychast Tradition and Culture*, trans. I. Bănică and C. Hâncianu Latiş (Whitby, ON: Cross Meridian, 2013).

Joseph, Elder, *Elder Joseph the Hesychast: Struggles – Experiences – Teachings*, trans. E. Theokritoff (Mount Athos: Monastery of Vatopaidi, 1999).

Kitromilides, P. M., *An Orthodox Commonwealth: Symbolic Legacies and Cultural Encounters in Southeastern Europe* (Aldershot: Ashgate, 2007).

Lemerle, P., *Byzantine Humanism: The First Phase*, trans. H. Lindsay and A. Moffatt (Canberra: Australian Association for Byzantine Studies, 1986).

Loch, S., *Athos: The Holy Mountain* (London: Lutterworth, 1957).

Louth, A., *Modern Orthodox Thinkers: From the Philokalia to the Present* (London: SPCK, 2015).

McGuckin, J. A., 'The Life and Mission of St Paisius Velichkovsky, 1722–1794: An Early Modern Master of the Orthodox Spiritual Life', *Spiritus*, 9: 2 (2009), 157–73.

Maloney, G. A., *Russian Hesychasm: The Spirituality of Nil Sorskij* (The Hague/Paris: Mouton, 1973).

Meyendorff, J., *Byzantium and the Rise of Russia: A Study of Byzantino-Russian Relations in the Fourteenth Century* (Cambridge: Cambridge University Press, 1981).

'Mount Athos in the Fourteenth Century: Spiritual and Intellectual Legacy', *Dumbarton Oaks Papers*, 42 (1988), 157–65.

St Gregory Palamas and Orthodox Spirituality (Crestwood, NY: St Vladimir's Seminary Press, 1998).

A Study of Gregory Palamas (Crestwood, NY: St Vladimir's Seminary Press, 1998).

Miller, D. B., *Saint Sergius of Radonezh, His Trinity Monastery, and the Formation of the Russian Identity* (DeKalb, IL: Northern Illinois University Press, 2010).

Morris, R., *Monks and Laymen in Byzantium 843–1118* (Cambridge: Cambridge University Press, 1995).

Murzaku, I. A. (ed.), *Monasticism in Eastern Europe and the Former Soviet Republics* (London and New York: Routledge, 2016).

Obolensky, D., *The Byzantine Commonwealth: Eastern Europe 500–1453* (London: Weidenfeld & Nicholson, 1971).

The Byzantine Inheritance of Eastern Europe (London: Variorum, 1982).

Byzantium and the Slavs (Crestwood, NY: St Vladimir's Seminary Press, 1994).

'Italy, Mount Athos and Muscovy: The Three Worlds of Maximos the Greek (c.1470–1556)', *Proceedings of the British Academy*, 67 (1981), 143–61 [= *Six Byzantine Portraits*, ch. 6].

'Late Byzantine Culture and the Slavs: A Study in Acculturation', *The Byzantine Inheritance of Eastern Europe*, ch. 17.

Six Byzantine Portraits (Oxford: Clarendon Press, 1988).

Patapios, Hieromonk and Archbishop Chrysostomos, *Manna from Athos: The Issue of Frequent Communion on the Holy Mountain in the Late Eighteenth and Early Nineteenth Centuries* (Oxford: Peter Lang, 2006).

Romanchuk, R., *Byzantine Hermeneutics and Pedagogy in the Russian North: Monks and Masters at the Kirillo-Belozerskii Monastery 1397–1501* (Toronto, Buffalo, London: University of Toronto Press, 2007).

Rose, Fr Seraphim (trans.), *Blessed Paisius Velichovsky: The Man behind the Philokalia* (Platina, CA: St Herman of Alaska Brotherhood, 1976).

Rose, Fr Seraphim and Fr Herman Podmoshensky (trans.), *The Northern Thebaid: Monastic Saints of the Russian North*, 3rd edn (Platina, CA: St Herman of Alaska Brotherhood, 2004).

Runciman, S., *The Great Church in Captivity: A Study of the Patriarchate of Constantinople from the Eve of the Turkish Conquest to the Greek War of Independence* (Cambridge: Cambridge University Press, 1968).

Sakharov, N. V., *I Love, Therefore I Am: The Theological Legacy of Archimandrite Sophrony* (Crestwood, NY: St Vladimir's Seminary Press, 2002).

(Sakharov), Archimandrite Sophrony, *On Prayer*, trans. R. Edmonds (Crestwood, NY: St Vladimir's Seminary Press, 1996).

Saint Silouan the Athonite, trans. R. Edmonds (Tolleshunt Knights: Stavropegic Monastery of St John the Baptist, 1991).

Speake, G., *Mount Athos: Renewal in Paradise*, 2nd edn (Limni: Denise Harvey, 2014).

Speake, G. and K. Ware (eds), *Mount Athos: Microcosm of the Christian East* (Oxford: Peter Lang, 2012).

Stanton, L. J., *The Optina Pustyn Monastery in the Russian Literary Imagination: Iconic Vision in Works by Dostoevsky, Gogol, Tolstoy, and Others* (New York: Peter Lang, 1995).

Strezova, A., *Hesychasm and Art: The Appearance of New Iconographic Trends in Byzantine and Slavic Lands in the 14th and 15th Centuries* (Canberra: ANU Press, 2014).

Tachiaos, A.-E. N., *Cyril and Methodius of Thessalonica: The Acculturation of the Slavs* (Crestwood, NY: St Vladimir's Seminary Press, 2001).

'The Greek Monk Maximus Trivolis between Eastern and Western Religious Tradition', *Studi Slavistici*, 7 (2010), 327–37.

'Gregory Sinaites' Legacy to the Slavs', *Cyrillomethodianum*, 7 (1983), 113–65.

'Le monachisme de Saint Sava et la tradition hésychaste athonite', *Historische Zeitschrift*, 1 (1966), 83–9.

'Mount Athos and the Slavic Literatures', *Cyrillomethodianum*, 4 (1977), 1–35.

Turdeanu, E. (ed.), *Etudes de littérature roumaine et d'écrits slaves et grecs des principautés roumaines* (Leiden: Brill, 1985).

Vaporis, N. M., *Father Kosmas, the Apostle of the Poor: The Life of St Kosmas Aitolos together with an English Translation of his Teaching and Letters* (Brookline, MA: Holy Cross Orthodox Press, 1977).

Ware, K., 'The Jesus Prayer in St Gregory of Sinai', *Eastern Churches Review*, 4: 1 (1972), 3–22.

The Orthodox Church: An Introduction to Eastern Christianity, 3rd edn (Harmondsworth: Penguin, 2015).

'The Spirituality of the *Philokalia*', *Sobornost*, 13: 1 (1991), 6–24.

Whittow, M., *The Making of Orthodox Byzantium, 600–1025* (Basingstoke: Macmillan, 1996).

Index

academy of Athos (Athonias), 200, 201
Acre
   monastery of St George, 89
Acts of the Apostles, 60
   commentaries on, 191
Adrianople, 100, 115, 204
Aetolia, 200, 202
Agathon, abbot of Vodiţa, 148
Aimilianos, abbot of Simonopetra, 259, 268
Akakij, bishop of Tver', 195
Alaska, 10, 223, 259
Alaverdi, monastery of, 55
Albania, 77, 143, 207, 211
Aldine press, 184
Aleutian islands, 10, 223
Aleuts, 259
Alexander Basarab, 150
Alexander Lăpuşneanu, voivode of Moldavia, 157
Alexander VI, Pope, 185
Alexios I Komnenos, Emperor, 149
Alexios II Komnenos, Emperor, 35
Alexios III Angelos, Emperor, 78, 80, 85
Alexis Apokaukos, Grand Duke, 114
Alexiy, metropolitan of Kiev and All Russia, 133,
   163, 165–6
Alexiy II, patriarch of Moscow, 198
Ali Pasha of Tepeleni, 211
Amalfitans, 270
Amalfitans, monastery of, 51–2, 56, 60, 80
America, North, 258, 263
Amirales, Bulgarian monk, 100
Amphissa, 200
Amvrosy, elder of Optino, 226, 228, 230
Anastasios, archbishop of Albania, 212
anathemas, exchange of in 1054, 52, 60
Andronikos II Palaiologos, Emperor, 93, 100,
   105, 186
Andronikos III Palaiologos, Emperor, 106, 109,
   113, 114, 115
animals, 35, 44, 46, 101, 151, 163
Anna Komnena, 62

Anne of Savoy, Empress, 114, 115, 118
Anthimos, patriarch of Jerusalem, 210
Anthimos Vardis, metropolitan of Paros and
   Naxos, 235
Antioch, 89
Antioch, patriarchate of, 54, 60
Antony, metropolitan of Sourozh, 257
Antony, prior of the skete of St John the
   Forerunner, 225
Antony of Kiev, St, 13, 66–75, 271
Antony the Great, St, 15, 19, 21, 102, 221
Apophthegmata Patrum. See Desert Fathers,
   sayings of the
Arabic, 265
Arabs, 18, 22, 41
Archdiocese of America, Greek Orthodox, 262
Aristotle, 186
Arizona, 262
Armenia, 49, 54
Armenians, 62
Arsenios, bishop of Ninotsmida, 58, 59
Arsenios, hermit in Scetis, 19
Arsenios, hesychast monk on Crete, 94, 97
Arsenios, patriarch of Constantinople, 105
Arsenios the Peloponnesian, monk, 243
Arta, 182, 200
   church of Panagia Parigoritissa, 182
Athanasios of Alexandria, St, 15
Athanasios, patriarch of Constantinople, 111
Athanasios, patriarch of Jerusalem, 88, 89
Athanasios Parios, 235, 240, 246
Athanasios the Athonite, St, 39–50, 55, 83, 171,
   234, 270
   abbot of Great Lavra, 42
   death, 48
   legacy, 48–50
   typikon for Great Lavra, 36, 44–8, 49
Augustine, St, 186
Auxentios, Mount, 31, 106, 111
Avlona, 143
Avraam, abbot of Optino, 225

Bachkovo, monastery of, 62, 128, 129
Bagrat IV, king of Georgia, 60
Balkan Mountains, 125
Balkan Wars, 7
Banjska, monastery of, 102
baptism, 77, 78, 97, 238, 268
Baramus, monastery of, 18
Bardas Phokas, 65
Bardas Skleros, 56, 65
Barlaam, abbot of the Caves monastery, 68
Barlaam, metropolitan of Moscow, 189, 191
Barlaam of Calabria, 109–14, 127
Barsanouphios of Gaza, St, 246
Barsky, Vassily, 215
Basil, St, spiritual father of Poiana Mărului, 219
Basil I, Emperor, 30, 41, 77
Basil I, grand prince of Moscow, 134
Basil II, Emperor, 56, 65
Basil the Great, St, 19, 20, 24, 58, 264
    rule, 36
Bayezid I, Sultan, 137
Bebis, George, 245
Bedouin, 18
Belgrade, 90
    cathedral of St Sava, 90
Bellefontaine, abbey of, 264
Beloozero, 172
Benedict, St, 18, 264
Benedict XIII, Pope, 139
Benedictines, 51–2, 264, 270
Berdyaev, Nikolai, 253, 254
Bersen'-Beklemishev, Ivan, 195
Bessarion, Cardinal, 184
Bessarion, companion of St Paisy
        Velichkovsky, 216
Bishoi, St, 18
Bistriţa, monastery of, 149, 156
Black Death, 18, 116
Bodbe, monastery of, 54
Bogomils, 87, 110, 126, 127, 128
Bogoroditsa, skete of, 66
Bogotin, monastery of, 149
Boris, passion-bearer, 67
Boris I, ruler of Bulgaria, 29, 31
Bouyer, Louis, 267
Braudel, Fernand, 8
Bucharest, 158, 203
    National Museum of Romanian History, 148
Bulgakov, Sergei, 253, 254
Bulgaria, 10, 26, 29, 31, 62, 100, 124–7, 273
Bulgaria, patriarchate of, 126
Bulgarian Church, 31
Bulgarians, 29, 79, 82, 84, 105, 124–44, 215, 271
Bulgars, 32, 50, 64
Byzantine Church, 129, 134

Calabria, 31
Calabrians, monastery of, 51
Cameron, Averil, 6
Canada, 261
Cantacuzino, Şerban, 159
Cappadocia, 19, 30, 31, 220
Casey, R. P., 69
Cassian, John, 18, 58
Catherine II, Empress, 259
Cavarnos, Constantine, 234
Caves, monastery of the. *See* Kiev
cenobitic monasticism
    at Great Lavra, 42–50, 270
    at Hilandar, 83
    at Koutloumousiou, 150
    at Stoudios, 24, 26
    at the Caves, 72
    at Trinity monastery of St Sergius, 163
    at Vatopedi, 79
    at Xylourgou, 66
    in Arizona, 262
    in Egypt, 16, 265
    in France, 264
    in Russia, 74, 165, 175
    preached by Gregory Palamas, 108
    preferred by St Maximos the Greek, 190
    revived by Paisy Velichkovsky, 217
    supported by St Basil, 19
Cephalonia, 207
Chalcedon, Council of, 54
Chalkidiki, 39
Chariton, abbot of Koutloumousiou, 149–54
chastity, vow of, 25, 45
Chelandarion, monastery of, 80
Chios, 100
Chordvaneli family, 56, 57
Christodoulidis, Sapphiros, 206, 211
Chrysanthos, brother of St Kosmas the Aetolian,
        200, 206, 234
Chrysoupolis, 35
Cistercian Trappists, 264
Civil War, Russian, 254
Clement of Alexandria, St, 28
Clement of Ohrid, St, 29, 31
Clement, monastery of, 56
Clogg, Richard, 210
Cluny, abbey of, 26
Coman, Fr Constantin, 154
Commonwealth, Athonite, 14, 39, 198, 253, 272
    Bulgarian ambassadors, 144
    defined, 8–11
    during Tourkokratia, 205
    embraces Albania, 212
    embraces Bulgaria, 101
    embraces Georgia, 54

embraces Romania, 154
embraces Russia, 66, 175, 233
embraces Serbia, 85
a global phenomenon, 274
St Sergius an honorary member, 168, 172
Commonwealth, British, 6
Commonwealth, Byzantine, 6, 29, 52, 54, 79, 85,
 131, 171
built on soft power, 271
embraces Russia, 65
embraces Serbia, 78
held together by hesychasm, 103, 126
spiritual unity strengthened, 135
terms of membership, 168
Commonwealth, Orthodox, 7, 132
communism, 10, 212
Constance, Council of, 139–42
Constantine of Kostenets, 130, 137
Constantine the Philosopher, St, missionary
 to the Slavs, 27–8, 129
Constantine VII Porphyrogennetos,
 Emperor, 77
Constantine IX Monomachos, Emperor
 typikon, 51, 59
Constantinople, 50, 100, 188
 Akataleptos monastery, 109
 Amalfitan quarter, 51
 besieged by Turks, 134
 Chalke gate, 30
 Chora monastery, 105
 Evergetis monastery, 34, 82, 88, 89, 242
 Hagia Sophia, 53, 65, 113, 116
 Hodegon monastery, 34
 Lips monastery, 31
 Myrelaion, 31
 Nea Ekklesia, 31
 palace of Blachernae, 118
 patriarchal academy, 206
 Petra monastery, 34
 St Mamas, monastery of, 126, 127
 threatened by Arabs, 22
Constantinople, patriarchate of, 7, 31, 101, 132,
 147, 187, 194, 222, 262
Copts, 15, 89, 265
Corfu, 183, 207
Corinth, Gulf of, 77
Cotroceni, monastery of, 158
councils, church, 113, 114, 116, 118, 120,
 178, 222
councils, ecumenical, 23, 120
Crete, 31, 41, 94
Crimea, 28, 65, 116
Crusade, Fourth, 52, 84, 85, 86, 182
Curtea de Argeş, monastery of, 156
Curzon, Robert, 249

Cuza, Prince Alexander of Romania, 158
Cyclades, 206
Cyprian, St, metropolitan of Kiev and All Russia,
 132–5, 136, 142, 166, 168
Cyprus, 31, 39, 93
Cyril. *See* Constantine the Philosopher, St
Cyril V, patriarch of Constantinople, 201
Cyrillic alphabet, 28, 29
Czech Republic, 26

D'Alessandri, Antonio, 158
Dandolo, Enrico, Venetian doge, 85
Daniel of Katounakia, Elder, 21
Daniil, abbot of Volokolamsk, 182
Daniil, metropolitan of Moscow, 191–6
Danube, river, 77, 146
Daphni, church at, 32
Dapontes, Kaisarios, 203–5
David, king of Israel, 33, 127
David Dishypatos, monk of Paroria, 116
David III Kouropalates, 56, 58
Davit-Gareja, monastery of, 55
Dawkins, Richard M., 250
de' Medici, Lorenzo, 183
Dečani, monastery of, 83, 137, 142
deification (*theosis*), 238
Demetrios Chomatianos, archbishop
 of Ohrid, 87
Denissoff, Elie, 186
Desert Fathers, 15, 35, 168, 264, 265
 sayings of, 18–19, 242, 265
desert of Athos, 40, 143, 248, 252, 256, 273
Diadochos, St, 221
Dimitri Donskoy, Grand Prince, 165, 166,
 168, 173
Dionisy, abbot of Spaso-Kamenny
 monastery, 173
Dionisy Glushitsky, St, 173
Dionysios, abbot of Philotheou, 155
Dionysios the Areopagite, Pseudo-, 134, 146
Dionysios the Areopagite, St, 109, 111
Dionysios Zagoraios, monk, 245
Dionysiou, monastery of, 156, 157, 236
Dioscorides, 34
Dnieper, river, 65, 68
Dobrotolyubie, 223, 225, 232, 240
Dochiariou, monastery of, 157
Domentijan, 83, 84, 88
Dominicans, 184
Dostoevsky, Fyodor, 225, 227–30
Dyrrachion, 102

Easter, 208
ecumenical patriarch, 133
Egypt, 15, 16, 19, 89, 265

elder, 16, 21, 82, 95, 131, 163, 177, 213, 216, 218, 228–30, 255
elders of Optino, 179, 224–33
Elijah, 102
Eliot, T. S., 241
England, 257–8, 263
Enlightenment, 201, 210, 222, 236, 240, 241, 242, 272
Ephraim, abbot of Philotheou, 260–3
Ephraim, abbot of Vatopedi, 198
Epiphanius the Wise, St, 162, 163, 169
Epirus, 77, 182, 207
eremitic monasticism, 19, 32, 41, 48, 49, 94, 225, 271
Esphigmenou, monastery of, 52, 66, 108, 113, 158
Eudokia, wife of Stefan the First Crowned, 78, 85
eunuchs, 44
Eustathios, archbishop of Thessaloniki, 36
Euthymios, monk of Stoudios monastery, 42
Euthymios of Athos, St, 55–9
  Life, 60
Euthymios the Great, St, 22
Euthymios the Younger, St, 40, 216
Euthymius of Trnovo, St, 63, 126, 127–32, 147
  literary reform, 128
  on Athos, 128
  patriarch of Trnovo, 128
Evagrios of Pontos, 15
Evergetinos, 222, 237, 242

Fennell, John, 67, 161
Feodor, bishop of Rostov, 172
Ferapont, monk, 172
Ferapontov monastery, 173
Ferrara–Florence, Council of, 183, 185
Ficino, Marsilio, 183
Filaret, metropolitan of Moscow and Kaluga, 225
filioque clause, 109, 185
Fillastre, Cardinal, 140
Florence, 183
  priory of San Marco, 184
Florovsky, Georges, 233, 254
foreigners on Athos, 47, 50, 51, 52, 60, 80
France, 263–9
Frank, Symeon, 254
Franks, 28
Frederick II, Holy Roman Emperor, 87
French, 269

Galesion, Mount, near Ephesus, 20
Gallipoli, 119
Gavriil, metropolitan of St Petersburg, 239, 259
Gavriil Preotul, 156
Gennady, metropolitan of Novgorod, 178, 189
George I, abbot of Iviron, 59

George II ('the Hagiorite'), abbot of Iviron, 59–61
Georgia, 10, 49, 54–63
Georgian, 54, 57
Georgian Church, 60
Georgians, 50, 54–63, 79, 80, 82, 270
Gerasimos, disciple of St Gregory of Sinai, 94
Gerasimos, monk of Little St Anne, 236
Germans, 26, 29, 64
geron. See elder
Ghyzis, Nikolaos, 200
Glagolitic, 27, 29
Gleb, passion-bearer, 67
Glorifiers of the Name, 254
Glossia, cell of, 107
Gogol, Nikolai, 225, 227
Goldfrank, David, 179
Golia, monastery of, 159
Gračanica, monastery of, 83, 102
Great Lavra, monastery of, 39–50, 83, 107, 113, 128, 156, 255
  adopts Stoudite rule, 25
  foundation, 39, 42, 270
  Georgians at, 55
  katholikon, 40, 42, 48
  landholdings, 35
  scriptorium, 34
  typikon of Athanasios, 36, 44–8
Greek, 27, 29, 199, 207, 209
Greek Catholic Church, 114
Greek Church, 196, 236
Greeks, 52, 64, 79, 82, 109, 126, 185
Gregory Akindynos, 109, 110, 114, 127
Gregory Palamas, St, 95, 106–21, 135, 164, 170, 177, 187, 236, 264, 272
  abbot of Esphigmenou, 108
  Apodictic Treatises, 108, 109
  archbishop of Thessaloniki, 117
  arrested, 115
  captured by Turks, 119
  death, 119
  early writings, 108
  edited by Nikodimos of the Holy Mountain, 246
  hesychast controversy, 99
  legacy, 120
  Life, 239
  mentor of Athonite renewal, 260
  on Athos, 93, 107–11, 117
  translated into Slavonic, 129, 146
  Triads, 111
  vindicated, 118
Gregory Tsamblak, 129, 135–42
Gregory V, patriarch of Constantinople, 243
Gregory XII, Pope, 139

Gregory of Nazianzos, St, 36, 58, 186
Gregory of Nyssa, St, 58, 264
Gregory of Sinai, St, 93–104, 118, 120, 131, 177,
    179, 221, 236, 271
  at Paroria, 100–4, 124, 142, 144
  death, 104
  legacy, 103
  on Athos, 94–9, 107, 108
  school of, 128
  translated into Slavonic, 125, 129, 146
Grigoriou, monastery of, 155

hagiography, 129, 169
Hagioritic Tome, 112
Haney, Jack, 185, 195, 197
Hasluck, F. W., 250
Hebrew, 27
Heppell, Muriel, 139
Herman of Alaska, St, 258
Herman of Solovki, St, 174
hermits, 16, 40, 44, 47, 68, 93, 101,
    173, 216
hesychasm, 10, 36, 93–104, 106–16
  and Andrey Rublev, 170
  and Gregory of Sinai, 94–104
  and Gregory Palamas, 106–21
  and Nil Sorsky, 179
  and St Maximos the Greek, 198
  and St Sergius, 168
  and St Silouan, 255
  and the Kollyvades, 236
  at Hilandar, 82
  at Optino, 225, 230
  basis of the Athonite Commonwealth, 272
  in Bulgaria, 124–7, 129
  in Romania, 145
  in Russia, 135, 164
  in Serbia, 144
  in the eighteenth century, 208
  revived by St Paisy, 213, 218
hesychast controversy, 99, 109–16, 203
hesychast international, 103, 131
hesychasts, 22, 43, 48, 99, 107–21
Hesychios, St, 221
Hesychios of Vatos, St, 220
Hierotheos, metropolitan of Nafpaktos and St
    Vlasios, 262
Hilandar, monastery of, 12, 52, 80–91, 113, 145,
    186, 216, 271
  cell of St Saba, Karyes, 83
    typikon, 83
  katholikon, 81, 102, 105
  library, 82, 219
  Milutin's tower, 102
  Panagia Tricherousa, 88

scriptorium, 82, 145
St Basil's by the sea, 102
  typikon, 82, 146
Holy Community, 41, 80, 151, 217, 261
Holy Trinity, monastery of, Jordanville, 260
Honorius III, Pope, 78, 86
Hosios Loukas, monastery of, 32
humanism, Byzantine, 30
humanists, 105, 184, 187
Humor, monastery of, 149
Hungary, 78, 84, 87, 136, 147
Hyacinth, metropolitan of Hungro-Wallachia, 146
Hydra, 235

Iakovos, bishop of Ierissos, 113
Iaşi, 158, 159, 203
iconoclasm, 23, 26, 29, 33
iconography, 78, 170
Ida, Mount, 31
idiorrhythmic monasticism, 49, 150, 155, 190, 215,
    217, 265
Ierissos, 41, 44
Ierotheos, bishop of Euripos, 244
Ignatios, abbot of Vatopedi, 159
Igor', prince of Kiev, 65
Ilarion, bishop of Kiev, 68
Ilarion, monk of Paroria, 142
Iosif, abbot of Volokolamsk, 178, 189
Iosifians. *See* Possessors
Irene, Empress, 23
Iron Curtain, 273
Isaac the Syrian, St, 58, 179, 220
Isaac I Komnenos, Emperor, 31
Isaiah, monk of Hilandar, 145, 155
  abbot of St Panteleimonos, 146
Isaiah, St, 221
Isaias, abbot of Koutloumousiou, 149
Isidore, patriarch of Constantinople, 107, 117
Islam, 22, 23, 64, 119, 202, 206, 207, 209
Italians, 79
Italy, 25, 49, 95
Ivan III, grand prince of Moscow, 189
Ivan IV ('the Terrible'), Tsar, 196
Ivan Alexander, tsar of Bulgaria, 63, 101,
    125, 128
Ivan Asen II, tsar of Bulgaria, 89
Iviron, monastery of, 3, 42, 54–63, 65, 83, 113,
    118, 158
  becomes Greek, 63
  foundation, 56
  Greek monks, 57, 59, 61
  katholikon, 60
  receives Romanian support, 156
  scriptorium, 34, 57, 58, 60
Izyaslav, prince of Kiev, 68, 139

Janković, Vladeta, 90
Jerusalem, 87, 94
Jerusalem *Typikon*, 88
Jesus Prayer, 104, 107, 177, 232, 258, 265
and Barlaam of Calabria, 113
and Gregory of Sinai, 94, 98
and Herman of Alaska, 259
and John Klimakos, 21
and Kosmas the Aetolian, 208
and Maximos of Kafsokalyvia, 99
and Nikephoros the Hesychast, 95
and Nil Sorsky, 177
and St Paisy, 213, 218
and the *Philokalia*, 239
Jews, 64, 90
Joachim III, patriarch of Constantinople, 7
Joantă, Metropolitan Serafim, 149, 157
John Chrysostom, St, 146
John Grdzelisdze, 58, 59
John Kalekas, patriarch of Constantinople,
     111, 114
John Klimakos, St, 20, 58, 98, 111, 129, 133, 134, 179
     Ladder of Divine Ascent, 20–2
John Kolobos, 40
John Tornikios, 56, 65
John XXIII, Pope, 139
John of Damascus, St, 23, 24, 58, 88, 186
John of Gaza, St, 246
John of Georgia, 42
John of Rila, St, 32
John the Evangelist, St, 58
John the Iberian, St, 47, 55–9
     Life, 60
John I Tzimiskes, Emperor, 42, 56
John III Doukas Vatatzes, Emperor, 88
John IV Laskaris, Emperor, 105
     deposed, 116
John V Palaiologos, Emperor, 114, 115, 117,
     118, 147
John VI Kantakouzenos, Emperor, 113–18, 186
Joseph of Vatopedi, Elder, 260
Joseph the Hesychast, Elder, 21, 216, 260, 263
Judaism, 23, 64, 193, 209
Judaizers, 178, 189
Justinian, Emperor, 20
Jvari, monastery of, 55

Kadloubovsky, E., 241
Kafsokalyvia, 220
Kallistos I, patriarch of Constantinople, 63, 94,
     96, 101, 118, 125, 126, 129
     deposed, 118
Kaloyan, tsar of Bulgaria, 85
Kapodistrias, John, 244
Kapsala, skete of, 243

Karakalou, monastery of, 83, 157, 261
Karoulia, 256
Karyes, 41, 42, 44, 237
     monastery of Skourtaioi, 243, 247
     Protaton, 43, 56, 83, 105, 112, 158
Kassian, abbot of Kirillo-Belozersky
     monastery, 176
Kern, Kiprian, 264
Khazars, 27, 64
Khomyakov, Aleksey, 226
Kiev, 12, 14, 26, 65, 133–5, 138, 213
     cathedral of St Sophia, 12
     monastery of St Demetrios, 69, 73
     monastery of St Michael, 12
     monastery of St Nicholas, 71
     monastery of the Caves, 12, 13, 26, 68–75,
          161, 214
          cathedral of the Dormition, 12, 13, 69, 73
          church of the Holy Trinity, 13
          Paterikon, 74
Kilifarevo, monastery of, 125, 131, 132
     typikon, 125
Kireevsky, Ivan, 225, 226
Kirill of Beloozero, St, 168, 172, 178
Kirillo-Belozersky monastery, 172, 175,
     176, 178
     scriptorium, 176
     typikon, 177
Kitromilides, Paschalis, 7, 201, 205, 209, 223
     An Orthodox Commonwealth, 7
Knights Templar, 87
Kodiak island, 259
Koliopoulos, John, 200
Kolkondas, 211
Kollyvades, 210, 221–4, 235–7, 240, 243
Kolobos, monastery of, 44, 56
Kolomna, 172
Konevitsa monastery, 174
Konstamonitou, monastery of, 154, 261
Kosmas the Aetolian, St, 199–212, 234, 240, 248
     death, 211
     Life, 206
Kosovo, 137
Kosovo, battle of, 131, 136
Kostroma, 173
Koutloumousiou, monastery of, 113, 149–54,
     156, 271
Kozelsky, monastery of, 229
Kubena, Lake, 173
Kulikovo, battle of, 165, 168
Kurbsky, Prince Andrey, 195
Kyminas, Mount, near Bursa, 20, 31, 41

Ladoga, Lake, 162, 174
Lakkou, skete of, 273

landownership, 34–6, 39, 158, 172, 176, 178, 182, 189–93, 194
Laodikeia, 93
Lash, Archimandrite Ephrem, 20
Laskaris, Janus, 183, 185
Latin, 27, 29, 33, 51, 140, 183, 188, 265
Latin Church, 185
Latin empire, 10, 85, 120
Latins, 27, 52, 109, 185, 247
Latros, Mount, near Miletus, 20, 31
lavra, 16, 35, 36, 40, 101
Lavrenty, abbot of Xylourgou, 66
Lazar, prince of Serbia, 136, 144, 146
Lazaros, artist, 30
Le Guillou, Marie-Joseph, 266
Leake, William Martin, 39, 249
Lear, Edward, 249
Lebanon, 100
Lemerle, Paul, 30
Leo III, Emperor, 23
Leo V, Emperor, 23
Leo of Benevento, 51
Leonid, elder of Optino, 224, 226
    Life, 227–30
Leontiev, Konstantin, 225
Leontios, metropolitan of Helioupolis, 246
libraries, 24, 33, 215, 219
Lithuania, 133–5, 166
Liturgy of St John Chrysostom, 134
Loch, Sydney, 250–1
London
    British Library, 33
Lossky, Nicholas, 253
Lossky, Vladimir, 253, 257, 264
Loyola, Ignatius, 247
Lucania, 31
Lupu, Prince Basil of Romania, 159
Lyons, Council of, 105
Lyubech, 66

Macedonia, 31, 39, 52, 78, 102, 207
Magarshack, David, 230
Magoula, skete of, 95, 96, 107, 113, 118
Magyars, 32, 50
Makarios Notaras, St, 222, 235, 237–9, 245
Makarios of Simonopetra, Hieromonk, 246
Makarios the Great, St, 17, 19, 58, 111
Makary, elder of Optino, 226
Makary, metropolitan of Moscow, 196
Makary, metropolitan of Novgorod, 194
Maloney, George, 180
Manasija, monastery of, 137, 144
Manuel I Sarantenos, Patriarch, 86
manuscripts, 25, 32–4, 36, 82, 130, 183
Manutius, Aldus, 184

Mar Saba. *See* St Sabas, lavra of
Marinescu, Florin, 159
Martin V, Pope, 140
Mary the Mother of God, 99
    appears to St Sergius, 164
Matthew, patriarch of Constantinople, 134, 136
Matthew the Poor, Elder, 265
Matthew I Kantakouzenos, co-emperor, 118
Mavrocordatos, Constantine, voivode of Moldavia and Wallachia, 203
Mavrogordato, John, 238
Maxim the Greek. *See* Maximos the Greek, St
Maximos of Kafsokalyvia, St, 99, 216
Maximos the Confessor, St, 58, 112, 264
Maximos the Greek, St, 182–98, 213, 272
    arrested, 193
    death, 196
    in Italy, 183–5
    in Moscow, 188–98
    legacy, 196–8
    on Athos, 185–8
Melana, 41, 143
Meletios, abbot of Vatopedi, 201
Menaion, 60
Menoikeion, Mount
    Prodromos monastery
        scriptorium, 34
Mese. *See* Karyes
Mesembria, 89
Mesolongion, 206
Messalians, 110, 112, 127
Meteora, 20, 264
Methodios, abbot of Hilandar, 12
Methodios, St, missionary to the Slavs, 27–9, 77, 129
Meyendorff, John, 132
Michael, abbot of Stoudios monastery, 33
Michael, *protopapas* of Hungro-Wallachia, 151
Michael Maleinos, abbot of Mount Kyminas, 41
Michael III, Emperor, 27
Michael VIII Palaiologos, Emperor, 105
Michelangelo, 183
Mileševa, monastery of, 83, 89
Miller, David, 170
Mircea, voivode, 147
Mirian, king of Iberia, 54
Mitrofan, monk of Neamţ, 214, 217, 221, 224
Moisey, abbot of Optino, 225
Moldavia, 130, 136, 141, 149, 204, 213, 219, 221, 233
Moldoveanu, Ioan, 158
Moldoviţa, monastery of, 149
Monastirica, monastery of, 146
Mongol invasions, 10, 74
Mongols, 13, 105, 161, 166, 272
Morava architectural school, 137

Moravia, 26–9
Morphonou, 51
Morris, Rosemary, 36, 50
Moschos, John, 183
Moscow, 133–5, 138, 187, 253
    Chudov monastery, 165
    monastery of the Theophany, 163
    Simonov monastery, 172
    Tretyakov Gallery, 169
Moscow, patriarchate of, 257
Moses, 94, 102, 129, 140, 199
Mother of God Hodegetria, monastery of, 142
Muscovy, 10, 166, 167
Muslims, 22, 31, 32, 50, 54, 64, 90
Mykale, Mount, 31

Naum, St, 29, 31
Naupactus, 206
Naxos, 234
Nazary, abbot of Valaam, 259
Nea Moni, Chios, 32
Neagoe Basarab, 156–7, 187
Neamţ, monastery of, 130, 147, 149, 223, 228, 240
Neilos Kerameus, patriarch of
    Constantinople, 153
Nekresi, monastery of, 55
Nemanjid dynasty, 77
Neophytos of Kafsokalyvia, monk, 201, 235, 242
Nestor, monk of the Caves monastery, 69, 74
New Diviyevo, convent of, New York, 260
New Skete, 260
New Valaam, hermitage on Spruce island, 259
Nicaea, 86, 88
Nicol, Donald, 184
Nikephoros Gregoras, 108, 118
Nikephoros the Hesychast, St, 95–6, 98, 111, 221
Nikephoros II Phokas, Emperor, 34, 39, 41–2
Niketas Stethatos, St, 221
Nikodimos, hesychast monk, 106
Nikodimos of Tismana, St, 145–9
    abbot of Hilandar, 146
    abbot of Vodiţa, 146
    monasteries founded by, 148
Nikodimos of the Holy Mountain, St, 179, 210,
    222, 234–48
    death, 247
    Handbook of Spiritual Counsel, 244
    Life, 236
Nikon Chronicle, 139, 141
Nikon, abbot of the Caves monastery, 73
Nikon, abbot of Trinity monastery, 169, 171
Nikon, patriarch of Moscow, 131, 197
Nil Sorsky, St, 175–81, 189, 213, 228
    death, 180
    on Athos, 176

Predanie, 180
Skete Typikon, 177
Ustav, 179
Nino, St, 54, 55
Niphon II, patriarch of Constantinople, 156, 187
Nitria, 17
Nizhny Novgorod, 165
Nomocanon, 189
Non-Possessors, 178, 189, 194, 195, 213
Novgorod, 26
Novi Pazar
    church of St Peter, 77
novitiate, 43, 72, 229
Novo Brdo, 78
nuns, 32, 71, 258, 268

obedience, vow of, 16, 25, 45, 49, 166, 229
Obolensky, Dimitri, 5, 8, 86, 131, 263, 270
    on Gregory of Sinai, 103
    on Rublev's icon of the Holy Trinity, 171
    on St Antony and the Caves monastery, 74
    on St Cyprian, 135
    on St Maximos the Greek, 191, 197
    on St Sava, 90
    on St Sava's Life of his father, 85
    on Stoudios monastery, 26
    The Byzantine Commonwealth, 5
Ohrid, 87
    monastery of St Panteleimon, 31
    monastery of Sveti Naum, 31
Oikonomides, Nikolaos, 103
Oleg, prince of Ryazan', 166
Ol'ga, princess of Kiev, 65
Oltenia, 148
Olympos, Mount, near Bursa, 20, 31, 50, 55, 56
Optino monastery, 223–33
Orlov revolt, 207
Ormylia, monastery of, 259
Orthodoxy, Triumph of, 24, 30, 120
Oshevensky monastery, 174
Oshki, monastery of, 56
Otkhta Eklesia, lavra of, 58
Ottomans, 10, 23, 90, 101, 116, 131, 200, 202, 272
Ouranoupolis, 83, 251

Pachomios, St, 16, 17, 24, 264
    rule of, 17
Paisy Yaroslavov, abbot of Trinity monastery, 176
Pakhomy the Serb, monk, 171, 172, 176
Pakourianos, Gregory, 61–3
Palestine, 22, 88
Palmer, Gerald, 241
Pandulf II, duke of Benevento, 51
panegyric, 129
pan-Orthodoxy

of Athos, 50, 79, 103, 186, 215, 269, 270
of hesychasm, 126
Panselinos, Manuel, 105
Pantokrator, monastery of, 156, 214, 216, 243
Papoulides, C., 222
Paraskevi, St, relics of, 159
Paris, 253, 256, 264
    Bibliothèque Nationale, 183
    Institut St-Serge, 253
Paroria, monastery of, 100–4, 108, 118, 124, 131, 142, 144
Patmos, 201
Patrikeev, Vassian, 189, 191, 195
Paul, St, disciple of St Sergius, 173
Paul of Xeropotamou, 43
Paul the Apostle, St, 45, 100, 129, 164
    Epistles, 60
Peć, 78
Pechenegs, 62
Pelion, 206
Pentecostarion, 60
Pereslavi, 165
Peter of Damascus, St, 220
Peter the Apostle, St, 100, 164
Peter the Athonite, St, 108
Peter the Great, Tsar, 213
Petrarch, 114
Phanariots, 203
Philokalia, 95, 219, 232, 234, 237–42, 259, 260, 272
    English, 241
    Romanian, 240
    Russian, 240
Philotheos, St, 221
Philotheos Kokkinos, patriarch of
    Constantinople, 106, 115, 118, 129, 132–5, 146, 163
Philotheos of Sinai, St, 220
Philotheou, monastery of, 83, 95, 155, 202, 208, 261
    scriptorium, 34
Photios, metropolitan of Kiev and
    All Russia, 138
Photios, patriarch of Constantinople, 27, 29
Pico della Mirandola, Gianfrancesco, 184
Pico della Mirandola, Giovanni, 183
Pinamonti, Giampetro, 247
Placide, Fr, 263–9
Plato, 183, 187
Platon, metropolitan of Moscow and Kaluga, 225
Poiana Mărului, 219
Poland, 140, 166
Polish–Lithuanian federation, 134
Poliziano, Angelo, 183
Poltava, 213
population of Athos, 48

Possessors, 178, 180, 182, 189, 194
poverty, vow of, 25, 34, 45, 47, 49, 178
Precista, monastery of, Galaţi, 159
Preslav, 31
Prilep, 145
printing, 184, 196
Prodromou, skete of, 273
Prophet Elijah, skete of, 216, 217, 233
Prosphori, dependency of Vatopedi, 83, 251
Protection of the Mother of God, monastery
    of the, Solan, 269
Protos, 43, 44, 66, 84, 100, 150
Provata, skete of, 107
Psalms, 46, 58, 177
    commentaries on, 188
Psalter, 60, 134, 190

Radonezh, 162
Radoslav, king of Serbia, 87
Radu I, Voivode, 147
Raiska architectural school, 85
Rastko. *See* Sava of Serbia, St
Ratislav, prince of Moravia, 26
Ravanica, monastery of, 144
Renaissance, Italian, 183
renaissance, Macedonian, 60
renaissance, ninth-century, 30
renaissance, Palaiologan, 105, 272
Revelation, Book of, 58
Revolution, Russian, 224, 225, 253, 254
Rhodope Mountains, 62, 128
Rila, monastery of, 32
Riley, Athelstan, 250
Robaia-Zdrelea, monastery of, 158
Roman Catholic Church, 78, 263–7
Roman Catholicism, 64, 95, 209
Romanesque architecture, 78, 84
Romania, 10, 129, 145–60, 204, 240, 273
Romanian, 218
Romanians, 126, 271
    dedicated monasteries, 158
    support for Athos, 154–60
Romanos I Lekapenos, Emperor, 31
Romanos III Argyros, Emperor, 59
Rome, 28, 30, 265
Romylos of Vidin, St, 125, 137, 142–4
Roslavl, 224
Rostov, 74, 162
Rublev, Andrey
    icon of the Holy Trinity, 169–72
Rudnik, 78
Runciman, Steven, 196
Rus', 10, 64–75, 133, 271
Russia, 10, 64–75, 129, 130, 161–81, 224–33, 273
    conversion to Christianity, 65

Russian, 188, 193, 225
Russian Church, 65, 133, 161, 168, 187, 194, 254
Russian Church in Exile, 262
Russian Primary Chronicle, 64, 66, 74
Russians, 29, 64–75, 79, 82, 211, 215
Russo-Turkish war, 235
Ryazan', 166

Sabas, St, 22
    pastoral staff, 88
St Anne, skete of, 220, 221, 235
St Antony the Great, monastery of, Arizona, 262
St Antony the Great, monastery of, St Laurent-
    en-Royans, 268
St Basil, skete of, 220
St Catherine, monastery of, Sinai, 20, 22, 32,
    89, 94
    typikon, 125
St Demetrios, monastery of, Galaţi, 159
St Demetrios, skete of, 220
St John the Forerunner, hermitage of,
    Optino, 225
St Nicholas of Poiana Sirctului, monastery of, 149
St Panteleimon, monastery of, 52, 66, 79, 186, 215,
    232, 254, 273
St Paul, monastery of, 143, 156, 158, 256
St Petersburg
    Public Library, 33
St Sabas, cell of, 107
St Sabas, lavra of, 22, 23, 88
Sts Antony and Cuthbert, monastery of, 2, 14
Sts Constantine and Helena, cell of, 216
Sakharov, Fr Nikolai, 257
Samos, 205
Samuel I, patriarch of Constantinople, 209
Sapunov, Boris Viktorovich, 67
Sava of Serbia, St, 271
    abbot of Studenica, 84, 86
    archbishop of Serbia, 86
    death, 89
    Life of his father, 81, 85
    Nomocanon, 87
    pilgrimage to Palestine, 88
    relics burnt, 90
Savonarola, Girolamo, 183
Savvas, monk of Vatopedi, 187
Savvaty of Solovki, St, 174
Scetis. *See* Wadi Natrun
schools, 24, 27, 62, 160, 175, 199–202, 207,
    209, 235
scriptoria, 24, 32–4
Scupoli, Lorenzo, 247
Serafim of Sarov, St, 227
Seraphim II, patriarch of Constantinople, 206

Serbia, 10, 39, 77–91, 101, 102, 129, 136, 144,
    146, 273
    conversion to Christianity, 77
    independent Church, 86
Serbian Church, 84, 86, 87, 147
Serbs, 29, 77–91, 102, 105, 107, 115, 116, 271
Sergius of Nurma, St, 173
Sergius of Radonezh, St, 162–72, 178, 227, 272
    abbot of Trinity monastery, 163
    cult of, 168–72
    death, 167
    visions, 164, 170
Serpukhov, 165, 172
Shamordino, 226, 231
Shepard, Jonathan, 5, 6, 131, 168
Sherrard, Philip, 241
Shiet. *See* Wadi Natrun
ships, 35, 51, 82
Siberia, 223, 224, 229, 259
Sicilians, monastery of, 51
Silouan, St, 255, 256, 263
silver mines, 78
Simon, bishop of Vladimir, 73
Simon, metropolitan of Moscow, 189
Simonopetra, monastery of, 158, 217, 251, 267
Sinai, 229
Sinai, Mount, 20, 30
Sinan Pasha, grand vizier, 90
sketes, 101, 177, 180, 225, 258
Skopelos, 203
Skopje, 102
Slavonic, 27–9, 77, 82, 101, 125, 129, 186, 188,
    218, 221
Slavophile movement, 226
Slavs, 26–9, 32, 50, 77, 126, 131, 186, 215
Slovakia, 26
Smyrna, 93, 235, 238
Sobolevsky, A. I., 130
soft power, 271
Solan, 269
Solesmes, monastery of, 264
Soloviev, Vladimir, 225
Solovki, monastery of, 174, 224
Sophronios II, patriarch of Constantinople,
    206, 236
Sophrony, Fr, 253–8, 263
    death, 257
    in England, 257–8
    in Paris, 253, 256
    on Athos, 254–7
Sopoćani, monastery of, 83
Sources Chrétiennes, 265
Sozopolis, 100
Spaso-Kamenny monastery, 173
Spiridon, abbot of Studenica, 89

spiritual father. *See* elder
Spruce island, 259
Stăniloae, Fr Dumitru, 240
Stanton, L. J., 226, 230
starets. See elder
Stefan, abbot of the Caves monastery, 78, 84, 86, 87
Stefan Dečanski. *See* Stefan Uroš III, king of Serbia
Stefan Dušan. *See* Stefan Uroš IV Dušan
Stefan Lazarevic, prince of Serbia, 136
Stefan Nemanja, 77–81
    death, 81
    relics returned to Serbia, 84
Stefan of Perm', St, 168
Stefan the First Crowned, king of Serbia, 73
Stefan the Great of Moldavia, St, 154
Stefan Uroš II Milutin, king of Serbia, 102
Stefan Uroš III, king of Serbia, 137
Stefan Uroš IV Dušan, ruler of Serbia, 117, 146
Stephen, brother of St Sergius of Radonezh, 162
Stoudios monastery, 24–6, 32, 42, 133
Stoudite rule, 24–6, 32, 36, 45
    adopted at monastery of the Caves, 72
    adopted at Trinity monastery of St Sergius, 163
    adopted in Russian monasteries, 165
Strandzha Mountains, 100, 124
Strezova, Anita, 126, 170
Stronym, 165
Studenica, monastery of, 78, 83, 102, 271
    katholikon, 84
    typikon, 81, 84
Sublime Porte, 193
Suceava, 136
Suda, 186
Suzdal', 73
Svyatopolk, prince of Kiev, 67, 75
Symeon, monk. *See* Stefan Nemanja
Symeon the New Theologian, St, 111, 129, 221, 236, 245, 262
Synaxarion, 60
Syria, 19, 93, 113
Syrians, 54, 55
Syrians, monastery of the, 18, 265

Tabor, Mount, 112, 113, 170
Tao-Klarjeti, 55
Tatars, 139, 165, 167, 168, 169, 193
Thalassios, St, 221
Thebaid, Egyptian, 89
Thebaid, Northern, 174
Theodora, Empress, 23
Theodore Angelos, ruler of Epirus, 88
Theodore Metochites, 106
Theodore Psalter, 33

Theodore of Edessa, St, 220
Theodore the Stoudite, St, 23–5, 32, 45, 146
    Catecheses, 60
Theodore I Laskaris, Emperor, 86
Theodoret of Cyrrhus, 192
Theodosius of Kiev, St, 13, 26, 69–75
    abbot of the Caves monastery, 72
    Life, 69, 74
Theodosius of Trnovo, St, 124–8, 144
    death, 126
    disciples, 127–35, 142–4
    Life, 125, 126
Theodosy, archimandrite of the St Sophrony hermitage, 220
Theoktistos, abbot of Esphigmenou, 66, 67, 68
Theoleptos, metropolitan of Philadelphia, 36, 106, 108, 111
Theophan the Recluse, St, 232, 240
Theophanes of Vatopedi, 99
theosis. See deification
Thessalonians, monastery of, 66
Thessaloniki, 27, 35, 88, 100, 107, 118
    cathedral of St Gregory Palamas, 120
    church of Hagia Sophia, 170
    monastery of Philokales, 86
    monastery of St Andrew of Peristerai, 42
    'Zealots', 117
Thessaly, 78, 115, 206
Thrace, 115, 204
Three Holy Hierarchs, monastery of, 158
Tismana, monastery of, 145, 147
Tmutarakan, 73
Tolleshunt Knights, monastery of St John the Baptist, 257
Tolstoy, Leo, 225, 231
Tourkokratia, 153, 205, 217
trade, 36, 51
Tragos of 972, 43–4
Transfiguration, 110, 170, 260
Transfiguration, monastery of the, Aubazine, 266
Transfiguration, monastery of the, Martel, 268
Transvolga hermits, 162, 178, 189
Transylvania, 148
Trebizond, 41, 55
Trinity chronicle, 166
Trinity monastery of St Sergius, 163, 178, 196
    church of the Holy Trinity, 171
Triodion, 60
Trivolis, Michael. *See* Maximos the Greek, St
Trnovo, 89, 130, 131, 135, 204
    Holy Trinity, monastery of, 128
    literary school, 128, 136, 141
Turdeanu, Emil, 147
Turks, 100, 102, 107, 143, 153

Turks (cont.)
  capture Gregory Palamas, 119
  guardians of Orthodoxy, 210
  support for Kantakouzenos, 115
Tver', 193
  Otroch monastery, 195

Ukraine, 10, 66, 214
uncreated light, 110, 164, 170, 253
Uniates, 266
union of Churches, 105, 108, 109, 121, 140
USA, 261, 263

Valaam, monastery of, 174, 224, 259, 260
Vasileios, abbot of Iviron, 3
Vasily III, grand prince of Moscow, 187, 189, 194
Vatican Council, Second, 265
Vatopedi, monastery of, 80, 113, 157, 158
  academy of Athos, 201
  and Gregory Palamas, 107
  and St Maximos the Greek, 185, 197
  and St Sava, 79
  and St Symeon, 79
  becomes idiorrhythmic, 190
  icon of the Holy Trinity, 170
  katholikon, 105
  library, 185, 223
  receives Romanian support, 154, 156, 159
Velichkovsky, St Paisy, 179, 213–26, 236, 239, 240, 243, 258
  death, 224
  legacy to Athos, 217–19
  legacy to Russia, 224–6
  Life, 215, 218
  on Athos, 217–19
Venice, 27, 116, 182, 184, 196, 222, 238
Veremis, Thanos, 200
Veroia, 107
Vidin, 124
Vienna, 34, 246
Vilnius
  Public Library, 140
Vîrşevăţ, monastery of, 149
Vitovt, ruler of Lithuania, 138–42
Vlachs. *See* Wallachians
Vlad the monk, Wallachian voivode, 155
Vladimir, 165
Vladimir II Monomakh, prince of Kiev, 74
Vladimir, prince of Kiev, 7, 53, 64, 67

Vladislav, king of Serbia, 88, 89
Vladislav-Vlaïcu, Voivode, 146, 149, 152
Vodiţa, monastery of, 146
Vologda, 173
Volokolamsk, monastery of, 193
Voulgaris, Evgenios, 202, 209
Vratna, monastery of, 146
Vukan of Serbia, son of Stefan Nemanja, 84, 86

Wadi Natrun, 17, 18, 89, 265
Wallachia, 130, 146–54, 187, 204, 213, 218
Wallachians, 150
War of Independence, Greek, 216
Ward, Sister Benedicta, 19
Ware, Metropolitan Kallistos, 16, 22, 97, 163, 219, 223, 237, 238, 241, 248, 260
Way of a Pilgrim, The, 231, 240
White Lake, 172, 177
White Sea, 162, 174
wine, 36, 44, 46, 64, 172
Wisques, abbey of, 264
World War I, 254
World War II, 13, 251, 256, 264
Wycliffite heresy, 139

Xenophontos, monastery of, 52, 158
Xeropotamou, monastery of, 52, 83, 156, 157, 204, 261
Xerxes' canal, 39
Xylourgou, monastery of, 66, 69, 176, 271

Yaroslav, prince of Kiev, 67, 68

Zagora, 142
Zakynthos, 207
Zedergol'm, Fr Kliment, 227
Zernov, Nicholas, 253
Žiča, 78
Žiča, monastery of, 83, 84, 87
Zographou, monastery of, 52, 128, 130, 155, 156, 157, 158, 186, 271
  lavra of the Moldavians, 155
Zonaras, historian, 30
Zosima of Solovki, St, 174
Zvenigorod, 172
Zygos, 41
Zygou, monastery of, 82